The Sound of Light

The Sound of Light:
A History of Gospel Music

Don Cusic

Bowling Green State University Popular Press
Bowling Green, Ohio 43403

This book is dedicated
to Charles K. Wolfe

Acknowledgments

Charles Wolfe, Judy McCullough and I had dinner one evening at the Wolfe's and at that dinner the seeds were planted for this book. I am grateful to Charles and Judy for the early encouragement.

It took over five years to finish this book and several typists and secretaries typed letters and chapters. I am especially thankful to Janice Burysek and Teresa Snow. Dr. Geoff Hull, the Chairman of the Department of Recording Industry Management at Middle Tennessee State University has been both encouraging and helpful, arranging my teaching schedule and allowing me time off for research. I would also like to thank Dr. Robert Wyatt, Dr. Alex Nagy, Dr. Ed Kimbrell, Dr. Michael Dunne, Dr. William Holland, Dr. William Beasley (deceased) and others down here for their encouragement and support.

I have interviewed a number of people involved in gospel music during the years and mention a number of these in the "Notes." However, I want to especially thank Bill Gaither, Amy Grant, Billy Ray Hearn, Bill Hearn, Don Butler, Jarrell McCracken, Marvin Norcross (deceased), James Blackwood, Johnny Cash, Barbara Mandrell, Larry Norman, Brock Speer, Joe Moscheo, Frances Preston, Les Beasley, Niles Borup, J. Aaron Brown, Ken Harding, Elwyn Ramer, Mosie Lister, W.F. "Jim" Myers, James Bullard, Lou Hildreth, Charlie Monk, Joe Talbot, Stan Moser, Roland Lundy, Dan Harrell, Mike Blanton, Karen Lafferty, Eddie Huff, John T. Benson III, Bob Benson (deceased), Robert Benson, Jr., Shannon Williams, Ricky Skaggs, as well as many others I have interviewed and conversed with through the years.

I must also thank John Sturdivant, my boss at *Record World*, John Styll, the editor of *Contemporary Christian Music*, Jim Sharp, my boss at *Cashbox*, and Neal Pond, the editor of *Music City News* while I was writing for those publications. Finally, I must thank my wife, Jackie, for her continuing encouragement and support, and Delaney, Jesse, Eli and Alex for providing a series of continuing diversions from such mundane things as doing research and writing books.

Contents

Introduction   i

Part I
Chapter 1
  Music in the Bible   3
Chapter 2
  Early Music in the Church   7
Chapter 3
  The Sixteenth Century:
  Roots of Contemporary Christianity   10
Chapter 4
  A Mighty Fortress:
  Martin Luther as Songwriter   15
Chapter 5
  First Seeds:
  Gospel Music in America   19
Chapter 6
  Isaac Watts   26
Chapter 7
  The Wesleys   32
Chapter 8
  The Secular Influence   40
Chapter 9
  Give Me That Old Time Religion   47
Chapter 10
  The Great Revival   56

Part 2
Chapter 11
  Billy Sunday and Homer Rodeheaver   69
Chapter 12
  The Rise of Radio and Records   77
Chapter 13
  Black Gospel   84
Chapter 14
  Southern Gospel   93
Chapter 15
  The Speers and The Blackwoods   100

Part 3
Chapter 16
  Spirit in the Sky:
  Gospel Music on Pop Radio   110
Chapter 17
  Elvis and Gospel   116

Chapter 18
  Mahalia Jackson and Sam Cooke   121
Chapter 19
  The Jesus Revolution   126
Chapter 20
  The Catholics in America   130
Chapter 21
  The Major Labels:
  Word and Benson   134
Chapter 22
  Bill Gaither   139
Chapter 23
  Fanny Lou Hamer and James Cleveland   143
Chapter 24
  Cathedrals, Florida Boys and Kingsmen   149
Chapter 25
  Sparrow Records and Keith Green   158
Chapter 26
  Music in the Church:
  George Beverly Shea and Sandi Patti   164
Chapter 27
  Jimmy Swaggart   170
Chapter 28
  Country and Gospel:
  Johnny Cash and Barbara Mandrell   177
Chapter 29
  Amy Grant   184
Chapter 30
  The Rock That Doesn't Roll:
  Imperials, Petra and Michael W. Smith   191
Chapter 31
  The Music Missionaries   200

Part 4
Chapter 32
  The Christian Culture   213
Chapter 33
  Rewards and Awards:
  Marketing the Movement   222
Conclusion   226
Notes   229
Bibliography   235
Index   247

Introduction

The first question is "What is Gospel Music?" The twentieth century answer is that "there is no such thing as gospel music." There is such a thing as a gospel song, which depends primarily upon the lyric to express its Christian message. The song carries the gospel, or "good news" in music, which qualifies it as a gospel song. But the vehicle—the music itself—may be rock, country, r&b, folk, classical, jazz or any other kind of music. Because Christianity always seeks to be contemporary, it adapts its structure to the music of the day (today's being the music of the popular culture) to carry its message.

Since American Christianity is basically divided between black and white churches, gospel music reflects this major division within the confines of black and white gospel music. Black gospel may be either traditional, featuring the large choirs with soloists from black churches, or contemporary, akin to the music heard on black radio stations. Its heritage is linked to the slave culture in this country while other influences come from the white culture (from British broadside ballads and hymns), as well as the black experience movement.

White gospel music may be divided into three broad categories: southern gospel, the sound akin to country music usually dominated by the male quartet sound; inspirational or church music, geared for the church audience and generally sung by choirs in the sanctuary during a service; and contemporary Christian music, songs of the popular culture with Christian lyrics marketed to consumers through the network of Christian bookstores.

The primary difference between musicians in the pop world and gospel musicians is that pop musicians see themselves as entertainers while Christian musicians see themselves as ministers. Therefore, the songs of the gospel singers, musicians and songwriters must be functional, expressing the Christian faith to attract new believers or edify established believers. Music outside the Christian culture, on the other hand, is generally viewed as entertainment.

The music for Christian revivals generally comes from the secular culture as revivalists seek out popular tunes and contemporary styles of music to entice new converts and infuse traditional religion with new life and make it contemporary. As the revival turns into a movement, and then into an accepted part of established Christianity, the music turns inward, seeking to edify believers rather than convert non-believers. Thus, the music first comes from outside the church to the members, then from the congregation to the church, where it is incorporated into the worship. After this metamorphosis, the church shuts its doors to new music and develops another tradition. This tradition will become entrenched, then challenged by a new revival led by music, which will alter the music of the church again. This has been the history of music in religious revivals from Martin Luther's day to the Jesus Movement of the 1970s.

i

Outside the framework of the church, music serves the function of attracting the attention of non-believers (or nominal believers) and leading them to a conviction of their sins or establishing a mood for an evangelist who will deliver a message which will cause the hearer to commit his life to Christ and embrace the Christian walk. This music will challenge or soothe, but it is primarily meant to move the hearer in the direction of the gospel, which he has either never heard before or ignored.

Inside the church there are three functions of music: to teach, to shape morals and to edify. It has long been accepted that great truths and Scriptures are most easily memorized when sung. Since music tends to reflect the order, stability and continuity of the universe, it may be used as a force for shaping morals. Edification—meaning the spiritual improvement and further instruction of church members—serves as a psychological sedative the church uses against the chaos and confusion of the secular world.

Music has been a part of religion since the earliest days of biblical history and has been important in the history of Christianity from the first century. But it was Martin Luther who freed music from strictly liturgical use in the sixteenth century and allowed it to play an important part in the Protestant Reformation, communicating the faith and making it a personal, rather than institutional, experience.

It was the sixteenth century that established the framework for contemporary American Christianity. As Martin Luther headed the religious reformation, John Calvin led a social reformation with his *Institutes*. Henry VIII provided the impetus for the political aspect of the reformation by putting Great Britain in religious turmoil and planting the seeds for the exodus of Pilgrims and others to America to establish this land as the "new Canaan."

Once in America, the early settlers used Luther's Reformation concept of grace and personal belief as well as Calvin's notions of a theocracy and the role Christianity should play in government to establish the United States as a "Christian nation." Since that time, the history of Christianity in America has been a history of revivals. Jonathan Edwards and George Whitefield led the Great Awakening and the people pushing westward led to the Kentucky Revival and the tradition of camp meetings as sources of religious movements.

The songs of Isaac Watts furthered the concept of the personal relationship with God. The missionary zeal of the Wesleys helped spread Christianity further and established a body of songs in print that churches would sing for years. After the Civil War, evangelists like Dwight Moody, accompanied by singer Ira Sankey, led urban revivals as America became an industrialized nation.

The blacks, whose work songs in slavery produced their own unique form of American music, took some of the old songs from the British/Scottish/Irish tradition and transformed them into their own gospel songs. Later, the holiness church produced the environment for the black experience to blossom within a religious context. The climate of the country was such that separate cultures—black and white—and separate musics developed, united by the theme of the gospel message.

In the twentieth century, the development of electronic media—radio and television—as well as the development of the phonograph record saw religious music spread through new forms. The Jesus Movement of the late 1960s and early 1970s is another example of a revival, once again led by music, which reunited America with its roots as a Christian nation and established a Christian culture as religion became big business.

There are two common denominators in all these revivals—the gospel and the music—and each depends on the other in order to thrive and take hold. Thus the history of gospel music in America becomes the history of Christianity in America as the faith uses music to grow and expand. It is the music that keeps Christianity ageless, timeless and contemporary and it is music that offers both tradition and renewal for believers. The church without music is a dead church and the American Christian church has thrived as long as this nation has been in existence largely because music has continually provided the means for the gospel message to find new audiences, convert new believers, and establish new churches.

American Christianity may be characterized as individualistic, independent, aggressive, and competitive. These four traits increasingly mark Christian revivals and individual believers as Americans have forged their own unique brand of Christianity from a diversity of ethnic, cultural and social influences.

The individualism has its roots in Martin Luther's Protestant Reformation which required an individual to make a personal commitment to God. It cannot be made for him by the church, state, or parents, but must be his own choice. This means that each believer can interpret the Bible and hear the voice of God without having it filtered through a religious bureaucratic hierarchy. It also means he can fit his religion to his own personal life, encompassing his own cultural and personal biases.

American Christianity is independent because the believer may break from his mold—he may come from a non-believing background or from a denomination—into a new strata. It is this "brand new start" from which a "brand new person" emerges after being "born again."

American Christianity is aggressive because it must seek to evangelize in order to win new converts. For this reason, it will use the airwaves of TV and radio, the print media, public halls, personal contacts and even door to door evangelizing or street evangelism to spread the message. And it is competitive because it not only competes against other religions and philosophies but also within its own ranks. For many, it is not a matter of simply being a Christian, but a Christian aligned with the right denomination, movement or church with the "correct" interpretation of Scripture and formulation of doctrine. This means American Christians will actively seek to "convert" believers from different denominations or those with a different interpretation of Scripture, doctrine, or tradition into "true" Christianity.

Music is important to Christianity because it is an expression of individuality and independence the believer must make before the world in order to join the body of Christ. It is used to aggressively pursue non-believers or nominal believers and bring them into the fold as "true" Christians, and it is important because it too is spiritual and can reach out and communicate spiritual truth or spiritual experience.

Great art often poses great questions, which is why it is often unsettling as well as comforting. It also poses great contradictions. Christian art, on the other hand, poses the Great Answer and this answer must be either accepted or rejected. For that reason, Christian art—particularly music—must be functional, conveying the Gospel in a simple form. When Christian music becomes "art for art's sake" it fails because it has lost its purpose, which is to convert souls.

When Christian music fulfills its purpose it finds its strength. From this strength comes the definition of Christian art: that which leads man to God. Music has filled that role since earliest biblical times and continues to do so today, a tribute to the power of music as well as its role in American Christianity.

Part 1

Chapter 1
Music in the Bible

The significance of the Bible to Christians is that it is viewed not as just a book of history and literature but as a handbook for life, the tool God uses to communicate with people. In that sense, it is not a book by people but a book authored by God. Therefore, the Bible is read by believers in a spiritual, not a literary, sense to understand God and live according to His design and intentions. Of course, not everyone who reads the Bible views it in a strictly spiritual context and there have been numerous studies and analyses of the Bible from those who view it as a work of literature, history, or even as a cultural and religious artifact. Still, the fact remains that fundamental Christian religious revivals have come from people and movements who read the Bible in a spiritual light and acted upon the principles and interpretations they deduced.

Throughout the Bible songs and singing play an important part of life. Music is used in religious services, in secular celebrations, in wars, as private prayer, a means of offering thanksgiving and praise to God, to record events, in apocalyptic visions of the final days of earth, and visions of life in heaven where songs will be used as a way to honor God with praise and thanksgiving, expressing awe and wonder.

The twentieth century has seen the Bible inspire new Christian revivals and songs have been an integral part of communicating the Biblical messages, introducing the unbeliever to God, and offering believing Christians new instruments of praise, worship, and thanksgiving for a closer communication with God. Indeed, a whole industry of songs has been born from this tradition of singing songs to, for, and about God.

The first mention of songs in the Bible is in Genesis, Chapter 31, when Jacob left Laban to return to his own land. Jacob and Rachel fled early one morning to go back to Canaan, the land of his father and grandfather (Isaac and Abraham) without telling Laban, whom they had been visiting. However, Laban, learning Jacob had left, pursued him for seven days, finally overtaking him and asked, "What have you done, that you have cheated me, and carried away my daughters like captives of the sword? Why did you flee secretly, and cheat me, and did not tell me, so that I might have sent you away with mirth and songs, with tambourine and lyre?" (v. 26-7). From this early time, it is clear that music was part of the culture, in this case used for festive occasions.

The first mention of singing used in a religious context occurs in Exodus, Chapter 15, after Moses had crossed the Red Sea when the sea was rolled back for the Israelites, then closed on Pharoah's army, assuring the Israelite's safety. It was at this time that Moses and the people of Israel sang a song of thanksgiving to the Lord for deliverance. The song begins, "I will sing to the Lord, for he has triumphed gloriously; the horse and his rider he has thrown into the sea" and continues with a description of what happened at the Red Sea and how the Lord had defeated his enemies. This was topical and apparently composed on the spot, probably by Moses who, if this is true, would be the first acknowledged gospel songwriter.

This first biblical song lasts 18 verses and served the purpose of thanksgiving, a celebration of praise and appreciation to the Lord for what he had done. Although it is not safe to assume that other biblical characters before Moses—Adam, Noah, Abraham, Isaac, Jacob, Joseph, etc.—never sang, at least there is no mention of it. It is also significant to note that a song of thanksgiving was established as an important part of the religious life of the new nation forming under the leadership of Moses.

From the earliest establishment of Israel as the nation of God and the Jews as the people of God, singing has been a vital part of communication with God by man. When the people were in the wilderness with Moses, without food and water, suffering from their rebellion, they reconciled themselves to God with singing and he provided water.

In establishing the nation of Israel, God commanded Moses to

Write this song, and teach it to the people of Israel; put it in their mouths, that this song may be a witness for me against the people of Israel. For when I have brought them into the land flowing with milk and honey, which I swore to give to their fathers, and they have eaten and full and grown fat they will turn to other gods and serve them, and break my covenant. And when many evils and troubles have come upon them, this song shall confront them as a witness (for it will live unforgotten in the mouths of their descendants); for I know the purposes which they are already forming, before I had brought them into the land that I swore to give. (Deut 31: 19-22)

So Moses wrote this song the same day and taught it to the people of Israel.

The song itself is Chapter 32 of Deuteronomy and tells the story of the formation of Israel and admonishes them to not forget the God who brought them out of Israel to be a special nation, warning them of the wrath and vengeance of God lest they forget their heritage. After singing the song, Moses commanded the people

Lay to heart all the words which I enjoin upon you this day, that you may command them to your children, that they may be careful to do all the words of this law. For it is no trifle for you, but it is your life, and thereby you shall live long in the land which you are going over the Jordan to possess. (Deut. 32: 45-47)

The Psalms, which are essentially a collection of songs from around the time of David, contain an abundance of references to songs and singing, with the emphasis being on communicating with God through singing. Many of the Psalms admonish the people of God to sing to show their faith with passages like "Come into his presence with singing" (100: 2), and "I will praise the name of God with a song" (69: 30). The Psalms also illustrate that singing and songs are part of everyday life—not just life in the assembly of worship or churches, but a continuous outpouring of faith and praise. There is also encouragement to compose new songs expressing faith with the passage "Sing to the Lord a new song" contained in several Psalms.

Contemporary Christianity tends to ignore one aspect of the Psalms—the themes of revenge, fear, doubting, frustration, and outrage. Yet these are all part of the Psalms, although modern songwriters prefer to use the praise aspects. Still, the Psalms show us songs of individual expression, of earthly concerns, of personal cries of pain and help. They also show the roots of Christianity to be strongly in Judaism—a fact that has been obscured along the way, particularly in the eighteenth and nineteenth centuries when an anti-Semitism arose and the Psalms were "Christianized" to fit the doctrines of denominations whose faith was rooted in the New Testament.

There are not a large number of examples of songs in the New Testament; still, it is obvious that singing and songs were considered an important part of the religious life of the Christian. It was a way to communicate with God as well as share a sense of togetherness among believers.

Perhaps the most significant mention of a song in the New Testament is after the last supper when it is noted that Jesus and his disciples sang a hymn before retiring to the Mount of Olives where he spent his last free moments with the group who had been the core of his earthly followers. There is no record of what they sang, but the implication is that the song was known by all of them and that they had sung together before, hence singing was not foreign to Jesus and his disciples, but rather a part of their spiritual life.

A significant example of the power of singing in the New Testament comes in Acts, Chapter 16, where Paul and Silas had been thrown in jail in Philippi after casting an evil spirit from a prophetess. It states,

About midnight, Paul and Silas were praying and singing hymns to God, and the prisoners were listening to them, and suddenly there was a great earthquake, so that the foundations of the prison were shaken; and immediately all the doors were opened and every one's fetters were unfastened. (v 25-26)

Clearly, singing was considered part of the spiritual life and the New Testament proves that by containing examples of both Jesus and his chief apostle, Paul singing. Once again, the song Paul sang was not mentioned, but the implication is that it was a known hymn.

Later, Paul in his letters admonishes new believers to "be filled with the Spirit, addressing one another in psalms, and hymns and spiritual songs, singing and making melody to the Lord with all your heart, always and for everything giving thanks in the name of our Lord Jesus Christ to God the Father" (Ephesians 5:19-20) and to "let the word of Christ dwell in you richly, teach and admonish one another in all wisdom, and sing psalms and hymns and spiritual songs with thankfulness in your hearts to God" (Colossians 3:16). Clearly, these are statements which show that singing is to be an important part of the spiritual life of Christians. It is interesting to note that Paul, in these two passages, cites "psalms, hymns, and spiritual songs," as three kinds of songs, but never defines the difference. It may be surmised, however, that the psalms and hymns were known songs while spiritual songs may be songs sung "in the spirit" or extemporaneously and in an improvisational and personal manner, thereby encouraging believers to create their own songs, tailored to fit their own experiences with God. This implication sets the stage for Christianity to continually produce new songs to fit with contemporary spiritual revivals and experiences throughout the generations since that time.

Not only are songs important in this world, they are also an important and vital part of the next world, according to Revelation. In the apocalyptic vision, a "new song" is sung (Rev. 5:9-10) in the final time. During the last days, as the scroll of life is opened, a song will be sung about the Savior,

Worthy art thou to take the scroll and to open its seals for thou was slain and by thy blood didst ransom men for God from every tribe and tongue and people and nation, and hast made them a kingdom and priests of our God, and they shall reign on earth.

There are also passages (14:3) where Jesus will stand on Mount Zion on the final day and the 144,000 who are chosen to be saved will learn a "new song" which "no one else could learn" (15:3). Also, the song of Moses is sung during this time and the song of the Lamb which says,

Great and wonderful are thy deeds, O Lord God Almighty! Just and true are thy ways, O King of the ages! Who shall not fear and glorify thy name, O Lord? For thou alone are holy. All nations shall come and worship thee, for thy judgments have been revealed. (15:3-5)

So it is that the God of Israel is still a source of inspiration for songs. With the concept of the Trinity and Jesus, the Son being equal to the Father, gospel music today reaches back through the Old Testament by reaching back to the New Testament. The theme of Christianity, therefore, runs throughout the Bible and Christian music encompasses the entire Bible by centering on the last part—the conclusion—because the ending brings into focus the entire book. So contemporary gospel music is not just songs of the Jesus born two thousand years ago, but of the God of eternity. The Jewish roots have been Christianized and the branches run through the ages, a testament to the timeless spiritual thread that runs through the history of mankind. Indeed, contemporary gospel music is really a circle with the Bible as both the starting and ending point; it may be said that the history of gospel music is a series of circles that has continually grown larger as the music has become more diverse and encompassed more styles and roles in the lives of believers and non-believers. Thus, the history of gospel music is also the history of Christianity, particularly in the United States where music has played such a vital role in Christian revivals throughout the history of the country.

Chapter 2
Early Music in the Church

The Christian church began as an extension of Judaism and the early church had no formal break with the Judaic tradition as the disciples assembled regularly in small gatherings modeled on that of the synagogue. With the passing of the Apostolic Age (c. 33 to 100) the young church entered a period of expansion as well as an age of controversy and persecution. The center had shifted from Jerusalem to Antioch to Ephesus and then, by the end of the second century, to Rome and Alexandria. Rome offered the world great wealth and prestige while Alexandria had the early literary pugilists, the thinkers, philosophers, and apologists.

For music, the early Christians used Hebrew melodies and cultivated the habit of antiphonal or responsive chanting of the psalms. But as the church grew, it became more organized and the shift from the homogeneous, democratic system of the apostolic age to a hierarchical organization occurred under the Western popes and Eastern patriarchs who developed "an elaborate system of rites and ceremonies" which were "partly an evolution from within, partly an inheritance of ancient habits and dispositions, which at last became formulated into unvarying types of devotional expression" (Dickinson 37). Music was part of this ritualistic movement and it rapidly became liturgical and clerical as the laity stopped sharing in worship through song. A chorus, drawn from minor clergy, took over the "highly organized body of chants" which were almost the entire substance of worship music and remained that way for a thousand years.

The independent songs of the people were replaced by the sacerdotal and liturgical movement and the people's part of the service became limited to responses at the end of the verses of the psalms. Originally, the singing of psalms and hymns by a group of worshipers was the custom of the early churches at informal assemblies but the progress of ritualism and growth of sacerdotal ideas put all the initiative of public devotion—including songs—on the clergy. This shift from a people-centered service to a clergy-centered-and-controlled service was complete by the middle of the fourth century, if not earlier. The reason appears fairly simple: doctrinal vagaries and mystical extravagances as well as unified teaching could serve as a control for the religion through these ritualistic, clergy-centered services. Too, Christianity was becoming a political as well as religious power.

The idea that songs should be used to instruct converts in the faith goes back to the first days of Christianity, to the time of the apostle Paul and his allusion to "psalms, hymns, and spiritual songs." Here, he divides songs into three categories, probably meaning ancient Hebrew psalms for "psalms," hymns taken from the Old Testament for "hymns" and songs composed by the early

7

Christians themselves for "spiritual songs." In 112, it was recorded that Christians were "coming together before daylight and singing hymns alternatively to Christ" (Dickinson 47).

This early music was a combination of Greek and Hebrew. Paul wrote his Epistles in Greek and the earliest liturgies are in Greek while the Hebraic influence was felt in the sentiment of prayer and praise. The use of songs for worship worked because it was impressive and easily remembered. Edward Dickinson in his *Music in the History of the Western Church* notes that "The injunction to teach and admonish by means of songs also agrees with other evidences that a prime motive for hymn singing in many of the churches was instruction in the doctrines of the faith" (43).

The history of music in the Catholic church begins with the establishment of the priestly liturgic chant, which had replaced the songs in public worship as early as the fourth century. This chant was exclusively vocal and evolved from the selection and integration of certain prayers, Scripture lessons, hymns, and responses woven together until a "religious poem" emerged which expressed the relation of Christ to the church. This great prayer was primarily composed of contributions from the eastern church during the first four centuries, which were adopted and transferred to Latin by the Church of Rome. Its form was basically completed by the end of the sixth century.

This "religious poem" or "great prayer" is the Mass and several kinds of Masses have since developed: High Mass, Solemn High Mass, Low Mass, Requiem Mass or Mass for the Dead, Mass of Presanctified, Nuptial Mass, Votive Mass, etc. However, there is little difference in the essential elements of these Masses and virtually no difference in the words of the High Mass, Solemn High Mass, and Low Mass, only in the performance and degree of embellishment.

As the church grew, so did the opposition to musical instruments. The prejudice against instruments came about primarily because of the association of these instruments with superstitious pagan rites and their connection with the theater and circus, two degenerate forms of entertainment. Thus purely vocal chants emerged as the dominant form of music in the church. This was a split from the Hebraic tradition where instruments were used in the temples and from the Greek and Roman song tradition. The Greeks and Romans sang songs that were metrical but the Christian psalms, antiphons, prayers, responses, etc. were unmetrical as church music moved away from rhythm to a mystical chant. As the music moved away from rhythm, it also moved away from the people to the sole authority of the clergy. At the Council of Laodicea—held between 343 and 381—it was decreed in The 13th Canon: "Besides appointed singers, who mount the ambo and sing from the book, others shall not sing in the church" (Dickinson 51, quoting from *History of the Councils of the Church* by Hefele, translated by Oxenham). Thus, the musical roles of clergy and laity were set by law.

A large body of liturgic chants had been classified and systematized by the middle or latter part of the sixth century. The teaching of the form and tradition of their rendering was the role of the clergy. The liturgy, which was basically completed during or shortly before the reign of Gregory the Great (590-604) was placed in a musical setting. This liturgical chant was made the law of the

Church, on equal footing with the liturgy itself, and the initial steps to impose one uniform ritual and chant upon all congregations of the West was completed.

The first six centuries of the Catholic Church were essential in the organization and structure of Christianity and the Church controlled the direction of her music, as well as all art. It was during this time that Christian music separated itself from the secular, pagan world by embracing a vocal music without the support of instruments, unencumbered by the antique metre which kept Greek and Roman music in strict prosodic measure. The result was a mystical music that was uniquely the Church's, centered on vocal melody, not on rhythm, which differed dramatically from any other music. Thus the music of the Church, like the Church itself, separated itself from secular culture and developed a music and culture all its own. This Church music defined a universal mood for prayer and reinforced the concept that the expression of the individual was to be subjugated to the whole body.

The first major split in the Christian church occurred in 1054 when the church separated into east and west with the west becoming the Roman Catholic Church and the east evolving to the Greek Orthodox Church. This split came after a long series of disagreements that involved differences in politics, geography, the expressions of faith, the way to worship, details of administration, and language. An unofficial boundary line was established, running the length of the Adriatic and extending south to the Gulf of Libya in Africa with all those living to the east primarily Greek-speaking, while those living to the west generally Latin-speaking. Although there are a number of differences between the two branches of Catholicism, the primary difference is that the Roman Church is headed by a pope while the Greek Orthodox prefer to be governed by a board.

Chapter 3
The Sixteenth Century:
Roots of Contemporary Christianity

The roots of contemporary American Christianity lie in the sixteenth century, particularly with three men: Martin Luther, John Calvin, and Henry VIII. The turning point is 1509—the year Henry VIII ascended to the throne of England, John Calvin was born in France, and Martin Luther, then an Augustinian monk in Wittenberg, Germany, read about the "justification of faith" in the epistle to the Romans and became transformed by the concept of "grace." Luther's pilgrimage would lead to his nailing ninety-five theses to the door at Wittenberg protesting the selling of plenary indulgences, which officially began the Reformation, while Calvin's life would provide Christianity with a book—the *Institutes of Christianity*—which would define and regulate Christianity for centuries. Henry VIII's reign would produce a break with the Catholic church in England, which created a climate for religious dissent—leading to the rise of Protestantism in England—and cause religious factions. This religious upheaval encompassed a spiritual awakening in England, resulting in the settling of America by religious dissenters who viewed the new land as a second Canaan and their mission akin to Moses leading the chosen people to a chosen land to create a God-ordained nation.

Religious movements are a result of spiritual awakenings, and spiritual awakenings are impossible to document in the historical sense because they spring not from "reason," but rather rise from mystical experiences, which are the antithesis of reason and cannot be factually documented. Religious movements are the historian's way of documenting spiritual awakenings, and the Protestant movement came about largely through the spiritual leadership of Martin Luther and John Calvin, and the political actions of Henry VIII. The "documentation" of this spiritual revival came later, through the development of religious movements and writings.

Martin Luther gave Christian theology an individualism; John Calvin gave it a legislation that transformed the individualism into a collective force. The two forces of individualism—through the single soul's spiritual awakening—and collectivism—through the concept of the "body" of Christ consisting of all believing Christians—would unite to pull against each other for centuries. Luther's influence provided an individual liberation that freed the bonds of society on man, setting the soul free to rule the body and serve heavenly purposes in the earthly realm. Calvin preached morality and moralizing, binding the soul to other believers, tying the souls of the elect into a tight bond. Both men believed an individual could communicate with God directly, but Calvin did not trust

10

all individuals to "interpret" this communication correctly. For that reason, the Catholic church's sin against which both men rebelled—the autocratic and authoritative directing of the spiritual life of individuals—became the same sin of the Reformed church under Calvin.

It is when theology is an individual event that it is most revolutionary and most freeing. However, the new liberation of theology by Luther was quickly harnessed by Calvin to live in accordance with the state. It is the state, more than the church, that has dictated the limits of modern Christianity while, at the same time, assuring its success. Most people believe morals are important and should be governed—specifically and most importantly, other people's morals. The success of Calvinistic Christianity can be attributed to the fact that its major goal—the regulation of public morals—is in line with the goals of the state. Certainly the state used Christianity, which exacted a trade-off and received protection and certain perquisites, such as tax free income and property, and access to the power holders of the state. It is under Calvinism that the radicalism of Christianity is tamed and the threat to society is thwarted and turned into cooperation. The result is that Christianity becomes a social code of being "nice" and "good," all within the state's definition of "nice" and "good."

Just as the apostle Paul virtually ignored the physical, earthly Christ and embraced the spiritual Christ to establish a code of behavior for Christians, so Calvin took the writings of Paul and further elaborated on this code. Whereas Paul had to fight the state because it was against Christianity, Calvin embraced the state and developed an alliance where the state and church co-existed in a theocracy. Luther, too, embraced Paul and the concept of the spiritual Christ, and tied the Protestant revolt with German nationalism to mute the threat the state held against Christianity. The net result was a state sanctioned—or at least tolerated and accepted—religion that worked with the state rather than against it. Henry VIII, in his anti-Catholic revolt, also sought to bring the state and religion together with himself as the head of the Anglican church, succeeding in making the state and religion one. However, because of his lack of spiritual leadership, the two forces could never really co-exist as one.

Paul and Luther used music as a means of communicating with God, singing "psalms and hymns and spiritual songs" as the means to express prayer, love, and thanksgiving. Calvin used the laws of the state to carry out the will of God and placed strict limitations on music, insisting it only be used as part of worship. Calvin saw music as a diversion the rest of the time, so music for Christians was limited to congregational singing and not to individual expression. That is why Paul and Luther encouraged music while Calvin frowned on it. The joy of Christianity—expressed by Paul and Luther—became a somber, serious commitment to a code of behavior. Calvin interpreted behavior as sin and placed man in the role of God in judging which behavior was acceptable. It is this emphasis on outward behavior for the inner spiritual life that made Calvinism so appealing to the state. For Calvin, the ideal Christian was a well-behaved person; for Luther, he was a rebel. Both were anti-papacy, but Calvin replaced the Catholic hierarchy with one of his own, giving different names to the offices (elders, deacons, etc. instead of bishops, priests, etc.) but keeping the bureaucracy of belief so that faith would be socially acceptable.

12   The Sound of Light

There was religious dissension in Europe before Martin Luther nailed his ninety-five theses on the Wittenberg door in 1516; however, it was this act—and the subsequent life and trials of Luther—that led to the Protestant Reformation in Europe and the rise of the Anglican church in England as the Catholic Church, headed by the Pope in Rome, lost its grip on Europe in a turmoil that would eventually affect all of Christendom.

Luther was born at Eisleben, Germany, on November 10, 1483, the eldest of seven children to Hans and Grethe Luther. His father, who was a peasant and later a miner, was described as "a hard father and strict judge, exacting a joyless virtue, demanding constant propitiation, and finally damning most of mankind to everlasting hell." Luther's father beat him "assiduously" while his mother was a "timid, modest woman much given to prayer" (Durant 341).

From early in his life, Luther sang well and played the lute. He disliked the academic life and found scholasticism disagreeable, but managed to obtain a master of arts degree at the University of Erfurt, then began to study law. However, after two months of study, Luther quit and decided to become a monk at twenty-two. His "conversion" was a road to Damascus experience, complete with lightning. It occurred as he was returning from his father's house in Erfurt (July 1505) and encountered a storm. Lightning flashed and struck a nearby tree, which seemed to Luther a warning from God that "unless he gave his thoughts to salvation, death would surprise him unshriven and damned...[so] he made a vow to St. Anne that if he survived the storm he would become a monk" (Durant 343). He took his vows of poverty, chastity, and obedience in September, 1506, and was ordained a priest in May 1507.

Luther was reading St. Paul's epistle to the Romans c. 1509 when he was struck by the passage in 1:17, "The just shall live by faith." These words eventually led him to a doctrine that man can be "justified" and saved from hell only by a complete faith in Christ and His atonement for mankind, not by good works, which are insufficient to atone for sins against an infinite deity. During the years 1512-1517 Luther's religious ideas moved away from the official doctrines of the Catholic church. At this time he began to argue that "the mere acceptance of the merits of Christ assured the believer's salvation" and identified the pope as the Antichrist (Durant 345).

There was an inner turmoil within Germany, an undercurrent of rebellion against the indulgences, with thousands ready to protest the corruption of the church, as well as a pent-up anticlericalism which found its voice in Luther. The theologian became the leader of the movement because he first articulated the frustration, then stood and fought a battle against Rome.

Meanwhile, in England, the Protestant Reformation was taking hold, but there was no spiritual leader the magnitude of Luther to lead it. Instead, the anti-papacy movement was led by a political leader, King Henry VIII.

When Henry VIII ascended the throne in England in 1509, he began a thirty-seven year reign that saw him become both a hero and villain during this dramatic time in history. He was eighteen when he became king and was good at athletics, theology, dancing, and literature. According to Sir Thomas More, the king "has more learning than any English monarch ever possessed before him" (Durant 523). However, from this promising beginning of the liberal and erudite young man, there emerged the "incarnation of Machiavelli's Prince" by the end of his reign (Durant 525). During the early part of his reign, Henry VIII protected the papacy; however, at the end of his reign, he was responsible for the decline of papal influence in England, primarily due to the pope's refusal to grant him a marriage easement.

At the beginning of Henry VIII's reign, Cardinal Wolsey controlled much of foreign policy and the government of England. This close relationship between church and state was as much a result of Wolsey's own power and ambition as an alliance between Rome and England. When Martin Luther broke from the Catholic Church in Germany, Henry VIII rushed to the papal defense, publishing his *Assertion of the Seven Sacraments* against Martin Luther in 1521, stating in this work that "the whole church is subject not only to Christ but...to Christ's only vicar, the pope of Rome" (Durant 532). For that, Henry and his successors were given the title of "Defensor Fidei" (Defender of the Faith) by the pope. Luther published his reply in 1525, calling Henry VIII the "King of Lies...by God's disgrace King of England" (Durant 532).

This incensed Henry and he never embraced the German Protestant rebellion and never forgave Luther, despite the latter's later apology. However, despite the King repudiating the German movement, Luther's influence spread in England through a London group called the "Association of Christian Brothers," which distributed tracts from Luther and others as well as English Bibles. At this time, most clergymen discouraged the reading of the Bible because "special knowledge" was needed for the right interpretation and the fact that excerpts from Scripture were being used to foment sedition.

There had been English translations of the Bible before this time (c. 1526) including those by Wycliff, but they were in manuscript form. The English New Testament, however, printed by Tyndale in 1525-6 and translated from the original Hebrew and Greek (as opposed to the Latin Vulgate by Wycliff) achieved epochal importance. Tyndale had gone to Wittenberg in 1524 to work under Luther's guidance on the Bible translation and when the Bible was released in England it was accompanied by a separate volume of notes and aggressive prefaces based on those by Erasmus and Luther. These copies were smuggled into England and "served as fuel to the incipient Protestant fire" despite the efforts of England's clergy to suppress the edition by publicly burning them and trying to silence Tyndale (Durant 533). Cardinal Wolsey ordered Tyndale to appear but the translator eluded English officials until he fell into their hands and was imprisoned for sixteen months near Brussels. Tyndale was burned at the stake in 1536, but the influence of his English translation of the Bible remained strong and heavily influenced the Authorized Version (King James) which was published in 1611.

Henry VIII's marital troubles actually began with Cardinal Wolsey's foreign policy. Wolsey had aligned England with Emperor Charles of Italy to fight France. The expense of the campaign hurt Wolsey with Parliament and the realization that the Continent would soon be under the rule of Charles caused England to align with France against the Emperor in 1528. Compounding this political problem for the control of Europe was the fact that Charles was the nephew of Catherine of Aragon, Henry's wife, whom he desired to divorce. Pope Clement VII, who could grant the divorce and had granted similar requests in the past, was under the control of Charles so, for reasons of state, the divorce would not be granted.

Henry's basic desire was to have a son. Cardinal Wolsey argued for the King here and the papacy had generally acknowledged this national need and had many precedents of granting annulments for this purpose. Emperor Charles, who "controlled" the pope, had an open hostility towards Henry, so "the Catholic Queen and the Catholic Emperor collaborated with the captive Pope to divorce England from the Church" (Durant 538). Historian Will Durant states, "The ultimate cause of the English Reformation was not Henry's suit for annulment so much as the rise of the English monarchy to such strength that it could repudiate the authority of the pope over English affairs and revenues" (538). There were some ideas for reconciliation: the proposal that Henry be allowed to have two wives (a principle that Luther supported later when he addressed the problem of barren wives) but all the appeals failed.

The Parliament and Convocation that convened in 1532 would have lasting historical and religious importance because it was at this time the British agreed to separate from the papacy. From this "Reformation Parliament" the Church of England was born and became an arm and subject of the state. This act would later be of prime importance in the religious toleration and separation of church and state when America was settled.

Since one church no longer dominated religion, no church could stand united and thus religion was split into factions, often warring against each other. A great amount of disorder prevailed in the church because "in some instances the prayer book was rigidly adhered to, in others psalms in metre were added; in some churches the communion table stood in the middle of the chancel, in others altarwise a yard distant from the wall; some ministers officiated at the sacraments in the surplice, others without it; some used a chalice in the communion service, others were content with a common cup; some favoured unleavened bread, others preferred leavened; some baptized in font, others in a basin; some made the sign of the cross, others dispensed with it; and so forth" (Black 192). There was a great rise in religious literature as numerous translations of the Bible as well as biblical commentaries appeared. The *Book of Common Prayer* was published in 1549 and "hours" or "primers," long series of books of devotion, became commonplace.

Chapter 4
A Mighty Fortress:
Martin Luther as Songwriter

More people have heard Martin Luther's songs than have read his essays, biblical commentaries, treatises, sermons, his German Bible or even his 95 theses. Although Luther wrote only thirty-seven songs, it is this body of work which has carried Luther's words and thoughts directly to people for over five centuries. His legacy left in song has lived longer and probably had as great an influence as any of the other works by this leader of the Reformation.

Martin Luther's greatest contribution to the music of the church was to return it to the people. For over a millennium—from the Council of Laodicea in the fourth century until the Reformation in the 1520s—congregations had not sung in church. There were hymns written, but their use was limited to special occasions such as processions, pilgrimages, and some major festivals, all held outside the sanctuary. Luther put music back into the church and in so doing made the congregation an active participant rather than passive onlookers in the church service.

Luther's formal music training began as a boy when he was a soprano in the choir at Mansfield. At the age of 13, in 1497, he attended a cathedral school administered by a religious brotherhood at Madgeburg and studied singing there. Later, at Saint George at Eisenach, he continued his vocal study. In 1501, Luther entered the University at Erfurt where he studied musical theory and composition and learned to play both the flute and lute. He learned the liturgy and plainchant in the Augustinian monastery he entered in 1501; while there, it is said his chief recreations were playing chess and the lute.

Martin Luther had a legendary love for music. He was an accomplished lutanist and could improvise accompaniments for singing. He often played after dinner with his family and guests and composed songs for his children. Throughout his life, he carried his lute with him on his travels and entertained friends and guests after dinner with his singing and playing. Music was not just a recreational tool for Luther—it was an integral part of his life and he found a source of strength and comfort in music. Like Bach, whom he influenced greatly, Luther viewed his music primarily as utilitarian, not as "art for the ages." He stated that we "should praise God with both word and music, namely by proclaiming (the Word of God) through music" and another time said "He who believes (the gospel) earnestly cannot be quiet about it. But he must gladly and willingly sing and speak about it so that others may come and hear it. And whoever does not want to sing and speak of it shows that he does not believe it." Luther's prophetic statement, "I intend to make...spiritual songs so that the Word of God even by means of song may live among the people" became a guiding philosophy in his life (Dinwiddie 19-21).

Luther wrote his first hymn, "Out of the Depths I Cry to Thee," in 1523 at the age of forty. He wrote twenty-three hymns that first year and thirty-seven which still survive. They were generally introduced as broadsheets at the church in Wittenberg and later collected into hymnals. He demanded a simple, straightforward German for his songs—and those by others composed for the new mass—so the people could readily understand them. Of the thirty-seven he composed, twelve were translations from Latin hymns, four from German folk songs, and at least five were "completely original hymns." Catherine Winkworth states,

They were not so much outpourings of the individual soul, as the voice of the congregation meant for use in public worship, or to give the people a short, clear confession of faith, easily to be remembered. But they are not written from the outside; Luther throws into them all his own fervent faith and deep devotion. The style is plain, often rugged and quaint, but genuinely popular. So, too, was their cheerful trust and noble courage; their clear, vigorous spirit, that sprang from steadfast faith in a Redeemer. (108)

In 1524, Luther invited Conrad Rupf, choirmaster to the Elector of Saxony, and Johann Walther, choirmaster to Frederick the Wise at Jorgau, to live with him to help reform and readapt the liturgy for popular use. These men studied the church music and selected tunes which lent themselves to this purpose. They transposed a large number of chorales from old Latin hymns and others from German origin—sacred and secular—while a larger number were composed. In Luther's time, it was customary to change secular songs into religious songs or older Catholic texts into Protestant ones, retaining the original melody. According to Paul Nettl, "Music was considered a functional art and not merely art for art's sake...It was not a question of who created the melody. The purpose counted" (29).

The first hymnal from Luther was given to the congregation in 1524 to read while the choir was singing. However, the people were so unused to joining in the public service "they could not at once adopt the new practice." It took four or five years before Luther taught the people of his own parish church in Wittenberg to sing in church. After this, the custom spread swiftly.

Luther was well aware of the power of music and insisted that its proper use was "to the glorification of God and the edification of man." He said, "We want the beautiful art of music to be properly used to serve her dear Creator and his Christians. He is thereby praised and honored and we are made better and stronger in faith when His holy Word is impressed on our hearts by sweet music." At another time, Luther said of music, "Next to the Word of God, music deserves the highest praise" and "I am quite of the opinion that next to theology, there is no art which can be compared to music; for it alone, after theology, gives us rest and joy" (Dinwiddie 21).

"A Mighty Fortress is Our God" is considered Luther's greatest song. It was based on Psalm 46 from the Vulgate Bible and has been called "The Battle Hymn of the Reformation" (Pollack 193). It first appeared in a hymnal in 1529 and by 1900 had over 80 English translations.

A Mighty Fortress is Our God

A mighty fortress is our God,
a bulwark never failing,
Our helper He amid the flood
of mortal ills prevailing,
For still our ancient foe
doth seek to work us woe;
His craft and power are great,
and, armed with cruel hate
On earth is not his equal.

Did we in our own strength confide,
our strength would be losing;
Were not the right Man on our side,
the Man of God's own choosing;
Dost ask Who that may be?
Christ Jesus, it is He;
Lord Saboath His name,
from age to age the same,
And He must win the battle.

And though this world, with devils filled,
should threaten to undo us;
We will not fear, for god hath willed
His truth to triumph through us;
The Prince of Darkness grim,
we tremble not for him;
His rage we can endure,
for lo! his doom is sure,
One little word shall fell him.

That word above all earthly powers,
no thanks to them, abideth;
The spirit and the gifts are ours
through Him Who with us sideth;
Let good and kindred go,
this mortal life also;
the body they may kill;
God's truth abideth still,
His kingdom is forever.

In this hymn, called "the greatest hymn of the greatest man in the greatest period of German history," Luther takes a stand against the Catholic church and the German state in the line "And though this world, with devils filled, should threaten to undo us" saying that those who opposed the Reformation movement were "devils." He solidifies his own stand with the line, "The spirit and the gifts are ours through Him Who with us sideth" leaving no doubt whose side God is on. This would be a common tactic of Christians in the Protestant movement throughout the centuries—they were in God's favor and all those who opposed them were instruments of the devil. It is an argument impossible to refute, and though it is also impossible to prove, the Christian refutes the question through the self-assurance of his stand.

Luther's first congregational hymn, "Dear Christians, One and All, Rejoice," summarizes his philosophy and own conversion experience. It begins,

> Dear Christians, one and all, rejoice,
> With exultation springing,
> And, with united heart and voice
> And holy rapture singing,
> Proclaim the wonders God hath done,
> How his right arm the victory won;
> Right dearly it hath cost Him.

Luther's hymn, "From Depths of Woe I Cry to Thee" was sung at the funeral of his friend, Frederick the Wise, and also sung at Halle in 1546 when Luther's body was being brought from Eisleben to Wittenberg. Luther's Christian philosophy is expressed in the line "Thy love and grace alone avail to blot out my transgression" while "Though great our sins and sore our woes, His grace much more aboundeth" applies Luther's concept of "grace" and "justification by faith" for all believers. The lines "Therefore my hope is in the Lord and not in mine own merit; It rests upon His faithful Word to them of contrite spirit" are anti-Catholic statements because they asset Luther's belief that God communicates to people through the Bible and not the clergy.

Martin Luther had an immense regard for the power of music and its compatibility with the gospel. He stated, "I should like to see all the arts, and especially music, used in the service of Him who gave and created them" (Dinwiddie 21). Luther's joy of life was expressed by his love for music and his strong belief was communicated through songs he composed. Those songs have been sung in religious revivals for hundreds of years, carrying the spirit of the Reformation all over Europe and on to other continents as Protestantism spread all over the world. Through the spread of Protestantism, a continuing appeal has been the songs it has generated while Luther's leadership in giving all people a chance to sing in church has made that religion come alive, infused with joy, for centuries. Because of the songs he composed, Martin Luther is not just an historical figure for Christianity but a current presence as well—vibrant, alive, and communicating his timeless message through the ages with his songs.

Chapter 5
First Seeds:
Gospel Music in America

For America, the 17th century was a time of settlement and each group of new settlers that arrived brought some new songs. There were songs from churches and songs from the taverns, traditional ballads, and new songs composed by people about timeless love or topical news events. A distinctive American voice would not truly emerge until the nineteenth century, but the musical roots of America were planted in the seventeenth and eighteenth centuries.

The settlers in the Jamestown and Plymouth colonies were not the first to come to the new world; in fact, the first Europeans to establish themselves in America were the Spanish explorers who came through Mexico and into the southwestern area of what is now the United States. The first gospel songs sung in the new world have been traced to the Roman Catholic church through the inhabitants of southern America and Mexico. Catholic service books were published in Mexico as early as 1556 and the main effect of this Catholic influence was to introduce to America the Gregorian chant, sung in Latin.

However, the true settling and growth of what became identified as the United States came from the European settlers who peopled the eastern seaboard and then began moving westward. To understand early American music, a knowledge of Europe and European music is necessary since the roots for America are embedded in the European culture these settlers left.

The Reformation in Europe brought a new song, sung in the vernacular (not in Latin) by the entire congregation. Two basic forms emerged here, the chorale (associated with the Lutherans and Moravians), and the psalm tune, which developed among the Calvinists. Both the French and English sang psalms which were paraphrased in meter, to which were added paraphrases of other lyric passages from scriptures. They sang "God's word," but welcomed devotional poems written by individuals. The Puritans of New England came from the Calvinist tradition and the transition in America from scriptural to devotional poems—psalms to hymns—was a long and gradual one, hindered by the Puritans' strict adherence to the psalms. Musically, there was a major difference as the Lutherans and Moravians made use of the organ and orchestral instruments in worship while the Calvinists and English dissenters limited their music to metrical poems sung in unison.

American Hymns Old and New records that psalms were sung at Port Royal, an island near Charleston, South Carolina, in 1562 by a party of Huguenots who landed there and that a short-lived settlement was established in Florida two years later. According to the authors, the Indians there remembered two

19

of the psalms long after the settlement was destroyed. The first English-sung psalms in the new world were noted by Francis Fletcher, the chaplain who sailed with Sir Francis Drake in 1577. He recorded the interest in singing of the Indians in the region now known as San Francisco.

When the settlers landed in Jamestown, Virginia in 1607, they brought with them the Este psalter, with some evidence that they also had copies of the Sternhold and Hopkins (The Old Version) psalter. The songbooks brought to the Plymouth colony were the Sternhold and Hopkins psalter, the Scottish psalter, and the psalter by Ainsworth.

The Sternhold and Hopkins psalter began with a group of psalms written by Thomas Sternhold and performed with his organ accompaniment. His *Certayne Psalmes* was the earliest version, published before his death in 1549. John Hopkins added seven more in 1551 and by 1562 it included all of the psalms. French tunes entered the English repertory in 1553 when many English refugees fled to Geneva after Mary Tudor became queen. It was at this time that the development of spiritual songs, or hymns, began, primarily due to the French influence on the English refugees.

The Scottish Presbyterians were the last to give up the exclusive use of psalms and the most vigorous in rejecting the inclusion of musical instruments. The earliest Scottish psalter appeared in 1564. The Ainsworth Psalter was brought from Holland by the settlers who landed at Plymouth in 1620. This was a collection of psalms with "suitable melodies" by Henry Ainsworth and was used during the early years of colonial America.

The first collection of gospel songs published in America was *The Whole Booke of Psalmes Faithfully Translated Into English Metre*, commonly known as *The Bay Psalm Book*. It appeared in 1640 in the Plymouth colony in Massachusetts and contained the first version of psalms made by Americans and used in American churches. The question of whether hymns ("Psalms invented by the gifts of godly men") were to be included in church services was raised in the preface (written by either Richard Mather or John Cotton) with the decision reached to sing only psalms or other paraphrases from passages in the Bible. Some hymns were added to the *Bay Psalm Book* in the 1647 edition.

The success of the *Bay Psalm Book* was immediate, with 1700 copies in the first printing and 2000 copies of a new edition in 1651. In all, there were twenty-seven editions of this book printed in New England and at least twenty in England (the last in 1754), and six in Scotland. The ninth edition, published in 1698, was the first to contain music to accompany the texts. Prior to that, only the words were printed and they were sung to a known melody with a handful of melodies fitting a large number of songs. According to Richard Crawford, "singers knowing a mere half-dozen tunes could sing the entire psalter. The evidence is that around the end of the seventeenth century many congregations actually knew no more than that" ("The Birth of Liberty").

Personal, devotional verse is predominant in the seventeenth century, with Cotton Mather and Jonathan Edwards both writing and singing hymns "unto the Lord." Examples of devotional verse are the poems of Anne Bradstreet, John Wilson's "Song of Deliverance," Michael Wigglesworth's "Day of Doom," and the "Meditations" of Edward Taylor.

In the eighteenth century, some changes evolved, basically reflecting the changes occurring in England. The Methodists and their Methodism brought the Wesley hymns to New Jersey and the later comers to New England imported Isaac Watts. Ironically, the initial resistance Watts encountered with his hymns in America was the same he had encountered in England; his "hymns of human composure" were not literal renderings of the psalms but rather from the human heart. During this time, the psalm was still the predominant form of gospel music, sung in churches as well as homes.

The Great Awakening was responsible for a large influx of hymns into church services, altering the traditional view of scriptural songs being the only music in church. Beginning in Wales, under Howell Harris (c. 1730), The Great Awakening witnessed an infusion of religion in society, producing laws that eliminated some of the exploitation and abuse of the poor as well as injecting a genuine spirit of revival into the souls of a great number of people, especially among the lower classes. It grew to epic proportions under George Whitefield (1736-1790) and the Wesleys (1739-1791). In America, The Great Awakening began with Jonathan Edwards in New England (c. 1734) and received an incredible boost under the leadership of George Whitefield, who came to America in 1740, met Edwards in Massachusetts, and travelled throughout the colonies preaching.

Hymn singing caught fire in America in 1740 during Whitefield's visit. According to Hamilton C. MacDougal in *Early New England Psalmody*, "It is easy to understand how welcome the new hymn tunes were, with their pulsating, secular rhythms, their emotional repetitions, the fugal tunes, the iterations of words to cumulative sequences after the 'sleep' of formalism" (137). The author continues that the Methodists with their hymns and singing burst "like heralds of new life." Crowds were drawn to the services by the irresistible charm of the music. The effect of this revival on hymns was felt for more than a hundred years, although the domination of Watts songs inhibited lyrical expression until well into the nineteenth century.

During the 1600s and early 1700s, the New England congregations were noted for singing their psalm tunes at a very slow tempo, known as the "old way." As with most religious customs, its adherents defended it as the "only proper mode" for performing music in church. This was challenged in the early part of the eighteenth century by advocates of the "new way," who encouraged singing by note instead of rote, briskly in harmony rather than slowly and in unison. The state of singing had sunk to a low from years of having no formal music training for singers and psalm books with texts but no melodies to read. In *America and Their Songs*, Frank Luther states, "By 1700 things had reached such a point that people could hardly sing together at all. Everybody had his own idea of the tune; and while it might sound well enough when one sang alone, when a hundred people in one room sang a hundred different versions of the same tune at the same time, it sounded like nothing so much as a three-cornered dog-fight" (25).

This problem was solved with the rise of the singing school, which gave instruction and training in the rudiments of music to members of a church or community. The first two manuals written to meet this need, both thin pamphlets, were written by ministers: John Tufts and Thomas Walter. The first edition of Tuft's *An Introduction to the Singing of Psalm-Tunes* probably appeared in 1721, the same year as Walter's treatise. The study of sight singing was taken up by Americans with "enormous zest" and there was a singing school in Boston in 1717. The eighteenth and early nineteenth centuries also saw the rise of the singing master. Not only were these classes for singing, but they were also social occasions for the youth in the area, a feature that caused many of the church fathers to frown on the desirability of these gatherings. The impact of the singing master was greatest in the rural areas and small towns; the congregations in the coastal towns retained a closer tie with English tastes. The methods of the singing master are described in *American Hymns Old and New*, which states, "The singing master generally canvassed the neighborhood, assembled a class, and engaged a large room which might be a schoolhouse, a church, or a tavern. He taught the rudiments of notation, a method of beating time, and solmization. These principles were applied to psalm tunes, and the session terminated with an 'exhibition' in which the class sang the tunes which they had learned to their assembled relatives, friends, and neighbors" (110).

While psalm singing dominated the seventeenth century and continued through the introduction of hymns in the eighteenth century, the nineteenth century was marked by the emergence of the denominational hymn. The order of service was planned to "give the congregational hymn its due place" (Christ-Janer 273). Although tenors generally sang the melody earlier, sopranos sang the melody in the nineteenth century. The use of the tuning fork or pitch pipe established the key. But because there was a prejudice against musical instruments in worship the pitch pipe was often disguised to resemble a psalm book.

Like the eighteenth century, the bass viol was often used as an accompanying instrument; it was generally a cello with a short neck and its introduction "caused violent controversies and schisms" (Christ-Janer, 274). In Salem, Massachusetts, the clarinet and violin were first played in church on Christmas Day, 1792, and a flute was played there in 1795. In 1814 in Boston the singing was accompanied by flute, bassoon and cello. Gradually, the organ was accepted as a proper instrument for the church, with small pipe organs and melodians being played. Still, the churches proved reluctant and slow to adapt any musical adornment to the plain singing of the congregation during the first 200 years in America.

In the early New England churches, social status was reflected in the seating of the congregation. In the seventeenth century, one person "set the pitch," then the entire congregation sang the psalm. However, the eighteenth century brought the emergence of the musical elite—the choir—which changed the seating pattern (and architecture) within the church. During this time, a gallery was erected over the entrance vestibule and sometimes on three sides of the church, with the choir sitting apart from the congregation. Wealthy churches with a highly developed liturgy often established professional choirs or choirs with some professional singers. Some of the churches which did not support a choir would hire a professional quartet of singers and an organist.

The influences of England remained strong throughout the eighteenth century in the American churches. This was because English tunes were republished in America as well as the fact that many American composers were born and trained in England. There were three types of music cultivated by the New England composers—the psalm tune, the fuguing tune, and the anthem. The voices tended to move together with little or no word repetition in the psalm tune; the fuguing tune was in two sections—the first more or less choral in texture and the second beginning with free imitative entries in each of the voices, which were repeated.

During the eighteenth century, the two most important psalters were by Tate and Brady and by Isaac Watts. The earliest American edition of Tate and Brady was published in Boston in 1713, although this book, called "The New Version," was originally published by Nahum Tate and Nicholas Brady in England in 1696. The Episcopal congregations in America adapted an abridged version of Tate and Brady after the Revolution. The Watts psalter first appeared in England in 1719. The first America edition, printed by Benjamin Franklin, was published in Philadelphia in 1729. It did not sell well. The major problem with the Watts psalter, according to the American religious establishment, was that Watts did not paraphrase all the psalms. He omitted the precatory psalms and he did not repeat himself when the psalms did. During this time Americans were accustomed to read or sing all of the psalms in numerical order, sung at one standing, regardless of the subject of the sermon. The second major problem with the Watts psalter was the laudatory lines to Great Britain and her ruler, which became increasingly unacceptable as America moved closer to the Revolution and the break with Great Britain. However, many religious leaders sought to complete Watts' version and adapt it for American use. Before his psalter appeared, Isaac Watts had published *Hymns and Spiritual Songs* in 1707, which soon found their way to the new world. The first American edition of this work was published in Boston in 1739, followed by editions in Philadelphia (1742) and New York (1752) and these hymns were welcomed, imitated, and incorporated into private devotions within Protestant denominations in this country.

American psalters during this time were developed by Thomas Prince, who revised the *Bay Psalm Book* in 1758 with such freedom as to nearly produce an entirely new version. Cotton Mather (1718) and John Barnard (1752) also produced versions of their own, while John Mycall (1775) and Joel Barlow (1785) endeavored to amend the patriotic lines in Watts and fill in the gaps he left. Henry Alline was among the early Baptist hymn writers in America whose *Choice Hymns and Spiritual Songs* was published in 1786. Samuel Holyoke published his *Harmonia American* in 1791 and *Village Hymns* of Asahel Nettleton were published in 1824. *The Divine Hymns or Spiritual Songs* by Joshua Smith was another favorite book with the Baptists, with many of these hymns set to music by Jeremiah Ingalls. The first Catholic hymnal in the United States was published by John Aitkin and titled *A Compilation of the Litanies, Vesper Hymns, and Anthems, as sung in the Catholic Church*. This was published in Philadelphia in 1787. For the Episcopals, collections of hymns included those by William Duke (1790) and Andrew Fowler (1798) titled *A Selection of Psalms with Occasional Hymns* published in Charleston in 1792. Hymn writers among the Universalists included John Murray, whose first hymns were published in 1782, Silas Ballouw, whose collection appeared in 1785, and George Richards, whose *Psalms, Hymns, and Spiritual Songs* appeared in 1792.

The development of tune books (books which contained melodies) was due primarily to enterprising individuals who developed these books for singing school classes, church choirs and, eventually, for the organist. There was an obvious convenience having the music associated with the words, although they were generally on opposite pages. After the mid-nineteenth century, the congregation hymnal with words and music appeared. The words were generally under the tune and sometimes several texts were given for one tune. The most convenient were the books where the words were printed between the staves, in upright form, a form still used today.

Sacred music had long felt the influence of secular music as congregations were exposed to both forms in their lives. According to Richard Crawford in his essay, "The Birth of Liberty," "Americans were used to singing a variety of sacred texts to a small number of psalm tunes. They also were likely to know by heart a stock of secular tunes from the English theatre and from the broadside-ballad tradition, and to be accustomed to singing those tunes to old and new texts." During this time, it was not unusual for one melody to be used over and over again with new verses written. This occurred in both religious and secular music with a handful of tunes being the source of countless songs, writers feeling that the familiarity of the tune helped people learn the verses quickly as well as the general belief that all music was public domain.

The eighteenth century, however, saw a secularization of sacred music occur that would help make that music more appealing to the masses of people as well as carry it outside the church where it would stand outside of worship. In his essay, "Make a Joyful Noise," Richard Crawford states, "The conflict between sacred music as a subordinate part of worship and as an independent art is a classic fact of Christian church history." He notes that the churches of New England adopted Calvinist practice by prohibiting musical instruments or choirs in their public worship, thus separating themselves from the professional music traditions of the Roman Catholics, the Lutherans, and the Anglicans. In the latter churches, the emphasis on the music had shifted from the congregation to a designated group of singers singing to a non-participating audience, like a theatre. The introduction of choirs led to more elaborate song, with a tendency towards "wide-ranging melodies, word repetitions, 'fuguing' (imitative voice overlapping), fast tempos and expressive treatment of text," which placed it in a totally different musical environment and framework than that known to Cotton Mather and his associates. Crawford states,

There is a crucial difference...between the transformation of eighteenth century Protestant Christianity and the transformation of its music in New England: the former was effected by the church leaders, the latter by musicians...The musicians took over sacred music, originally under the clerical control, not by the usual means of effecting change—defining an issue and debating it and deciding it by action of the clergy or congregation—but by gradual encroachment...It grew from a tradition rooted in religious ritual, but it has held the interest of later musicians for precisely the reasons that religious leaders objected to it in its own day: it transcended the ritual of public worship and came to flourish as an independent art. ("Joyful Noise")

The emergence of sacred music from a part of the church service, integral but subordinate to the preaching, to a form of art that stands on its own is a vital ingredient in looking at the history of sacred music in America, especially the developments in the latter part of the twentieth century. This affected audiences as well as musicians and Crawford notes, "Americans in the 1760s came for the first time to recognize psalmody as an art, as an activity demanding creative inspiration (composing) as well as performance (singing) and requiring technical proficiency of both creator and performer" ("Joyful Noise").

The secular influence was felt strongly in sacred music as the church began to be dominated by the culture in much the same way the Puritan church dominated the secular culture in early New England. Alan Lomax in "White Spirituals from the Sacred Harp," states,

The editors of the early New England hymnbooks largely included the more formal hymns and psalms from British sources; but from the time of the Revolution forward, more native and more folk-originated material was included...a large proportion of these tunes were simply religious remakes of secular love songs and dance tunes, exhibiting the traits of traditional folk music in their gapped modal scales and their use of the lowered seventh...the radical Methodists, like John and Charles Wesley...brought many British folk and popular tunes into the hymnals by setting religious words to them; and, all-pervasive...the Baptists, who led the way in the popular religious revivals in Britain and America and thus introduced many folk tunes and much folksy singing into the church.

This influence of folk music, as well as the establishment of singing schools and the Great Revival of the nineteenth century, established the roots of the Sacred Harp and white spiritual traditions and paved the way for twentieth century southern gospel music.

Chapter 6
Isaac Watts

The songs of Isaac Watts can be considered rhymed Calvinism. Ironically, though, it was the break from the Calvinist code which insisted that songs should only come directly from Scripture, that made Isaac Watts such a radical and influential writer of hymns. Still, except for this break with Calvinism in his view of music, (although Calvinists and fundamentalists later agreed and joined him) Isaac Watts presented a body of work for the believers which embodies the fundamental Christian faith espoused by Martin Luther and John Calvin.

It is difficult to imagine a small, sickly man, standing five feet five, with a hooked nose, small beady eyes and a head made even larger by the powdered wig topping a frail, sickly body as a "giant." Yet Watts was (and still is) a giant among hymn writers. He dominated the field in his day and his hymns continue to hold a preeminent place in gospel music. Time is a great editor and the fifty or so hymns which congregations still sing may be considered his definitive hymns.

Watts was born in 1674, son of a religious father whose dissenting views caused him to be jailed several times while Isaac was a youth. Later, his father moved to London and became a wealthy clothier. Isaac's father taught his son at home and the youth learned Latin at four, Greek at eight or nine, French when he was eleven, and Hebrew at thirteen. From his earliest days, Isaac had a penchant for rhyming, a talent that drove his father to frustration and exasperation.

In 1701, at the age of twenty-six, Watts began as pastor for the Mark Lane Independent Chapel in London. His parishioners loved him and soon hired an assistant pastor because Watts' ill health would not allow him to preach every Sunday. Still, Watts remained in the Mark Lane pastorate for twenty-two years, holding no other pastorate in his life. The congregation was largely wealthy and prominent, consisting of merchants and politicians. One parishioner, Sir Thomas Abney, was elected Lord Mayor of London in 1700 and once invited Watts to spend a week at his country estate. Watts accepted the invitation and remained there thirty-six years, until Abney died, then moved with the family to another estate until his own death. Except for the earliest hymns, Watts wrote most of his hymns on these luxurious estates.

Isaac Watts was a man of considerable learning. In addition to his hymns—which were really religious poetry set to common known melodies—Watts wrote a number of books, including *Logic, The Knowledge of the Heavens and Earth Made Easy, Divine and Moral Songs*, books on grammar, pedagogy, ethics, psychology, three volumes of sermons, and twenty-nine treatises on theology—fifty-two works in all in addition to his poetry. He received the Doctorate of

Divinity from both Aberdeen and Edinburgh universities and was considered the leading religious poet of his day. A lifelong bachelor, Watts became like a member of the Abney family as he shared their home.

Watts began writing hymns at fifteen. Appalled by the horrendous and lamentable singing in churches he attended, he stated, "The singing of God's praise is the part of worship nighest heaven, and its performance among us is the worst on earth." After returning from a service one Sunday morning, Isaac complained to his father about the singing; his father replied, "Give us something better, young man." Before the evening service, Watts had written his first hymn, "Behold the glories of the Lamb,/ Amidst his Father's throne;/ Prepare new honors for his name,/ And songs before unknown" (Bailey 48). That evening, the hymn was lined out (a practice where the clerk announced a line, then the congregation sang it) and sung.

Isaac Watts created a revolution in hymn writing by breaking the stranglehold of David's Psalms on the liturgy and substituting "hymns of composure." He was not the first writer of English hymns, although he is given the title, "Father of English Hymnology," but he was the first to thoughtfully develop a theory of congregational praise and provide a well-rounded body of material to be used in the church. Watts' theory was that our songs are a human offering of praise to God, and therefore the words should be our own. This contrasted with the Calvinistic theory, which the Church had held, that the inspired words of the Bible, particularly the Psalms, were the only fit offerings of praise that man could make. Watts' arguments were sound and finally won out against long and determined opposition. Secondly, Watts maintained that if the Psalms were to be sung, they should be Christianized and modernized.

Watts took his two theories and two kinds of hymns—the hymns of "human composure," which were his own, and hymns based on the Psalms—and infused his own interpretations and imagination. In these "Imitations of the Psalms," Watts replaced the allegiance to Israel and Judah with a patriotism for England and made the Psalms' author speak like the King of England.

Watts' hymns were composed in simple meter and sung to whatever familiar tune was chosen by the Clerk. They were sung in the church where Watts preached and composed for the practice of "lining out." According to Watts, "I have seldom permitted a stop in the middle of a line, and seldom left the end of a line without one, to comport a little with the unhappy Mixture of Reading and Singing, which cannot presently be reformed" (Bailey 49).

The first collection of Watts' songs, *Hymns and Spiritual Songs*, was published in 1707. The composer's intention was "to write down to the Level of Vulgar Capacities, and to furnish Hymns for the meanest of Christians." The poetry should be "simple, sensuous, and passionate" (Bailey 49). The simplicity is apparent as anyone with a basic intelligence can understand what he means with his verse while his meters were standard—common, long, and short. Watts' sensuousness is obvious as he uses words to conjure pictures in the mind with images from the Bible, nature, and everyday occurrences and experiences. His hymns are passionate because they are charged with the emotion of a true believer. According to Albert Bailey in *The Gospel in Hymns*,

They shed a glow of joy or resound with praise. Even the cold logic of Calvinism catches fire: God is apprehended emotionally, in awe, or dread, or fear; as love, or power, or infinity; Christ is full of human sympathy that evokes from the individual a personal response; a man is filled with hope or fear, with joy or penitence; he is torn by doubts or enraptured by the certainties of heaven. In Watts at his best there is nothing drab or passive; all is vivid and active. (61)

The theology of Watts and Calvin is sung in the hymns. God is an arbitrary and absolute ruler, man is totally depraved, and people fall under considerable conviction of sin. There is no appeal to the lost souls because the concept of predestination precluded a sinner's option to change. Foreordination and election meant that man was powerless to change the status determined for him before the foundation of the world, so it was an exercise in futility for a hymn writer to seek out those souls and attempt to convert them. Not until the Wesleys came with their missionary zeal and songs of evangelistic outreach did this concept of Christianity change.

Watts' theology came directly from John Calvin, whose theology was inspired by St. Augustine and the Apostle Paul—the author of basic precepts of earthly Christianity. The followers of these theologians found a dreadful religion with a monster God who outrages our sense of justice and contradicts reason. In the tragedy of human history, Christ is a figure of redemption only for the privileged few chosen for heaven even before their birth. Of course, one can never tell if he is among the elect, he must put his total trust in Christ then wait to see what happens. If you are not among the elect, you will not be able to put your full trust in Him; however, if you feel a trust it may be a deceit of the Devil to give you that sense of security. In the end, the believer hopes for election with fear and trembling, always sure but never assured.

One of the greatest of Watts' hymns is "When I Survey That Wondrous Cross," written for communion service in 1707. It was inspired by the line in Galatians 6:14, "But far be it for me to glory save in the cross of our Lord Jesus Christ, through which the world hath been crucified to me, and I unto the world." The melody used today is an eighteenth century English melody.

When I Survey the Wondrous Cross
When I survey the wondrous cross
On which the Prince of Glory died,
My richest gain I count but loss,
And pour contempt on all my pride.

Forbid it, Lord, that I should boast,
Save in the death of Christ, my God:
All the vain things that charm me most,
I sacrifice them to his blood.

See, from his head, his hands, his feet,
Sorrow and love flow mingled down!
Did e'er such love and sorrow meet,
Or thorns compose so rich a crown?

Were the whole realm of nature mine,
That were an off'ring far too small;
Love so amazing, so divine,
Demands my soul, my life, my all.

The song is an example of the complete surrender of the believer to the crucified Christ, whose death atoned for mankind's sins. The term "survey" indicates that Watts (and all who sing the hymn fervently) study the crucifixion, deeply contemplating the meaning of this great sacrifice.

Watts did not write any Christmas songs because the Dissenters believed Christmas to be the celebration of a pagan holiday. However, his "Joy to the World," written from Psalm 98:4, is used almost exclusively as a Christmas carol in the twentieth century.

Joy to the World! The Lord is Come
Joy to the world! the Lord is come;
Let earth receive her King;
Let every heart prepare Him room,
And heaven and nature sing,
And heaven and nature sing,
And heaven, and heaven and nature sing.

Joy to the world! the Saviour reigns;
Let men their songs employ;
While fields and flood, rocks, hills and plains
Repeat the sounding joy,
Repeat the sounding joy,
Repeat, repeat the sounding joy.

He rules the world with truth and grace,
And makes the nations prove
The glories of His righteousness,
And wonders of His love,
And wonders of His love,
And wonders, and wonders of His love.

Watts was well aware of the treasure of praise songs in the Psalms but objected to the indiscriminate use of the Psalms. The Church failed to discard the obsolete and un-Christian elements in the Psalms. There was a tendency towards anti-Semitism in Watts' time because the Jews had rejected Jesus as the Savior and Watts sought to eliminate the strong Judaism in the Psalms and replace it with Calvinist Christianity. Watts tried to "improve" the Psalms for ten years and in 1719 published *The Psalms of David Imitated in the Language of the New Testament, and Apply'd to the Christian State and Worship.* This was a radical work because Watts did not provide a metrical translation or paraphrases but produced songs "inspired" by the Psalms which followed the general thought of the original. According to Watts, "Tis not a translation of David that I pretend, but an imitation of him, so nearly in Christian hymns that the Jewish Psalmist may plainly appear, and yet leave Judaism behind"

(Bailey 52). Watts' work eventually dominated the field of Psalmody and superseded the Old Version of Sternhold and Hopkins and the New Version of Tate and Brady.

A good example of Watts' use of the Psalms as inspiration is his use of Psalm 23 to produce "My Shepherd Will Supply My Need."

My Shepherd Will Supply My Need (Psalm 23)
My shepherd will supply my need;
Jehovah is his name:
In pastures fresh he makes me feed,
Beside the living stream.
He brings my wandering spirit back,
When I forsake his ways;
And leads me, for his mercy's sake,
In paths of truth and grace.

When I walk through the shades of death
Thy presence is my stay;
One word of thy supporting breath
Drives all my fears away.
Thy hand, in sight of all my foes,
Doth still my table spread;
My cup with blessings overflows,
Thine oil anoints my head.

The sure provisions of my God
Attend me all my days;
O may thy house be my abode,
And all my work be praise.
There would I find a settled rest,
While others go and come;
No more a stranger, nor a guest,
But like a child at home.

In "Before Jehovah's Awful Throne," Watts uses Psalm 100 to present Calvinism and the concept of predestination. The concept of the chosen elect, the concept of the all-powerful, arbitrary God, and the replacement of Israel with Europe (in this case Great Britain) as God's chosen land are all found here. Fortunately, the first verse was edited out by the Wesleys before they published it.

Before Jehovah's Awful Throne
Sing to the Lord with joyful voice;
Let every land his name adore;
The British Isles shall send the noise
Across the ocean to the shore.

Before Jehovah's awful throne,
Ye nations, bow with sacred joy;
Know that the Lord is God alone;

He can create, and He destroy.

We are His people, we His care,
Our souls and all our mortal frame;
What lasting honors shall we rear,
Almighty Maker, to Thy name?

We'll crowd Thy gates with thankful songs,
High as the heavens our voices raise;
And earth with her ten thousand tongues,
Shall fill Thy courts with sounding praise.

Wide as the world is Thy command,
Vast as eternity Thy love;
Firm as a rock Thy truth must stand,
When rolling years shall cease to move. Amen.

Isaac Watts wrote from both his head and his heart. He was an intelligent man who mastered the mechanics of writing what he fervently believed. This combination of a skillful writer writing songs from the heart, expressing his deep faith, is what makes the hymns of Watts remain so powerful today. In "Begin, My Tongue, Some Heavenly Theme", Watts could have been expressing his heart, mind, and soul when he wrote the lyrics. It is certainly his personal philosophy as well as that of fundamentalist Calvinism and an admonition to all who compose hymns.

Begin, My Tongue, Some Heavenly Theme
Begin, my tongue, some heavenly theme,
And speak some boundless thing,
The mighty works, or mightier name,
Of our eternal King.

Tell of His wondrous faithfulness,
And sound His power abroad;
Sing the sweet promise of His grace,
The love and truth of God.

His very word of grace is strong
As that which built the skies;
The voice that rolls the stars along
Speaks all the promises.

O might I hear Thy heavenly tongue
But whisper, "Thou art Mine!"
Those gentle words should raise my song
To notes almost divine.

Chapter 7
The Wesleys

The Wesleys, like Isaac Watts, are known for their songs of personal experiences; however, while Watts remained amongst the rich, the Wesleys were involved with the poor as the Great Awakening brought a deep concern for the individual. This contrasted with the apathy of the established church towards the social and economic degradation of the masses of poor who inhabited England at that time. Still, the Wesleys were influenced by Watts (their first hymnal had 70 selections—half by Watts) and they encountered some of the same difficulties with the established churches in getting their hymns accepted.

In 1660, the Anglican Church was restored to power in England; naturally, it was a strong defender of the monarchy from which it derived its privileges, class distinctions, wealth, and power. Being political, the higher church offices were for sale and ambitious men, regardless of character or ability, filled these offices. However, the ordinary, working rector who did the day-to-day duties of the church was paid little; the Wesleys' father, Samuel, was a clergyman who spent months in prison because he could not pay debts incurred for the basics of life.

There was a need for a revolution in the social structure: beneath the upper class was a worldly, amoral middle class dedicated to making themselves rich merchants at the expense of the poor, lower class. Four out of five children born in England died during this time—but among the poor it was worse, only one in 500 illegitimate children survived while gin factories, gambling dens, and harlotry all contributed to a national degeneracy.

Three great evangelists—John and Charles Wesley and George Whitefield—all confronted these societal problems. Albert Bailey, in his book *The Gospel in Hymns* states,

(They) tackled the problem of reform, not from the economic or social point of view, but from the religious. They believed that the spirit of God could change the hearts of men, could make them desire a better life there, and, trusting in the saving power of God through Christ, could break the chains of sin and cause them to rise to a sobriety and dignity which was theirs by right. Historians can trace the revolutionary effects of their preaching in all fields: personal morality, health, politics, the penal code, class barriers, economic and personal slavery, education, literature, music, and the religious life of all sects. (76)

To the established church in England, these evangelists were forbidden to preach in any church and their enthusiasm was "condemned as an excitation of the devil" (Bailey 77). Despite several prominent clergymen of the time condemning the Wesleys, both John and Charles died in full communion with the Church of England; Methodism was not established as a separate dissenting sect until 1808, 17 years after the death of John Wesley.

John Wesley (1703-1791) travelled over a quarter of a million miles (mostly on horseback) while preaching approximately 40,000 sermons and converting at least 100,000 people. He was known for rising at four in the morning, retiring at ten at night, and never wasting a minute, reading hundreds of volumes while travelling on horseback—in spite of being undersized with a frail appearance. He wrote 233 original works, kept a diary for 66 years that accounted for every hour in every day, could read in Hebrew, Greek and Latin, and could preach in English, German, French, and Italian, mastering Spanish enough to pray in that tongue.

On his first voyage to America with younger brother Charles, he learned there were some Moravians on board; immediately he set out to learn German so he could converse with them. The Moravians loved to sing and their services convinced Wesley of the immense value of singing. At this time there was no hymn singing in the Church of England and psalm singing was "in its worst estate" (Bailey 79). Wesley would translate a number of German hymns and sing them in his early morning devotions, in sickrooms, and in larger gatherings on weekday nights and on Sundays.

In 1737, in Savannah, Georgia, John Wesley printed these hymns and psalms in *Collections of Psalms and Hymns*, which was the first hymnal ever used in an Anglican church. Five hymns came from Wesley's father and another five from his brother, Samuel; Charles had not yet begun to write. All was not well with Wesley's parishioners, however, as most objected to anything but the psalms to sing.

Although John Wesley was a known preacher, his real 'conversion' did not come until after his initial American trip when he returned to London and attended some more Moravian meetings. Brother Charles had been converted at a Moravian meeting three days earlier and the two would form a team after this with a passion for spreading the gospel.

John Wesley's major contribution to gospel music was editing, organizing and publishing the hymns of Charles. This body of work became one of the most powerful evangelizing tools that England ever knew. He also extensively translated German hymns into English, especially those by Paul Gerhardt, Tersteegen, and Zinzendorf.

Charles Wesley (1707-1788) attended Christ Church, Oxford, then went to Georgia as a private secretary to Governor Oglethorpe. However, he soon fell out of favor with the Governor and others because of some escapades with adventuring females and returned to England. After his conversion at the Moravian rooms at Aldergate, Charles met with his brother, John, and they discussed their mutual experiences; afterward they resolved to become partners to reach the poor and outcast in the United Kingdom. Beginning with prisoners in London, the brothers preached, encountering hostile mobs and more subtle persecutions while exhibiting tremendous energy, courage, self-sacrifice, and a power in preaching. The converts of the Wesleys fared no better, often they were "outrageously treated— stoned, mauled, ducked, hounded with bulldogs, threatened; homes looted, businesses ruined" (Bailey 83).

Charles Wesley wrote his first hymn the day after his conversion, "Where Shall My Wandering Soul Begin." After this hardly a day or an experience passed without him putting it into a song. He composed in his study, his garden, on horseback—anywhere. In the end, he had composed 6500 hymns of Scripture texts on every conceivable phase of Christian experience and Methodist theology. John began to select and publish hymn tracts in small collections. Later he published larger collections. In 53 years, there were 56 publications. The culmination of the series was the hymnal of 1780, *A Collection of Hymns for the Use of the People Called Methodists*. Not only was this a complete collection of songs, it was also a complete manual for religious education. It was a religion that was "intense, introspective, and yet so socially concerned; humble yet militant—as if religion, salvation, character, the will to save others, were the most important things in the world" (Bailey 85).

In discussing the effect of the Wesleys' Methodist movement, Albert Bailey states,

The Methodist Revival did not concern itself with the reformation of social institutions. It did not tackle evils from the legislative end. It did work a moral transformation in the lives of thousands of people and thus prepared the public conscience and raised up the leaders to enact the legislative reforms of the nineteenth century. John Wesley has expressed the rationale of it: 'The sure hope of a better age is a better man.' Yet the Wesleys were perfectly conscious that institutions needed reformation. They spoke fiercely against human slavery, war, inhuman prisons, barbarous laws, the abuse of privilege, power and wealth, the liquor traffic. (88)

The Wesleys' Methodist theology contrasted sharply with the Calvinistic theology of the day in the issue of "election." Isaac Watts represented the Calvinists, who believed that God had chosen some men to be saved and some to be damned and man could do nothing to change his foreordained state while Wesley, following the Dutch theologian Arminius (1560-1609) believed man is free and that he himself can decide whether he will be saved. Therefore, Christ's death on the cross atoned for the sins of all men, not a chosen few. This meant that men are subject to persuasion and the function of the Christian is to endeavor to bring men to a decision.

The Wesleys took their songwriting seriously, and set a high standard in their work. John stated:

In these hymns there is no doggerel; no botches; nothing put in to patch up the rhyme; no feeble expletives. Here is nothing turgid or bombast, on the one hand, or low and creeping, on the other. Here are no words without meaning. Here are purity, the strength, and the elegance of the English language; and, at the same time, the utmost simplicity and plainness, suited to every capacity. (Dinwiddie 30)

Richard Dinwiddie, in an article on the Wesleys in *Christianity Today*, quotes Erik Routley, an English hymn authority, who summarized three purposes to Charles Wesley's hymn writing: (1) to provide a body of Christian teaching as found both in the Bible and in the Book of Common Prayer; (2) to provide material for public praise; and (3) to objectify his rich personal faith (31).

John Wesley's method of choosing hymns for public worship involved singing them by himself and then trying them out with a few people during early morning devotionals. Visiting the sick he would sing the hymn with them and finally use the hymn during a weeknight service or a Sunday meeting. After using the hymn extensively, he would determine whether it would be printed or not.

Jesus, Lover of My Soul

Jesus, lover of my soul,
    Let me to Thy bosom fly,
    While the nearer waters roll,
While the tempest still is high;
    Hide me, O my Saviour, hide,
    Till the storm of life is past;
Safe into the haven guide,
    O receive my soul at last.

Other refuge have I none,
    Hangs my helpless soul on Thee;
    Leave, ah, leave me not alone,
    Still support and comfort me!
    All my trust on Thee is stayed,
    All my help from Thee I bring;
Cover my defenseless head
    With the shadow of Thy wing.

Plenteous grace with Thee is found,
    Grace to cleanse from all my sin;
    Let the healing streams abound,
    Make and keep me pure within.
        Thou of life the fountain art;
    Freely let me take of thee;
    Spring Thou up within my heart,
    Rise to all eternity.

This hymn was published in *Hymns and Sacred Poems* in 1740 and was probably connected to his conversion in 1738. A number of myths surround this hymn: a bird at sea flew to Wesley during a storm, a dove pursued by a hawk took refuge in his room, or Wesley himself escaped in a time of peril. The melody in contemporary hymnals was written by Simeon B. Marsh (1798-1875), an upstate New York singing teacher.

Christ The Lord Is Risen Today

Christ the Lord is risen today; Alleluia!
    Sons of men and angels say; Alleluia!
Raise your joys and triumphs high; Alleluia!
    Sing, ye heavens, and earth, reply; Alleluia!

Vain the stone, the watch, the seal; Alleluia!
    Christ has burst the gates of hell; Alleluia!

Death in Vain forbids his rise; Alleluia!
Christ hath opened Paradise. Alleluia!

Lives again our glorious King; Alleluia!
Where, O death, is now thy sting; Alleluia!
Once He died, our souls to save; Alleluia!
Where thy victory, O grave? Alleluia!

Soar we now where Christ has led; Alleluia!
Following our exalted Head; Alleluia!
Made like Him, like Him we rise; Alleluia!
Ours the cross, the grave, the skies. Alleluia!

Hail, the Lord of earth and heaven! Alleluia!
Praise to Thee by both be given; Alleluia!
Thee we greet triumphant now; Alleluia!
Hail, the Resurrection Thou! Alleluia!

This song first appeared in Hymns and Sacred Poems in 1739. It is considered an Easter hymn and usually sung at Easter services as the resurrection is celebrated.

Rejoice, The Lord is King

Rejoice, the Lord is King!
Your Lord and King adore!
Mankind, give thanks and sing,
And triumph evermore.
Lift up your heart!
Lift up your voice!
Rejoice! again I say,
Rejoice!

The Lord the Saviour reigns,
The God of truth and love;
When he had purged our stains,
He took his seat above.
Lift up your heart!
Lift up your voice!
Rejoice! again I say,
Rejoice!

His kingdom cannot fail;
He rules o'er earth and heaven;
The keys of death and hell
To Christ the Lord are given.
Lift up your heart!
Lift up your voice!
Rejoice! again I say,
Rejoice!

Rejoice in glorious hope!

Our Lord the Judge shall come,
And take his servants up
To their eternal home.
   Lift up your heart!
   Lift up your voice!
   Rejoice! again I say,
   Rejoice!

This text comes from *Hymns for Our Lord's Resurrection*, published in 1746 and the melody comes from John Darwall, an English clergyman and amateur musician.

Hark! The Herald Angels Sing

Hark! the herald angels sing
Glory to the newborn King!
Peace on earth and mercy mild,
God and sinners reconciled!
Joyful, all ye nations, rise,
Join the triumph of the skies;
With the angelic host proclaim
Christ is born in Bethlehem!
Hark! the herald angels sing
Glory to the newborn King!

Christ, by highest heaven adored;
Christ, the everlasting Lord;
Long desired, behold Him come,
Finding here His humble home.
Veiled in flesh the God-head see;
Hail the incarnate Deity,
Pleased as man with man to dwell;
Jesus, our Emanuel!

Mild he lays his glory by,
Born that man no more may die,
Born to raise the sons of earth,
Born to give them second birth.
Risen with healing in his wings,
Light and life to all he brings;
Hail, the Son of Righteousness!
Hail, the heavenly Prince of Peace!

The first lines of this hymn were originally "Hark, how all the welkin ring! Glory to the King of Kings," but were changed by George Whitefield. It's use as a Christmas hymn was established about 1810 after a number of others had tinkered with the lyrics—a practice that made the Wesleys irate. Charles Wesley once stated about his lyrics, "Let them stand just as they are...or add the true reading in the margin or at the bottom of the page, that we may no longer be accountable either for the nonsense or for the doggerel of other men" (Leiper 77). Ironically, he had tampered with the lyrics of George Herbert and

Isaac Watts to suit his own purposes. The melody came from Felix Mendelssohn-Bartholdy from his "Festgesang." Ironically, Mendelssohn did not feel that sacred words were appropriate for his melody.

Love Divine, All Loves Excelling

Love divine, all loves excelling,
Joy of heaven, to earth come down,
Fix in us thy humble dwelling,
All thy faithful mercies crown.
Jesus, thou art all compassion,
Pure, unbounded love thou art,
Visit us with thy salvation,
Enter every trembling heart.

Come, almighty to deliver,
Let us all thy life receive,
Graciously return, and never,
Never more thy temples leave.
Thee we would be always blessing,
Serve thee as thy hosts above,
Pray, and praise thee without ceasing,
Glory in thy perfect love.

Finish, then, thy new creation,
Pure and spotless let us be,
Let us see thy great salvation,
Perfectly restored in thee.
Changed from glory into glory,
Till in heaven we take our place,
Till we cast our crowns before thee,
Lost in wonder, love and praise.

The concept of "God as love" was not used much by early hymn writers so Wesley's lyrics were fresh. "Love Divine" first appeared in 1747 in *Hymns for Those That Seek and Those That Have Redemption in the Blood of Christ.* The melody was composed by John Zundel, who was organist of Plymouth Church, Brooklyn, which was pastored by Henry Ward Beecher.

O For a Thousand Tongues to Sing

O for a thousand tongues to sing,
My great Redeemer's praise;
The glories of my God and King,
The triumphs of His grace.

Jesus, the name that charms our fears,
That bids our sorrows cease;
'Tis music in the sinner's ears,
'Tis life, and health, and peace.

He breaks the power of reigning sin,

He sets the prisoner free;
His blood can make the sinful clean,
His blood availed for me.

My gracious Master and my God,
Assist me to proclaim;
To spread through all the earth abroad,
The honors of Thy name.

Glory to God and praise and love,
Be ever, ever given;
By saints below and saints above,
The church in earth and heaven.

This hymn originally had eighteen stanzas and was written to commemorate the anniversary of Wesley's conversion. The lines "He sets the prisoner free/ His blood can make the sinful clean" are indicative of the Wesley's theology that salvation was available to all, not just the "elect." This split in the theology of the "elect" vs. the "free will" of man to choose salvation also caused a split between the Wesleys and George Whitefield; after meeting with Jonathan Edwards in 1740, Whitefield believed in the theology of the "elect."

Chapter 8
The Secular Influence

During this country's first hundred years, religious music dominated America; however, in the eighteenth century, popular music began to grow and blossom and establish itself, although the identity of American music would remain an extension of Europe until the mid-nineteenth century.

There was, of course, secular music from the time of the first settlers, but it was frowned upon by the religious leaders and churches that dominated early society, especially in New England. Still, there is evidence of secular music's popularity in New England. In *American Hymns Old and New*, the authors note that Seaborn Cotton, while a student at Harvard (he graduated in 1651), copied three ballads into his notebook: "The Love-Sick Maid," "The Last Lamentation of the Languishing Squire," and "Two Faithful Lovers." The Puritan leaders were known to have spoken against ballad singing as well as "filthy songs," although some noted that a number of popular tunes were used with religious verses inserted, a practice that drew mixed responses but which seemed to be commonly accepted. Cotton Mather noted the "fondness of people for ballad singing" could be used for religious instruction, observing further that "the minds and manners of many people about the country are much corrupted by the foolish airs and ballads which the Hawkers and Peddlers carry into all parts of the country" (Christ-Janer 7).

Oscar G.T. Sonneck, in his book *Francis Hopkinson and James Lyon*, states that sacred and secular music developed "simultaneously" throughout the colonies, with sacred music "dominating" in the north (Boston) and secular dominating in the south (Charleston) while in the middle colonies (New York and Philadelphia), both were of "equal weight" (11).

The Great Awakening, which began in about 1734 in New England with Jonathan Edwards and gradually moved south and westward, infused a new life into sacred music. It introduced "hymns" into religious music, which had been dominated by psalms taken directly from scripture and usually sung in a slow, drawn-out style. The hymns were more lively and, under the influence of Isaac Watts and the Wesleys, full of personal expressions of faith. In Cotton Mather's time the words dominated the music and there were only a handful of tunes to fit a large body of texts, all of which were marked according to their "meters" or metrical structures.

The rise of the singing schools, which began c. 1717 in Boston, helped re-establish musical literacy and expanded the number of tunes that people knew. In addition, it corrected the mistakes Americans had injected into the old ones. According to Richard Crawford in his essay "Make a Joyful Noise," the establishment of singing schools and the publication of tunebooks (which

40

contained melodies as well as texts) were "seminal events in American musical history" because they saw the church commit "for the first time on record" to "supporting the development of musical skill." Crawford notes that some of the results of the success of the singing schools were

the spread of musical literacy, the greater availability of notated music...many Americans were composing their own music...(but) congregational singing was once again in the doldrums. The problem was no longer a lack of capable singers but rather that singers in many congregations were forming choirs that dominated the music of public worship. As some improved their skill in singing schools, others lost interest in singing at all.

One of the early singing masters, William Billings, is considered the first major composer in North America and his book, *New England Psalm Singer*, published in 1770, one of the first books from a singing master. He has been described as "without doubt the most popular composer of the day." A tanner by trade, he loved music, especially choral composition and performance and had an "enormous vitality," although he was "not a great singer" and had "no gift as an instrumentalist." He did, however, have administrative gifts and a sense of the dramatic and emotionally effective performance. He was somewhat deformed, blind in one eye, one leg shorter than the other, one arm withered and "given to the habit of continually taking snuff." Musically, he was unsophisticated but possessed a "vast amount of self-confidence" (MacDougal).

Billings established a "Sacred Singing School" in Stoughton, Massachusetts in 1774 with about 48 pupils. He formed the Stoughton Musical Society in 1786 and between 1770-1786 published music books, including *The New England Psalm Singer* (1770), *The Singing Master's Assistant* (1778), *Music in Miniature* (1778), and *The Suffolk Harmony* (1786). He spent his last years in poverty, a victim of his love for music. Credited with composing 263 hymns and psalms, his best known work is "Chester," a patriotic hymn that was the anthem for the Revolutionary War, and "Columbia," considered one of the "camp songs" of that period. According to Richard Crawford, Billings was the first American to see "psalmody as an art and himself as an artist."

The first secular composer in the colonies was Francis Hopkinson. Born in Philadelphia, Hopkinson was a member of the first graduating class at the University of Pennsylvania and was known in the colonies as a painter as well as a musician. A signer of the Declaration of Independence, he numbered among his closest friends George Washington, Thomas Jefferson and Benjamin Franklin. His best known song is "My Days Have Been So Wondrous Free" and though he is sometimes credited with composing "Yankee Doodle," perhaps the most popular song of the Revolutionary War, no conclusive evidence exists that affirms that conclusion.

Hopkinson was an accomplished musician, performing on the harpsichord, and was a leader in the music life of Philadelphia, organizing subscription concerts as well as public concerts where amateur musicians performed. In addition to concerts, music was also performed in the theater between acts of plays as well as at dances. The subscription concerts, c. 1764, featured choral music by and for young people as well as chamber music, performed by about a dozen of the top amateur musicians in Philadelphia, including Gov. John Penn, who played the violin.

A key year for music in the American colonies was 1759 when Hopkinson composed "My Days Have Been So Wondrous Free" and James Lyon composed music for an ode sung at his graduation from Princeton. Lyon is the second major secular composer in the colonies, best known for compiling *Urania*, a landmark volume of American music. Much larger than any preceding American musical publication, Lyon's book contains 198 pages and 98 compositions. According to Richard Crawford, in his essay "The Birth of Liberty," it is significant for a number of reasons.

It represents the earliest American printing of anthems (extended settings of prose text), 'fuging' tunes (psalm tunes with at least one section involving text overlap), and hymn tunes (settings of nonscriptural devotional text). It is also the earliest work to identify compositions as 'new'—that is, composed in the colonies (six pieces in the collection are so identified). Perhaps *Urania's* most significant innovation is that 28 of its pieces are underlaid with text. It is the first American publication to print text with music.

Urania was published in the 1760s, the most fruitful time for music in the colonies, with Hopkinson, Lyon and other composers and musicians bringing music to the public. However, earlier in the century there were some significant developments in secular music too. One of the earliest collections of secular songs in the colonies was the "Mother Goose" rhymes, which established a traditional set of songs that have remained an integral part of childhood since their publication. The book was assembled by Thomas Fleet, who had married Elizabeth Goose in 1715 and to whom a son was born the following year. Fleet's mother-in-law came to live with them and sang to the child constantly. Fleet soon grew weary of her singing; however, he wrote down the words to her songs and published them in a book titled *Songs for the Nursery or Mother Goose Melodies for Children*. Published in Boston in 1719, this book contained songs such as "Little Boy Blue," "Baa Baa Black Sheep," "To Market, To Market," "Little Robin Redbreast," "Sing a Song of Six Pence," "One, Two, Buckle My Shoe," "Snail, Snail," "Bye Baby Bunting," "Peter, Peter Pumpkin Eater," "Jack Spratt," and "Hickory Dickory Dock."

Songs brought from England, Scotland and Ireland dominated the early 1700s and George Washington reportedly danced for three hours "with one fair lady" to the music of fiddlers playing "Clock O' the North," "Sellingers' Round," "Strathspeys' Reel," and "Greensleeves" in the Apollo Room at Williamsburg's Raleigh Tavern. In the late 1700s, "The Way-Worn Traveller" is cited as Washington's favorite song, and he reportedly requested it played a number of times (Luther).

Richard Crawford lists two kinds of secular songs that circulated in eighteenth century England and the colonies. The oldest was the oral-tradition English and Scottish balladry, which was brought over by the earliest settlers and flourished primarily in the south, unaffected by topical currents. The other type was broadside ballads, which developed from Elizabethan times into the eighteenth century and was the earliest commercial popular music. Crawford states, "Broadside balladry depended partly on written practice. Texts circulated in broadsides—single sheets printed on one side and sold cheaply—and also in collections, occasionally with melodies but more often only with tune indications" ("Birth of Liberty"). The broadsides brought forth songs of news events, disasters, dying confessions, moralizing poems and hymns. The Wesleys' "Ah Lovely Appearance of Death," Samuel Sewall's "Once More Our God Vouchsafe to Shine," and the anonymous "Is There No Balm in Christian Lands" were originally published as broadsides.

The ballad opera, which began with John Gay's "The Beggar's Opera" in London in 1728, brought broadside tunes to the theatre. The heyday of the ballad opera was the 1730s and it helped establish the vernacular English musical theatre, which provided another kind of secular music that circulated in the colonies. The 1730s are also noted as the time of the first American music concert on record, held in Boston in 1731. The ballad operas were popular in New York, although their growth was inhibited by the disdain of the religious establishment which perpetuated the notion that the theatre was a den of iniquity and a haven for sin. However, as more and more people immigrated from Europe and the population of the new country grew, there was a growing sense of liberalism and a loosening of the stronghold religion held over seventeenth and early eighteenth century Americans so that music became more accepted and more prevalent as the nation developed.

In "The Birth of Liberty," Richard Crawford states:

Culturally as well as politically, pre-Revolutionary America was a colony of Great Britain; several different kinds of music-making flourished in the colonies, but the most widespread creative response of Revolutionary period America to the war lay in making verses to well-known tunes rather than in composing the tunes themselves.

The period just prior to the Revolutionary War marked the emergence of a society dominated by secularization. Alan Lomax states in his essay on "The Sacred Harp," "The Revolution was, for the common man, as much a throwing off of religious as of secular authority." In terms of music this meant the growing acceptance of musical instruments in homes as well as in churches, which had generally taken a strong stand against the use of instruments with sacred music. The acceptance and use of instruments for composing and performing music provided a striking difference in sacred and secular music during this time. Crawford states, "The lack of a keyboard instrument can be a decisive determinant of style...(it is) clearer why secular music, rooted in a tradition of melody with keyboard accompaniment, is stylistically distinct from most American psalmody." That difference may be heard in the music of Francis Hopkinson, who composed on the keyboard and William Billings, who did not, writing instead for four voices which he added successively to the song.

During the Revolutionary War, a number of songs were composed, most of them new texts set to old tunes, primarily concerned with patriotism and the struggle with Great Britain. In "The Birth of Liberty," Crawford states:

When the colonies went to war with Great Britain, a small amount of new music was composed to commemorate the struggle; a larger amount of propagandist verse was written and sung to well-known British tunes; and an even larger amount of traditional Anglo-

American dance music, song, and hymnody having nothing particular to do with the war continued to be played and sung and enjoyed, creating a musical continuity...The music was functional and hence existed in an unreproducible social context. It relied heavily on oral means for its circulation; its creators' identity was a matter of indifference to its performers. (The songs are likely to be timely parodies rather than original creations.) It addressed a cultural need and was hence accessible. The people whose feelings it expressed were preoccupied with survival rather than art; anxious to feel morally superior to their enemy; willing to be diverted and entertained...The music of the Revolution...was composed not so much to be listened to as to be sung, played, marched to, danced to.

After the Revolutionary War, Americans continued to look to Europe for their music and culture. Immigrants continued to come to the new country in large numbers and urban Americans grew wealthier and more desirous of luxury. European musicians took up residence in the major cities and these professionals replaced the native amateur musicians who had dominated the colonial period.

With the establishment of the European professional came the attitude that native American musician and music was unacceptable. There is some truth to this, as Oscar G.T. Sonneck states in *Francis Hopkinson and James Lyon*:

Our early musicians lacked opportunities accumulated abroad during centuries of musical activity. Their own efforts were restricted to a feeble imitation of European conditions and to the development of our musical life out of a most primitive...state of affairs.

In *Yesterdays,* Charles Hamm traces American popular music back to English garden music in the seventeenth century. He also notes that no secular sheet music was printed in this country before the 1770s. He attributes the lack of American songs to two reasons: the first national copyright act was not passed until 1790 and there was a ban on theaters and "Play Houses" from 1778 until 1789 because the Continental Congress had declared that these activities had "a fatal tendency to divert the minds of people from a due attention to the means necessary for the defense of their country and preservation of their liberties" (Hamm 2).

The English pleasure gardens were located in or near cities, were privately owned, filled with walks, waters, trees, and birds. Those who frequented these gardens paid an admission price and were treated to musical entertainment, food and drink, and the joys of walking through nature tamed and cultivated for civilized man. Musicians who composed for these gardens include Bach, Handel, and Thomas Arne, who was particularly adept at writing popular songs. Hamm notes that Arne was successful because he wrote music with "immediate accessibility." Knowing it would be

judged on first hearing...[Arne] did not fill his songs with complex and difficult passages that would interest and challenge other composers and professional musicians,...He wrote strophic songs, so listeners would hear the same music three, four, five, or even more times at a song's first hearing. His songs had simple internal structures, so listeners would hear the chief melodic phrase two or three times within each strophe. They often concluded with a refrain line that was catchy or easily memorable. By the time an audience had heard one of his songs for the first time, they might not be able to sing it from memory, but at the very least they would have some memory of it, could recognize it if they heard it again, and by the end of the song very likely could sing the refrain line at the end of each stanza with the performer. (Hamm 11)

This garden music never achieved the success in America that it did in England because of the Revolutionary War and because American taste and lifestyle was different from the English. Still, British musicians and composers came over to America to write and perform popular music and Americans generally welcomed them. Before the war, the Philadelphia newspapers were full of advertisements by musicians for music lessons as well as for dancing masters to teach lessons. This showed a growing interest by Americans to learn music. After the war these musicians were generally European professionals and while Americans desired to learn music, they wanted to learn European music. These professionals were classically trained and classical music has never been "popular music" in America like it has in Europe—the cultures can influence each other but they cannot be transplanted. Although the classically oriented music and musicians held a place in America, popular music gravitated towards a folk music that had been brought over a century earlier and nurtured on native soil. These folk melodies would influence secular music as well as sacred music, through the hymns of the Wesleys, Isaac Watts and Bach as well as the music from native composers.

In sacred music Alan Lomax notes four general classes—folk tunes, psalm tunes, revivalist hymns and fuguing tunes. The oldest are the folk tunes, originating with the English, Scotch, Irish and Welsh and passed by oral tradition through the people; the psalm tune is the next oldest, coming from an extensive tradition of church music in northern Europe and passed along by the churches. The revivalist tunes date from the period of the Great Revival (c. 1780-1840) when "many songwriters sought to bring to their music the rousing fervor of the revival meetings." These songs show a clear relationship to the older folk and psalm tunes but usually feature the use of "refrain, lively tempos, syncopated choral effects, and a structure that consciously ascends toward a stirring climax." The largest single category was the fuguing tunes, generally older songs from other types put into the new style "by popular demand." The introduction of new tunes, lively, active and vibrant, brought new life to sacred music and threw off the chains of tradition that held religious music in a straitjacket of formalism, sobriety and conservatism. Secular music, too, felt the influence of the Great Revival as it began to develop a distinctive American voice in the nineteenth century.

After the Revolutionary War, several songs emerged that would influence American music for years. "Hail, Columbia," a song that has been considered one of the most significant written during that period of time, was composed in 1794 by Judge Joseph Hopkinson of New Jersey, son of Francis Hopkinson. "To Anacreon in Heaven" was written in London by either John Stafford or Samuel Arnold at the end of the Revolutionary War and became the theme song for the first three American presidents. In 1814, Francis Scott Key, an attorney on board a British ship to arrange the release of a client, wrote the lyrics for "The Star Spangled Banner" to this melody and this became the national anthem.

The beginning of the nineteenth century marked the end of the first two stages of American musical growth—the psalmody of the seventeenth century and the hymns and secular songs of the eighteenth century. The next era of American popular music began on July 4, 1826, the day two former presidents, Thomas Jefferson and John Adams died. On that day, while "The Star Spangled Banner" played (according to legend), Stephen Foster was born. He would live to become the first major American composer with a distinctive American voice and an extensive body of musical work that would change America's music and set it apart from the music of the European heritage.

Chapter 9
Give Me That Old Time Religion

The revival that followed the Revolutionary War was not a highly organized affair and cannot be traced in a logical, sequential manner; rather, it was a number of religious freedom fires "which ignited as it would seem by spontaneous combustion" (Jackson, *White and Negro Spirituals* 11). As the country pushed westward, these revivals sprang up in various areas of the country, offending organized religion because revival preachers paid no heed to denominational lines, preaching wherever they could gather a crowd.

The Revolutionary War had capped the great concept of "freedom" that had been raging in the colonies. This meant there was freedom of religion as well as freedom from religion. Many early leaders—George Washington, Thomas Jefferson, and Benjamin Franklin, for example—were quite Deistic and preferred a more distant and rational God than the emotional Puritans. In the urban areas the rationalism that fueled the French Revolution and provided new breakthroughs in science and philosophy caught hold. However, in the untamed parts of the country, this rationalism had little appeal—the settlers had neither the time nor inclination to ponder intellectual enlightenment. The people needed a faith that was vibrant and alive, full of emotion and comfort, that let them relate to the lonely, danger-filled wilderness and a life steeped heavily in individualism. Thus, it was a "free" religion that took hold.

Socially, the new free religion was perfect for the common man who was poor. Sinful things were from the rich and were to be condemned—hence the rich pursuits of gambling, drinking and such were quickly labelled as sin and railed against. The large urban areas became dens of iniquity while rural America provided the most fertile soil for folk religion. Here it grew and spread, watered with an emotional spirituality that provided a comfort to the lonely settlers while fanning the flames of hell. While this folk religion came under no organizational guidelines, one basic tenet ran through it—all institutional mediacy between a man's soul and his redeemer must be rejected—every individual, no matter what his station in life, had access to God.

As the settlers moved westward, they moved beyond the influence of established churches and were served by a new kind of preacher, born on the frontier, or at least familiar with frontier life. Although they generally had little formal education, they did have the ability to move audiences and would preach wherever a group could be assembled. The "camp meeting" was born from the lack of a central church in the vast rural regions and because the settlers lived so far apart. These camp meetings brought people together for several days from a large area with families bringing food and living in their wagons, the women sleeping inside and the men on the ground underneath or in improvised shelters.

47

The Baptists were a particularly free group with dissensions breaking out within their sect about predestination, grace and other theological questions. They were the folksy sect of both Britain and America, never accepting a central church authority; in music this meant they were devoted to "free" singing rather than singing songs prescribed to them by a central authority. The spirit of the folk Baptists dominated this time of revivals after the Revolutionary War and the songs they chose to sing differed greatly from the psalms of the Puritans with their long texts. The revival spirituals, born from these mass meetings, emphasized choruses, burdens, refrains, and repeated lines.

In the period 1780-1830 a great body of folk texts appeared in the country-song tradition. Great Britain and the young United States were full of folk tunes and religious folk often put religious verses to popular secular tunes. The wedding of religious lyrics and folk tunes probably began around 1770 and continued strongly through this period. The composed tunes of the pre-Revolutionary War time in America remained unknown to the rural Americans who had moved westward, so they used tunes from the folk tradition for their worship. The source for these American folk tunes was primarily British—from England, Scotland and Ireland mainly—with only a handful from other sources.

The Kentucky Revival of 1800 established the revival spiritual in America. The Kentucky Revival was not the first and was similar to a number of other revivals that preceded it; however, the flames here seemed to burn higher and brighter because of a number of favorable conditions. One was the ethnic background of the population—primarily Gaels (Irish, Scots-Irish, Scottish, Welsh) who were known as highly emotional people. Another factor was climatic-geographic. The Kentucky farmers had a period of leisure during the summer from the time their crops were planted until harvesting time (as opposed to their New England counterparts who had a short summer) and the dry roads and trails invited long trips to big gatherings. Too, the dry hot summers lent themselves to meeting outdoors, thereby accommodating large numbers of people. The final factor was the lack of organized, established religion in that area, which meant no religious or civil authorities had to be battled for these revivals to occur.

The revivals were charged with spiritual emotionalism and George Pullen Jackson in *White and Negro Spirituals* describes a gathering in Kentucky, near Lexington, in 1801, where approximately 20,000 gathered. He states:

It was a night that the most terrible scenes were witnessed when the campfires blazed in a mighty circle around the vast audience of pioneers...As the darkness deepened, the exhortations of the preachers became more fervent and impassioned, their picturesque prophesies of doom more lurid and alarming...The volume of song burst all bonds of guidance and control, and broke again and again from the throats of the people while over all, at intervals, there rang out the shout of ecstasy, the sob and the groan. Men and women shouted aloud during the sermon, and shook hands all around at the close in what was termed 'the singing ecstasy.' The 'saints' and more especially those who were out to see the show would rush 'from preacher to preacher,' if it were whispered that it was 'more lively' at some other point, swarming enthusiastically around a brother who was laughing, leaping, shouting, swooning...The whole body of persons who actually fell helpless to the earth was computed...to be three thousand...These were carried to a nearby meeting house and laid out on the floor. At no time was the floor less than half covered. Some lay quiet unable to move or speak. Some talked but could not move...Some, shrieking in agony, bounded about like a fish out of water. Many lay down and rolled over and over for hours at a time. Others rushed wildly over stumps and benches and then plunged, shouting 'Lost! Lost!' into the forest...other 'physical exercises'...included 'jerks' (where) the victims snapped their heads from side to side and front to back with unbelievable rapidity and vim; the 'hops' where frogs were imitated; the 'holy laugh' and the 'barks' whose usually involuntary addicts would 'tree the devil' and then get down on all fours at the foot of the tree and snap and growl. (81)

The crowds at these gatherings had to sing from memory or learn songs that were easily repetitive and took little effort to learn because there were no song books. The revival songs were in the hands of the people as the real exhortational activity—praying, mourning and other physical exercises—was by and for the crowd. The singers controlled the songs but the crowds would join in the chorus, on a short-phrase refrain or on a couplet which struck their fancy. This led to the development of revival songs with repetitive passages.

The verse-with-chorus idea spread quickly with some choruses proving so popular they were interjected into other songs with different verses. There developed two types of revival songs at this time—the repetitive chorus and the call-and-response where a line was sung by the singer and the crowd sang the responding line, which always remained the same. George Pullen Jackson states the revivals spread throughout America and England because they provided "avenues of escape from a present world which had become unbeautiful, unsatisfying, if not quite unbearable" (*White and Negro Spirituals* 91).

This was the time when the folk tradition of song—an oral tradition that began in Britain and other parts of Europe—took over in religious music. The settlers moving west had little if any music training and neither song books nor established churches. When the revivals caught hold, music was returned to the people who responded with a congregational type of singing reminiscent of the earliest Puritans, albeit much more emotional and active. They had to depend upon tunes they already knew—much as the first Puritans did with their songs. But the nature of the revivals caused a major change—the melodies had to be altered to accommodate choruses that everyone could learn quickly. Thus the song leader would know the verses but everyone could know the chorus and would join the song on these choruses or on lines that repeated themselves.

This was democracy in action; everyone could feel a part of this religion and singing. The choruses also spoke the feelings of the settlers. According to Jackson, the early religious folk-singing practice took hold in the period 1780-1830, during which time it enjoyed its greatest vigor. He states:

This was the period...when the folk participated most widely in, and enjoyed most undisputed control—for better or worse—over its own private and institutional religious affairs. All the evidence had pointed moreover toward the interdependence during these decades of that mass-controlled religion and mass-controlled song. (*White and Negro Spirituals* 126)

As the Kentucky Revival followed the Great Awakening, the great Millenial Excitement followed as the religious revival continued to spread across America. This was not the first millenial expectation by American Christians—the Salem witch trials in the 1690s came from a religious fervor heavily doused with the projection of a coming millennium supposed to start in 1700. The millenial movement generally accompanies religious revival in America and centers on the belief that Christ will come back and the true believers will either be transported bodily to heaven or an earthly kingdom will be established where peace will reign for a thousand years.

The leader of the Millenial Excitement was William Miller (1782-1849) who declared, the world would end in the spring of 1843. When Judgment Day did not arrive at the appointed time, the faithful reset the date for October 22, 1844. When that date failed to yield the projected result, many committed suicide or entered insane asylums with "Miller Madness." Although the earth remained intact after this date, a new sect was born, the Seventh-Day Adventists, founded by Miller, after an evolution that produced a variety of "Adventists" before taking its present form. In addition to the millennialists, there also arose during this time religious factions against drinking, war, slavery, the Masons, and the Catholics.

The old-time religion was a personal, highly emotional affair between an individual and God; the rise of modern Protestantism brought forth a social-ethical-esthetic gospel. Thus the religions that were tribes of radicalism became cornerstones of the establishment. Methodists and Baptists, Mormons and Seventh-Day Adventists were no longer positioned outside mainstream society; they were now large denominations whose members occupied places of honor and respect and whose denominations now spanned the globe.

As the first half of the nineteenth century ended, the old-time religion faded as the cultural environment gave way to the Industrial Revolution and the Civil War. The second half of the nineteenth century witnessed a new religious trend appear as the wild, emotion-packed camp meeting style of religion gave way to a more solemn, sober movement, centered in the urban areas with the music of the gospel hymns.

The folk hymns and spirituals were the last gospel songs to be perpetuated solely in the oral tradition, although they survive now because they were collected in print and because folklorists collected them on tape. Although some were written by individuals, many of the hymns come from the broadside ballad tradition and the folk songs brought to this country from Europe. The spirituals are often black adaptations of white songs, influenced heavily by the African origins of black Americans but reflecting the culture of a people united and suppressed in America.

The "all day singing" was unique to the south and families often gathered at the county courthouse to sing from copies of the *Sacred Harp* or *Southern Harmony* and eat picnic lunches together. There was a great deal of harmony singing and most of the songs were written for three or four parts with the tenor generally carrying the melody line. Some of the ballads are reminiscent of the broadside ballads which present the confessions of criminals. One such religious ballad is "Remember, Sinful Youth," which is reminiscent of an earlier song about the fate of the pirate, Captain Kidd.

Remember, Sinful Youth
Remember, sinful youth, you must die, you must die,

Remember, sinful youth, you must die;
Remember, sinful youth, who hate the way of truth
And in your pleasures boast, you must die;
And in your pleasures boast, you must die.

Uncertain are your days here below, here below,
Uncertain are your days here below,
Uncertain are your days, for God hath many ways
To bring you to your graves here below, here below,
To bring you to your graves here below.

The God that built the sky, great I am, great I am,
The God that built the sky, great I am;
The God that built the sky, hath said (and cannot lie),
Impenitents shall die, and be damned, and be damned,
Impenitents shall die, and be damned.

And, O my friends, don't you, I entreat, I entreat,
And, O my friends, don't you, I entreat;
And, O my friends, don't you your carnal mirth pursue,
Your guilty souls undo, I entreat, I entreat,
Your guilty souls undo, I entreat.

Unto the Saviour flee, 'scape for life! 'scape for life!
Unto the Saviour flee, 'scape for life!
Unto the Saviour flee, lest death eternal be
Your final destiny, 'scape for life! 'scape for life!
Your final destiny, 'scape for life!

The travelling preacher, Peter Cartwright, is credited with writing "Where Are the Hebrew Children." In his autobiography, Cartwright presents one of the rare early accounts of southern folk singing. He wrote that he was in the Allegheny mountains, had not wanted to travel on the Sabbath and so had been directed to a home where he was invited to preach. In *American Hymns Old and New*, the authors relate that

at the conclusion of his sermon Cartwright 'called on our kind local preacher to conclude. He rose and began to sing a mountain song, and pat his foot, and clap his hands, and ever and anon would shout at the top of his speech, 'Pray brethren.' In a few moments the whole house was in an uproarious shout.' (Christ-Janer 294)

The Hebrew Children
Where are the Hebrew children?
Where are the Hebrew children?
Where are the Hebrew children?
Safe in the promised land.
Though the furnace flamed around them,
God, while in their troubles found them,
He with love and mercy bound them,
Safe in the promised land.

Where are the twelve apostles?
Where are the twelve apostles?
Where are the twelve apostles?
Safe in the promised land.
They went up through pain and sighing,
Scoffing, scourging, crucifying,
Nobly for their master dying,
Safe in the promised land.

Where are the holy Christians?
Where are the holy Christians?
Where are the holy Christians?
Safe in the promised land.
Those who've washed their robes and made them
White and spotless pure and laid them
Where no earthly stain can fade them,
Safe in the promised land.

The form is reminiscent of the 12 bar blues lyric format at the beginning of the verse as the singer sings the same line three times before the phrase, "Safe in the promised land," which also occurs at the end of the verse. The second half of each verse has an a-a-a-rhyme before the repeat of the "safe in the promised land" line, thus making it easy to learn. Indeed, people could often learn the song as it was being sung and, after a few times through, could sing it fluently.

Cartwright preached to both white and black audiences on southern farms because small congregations were often not segregated. This meant that both whites and blacks heard the same songs, although musically the spirituals, born from slavery, became separate from the southern folk songs primarily because of the differences in the black and white cultures and the aptitude of the Afro-Americans for rhythms. The first major collection of spirituals was *Slave Songs of the United States*, followed by *Jubilee Songs*, issued by the Fisk Jubilee singers, whose performances raised money for their school and helped it survive in the post Civil War years when the black education movement was struggling to survive and thrive. "Hurry on, My Weary Soul" is taken from *Slave Songs*.

Hurry On, My Weary Soul
Hurry on, my weary soul,
And I heard from heaven today,
Hurry on, my weary soul,
And I heard from heaven today.

My sin is forgiven and my soul set free,
And I heard from heaven today,
My sin is forgiven, and my soul set free,
And I heard from heaven today.

Hurry on, my weary soul,
And I heard from heaven today,

Hurry on, my weary soul,
And I heard from heaven today.

My name is called and I must go,
And I heard from heaven today,
My name is called and I must go,
And I heard from heaven today.

Hurry on, my weary soul,
And I heard from heaven today,
Hurry on, my weary soul,
And I heard from heaven today.

De bell is a-ringin' in de oder bright world,
And I heard from heaven today,
De bell is a-ringin' in de oder bright world,
And I heard from heaven today.

The line "And I heard from heaven today" could have several meanings, a trademark of many spirituals which served as communication between blacks as well as gospel songs. The song can easily be improvised by singers who add "And I heard from heaven today" after a new line. This would make a song constantly change to fit the mood of the worshipers as well as the individuality of the singer and congregation. It also invited congregations to join as "And I heard from heaven today" remains every other line.

The songs "Didn't My Lord Deliver Daniel" and "When Israel Was In Egypt's Land (Go Down, Moses)" come from *Jubilee Singers and Their Songs*, issued in 1872.

Didn't My Lord Deliver Daniel
Didn't my Lord deliver Daniel,
d'liver Daniel, d'liver Daniel,
Didn't my Lord deliver Daniel,
And why not every man?

He delivered Daniel from the lion's den,
Jonah from the belly of the whale,
And the Hebrew children from the fiery furnace,
And why not every man?

Didn't my Lord deliver Daniel,
d'liver Daniel, d'liver Daniel,
Didn't my Lord deliver Daniel,
And why not every man?

The moon run down in a purple stream,
The sun forbear to shine,
And every star disappear,
King Jesus shall be mine.

The wind blows East, and the wind blows West,
It blows like the judgment day,
And every poor soul that never did pray,
Will be glad to pray that day.

I set my foot on the Gospel ship,
And the ship it begin to sail,
It landed me over on Canaan's shore,
And I'll never come back any more.

When Israel Was In Egypt's Land
When Israel was in Egypt's land,
Let my people go;
Oppressed so hard they could not stand,
Let my people go.

Chorus: Go down, Moses, Way down in Egypt land,
Tell ole Pharoah, Let my people go.

Thus said the Lord, bold Moses said,
Let my people go;
If not I'll smite your first born dead,
Let my people go.

Chorus

No more shall they in bondage toil,
Let my people go;
Let them come out with Egypt's spoil,
Let my people go.

Chorus

O let us all from bondage flee,
Let my people go;
And let us all in Christ be free,
Let my people go.

Chorus

We need not always weep and moan,
Let my people go;
And wear these slavery chains forlorn,
Let my people go.

Chorus

It is easy to see why both of these songs would appeal to slaves with the lines "and why not every man" and "let my people go." These phrases not only speak of Biblical stories, they tell the slave's story as well. "When Israel

Was In Egypt's Land" equates the plight of the slave with that of the Israelites before Moses led them out. The analogy between America and Israel as God's land, housing God's chosen people, was one employed by the Puritans as well who escaped the religious persecution in seventeenth century England. It is only fitting that Afro-Americans would also use the parallels between themselves and the Israelites as they sought comfort through their songs and their religion.

It was not until the twentieth century that denominational hymnals included spirituals. "Were You There" was included in *The Hymnal 1940* and thus entered the white culture as a church hymn after its long life as a spiritual.

Were You There?
Were you there when they crucified my Lord?
Were you there when they crucified my Lord?
Oh! Sometimes it causes me to tremble, tremble, tremble.
Were you there when they crucified my Lord?

Were you there when they nailed him to the tree?
Were you there when they nailed him to the tree?
Oh! Sometimes it causes me to tremble, tremble, tremble.
Were you there when they nailed him to the tree?

Were you there when they laid him in the tomb?
Were you there when they laid him in the tomb?
Oh! Sometimes it causes me to tremble, tremble, tremble.
Were you there when they laid him in the tomb?

The songs of this period reflect the oral tradition as well as the revival spirit of singing "spontaneously," without books, led by a singer with the congregation joining on key lines, phrases, or the chorus. These are songs easily learned and easily remembered. They are also easily changed and adapted from singer to singer, congregation to congregation, with the chorus or key lines remaining and the verse lyrics subject to individual changes. They are timeless songs because of the repetitiveness but also because of their emotional appeal— they are songs that can inspire joy or comfort in sorrow, a verbalizing of people's feelings and thoughts. Within these songs are the roots of blues, country, modern gospel and rock 'n roll. Musically and lyrically simple, their power rests in their emotional impact and their ability to be learned and sung easily.

Chapter 10
The Great Revival

The nineteenth century saw America expand geographically and politically and its religion and politics reflected the country as the "home of the free and the brave." Along with the political expansion came moralistic crusades, laissez faire individualism, the Industrial Revolution and the Civil War. The two great forces of Christian revivalism and democratic nationalism set the stage for another great revival after the Civil War, which would center on the urban areas and stress a crusade among equals.

The Baptists and Methodists had been most active on the frontier and the religious awakening of the settlers put the principle of voluntarism (churches being supported freely by their members) before liturgy, democracy before orthodoxy, and emotionalism before an intellectual, rational approach to religion. Denominational lines were broken and crossed as the church reached the masses. The camp meeting became a social institution which supported the politics of manifest destiny while revivalism stressed the work of man in salvation as it stressed the doctrine of the sovereignty of God. There was a democratic character to the idea of a personal encounter with God as well as a linking of politics with religion through the belief that God was active and present in America.

During this period, America was a growing nation with a population that swelled from 31 million in 1860 to 106 million in 1920. There was an increase in farmers, from six to nine million, but the greatest growth came from the cities as factory workers increased from two million to eighteen million from 1860 to 1880. Even the definition of the city changed from "large village" to "metropolis" during this period. In 1850, only six cities contained more than 100,000 people; there were forty-one by 1900. For religious leaders the problem of growth was also compounded by the diversity within these cities—there were Catholics, Jews, atheists, and agnostics as well as Protestants.

In addition to competition from other sects, Christianity also had to deal with science, particularly Darwin's theory of evolution that questioned the Divine origin of man, as well as biblical criticism and the religion of economics, personified in Andrew Carnegie's book, *The Gospel of Wealth*. Americans were worshipping money and their leaders were the self-made entrepreneurs.

The role of the evangelist during the rapidly changing times of the nineteenth century was to assure believers of the continuity of the ageless faith in a rapidly changing world. It was to convince believers that all good came from God, so the changes that advanced America were proof that God was smiling on the nation. Too, the gap between modern science and old time religion was just a bridge where scriptural proofs were being revealed and the great truth was again being confirmed.

56

In London William Booth, an itinerant minister, found his calling in 1865 and began the Salvation Army. The Army began in London, amongst the poor and outcast who had no notion of religion. While other movements sought to mobilize those asleep in church pews, Booth's movement brought religion to the streets, bringing the church to the people instead of drawing people to the church. Along the way, through the Salvation Army, he revolutionized the use of instruments with religious music.

Booth loved singing and would "sit up singing until 12 after a hard days work," according to biographer Richard Collier. The General, as he became known, stated, "I am for the world's salvation; I will quarrel with no means that promises help" (31). It was this intense devotion to the world's salvation that gave Booth the strength to overcome adversity and immense odds to carry the gospel to the streets. Opposed by the churched as well as the unchurched, scorned by the respectable and the derelict, Booth nevertheless made an impact on London—and later the world—through his single-minded devotion to the gospel and his fervor for preaching this message to all listeners.

The Salvation Army band began in the same haphazard devotion that spread the Army's cause. In Salisbury, England in 1879, a local builder named Charles William Fry offered Booth the services of himself and his three sons, Fred, Ernest, and Bertram. The Army had been troubled with hooligans roughing up their members and Fry and his sons stepped in as bodyguards, bringing along their instruments as an afterthought. Since Fry and his sons played brass instruments while the Army marched through the streets, the first Salvation Army band was born. It brought attention to the Army's cause and attracted a crowd. The instruments accompanied Army members when they sang their songs—Booth banned the word "hymns" because it sounded "too churchy"—using concertinas, tambourines, brass horns, and anything else that made music. The players were mostly spare-time musicians, with the result that the music often sounded "as if a brass band's gone out of its mind" (Collier 59).

Booth was a maverick in his approach to evangelism as well as in his use of music. He regularly insisted that well-known secular tunes be used with Christian lyrics, reasoning that if someone knew "Here's To Good Old Whiskey," they could learn "Storm the Forts of Darkness." If they knew "The Old Folks at Home" they could learn "Joy, Freedom, Peace and Ceaseless Blessing" because the same tunes were utilized. Booth stated, "Why should the Devil have all the best tunes" and regularly took the secular and made it sacred (Collier 60). Through songs like "There Are No Flies on Jesus," Booth brought Christianity to the street and made it a religion for the poor, the wretched, the socially undesirable and the outcast. The Army's music reflected their tactics of spreading the gospel— loud, dramatic, and full of gusto. Meanwhile, in America there arose two preachers in the nineteenth century who would dominate evangelism on this continent— Henry Ward Beecher and Dwight Moody.

Beecher was a moderate, mainstream Protestant who attempted to prod Christianity toward modernity. For him the good in the world was produced by a loving God, therefore, Christian thought should be flexible enough to pull in new ideas. From his platform at the Plymouth Church in Brooklyn, Beecher attracted a national following. He injected a healthy dose of humanism into the gospel, urging his members to seek perspiration as well as inspiration, a good day's work to go along with Divine grace. Ward Beecher appealed to the middle class who aspired towards riches, arguing that poverty was a result of sin and that "if a man did not smoke or drink, he could feed his family on a dollar a day" (Marty 312). This concept of subordination of the poor by the rich was applauded by Beecher's followers.

The concept of the religious leader as a spiritual salesman was refined by Dwight Moody, a former shoe salesman who used the pulpit to sell Christianity to the masses. Moody was born February 5, 1837, in Northfield, Massachusetts, son of a Unitarian father who died when the boy was four. Moody was converted to Christianity in 1855 at the age of 17 by his Sunday School teacher, Edward Kimble. Ironically, Moody's request to join the Mount Vernon Congregation was turned down for a year because of his ignorance of the Christian faith.

In 1865 Moody moved from Boston to Chicago and became a successful businessman selling shoes and an active member of the Plymouth Congregational church. Every Sunday, Moody reportedly filled four pews he rented with those he had recruited. He was so successful at recruiting members for Sunday School that at the age of twenty-three he founded his own Sunday School where he served as administrator and recruiter. Moody was a forceful, though not an elegant speaker, and he was cautioned against speaking by members of his church. However, he began preaching one night after the scheduled speaker did not show up and he soon devoted himself full time to Christian work. He spoke at Sunday School conventions and to troops. He established a church of his own and served as president of the Chicago YMCA.

Moody could not sing but knew the value of songs and singing in his evangelistic work. He enlisted the support of Ira Sankey in 1871 and together the two travelled to England as well as urban areas in the eastern United States, "reducing the population of hell by a million souls." Moody was clearly the guiding light and visionary for the evangelistic endeavors, but he needed Sankey's songs to attract crowds and set the stage for his message. He would let Sankey begin with song, he would then preach and finally Sankey would conclude with a song as the sinners came forth. Moody viewed the Christian conversion as a successful sale—the set up, the hard pitch, and the closing or wrapping up where the convert must make his decision and act on it.

By the end of their careers the names Moody and Sankey were linked and shared equal billing. A testament to the power of song is that the gospel singer Sankey was as important as the evangelist preacher Moody, their roles supplementing each other and each indispensable to the cause.

The Great Revival brought the evangelistic fervor of conversion to the urban areas and in so doing united Christianity with the Industrial Revolution. Americans began to equate upward mobility with Christian ethics, the blessings of materialism with God's blessings, and the emergence of America as a nation that would dominate the world with the belief that God had chosen the nation for such a role and was guiding her wealth and creating her power. This "Great Revival" closed the nineteenth century by giving believers an assurance of their salvation and America an assurance of her destiny. The Protestant ethic of hard work, self-discipline and material blessings became an integral part of Christianity as the country moved towards the twentieth century as one nation under God, represented by a number of religious denominations. It was a religious fervor that saw people united in their nationalism but divided in their theology, finding in God a source of spiritual as well as material blessings and comforts.

Ira Sankey, as song leader for Dwight Moody's revivals, made the gospel hymn a popular song, presenting the format of verse-chorus-verse-chorus in a way that gave the songs emotional appeal and memorability. In making the hymn a popular song, Sankey evoked the charm of popular music and used the song as an instrument for religion to convict and convert people.

There were revivals in settled communities as well as in churches on the frontier, although the Great Revival came later in the nineteenth century than the "old time religion" that caught fire in the west. From these urban revivals, the gospel hymn developed to meet the needs of these revivals and prayer meetings. The camp meeting hymn was often the work of anonymous singers or the folk tradition but the gospel hymn was created by individual writers and musicians. The camp meeting hymn was characteristic of the frontier and rural areas; the gospel hymn of the great cities.

The gospel hymn is uniquely American. It is evangelical in spirit and focuses on the winning of souls through conversion. Its primary use was in revivals but it was gradually taken over by Sunday schools, Christian associations and churches made up of less educated members who preferred the appeals of emotion over literary form and quality.

The gospel hymn had certain characteristics that made it appealing to crowds. The mood might be optimistic or pleading, but the music was tuneful and melodic and easy to grasp and learn. A march-like movement was typical and the device of letting the lower parts echo rhythmically a line announced by the sopranos in a fuguing form became a mannerism.

Sankey preferred a small reed organ to accompany his singing. He did not like a professional quartet choir or putting the singers behind a screen in back of a minister. He preferred a choir of the best singers placed in front of the congregation, near the minister. Part of this desire stemmed from his own view that singing was as important as preaching and that he was as important as the evangelist, a view supported by the popularity of the hymns he sang.

Sankey was born at Edinburg, Pennsylvania on August 28, 1840 and throughout his childhood sang hymns with his family. He was a regular church attendee, singing in the choir, and was "converted" at the age of sixteen during a revival at The King's Chapel, a church about three miles from the Sankey home. Sankey's family moved to Newcastle in 1857 where his father was president of a bank. There Sankey finished high school and began working at the bank as well as singing and playing organ at the Methodist Episcopal Church, where he was the leader of the choir.

Sankey joined the Union army in 1859 and, after his discharge, joined his father again, who was now a collector for the Internal Revenue Service. He married Fanny Edwards in September, 1863, and became known for his singing at Sunday school conventions and political gatherings. In 1867, a Young Men's Christian Association was formed in Newcastle and Sankey became involved, first as secretary and later as president of that organization. In 1870, he was appointed a delegate to the YMCA's annual convention, held in Indianapolis that year, where he met Dwight Moody, whom he had heard about because of Moody's work in Chicago.

Moody and Sankey met after a morning prayer meeting where Sankey had led the singing of "There is a Fountain" after Moody had spoken. According to Sankey in his autobiography, *My Life and the Story of the Gospel Hymns,* Moody's first words to him, after an introduction, were, "Where are you from? Are you married? What is your business?" Sankey replied he lived in Pennsylvania, had a wife and two children and was employed by the government, whereupon Moody replied, "You will have to give that up." Sankey was reluctant to give up his job but Moody pressed him, saying "You must; I have been looking for you for the last eight years" (21).

Sankey stated that Moody could not sing and "therefore had to depend upon all kinds of people to lead his service of song, and that sometimes when he had talked to a crowd of people, and was about to 'pull the net,' someone would strike up a long meter hymn to a short meter tune, and thereby upset the whole meeting." (Sankey, *My Life* 22). The day after their meeting, Moody sent a note to Sankey, asking him to meet on a certain street corner. He complied and when he arrived, Moody produced a box and asked Sankey to climb up and sing a hymn. Never one to require much prompting to display his glorious voice in song, Sankey did so and a crowd gathered. After the song, Moody got on the box and delivered a short sermon, then invited everyone present to attend a meeting. He asked Sankey to close with another hymn and to sing while the crowd was led to the Opera House in Indianapolis where the YMCA was holding its convention.

Moody continued to press Sankey to join him but the singer returned to his home in Pennsylvania. Six months later Moody sent an invitation for Sankey to join him in Chicago and the two met at Moody's home where Sankey once again sang. During the week they were together, the two went around to visit the sick and held meetings with Sankey singing and Moody preaching. The first song Sankey sang at the first house they visited was "Scatter Seeds of Kindness." This was also to be the last song Sankey sang at a public meeting with Moody 28 years later in Brooklyn in September, 1899. The song, written by Mrs. Albert Smith with music by S.J. Vail, was popular at the time and was written in the format of verse-chorus-verse-chorus that Sankey would use throughout his singing. It expressed a philosophy of Christianity that made the faith a code of conduct, a religion of gentlemen and ladies. It contained the emotional sentimentality that many of Sankey's hymns did and compared the best of Christianity to the best of nature.

Scatter Seeds of Kindness
Let us gather up the sunbeams,
Lying all around our path;
Let us keep the wheat and roses,
Casting out the thorns and chaff,
Let us find our sweetest comfort
In the blessings of today,
With a patient hand removing
All the briars from the way.

Chorus:
Then scatter seeds of kindness,
Then scatter seeds of kindness,
Then scatter seeds of kindness,
For our reaping by and by.

Strange we never prize the music
Till the sweet-voiced bird is flown!
Strange that we should slight the violets
Till the lovely flowers are gone!
Strange that summer skies and sunshine
Never seem one half so fair,
As when winter's snowy pinions
Shake the white down in the air.

(Chorus)

If we knew the baby fingers,
Pressed against the window pane,
Would be cold and stiff tomorrow
Never trouble us again
Would the bright eyes of our darling
Catch the frown upon our brow?
Would the prints of rosy fingers
Vex us then as they do now?

(Chorus)

Ah! those little ice cold fingers,
How they point our mem'ries back
To the hasty words and actions
Strewn along our backward track!
How those little hands remind us,
As in snowy grace they lie,
Not to scatter thorns but roses
For our reaping by and by.

(Chorus)

Again Moody pressed Sankey to join him but again the singer declined, returning to the security of his job and life in Pennsylvania. However, upon discussing the offer with his minister and some friends, Sankey was urged to join the evangelist, moving to Chicago in 1871. Based at Moody's Illinois Street Church, the two made the rounds in Chicago, singing and preaching at daily noon prayer meetings as well as regular services.

During the great Chicago fire Moody's church and home burned. In his autobiography, Sankey goes into great detail about how he labored all through the night to save his material belongings, finally procuring a boat so he could sit safely in Lake Michigan with his possessions. Moody was involved in waking up the neighbors and helping them flee, saying later "All I saved was my Bible, my family and my reputation" (Sankey, *My Life* 38). After the fire, Sankey left Chicago for Pennsylvania and did not see Moody for two months. The evangelist finally called him back though and they began to rebuild the church, using his skill at raising money to provide the funds.

Dwight Moody and Ira Sankey visited England for the first time together in June, 1873, and, beginning with some small gatherings in York, soon achieved fame that saw them preaching and singing before 20,000 in London. Sankey had begun compiling a musical "scrapbook" with words and music to use during his singing. People often wanted to borrow it, sometimes not returning it in time for Sankey to lead the next service, so he had some words of hymns printed on small cards. Soon he compiled a book containing some of the hymns and began selling them for sixpence each; there was a quick demand and he soon sold all he had printed. This was the start of his songbook, which popularized numerous songs, including "Rock of Ages," "Onward, Christian Soldiers," "Whiter Than Snow," "It is Well With My Soul," "Jesus Loves Me," "Blessed Assurance" and others and caused the hymns he sang to be popularized in the print tradition as well as the oral tradition. It was Sankey's songbooks which perpetuated his songs—and furnished a healthy income—and the popularity of these songs is directly attributed to the fact he not only performed them during revivals but made them available in print as well.

Sankey was a large man, pompous and impressed with his own singing talent. He obviously had a full, rich voice and was quite proud of that fact and the recognition he received from it. He seemed to be a vain man about his singing as well as full of the assurance of salvation and his own election as one of God's chosen. He was born in the privileged upper middle class and remained there all his life. The Christianity he sang about was a social gospel but a social gospel for the middle and upper classes, drawn from the urban areas. For Moody and Sankey, Christianity was like a club, with members entitled to the privilege of Heaven as well as earthly benefits of peace and prosperity. All those not members were infidels, hopelessly lost and living in error.

One of Sankey's most popular songs was "The Ninety and Nine" and reflected the concept of conversion as joining the elect. Sankey sang it often and his rendition is reported to have convicted many who had strayed from the fold of righteousness.

The Ninety and Nine

There were ninety and nine that safely lay
In the shelter of the fold,
But one was out on the hills away,
Far off from the gates of gold—
Away on the mountains wild and bare,
Away from the tender Shepherd's care,
Away from the tender Shepherd's care.

"Lord, Thou hast here Thy ninety and nine;
Are they not enough for Thee?"

But the Shepherd made answer: "This of mine
Has wandered away from me,
And, although the road be rough and steep,
I go to the desert to find my sheep,
I go to the desert to find my sheep."

But none of the ransomed ever knew
How deep were the waters cross'd'
Nor how dark was the night that the Lord pass'd thru'
Ere He found His sheep that was lost;
Out in the desert He heard its cry—
Sick and helpless and ready to die,
Sick and helpless and ready to die.

"Lord, whence are those blood-drops all the way
That mark out the mountain's track?"
"They were shed for one who had gone astray
Ere the Shepherd could bring him back,"
"Lord, whence are Thy hands so rent and torn?"
"They are pierced to-night by many a thorn."
"They are pierced to-night by many a thorn."

But all thro' the mountains, thunder-riven,
And up from the rocky steep,
There arose a glad cry to the gate of heaven,
"Rejoice! I have found my sheep!"
And the Angels echoed around the throne,
"Rejoice! for the Lord brings back His own!"
"Rejoice! for the Lord brings back His own!"

Since Moody and Sankey conducted "revivals" where the stated purpose was to convert souls, it is obvious there would be many songs intended to convince the wayward sinner to return to the fold of Christianity. The story of the prodigal son is an ideal topic for such a sermon and Moody delivered it a number of times while Sankey sang this song, based on the prodigal son story. There are three characters in the story—the father and two sons. One son left and the other remained faithful to the father. When the lost son returned the father was overjoyed and the son who remained was jealous of the attention received by the "other" son who was, in a sense, rewarded for squandering his father's wealth. It can be read as a parable where the father is God, the faithful son the church which has remained with God and the errant son the lost sinner who abandons Christianity. Moody and Sankey put themselves in the role of the father—God—inviting the wayward son to return, ignoring the angry faithful son in this story. Since Sankey adapted the songs he sang to himself, expressing his point of view, it seems obvious he viewed himself and Moody as father figures in Christianity and the sinners as lost children. The jealous son, in the form of the church, did cause the evangelist and singer some problems throughout their careers, disliking some of their tactics and accusing them of "sheep stealing" on occasion.

The Prodigal Child
Come home! come home!
You are weary at heart,
For the way has been dark,
And so lonely and wild;
O prodigal child!
Come home! oh, come home!
Come home! Come, oh, come home!

Come home! come home!
For we watch and we wait,
And we stand at the gate,
While the shadows are piled;
O prodigal child!
Come home! oh, come home!
Come home! Come, oh, come home!

Come home! come home!
From the sorrow and blame,
From the sin and the shame,
And the tempter that smiled,
O prodigal child!
Come home, oh, come home!

Come home! come home!
There is bread and to spare,
And a warm welcome there,
Then, to friends reconciled,
O prodigal child!
Come home, oh, come home!

Although Moody and Sankey often seem Calvinistic in their rigid approach to religion and the self-imposed discipline of the believer, the Lutheran concept of justification by faith was deeply imbedded in them. Yet, somehow, they managed to be among Calvin's chosen elect, divinely ordained from the beginning of time, and saved by the merciful grace of God, too. It almost seems as if they adapted Calvinism's concept of preordination to include a moment of self-revelation where grace allowed them to see their salvation and become aware of their predestined fate.

The song "Saved By Grace" was written by Fanny J. Crosby with music by George C. Stebbins. Crosby and P.P. Bliss were particular favorites of Sankey and he sang and printed a number of their songs in his songbooks, setting a number of Crosby's lyrics to music as well.

Saved By Grace
Some day the silver cord will break,
And I no more as now shall sing,
But, O, the joy when I shall wake
Within the palace of the King!

(Chorus)
And I shall see Him face to face,
And tell the story—Saved by grace;
And I shall see Him face to face,
And tell the story—Saved by grace.

Some day my earthly house will fall,
I cannot tell how soon 'twill be,
But this I know—my All in All
Has now a place in heav'n for me.

(Chorus)

Some day, when fades the golden sun,
Beneath the rosy-tinted west,
My blessed Lord shall say, "Well done!"
And I shall enter into rest.

(Chorus)

Some day, till then I'll watch and wait,
My lamp all trimm'd and burning bright,
That when my Saviour ope's the gate
My soul to Him may take its flight.

Sankey provided the music for many poems and hymns he found from various sources, including periodicals, songs in other versions, or poems sent to him. He did, however, write several songs, including "Out of the Shadow-Land."

Out of the Shadow-Land
Out of the shadow-land, into the sunshine,
Cloudless, eternal, that fades not away;
Softly and tenderly Jesus will call us;
Home, where the ransom'd are gath'ring to-day.

(Chorus)
Silently, peacefully, angels will bear us
Into the beautiful mansions above;
There shall we rest from earth's toiling forever,
Safe in the arms of God's infinite love.

Out of the shadow-land, weary and changeful,
Out of the valley of sorrow and night,
Into the rest of the life everlasting,
Into the summer of endless delight.

(Chorus)

Out of the shadow-land, over life's ocean,

Into the rapture and joy of the Lord,
Safe in the Father's house, welcomed by angels,
Ours the bright crown and eternal reward.

This song—words and music—was written by Sankey alone. It was the last song he wrote and he did so for the occasion of Dwight Moody's funeral in 1899. The self-assurance of salvation by Christians is obviously present and Sankey has no doubt of his or Moody's reward with phrases like "Safe in the arms of God's infinite love" and "Into the summer of endless delight" giving proof that he knew the fate of the believer. There is also the philosophy of the monarchy of believers—that God is a King and those who enter heaven are welcomed as royal subjects in lines like "Ours the bright crown and eternal reward" and "Into the beautiful mansions above." Like many of Sankey's hymns, there is an abundance of emotional sentimentality in the lyrics and a romantic view of religion that contrasts with the harsh darkness of life on earth. Perhaps it was Sankey's intense devotion to the sentimental view of salvation and heaven that made it so appealing and struck an emotional chord in listeners' hearts.

Part 2

Chapter 11
Billy Sunday and Homer Rodeheaver

In the early 1900s one of the most famous people in America was Billy Sunday. Born on November 19, 1862 in Ames, Iowa, William Ashley Sunday was the son of German immigrants whose name had originally been Sonntag. His father, a private in the Union army at the time of his son's birth, died about a month after the birth and never saw his son. At home were three older brothers. About six years afterward, his mother married someone named Heizer, who fathered two more children and then disappeared in 1874. Young Willie lived with his grandfather and at the Soldiers' Orphan Home in what is now Davenport, Iowa.

Willie left the orphanage when he was fourteen and moved back with his grandfather. After a hot-tempered dispute, he left for Nevada, Iowa, where he landed a job as a hotel errand boy. He never returned home. Fired from his first job, Sunday landed a job as stableboy for Colonel John Scott, who had been lieutenant-governor of Iowa, and the Scotts helped send him to high school, where he attracted attention as a fleet track star. He came to the attention of the Chicago Whitestockings baseball team in 1883 after the Marshalltown team he played on won the state championship. In the major leagues for eight years—1883-1891—Sunday was known as a daring base stealer (he reportedly held the record for most stolen bases until Ty Cobb broke it in 1915) and a poor hitter, carrying a .259 lifetime average.

Billy Sunday's conversion occurred in 1886 when he went to the Pacific Garden Mission in Chicago after first hearing a group from the organization singing hymns outside the saloon where he and his teammates had been drinking. Married in 1888, Sunday continued to play baseball, moving to Pittsburgh and then Philadelphia. During this time, Sunday gave up drinking, swearing, going to theaters, and playing baseball on Sundays. In the towns where he played, he often spoke to groups of young men at the YMCA, telling of his conversion and lecturing on "Earnestness in Christian Life."

Sunday began working full-time for the YMCA in the winter of 1890-1891 where he was assistant secretary of the religious department. In 1893, he was offered a job with a well-known evangelist, J. Wilbur Chapman, and assisted with the setting up of revivals in the mid-west through the last part of the nineteenth century. Sunday was the "advance man" for Chapman—who was considered one of the leading evangelists of his day. Sunday worked for Chapman from 1893-1895. In December, 1895, Sunday received a telegram from Chapman, who said that he was quitting revivalism in order to pastor a church in Philadelphia. This left Sunday with a wife, two children, and no job. This was remedied when an offer came from the town of Garner, Iowa, for Sunday to conduct a revival campaign.

Chapman had taken Sunday under his wing and attempted to train him as an evangelist, but the young man was a poor speaker and suffered from stage fright when he had to speak before a large crowd. He could not sing either and had no singer to travel with him (Chapman worked with P.P. Bilhorn). Still, the revival was a small success and Sunday was asked to speak in other small towns in Iowa. Along the way he hired Joseph E. Van Winkle to lead the singing.

Sunday quickly became a successful evangelist and a number of people were converted during his revivals. By 1900, Sunday was successful enough to hold revivals in large tents and hire a gospel singer—Fred Fischer—full-time. Fischer sang familiar hymns like "When The Roll Is Called Up Yonder," "In the Sweet By and By," and "We'll Gather By the River." He was with Sunday for ten years.

During this time, Sunday's revivals were beginning to be criticized because of their entertainment aspect. Like Dwight Moody, Sunday advertised his revivals in the entertainment section of the newspaper, and also like Moody, he hired a handsome singer. He also sometimes employed a female singer, Miss Mamie Lorimer. But Moody was a man of proven devotion and his singer, Ira Sankey, always prefaced his songs with a prayer—which Fischer did not do—and accompanied himself on the reed organ. Fischer used a piano accompanist and encouraged local cornet and trombone players to join him on stage during the hymns. Encouraging audience members to compete with each other in singing (the men vs. the women) and turning the music portion of the revival into a community songfest were techniques also used by Charles Alexander, the chorister for Reuben A. Torrey and later Chapman, who was considered the leading gospel singer of the day. But Alexander performed mostly in urban areas while Sunday held most of his revivals in rural areas.

Billy Sunday continued to gain steam with his revivals and attracted larger and larger crowds. Musically, his revivals took a major turn when he hired Homer Alvin Rodeheaver to replace Fred Fischer in 1910. It was Rodeheaver who revolutionized the musical portion of the revivals and began, in essence, the gospel music industry of the twentieth century with his mixture of ministry and entertainment and his creation of an independent record company as well as publishing interests.

Rodeheaver was born in Cinco Hollow, Ohio in 1880 and grew up in Jellico, Tennessee. He learned to play the cornet as a boy and, when he went to Ohio Wesleyan in 1896, switched over to the trombone while playing in the college band, serving as a cheerleader and taking a number of music courses. His education was interrupted by the Spanish-American War, so Rodeheaver never obtained a degree, although he stayed at Ohio Wesleyan until 1904. At this time he left school to work for evangelist William E. Beiderwolf, where he served for the next five years as chorister.

Rodeheaver was the perfect man for the job with Sunday. He was genial and created an atmosphere of enthusiasm and friendliness which gave the revivals a tremendous popular appeal and made them entertaining. He had a rich baritone voice and incredible stage presence with his dark, wavy hair, moderately handsome face, and what has been described as an "ingratiating" personality. Always smiling, he was affable and mixed well socially with a wide range of people, perfecting the chorister role that Charles Alexander had first established. But Rodeheaver had more than just flair and style—he soon proved to have skill as a singer and trombonist. He had a talent for evangelistic speaking and the ability to coordinate and direct both children's and adult choirs. Musically, he was a bit more daring than his predecessor and sought out new gospel songs instead of relying solely on old hymns. He also experimented extensively with group singing.

A premier showman, Rodeheaver had the ability to win over a large crowd with a funny story, a magic trick producing various "noises" from his trombone, and pulling a practical joke on another team member on the stage. He encouraged his choirs to be enthusiastic and advised them to "go at it like selling goods." A bachelor, Rodeheaver was the first chorister to have an overt appeal as a "lady's man" or sex symbol. That, combined with a lively sense of humor, his musical ability, a thick southern accent, and ability to catch the feeling of a crowd made him an invaluable asset to Sunday. It is not fair to say that Billy Sunday would not have succeeded without Homer Rodeheaver, but it must be acknowledged that the chorister was a major drawing card and source of appeal for Sunday's revivals. His polish and grace served as a marked contrast to Sunday's physical acrobatics and hoarse shouting. Rodeheaver lent a tone of dignity to the meetings. Although a number of newspaper reporters privately felt him to be a little too smooth, suave, and unctuous to be sincere, the public crowds loved him and affectionately called him "Rody."

The songs Rodeheaver used were not very different from those of Ira Sankey in terms of doctrinal content, but differed greatly in terms of tone, tempo, and style. Rody tended to favor the lively, optimistic songs rather than the sentimental songs of Sankey's preference. For example, one of Sankey's favorite numbers was "The Ninety and Nine" while joyous numbers like "Brighten the Corner" tended to dominate Sunday's revivals. There were a few songs popular in both eras—"Ring the Bells of Heaven," "Bringing in the Sheaves," and "Pull From the Shore" are examples. Songs such as "Safe From the Law," "Christ Is My Redeemer," and "There is a Fountain Filled With Blood" were less popular with Sunday than in Moody's time. Dwight Moody had tended to favor songs of humility such as "Oh, to Be Nothing" while Sunday preferred the self-confidence of "Onward Christian Soldiers," "I Walk with the King, Hallelujah!," "The Battle Hymn of the Republic," and "The Fight is On." The atmosphere in the revivals of these two great evangelists was markedly different as well: for Moody, salvation was a lonely wailing while Sunday struck up a militant pose that encompassed the brashness of a righteous right. In fact, the songbook Homer Rodeheaver compiled and published contained an entire section entitled "Warfare" that contained a number of militaristic songs, equating the Christian walk with open warfare against sin, the secular world, and the ways of the Devil.

Rodeheaver went into the publishing business in 1910. Inspired by the example of Ira Sankey, it was perfectly natural for a chorister to compile songs, old and new, and sell them at revivals. Rodeheaver wrote a number of hymns and employed the services of such quality songwriters as B.D. Ackley and Charles Gabriel. In the thirty-minute musical program before the sermon, designed to warm up the crowd and get them in the proper mood for Sunday, Rodeheaver would generally begin with some old hymns, which the crowd already knew, and gradually introduce newer compositions. As a result, these newer gospel songs became popular and a demand for the songbooks was created and sustained. One of those songs, "Brighten the Corner," written by Gabriel, was initially criticized because of its entertainment appeal. Rodeheaver answered the critics, stating:

(This song) was never intended for a Sunday morning service, nor for a devotional meeting— its purpose was to bridge that gap between the popular song of the day and the great hymns and gospel songs, and to give to men a simple, easy, lilting melody which they could learn the first time they heard it, and which they could whistle and sing wherever they might be. (McLoughlin 85).

Brighten the Corner
Do not wait until some deed of greatness you may do,
Do not wait to shed your light afar,
To many duties ever near you now be true,
Brighten the corner where you are.

Brighten the corner where you are
Brighten the corner where you are
Someone far from harbor you may guide across the bar,
Brighten the corner where you are.

Just above are clouded skies that you may help to clear,
Let not narrow self your way debar
Tho' into one heart alone may fall your song of cheer,
Brighten the corner where you are.

(copyright 1913, renewed 1941, The Rodeheaver Co.)

There was an obvious secular appeal to this song as well as others, such as "If Your Heart Keeps Right" and Rodeheaver knew he was appealing to the audience's need for entertainment with these tunes. Too, he was firmly and confidently establishing an area for gospel songs outside the church, independent of a religious service, and congruent with the American spirit of optimism, democracy, and success through hard work.

If Your Heart Keeps Right
If the dark shadows gather as you go along,
Do not grieve for their coming, sing a cheery song,
There is joy for the taking, it will soon be light—
Ev'ry cloud wears a rainbow, if your heart keeps right.

If your heart keeps right,
If your heart keeps right,
There's a song of gladness in the darkest night;
If your heart keeps right,

If your heart keeps right,
Ev'ry cloud will wear a rainbow, If your heart keeps right.

Is your life just a tangle full of toil and care;
Smile a bit as you journey, others' burdens share;
You'll forget all your troubles making lives bright,
Skies will be blue and sunny if your heart keeps right.

(copyright 1912, renewal 1940, The Rodeheaver Co.)

A major reason for the popular appeal of gospel songs in revivals during this time was phonograph records and Homer Rodeheaver probably began the first gospel label, although there is some evidence that suggests James Vaughn in Lawrenceburg, Tennessee may have been responsible for the first gospel recordings. At any rate, the time was ripe for gospel music to be marketed with the new technology and Rodeheaver's company, Rainbow Records, was instrumental in presenting many of the new gospel songs and actively competing for the consumer's dollar with the secular labels. When Rodeheaver began with Sunday, the major source of revenue for music came from the copyrights in the songbooks; however, shortly after 1916, when he began his record company, the sales of records accounted for more income than sheet music sales. It was a sign of the times and the times to come that the new technology would dominate the music industry and records would replace song books and sheet music as the financial backbone of this industry. It was also a harbinger for the emergence of gospel music on independent labels later in the century, which assured the development of the music towards a Christian consumer rather than attempting to appeal commercially to the culture-at-large. Rainbow Records was only the first of a number of small labels which recorded only gospel music and which nurtured this music by allowing each artist creative control.

During the time just before World War I, a number of patriotic songs also were sung at revivals and found their way into the songbooks. Patriotism has long been a civil religion in America and Christians have often equated the love of God with the love of country and the flag as nearly equal to the Bible, so it is not surprising that songs such as "America," and "Song to the Flag" were often part of the services. Also during this time, temperance was a major issue and Billy Sunday (as well as a number of evangelists) ushered in the era of Prohibition by a steady stream of sermons against liquor. Rodeheaver had songs about "Temperance" listed in the topical index of his songbooks. One of these was "De Brewer's Big Horses," written in Negro dialect, apparently from the influence of vaudeville shows popular during this time.

De Brewer's Big Hosses
Oh, de brewer's big hosses comin' down de road,
Totin' all around ole Lucifer's load;
Dey step so high, an' dey step so free,
But dem big hosses can't run over me.

Oh, no, boys, oh, no!
De turnpike's free wherebber I go,

> I'm a temperance ingine, don't you see,
> And de brewer's big hosses can't run over me.
>
> Oh, de licker men's actin' like dey own dis place,
> Livin' on de sweat ob de po' man's face,
> Dey's fat and sassy as dey can be.
> But dem big hosses can't run over me.
>
> Oh, I'll harness dem hosses to de temp'rance cart,
> Hit 'em wid a gad to gib 'em a start,
> I'll teach 'em how for to haw and gee,
> For dem big hosses can't run over me.

This song was written in 1887 but first introduced into revivalism by Rodeheaver in 1911 and soon proved immensely popular with its rousing melody and fighting lyrics.

Songs like this were aimed at entertaining audiences. Since Sunday's services were not held in a church—they were generally held outdoors in a specially built 'tabernacle'—Rodeheaver actively used all the tools of secular entertainment without fear of disrupting the decorum of the sanctuary. He also employed various show biz tactics, such as encouraging audiences to sing and making them an active part in the musical program, encouraging competition among choirs, and of course, exercising his own considerable talents in showcasing his show biz tendencies.

The choirs between 1912-18 were generally large and this allowed Rodeheaver to popularize numerous new songs with them. With a large number of voices, the chorister could create jazzy arrangements, do call and answer type numbers (often by placing some members of the choir in the back of an auditorium), and manipulate a song so that it contained many melodramatic flourishes and effects. Since a large number of people learned the new songs and often sang them after the revivals left town, the popularity of new songs was assured.

Although local talent was encouraged to participate on the revival stage, and although Rodeheaver made use of large choirs during the services, it was Rody himself who provided the key thread which tied it all together. He served as host and master of ceremonies for the revivals in addition to his role as soloist and chorister. He also welcomed the delegations who held special seats each evening and required special attention from the revival team. And, of course, when Billy Sunday made his plea for converts, Rodeheaver was responsible for selecting the right song and leading it as the people came forth as an act of faith.

In many ways, Homer Rodeheaver set the standard for the gospel music industry in the twentieth century. Through the creation of his publishing company he promoted and popularized a number of new songs (including "The Old Rugged Cross") and through the formation of his record company he reached large numbers of people with new gospel songs, establishing the independent label as the primary outlet for gospel music.

During the early days of recording—in the early twentieth century—the major record labels (e.g. Columbia, RCA Victor, etc.) often went into the field—recording singers in rural areas of the south. They collected a large number of hymns.

These were mostly old songs carried from the oral tradition or learned from songbooks. But it was the records produced by independent companies like Rodeheaver's which began to create the Christian culture in twentieth century America, as the gospel consumer became part of a segmented market. As radio and secular records created a national market for recordings, gospel music passed from being a separately identifiable form of music—such as the hymns of Sankey or the spirituals—to songs which sounded like their pop counterparts with only a difference in lyrics. Homer Rodeheaver was the first to bridge this musical gap and establish the trend of religious music mimicking pop music in an attempt to draw a large audience and to appeal to those both in and out of religion.

A major religious movement which began at the turn of the century played an active role in guiding American Christianity in the twentieth century. Pentecostalism would have a major effect on religion in this country as well as music—particularly in the south—as a number of musicians came from this movement. This period also marked the beginnings of "Fundamentalism." Although it may be argued that most of the major Christian revivals in this country since the Great Awakening have been fundamental in nature, it was not until the twentieth century that this became a doctrine and a widely used term.

The roots of Pentecostalism have been traced to two sources in the United States. Charles Fox Parnham began Bethel Bible School in Topeka, Kansas in October, 1900. In late December, 1900, before he made a trip to Kansas City, Parnham instructed his students to study the Bible individually and learn about the baptism of the Holy Spirit. When he returned, the students told Parnham that in Apostolic times, whenever believers were baptized with the Holy Spirit there was speaking in tongues.

The source for this is Acts, chapter two. After this meeting members of the college began to pray and seek for this baptism and gift of tongues. On New Year's Eve, as about forty students and seventy others outside the student body gathered for the traditional "Watch Night" service, Miss Agnes Ozman requested that members lay lands on her so she might receive the Holy Spirit. Parnham demurred but, after repeated urgings, consented. After only a few moments of prayer, Miss Ozman began to speak in Chinese and could not speak English for the next three days. The significance of this was that believers accepted speaking in tongues, or glossolaia, as the outward sign that someone had received the gift of the Holy Spirit. The rest of the student body began to pray earnestly and soon most were speaking in tongues. This lead to a major evangelistic effort by Parnham and his students which resulted in Pentecostalism spreading through the midwest, south, and southwest.

Parnham opened another school in Houston, Texas in 1905. Like the one in Topeka, there was no tuition charged (just "faith" offerings), the only textbook was the Bible and the only lecturer was Parnham. One of his students there was William J. Seymour, a black holiness preacher. Seymour was invited to preach at the Nazarene mission in Los Angeles after another student, Neeley Terry, also black, had received the Holy Spirit baptism in Houston and began speaking in tongues. She had recommended Seymour to her home church after returning from Houston.

Parnham's first sermon offended a church member and he found the doors barred to him after that service. Invited to the home of Richard and Ruth Asberry (relatives of Neeley Terry) he conducted services there. On April 9, 1906, seven of the worshipers received this baptism of the Holy Spirit and began speaking in tongues, shouting and praising God for three days and nights, according to records. Soon, the small congregation moved into an old frame building, which once served as a Methodist Church, on Azusa Street and here The Apostolic Faith Gospel Mission under the leadership of the one-eyed preacher, William J. Seymour, heralded in a revival whose effects would be felt all over the world.

American fundamentalism began as an ideology among urban intellectuals and sought to keep modernism at bay through conservative and traditional values and ideology during a time when America was undergoing radical social changes. The term came from a series of booklets issued from 1910-1915 which defined the proper Christian doctrines and dogma as belief in the deity of Christ, the Virgin birth, bodily Resurrection of Christ, imminent Second Coming, substitutionary atonement, and the verbal inspiration and inerrancy of the entire Bible. These doctrines would not only come to define and dominate American Christianity, they would also be the central themes of the gospel songs throughout the century.

Pentecostalism also had a direct influence on rock'n roll music because so many of the pioneers of rock—Elvis, Jerry Lee Lewis, Little Richard and others— came from a Pentecostal background, transferring the Pentecostal energy to the rock'n roll stage. This movement also had a major affect on televangelism in the latter half of the twentieth century because a number of the major stars— like Jimmy Swaggart and Jim Bakker—came from Pentecostal backgrounds and part of their success came from their ability to carry the Pentecostal fervor into living rooms via the TV set.

Chapter 12
The Rise of Radio and Records

The twentieth century began with the development of two technologies which transformed music by taking it from the oral tradition to the electronic tradition. These two developments—the phonograph and the radio—would preserve music in a fixed, definitive form—the recording—rather than letting it be subjected to the nuances of each performer and performance. They would also let music reach the masses in a way it had never reached them before, creating national trends in music as well as national acceptance and popularity. Thus, music went from a local event to a national stage.

Thomas Edison invented the phonograph in 1877 and by the 1890s there were a number of firms competing in the phonograph market. Edison originally envisioned his invention as a business machine but it was soon apparent the real potential lay in the entertainment field. Edison's company, The Edison Phonograph Company, soon began making their own recordings for sale with the phonographs. These original recordings were on cylinders and caused problems with storage as well as with bootlegging. With recordings so easy to make—it could be done on the same machine that played the cylinders—the market soon became flooded with recordings made by nearly anyone who had a machine. The recording quality was not particularly good, but neither was the playback quality, and since this was such a new phenomena, consumers tended to overlook the quality problems in the first recordings. It wasn't until 1902 that the obvious superiority of studio recordings became apparent and the control of recordings came to rest with the record manufacturing companies. These companies, which manufactured discs for 120 or 160 rpm, included The National Phonograph Company (an extension of Edison's original company), Columbia, and Victor (later RCA).

Emile Berliner introduced commercial discs in 1895. By 1898, the quality of the discs had improved with the substitution of wax for zinc in the recording and shellac for rubber in the records and an important advantage began to emerge—storage space. Fifty of the discs could be stored in the same space allotted to four standard cylinders or one concert cylinder.

In 1903, Victor began manufacturing a twelve-inch disc which increased the playing time of recordings to three and a half minutes. The cylinders had previously recorded about two minutes. The significance of this development is that it defined the length of a popular song, which has remained around three minutes throughout the twentieth century.

The development of the coin-slot phonograph, or jukebox, let recorded music become public as these machines were placed in public places, particularly saloons. Comic songs, monologs, whistling and band records tended to attract

77

the most popularity initially, although hymns were also popular in a number of saloons. The coin-slot phonographs were also becoming popular in movie houses during the early 1900s as that industry was beginning to develop. The chief rival to these early jukeboxs were coin-operated player pianos, first introduced in 1908. The initial heyday for these jukeboxes was 1890 to 1908, but their major boost to the record industry came during the Depression years of the 1930s when record sales dropped and the coin-operated machines created a market which virtually saved the recording industry. They also provided a key outlet for minority music not on the radio. Thus these machines were extremely instrumental in the development of the market for country or "hillbilly" music for rural whites and "race" records for blacks.

The development of the technology for radio occurred about the same time Edison was developing the technology for the phonograph and the first radio communication signals were sent by Guglielmo Marconi of Italy in 1895. At first, the technology was developed for ship-to-shore communication but experimental broadcasts in the United States began around 1910. That was the year Lee De Forest produced a program from the Metropolitan Opera House in New York featuring Enrico Caruso. Other stations began to broadcast as well and the United States issued the first broadcast license for radio in 1921. Soon network broadcasting, begun by RCA-owned NBC, began to link the country.

The Golden Age of Radio broadcasting is generally considered to be from 1925 to 1950 when radio was the primary source of family entertainment. During the 1930s, in particular, radio came into its own with live musical shows, soap operas, comedy shows and dramatic series and news, especially Roosevelt's "Fireside Chats" from 1933 to 1945, which linked the Presidency to the people in a way that had never been done before. The Golden Age of Radio ended in the early 1950s with the advent of television, which replaced radio as the chief source of family entertainment in the home. However, radio emerged as the primary carrier of music to teenagers in the mid-1950s with the rise of rock 'n' roll. This gave radio a new direction—to the youth—and a new, important function—the spread of new kinds of music which had mostly been kept off the airwaves when the networks controlled radio.

Two other events in the early part of the twentieth century also had a profound effect on music: the Copyright Act of 1909 and the formation of the American Society of Composers, Authors and Publishers (ASCAP) in 1916. The Copyright Act provided protection for songwriters and legitimized the song as both a commercial and literary form. But it also demanded that compositions be "original," and thus the long tradition of "borrowing" from other sources began to come to an end. No longer could songwriters take old songs, or other people's songs, change and adapt them, and use them as their own (although this folk tradition still continued through World War II); now they had to create totally new material. The formation of ASCAP provided a means for songwriters and publishers to make money from music performers. By World War II there were a number of white performers on radio making their living as musicians. (Later, other performing rights organizations, Broadcast Music, Inc. [BMI] and [SESAC] would form and also have a major impact on music.) Again, this moved music from a mostly amateur status to that of a full-fledged occupation. Both of these events affected popular music immediately and directly but gospel, folk, blues, and country really did not feel the full effect until after World War II when the United States became an urban nation and the rural population began declining. Although the Industrial Revolution had begun a hundred years earlier, it was the boost in the economy from the after-effects of World War II that quickly changed this country in a short period of time.

Science and technology played a key role in America developing as a world power in the twentieth century, although these scientific advances often played a divisive role in the Christian community. The roots again date back to the sixteenth century and the Copernican Revolution, which took man out of the center of the universe and made him just one speck in the cosmos. This change in the position of man in the universe also changed man's view of God and the scientific revolutions during the next 500 years produced a chameleon God whose image and role changed with new scientific discoveries.

The scientific revolution which has provided the most dissent within the Christian community is the one begun by Darwin with his theory of evolution in the latter part of the nineteenth century. Man was not only removed from the center of the universe—holding the key position in God's creation—but was descended from God's lesser creature—the monkey. This was more than most Christians could handle and they argued from Genesis in the Bible against science. The landmark Scopes Monkey Trial in Dayton, Tennessee in 1925 provided a national platform for creationism vs. evolution theory that did not resolve the conflict but whose implications still resound today.

But science and religion did not always clash when science was used for practical applications. Christianity quickly embraced radio and preachers began to broadcast their sermons over the airwaves taking sacred music outside churches and revivals and putting it into the American home.

Religion discovered radio very early. The first commercially licensed radio station, KDKA in Pittsburgh, Pennsylvania, began broadcasting on November 2, 1920; on January 2, 1921, it broadcast a church service. The service was from the Calvary Episcopal Church and was a Sunday evening service conducted by Rev. Lewis B. Whittemore. The broadcast came about because one of the Westinghouse engineers at KDKA was a member of the church choir. The broadcast proved successful and soon the services were a weekly, Sunday feature. Other evening services were aired in Chicago by Paul Radar in 1922 and Omaha, Nebraska by R.R. Brown in 1923, whose "Radio Chapel Service" was the first nondenominational service.

During these early years of broadcasting, religious broadcasting generally occurred on Sunday and most of the programs were worship or church services. During this time, the Federal license requirements were minimal and stations could operate at whatever level of power they wished over whatever frequency they chose. That ended in 1927 when the Federal Radio Commission (FRC) was formed. The FRC established regulations that required regular broadcast schedules, an assigned frequency and channel, and the use of modulation equipment. This ended the era of radio mavericks, including religious broadcasters who could not keep up financially because of the cost of equipment. However, some pioneers hung on, including KFUO in St. Louis, which began in 1925; KFGQ in Boone, Iowa, which began in 1927; KPOF in Denver, which began in 1928; WWBL in Richmond, which began in 1924; KPPC in Pasadena,

California and WCAL in Northfield, Minnesota, which ᴜᴄgan in 1922 (Armstrong 25).

The first program of gospel music on radio was begun by two students from the Moody Bible Institute in Chicago who produced a Sunday evening program in 1925 over the school's radio station, WMBI. Wendall Loveless, a gospel composer, was the station's first program manager and served as announcer, pianist, vocalist and preacher on a number of programs. However, there was always music on gospel radio when the services were broadcast because singing was always a part of the service, traditionally preceding the sermon. At this time the music of the two students was confined to standard hymns and classical numbers.

As the FRC regulations essentially ended any individual beginning a radio station, religious programming moved over to secular radio where it purchased time on established stations. This was the era of network radio and Donald Grey Barnhouse was the first to purchase network radio time for a religious program. During the 1930s, a number of others also did this as shows such as "Radio Bible Class," "Radio Revival," "Heaven and Home Hour," "Haven of Rest," "Back to God Hour" and "Back to the Bible" were heard.

Walter A. Maier, a key figure in early religious radio programming, began The Lutheran Hour, which was broadcast over the CBS network. The price for broadcasting a season of half-hour weekly shows in 1930 was $200,000 and Maier provided $100,000 in seed money from his own church. The other half came from listeners after the show began in October, 1930, on WHK in Cleveland. Thus, the marketing of religion in the electronic media began. Barnhouse also received money from listeners. Charles Fuller, who began the Gospel Broadcasting Association, was so successful that in 1943 he spent $1,556,130 for time buys and was the Mutual Broadcasting Network's best customer (Armstrong 44). This year—1943—was the peak year for religion on radio as contributions reached an all-time high.

At this time the networks banned paid religious broadcasts, basically because Father Charles E. Coughlin and Rev. Robert "Fighting Bob" Schuler were proving to be too popular and too controversial with their broadcasts. This forced the religious programmers to purchase time on independent stations and this trend continued from 1944 until 1949 when the drop in radio advertising revenue because of the introduction of television saw radio look again to the religious broadcasters for time buys.

The beginning of the television era in 1950 meant the decline of network radio but not the decline of radio, which became even more influential and pervasive as it became more independent. It was here that radio had to play records because they did not have the income to support a live band. Too, they had to program music because they could not compete with television's shows— thus radio became the dominant medium for records and the dominant medium to reach those with differing tastes in entertainment as America became an increasingly pluralistic nation.

Musically, the turn of the century is marked by the emergence of the first truly "American" voice in songs. These songs are often linked directly to the theater, which has always been a leader in introducing new styles and trends in American music. The year 1890 serves as a good starting point, although there were breakthroughs in American music before that. This period is when America came of age with popular music, although this date fails to acknowledge the tremendous influence Stephen Foster had earlier in the nineteenth century as he became the first composer to be uniquely "American" in the field of song writing.

Stephen Collins Foster was born near Lawrenceville, Pennsylvania, which is now part of Pittsburgh. He had little formal music training but taught himself to play clarinet at six and soon could play any song by ear. He began composing at fourteen and eventually wrote over 200 songs. He called his minstrel songs "Ethiopian songs" and began composing them in 1845 to take advantage of the minstrel shows becoming popular in the United States at that time. Foster worked with E.P. Christy and the Christy Minstrels, who introduced most of Foster's songs to audiences across the country. The songs proved to be so popular that many of them were adapted for Sunday School use, with the words changed to fit the Christian message but the same melodies retained. His material is an example of Christian churches taking advantage of popular music to incorporate new tunes in the church with the old message, thereby making the ageless story contemporary and relevant to a new generation.

Foster's downfall was that he was a poor businessman, selling most of his songs, which soon became famous, for not enough money. He moved from Cincinnati to New York in 1860 and lived there fighting illness, poverty and alcoholism, until his death in 1865, after the Emancipation Proclamation and just before the end of the Civil War.

In his book, *American Popular Song*, author Alec Wilder points out that Foster approached his music from two points of view, the formal and the native. Examples of the "formal" are "Jeannie With The Light Brown Hair" and "Beautiful Dreamer" while examples of the "native" include "Old Black Joe," "De Camptown Races," and "Oh! Susanna." Wilder notes the latter style was deeply rooted in Negro music and Negro life. Foster was also influenced by early minstrel shows, which were white versions of black music. However, the black church affected Foster directly as well, so the songwriter drew from both white and black versions of black music for his own songs.

One of the reasons Foster was unique was that he was so sensitive and aware of black music and fused this influence into his own music. His death, during the time period of the Civil War, left a musical gap that no one filled until the late 1880s. Wilder states that "I feel sure that for a long while after the war had ended, the vital, creative energies that had nourished plantation music were subdued." Indeed, the whole country was more concerned about rebuilding itself and reestablishing individual lives than in songs and entertainment. Too, the Negro—who was homeless, jobless, uneducated, and untrained—had to learn how to survive in a world that was both hostile and indifferent to him. When the plantations were gone, the social structures that both hemmed in the Negro and allowed him the freedom to play and sing his own music were also gone.

The music from the plantations—jig and cakewalk music, blues and spirituals—would surface later in the nineteenth century as ragtime, jazz, popular blues, and the original spirituals from the church. However, during the 30-40 years after the Civil War there was a musical isolation imposed on both the black and white cultures as whites were no longer exposed to music in the slave quarters and blacks were excluded from white publishing houses. This period also marked a sharp division in the church life of Americans as blacks established their own churches outside and away from white culture while white churches by and large developed unwritten codes and practices which effectively barred blacks from their churches. Thus the music of the white church and the music of the black church were separate and one did not influence the other until black music influenced popular songs, which in turn influenced church music later in the twentieth century.

The key to the popularization of black music in the white culture lay in getting white publishing houses to present black music. The first black composer to do this was James A. Bland, who wrote songs such as "Carry Me Back to Old Virginny" (1878), "Oh, Dem Golden Slippers" (1879), and "In The Evening By The Moonlight" (1880). Bland was a northern Negro and the doors he opened led white publishers to "discover" people like Eubie Blake and the music that became jazz and ragtime.

Wilder points out that black music was first exposed to white audiences in brothels where black musicians played "party" music for the white customers. As America entered the twentieth century, Prohibition also played a key role in the development of black music as speakeasies employed black musicians and customers requested black music in the loose, easy-going atmosphere.

A major difference between Americans and Europeans at the turn of the century is that Americans were less formal, less inhibited, and more inclined to create wild dances outside the European tradition of waltzes, polkas, and gallops. These "informal" dances needed a music that was less structured than European music and Americans found it in the music of blacks. Thus, popular music and popular dance evolved together as often a dance created demand for a song or vice versa.

In 1912 W.C. Handy published the first blues song. Handy, called "the father of the blues" was actually the promoter and publisher of the blues, a music which had been around since before the Civil War and dates back to early work songs. Handy had the first successful black-owned publishing company which put down on paper the music of blacks, allowing white musicians to play the music. Musicians such as Eubie Blake and James P. Johnson—whose piano-playing style was later made famous by Fats Waller—influenced white musicians and audiences directly as well as songwriters. Irving Berlin published "Alexander's Ragtime Band" in 1912 (which was really not a "ragtime" song) and the floodgates were opened as songs from white songwriters influenced by black music poured through.

The early part of the twentieth century was particularly rich with musical developments as cowboy music in the west, folk music from immigrants, black spirituals (first popularized by the Fisk Jubilee Singers), hillbilly music from whites in the south, blues from blacks in the south, and the musical theater on Broadway all began to grow into their own and influence each other. The technology of phonographs and electricity as well as the practice of doing field recordings of musicians playing different forms of music in their own genre and culture let Americans all over the country hear the music that had previously been limited to a particular race, sub-culture, or region. Thus, music and technology grew hand in hand throughout the first half of the twentieth century.

Chapter 13
Black Gospel

Those who have traced some of the earliest black spirituals have discovered these songs are primarily from the white culture, from the British and European folk song tradition brought to America in the seventeenth and eighteenth centuries. So, in one sense, the tap root for black gospel could be considered 'white' or the white American-European culture. However, more important than individual songs is the "Black experience," specifically the history and concept of the slave culture and the rise of the "holiness church" in the nineteenth century.

There have been attempts made to trace black gospel back to African roots. One of the problems with tracing music to African roots is that Africa is a large continent with many different countries, cultures, languages and music. Americans tend to look at Africa as a country rather than a continent—a concept that further blurs the immense diversity of this vast land. Slaves were brought to America from a number of different areas in Africa and did not share a common culture or language or produce a single form of music. However, it is easy to show that the music of the British Isles, which was the basis for folk music and the music of the gospel revivals in the early 1800s in America, was adapted by blacks, who modified it to their black American culture and language—to become part of the "Black experience"—in America.

The first slaves were brought to Virginia by Dutch traders in 1629. Soon a whole economy and way of life was based on slavery, particularly in the south where large plantations grew acres of cotton and needed slave labor to keep them going. For thousands of years—even before America was founded—people of many cultures—including Christians—took the practice of slavery for granted and amassed scriptural texts to justify it. Many humane people saw no inconsistency in the practice of slavery and supported it; it was a very slow and painful awakening that cast slavery in the light of injustice and inequality.

Slavery grew quickly in America and soon there was a bustling slave trade spawned by Europeans between Africa and America. From 1720 to the 1760s over 150,000 African slaves arrived in America. Many Christian whites perpetuated the myth that blacks were descendents of the biblical Ham, wicked son of Noah, and that their bondage was a mark of sin from God. This theory received support from plantation masters as well as scientists from northern universities and some scholars used research from anthropology, history, sociology, and biology to prove Negroes were inferior, measuring and weighing brains in an attempt to "prove" inferiority because their brains were smaller or lighter.

There was, however, some early concern among white colonial Christians about the salvation of blacks. Cotton Mather, the venerable New England preacher, argued that blacks had souls, but many whites refused to baptize blacks because this act conferred certain liberties on black individuals that whites were reluctant to bestow. Mather solved the problem somewhat by offering the alternative of huge indentures imposed by masters on Negroes which would insure slavery after baptism. Also, he suggested black children be made to memorize lines like "I must be patient and content with such condition God has ordered for me" (Marty 111). The belief that African blacks were slaves because God had ordained it—in spite of evidence to the contrary—was a concept American whites openly embraced and promulgated. Whites also demanded that blacks accept this divine interpretation as well, which most blacks reluctantly did at the time of their Christian conversion.

Even after the Civil War, which officially abolished black slavery, many white Protestants continued in their quest to build a "righteous Empire." However, only certain people belonged in this empire so, although blacks were no longer slaves, they were still not equals. Thus slavery continued to be a religious doctrine and inequality a way of life among Christians.

A pivotal figure in the development of the black church is Richard Allen, born a slave in 1760. Allen's family was sold, one by one, by their owner who had fallen on financial hard times. Allen heard the circuit riders—preachers who travelled on horseback from plantation to plantation and community to community—and was influenced by them. He experienced a spiritual rebirth and showed a talent for preaching to his companions. The Methodists, under John Wesley and Francis Asbury, often taught their congregations to set goals for themselves as they sought perfection. Allen's goal was to purchase his freedom so he and his owner agreed on terms for his freedom. Both Allen and his brother became free after meeting the price.

Richard Allen lived in Philadelphia and did a series of odd jobs to support his preaching. He formed a Free Africa Society and founded a church, named Bethel. In 1816 there were five congregations of the church. This group formed the first Methodist General Conference for free blacks who chose to follow the Methodist Episcopal church doctrine.

Bishop Allen, as he was known, oversaw the 6,748 Methodists in his care around Philadelphia, Baltimore, and Charleston, and though he sought unity amongst freedmen, he saw them oppose each other within black denominations that were beset with disagreements and riddled with conflicts like those of their white counterparts. Still, he channelled his considerable energies into welfare work, mutual aid and preaching as he and his colleagues "inspired members with hopes of heaven while they imparted dignity to blacks in their daily struggles" (Marty 240).

Even during the early days of the freedom churches, there were militants who inspired slave revolts. These revolutionaries used biblical phrases learned on the plantations to inspire followers and often saw themselves as a Moses, leading the chosen and faithful to an exodus out of Egyptian slavery to the new Canaan, much in the same way the early American Puritans visualized their flight to the new world. These slaves often combined Christianity with African folk religion for a hybrid religion. Two of the more famous—Denmark Vesey and Nat Turner—were killed in 1822 and 1831, respectively, for leading slave uprisings.

Blacks also had to face a move by whites through the American Colonization Society, formed in 1817, to have them transported back to Africa. However, by then Blacks were several generations removed from being Africans and viewed themselves as Americans, with as much right to this country as their white counterparts. These blacks countered with a plea for black Americans and communicated via a "grapevine" that let others know about their movement. This was particularly needed on southern plantations, which were so far apart that no Blacks could effectively congregate. Still, their mixture of African religion and Christianity continued to grow and help them cope with their daily struggles. Indeed, their spirituals often had double meanings—the same songs spoke openly of eternal hope beyond the earthly life as well as underground railroads which could lead them to freedom.

The conversion of blacks was guided by the same principles as those of whites—each individual was expected to confront God and make his decision for Jesus, be "born-again" or "get religion." Many white settlers carried their black slaves with them during the early camp meetings at the beginning of the 1800s and the Blacks heard psalms and camp meeting songs. The slaves made a number of conscious attempts to reproduce the songs they heard but often sang these songs in a different manner, affecting rhythms which were different from the original and, because of an insufficient vocabulary or inability to recall the words correctly, different lyrics or lyrics which have been reproduced as Negro dialect, markedly different from white speech.

While the early white settlers placed a heavy emphasis on the words with the music being incidental—a handful of tunes were used, often interchangeable with different sets of lyrics—the black American felt a need to emphasize music over the words. But it was more than just a different melody—it was a whole new rhythm, an entirely new "feel" to the songs which became defined as black gospel. So, even though the Blacks and whites often sang the same words, learned from the same sources, the results were two entirely different songs, with the black gospel songs rhythmical in a way the white songs never were. These rhythms, often complex, are attributed to the African influence.

The spirituals were created by a people bound in slavery and were an integral part of the culture in the early nineteenth century. However, it was not until after the Civil War that the spiritual was first recorded. The first major book containing words and music of spirituals was *Slave Songs of the United States* in 1867, but the first real awareness of the black spirituals came when the Fisk Jubilee Singers undertook a tour of northern cities in order to raise money for their financially strapped institution. Still, the black's gospel music was virtually ignored by white Christians and it was not until the twentieth century that denominational hymnals included spirituals.

Musicologist and folk music collector George Pullen Jackson noted in the early part of the twentieth century that most of the black spirituals had white origins and could be traced back to the British folk song tradition and early American camp meetings. Many later called his conclusions racist for denying African origins for these songs. But Jackson was correct in tracing these songs to their source; however, he ignored the musical rhythms that define black gospel, tracing only words and melodies. Too, he overlooked the development of the "holiness" movement in the latter part of the nineteenth century which was a source of the essential difference between black and white gospel music.

The holiness church is most prevalent in black ghettos. Even within the black culture, and particularly within the Christian culture, it is a world all its own. Its roots go back to the 1890s and the "Latter Rain Movement" which sought to "irrigate the dry bones" in churches. Pentecostal congregations, characterized by this intense emotionalism in the worship service, developed all over the country, especially among the poor and depressed. The term "holy rollers" comes from this movement because people are liable to scream, shout, dance, jump or roll on the floor for Jesus. These churches place a heavy emphasis on "saved, sanctified, and filled with the Holy Spirit" which means a possession by the spirit, so the person is not chained to this world but free to act or say whatever God wants done or said, using the individual's voice and body. Speaking in tongues, or glossolalia (a fluent gibberish with a number of Hebrew-like sounds) is often practiced. There are an estimated 20 million Americans who have had significant exposure to holiness churches, with about an equal division between black and white. However, the holiness churches, like American Christianity in general, remains mostly segregated.

The black holiness churches feature a great amount of singing and dancing in their services, with half of the service usually comprised of music. These churches were the first to use musical instruments in the service, instruments that churches had long considered "of the devil." Conservatism has been a staple of American Christianity and the mainstream black churches, while usually more emotional than white churches, generally reject the intense emotional involvement and extreme physical activities the holiness churches introduced as a regular part of their service.

There are foot-stomping and hand-clapping up-tempo songs in holiness churches, songs replete with complex rhythms, but the archetypal holiness song is a slow chant, often begun as church starts or later, during a prolonged series of shouts and outbursts. The ministers, with their strong personal charisma and elaborate showmanship, are the key factor in the holiness churches and they are required to lead the church to a spiritual high during the service that will enable the congregation to face six hard, troublesome weekdays. For those attending, religion is a way of life and almost every night is filled with some church-related activity. These people come well-prepared for the Sunday service, ready and willing to begin the shouting and praise when they enter the door. There is a strong current of anti-intellectualism and, with all the physical and emotional activity at a fever pitch, the air is often heavy with repressed sexuality. The faith is composed of mystery, divinely inspired intuition, and visions that cannot be explained in this world. Holiness church is the antithesis of rationalism.

By definition and nature the holiness churches are usually small and generally "store front" churches, without elaborate trappings or extensive networks of denominations. Each church, like each individual, is intensely individualistic in its faith and expression of that faith. Yet, with all the rampant expression of faith in physical and emotional terms and an overriding commitment to living the Godly life, there are a number of paradoxes and ironies within the black holiness churches. The congregations are primarily composed of females and children with generally only a handful of males in attendance. The youth are a vital part because of their mothers and because of the music, which is loud, vibrant, and energetic. It's no wonder so many black pop music starts have come from the black holiness churches.

The songs sung in these churches derive primarily from old hymns from the Moody-Sankey collections and songs from the spiritual-jubilee tradition, all sung in a contemporary style. The music is very rhythmic and often inspires outbursts of emotion from members of the congregations. Again, the irony is that blacks have taken so many hymns popularized by Moody and Sankey— whites—and adapted them to their own services. However, the result is a brand new song from an old lyric and melody, a distinctively black gospel song.

The spiritual jubilee tradition and the jubilee singers' tradition come from the songs developed amongst the black population at the beginning of the nineteenth century. While these songs were established before the Civil War, the Moody-Sankey hymns came along after the Civil War, which serves as a convenient dividing place for these two kinds of black gospel songs. However, the black gospel music tradition that has evolved really began to take form at the beginning of the twentieth century, when blacks began to publish their own music.

The key figure in black gospel songwriting and publishing is Thomas Dorsey, who became known as a great personality, composer, publisher, performer, teacher, choir director and organizer as well as minister of music for the Pilgrim Baptist Church in Chicago. More than any other individual, Dorsey defined contemporary black gospel music, even though he was not the first black to have his gospel songs published. That honor belongs to C. Albert Tindley, who wrote during the early 1900s and was a great influence on the young Dorsey, particularly with his great classics "I'll Overcome" (later altered to become "We Shall Overcome") and "Stand By Me." But it was Dorsey himself, as well as his songs, that unified the movement which became black gospel, giving a definition to the music that has survived through the twentieth century.

Thomas Dorsey was a great songwriter, able to capture the spirit and essence of "soul-singing" and compose in the unique black idiom. But his influence and popularity is also attributed to his practice of reproducing his words and music on single sheets for sale, selling them directly to churches and singers, whose alternative was to purchase large collections of songs in books. W.C. Handy, the "Father of the Blues," also did this in the field of secular music.

Dorsey, of course, was a gigantic figure in gospel music outside his publishing. He trained and accompanied countless singers and fought for recognition against ministries and church musicians who were opposed to adding his songs in churches. Finally, the National Baptist Convention (Negro), which convened in Chicago in 1930, allowed the performance of two Dorsey songs and the reaction from delegates charted the direction for black gospel. George Robinson Ricks quotes Mahalia Jackson, who states,

When the Baptist convention met in Chicago in 1930, that was the first time gospel music was expressed officially in that body. Dorsey had written two songs, 'How About You' and 'Did You See My Savior.' These songs swept the convention and it seems that there was a frantic expression all over the place the whole week and then it swept the nation.

The style started from Chicago with the...true, honest, sincere expression in gospel music. (Ricks 136-137)

Dorsey had first made a name for himself in secular music, under the name "Georgia Tom," writing "The Stormy Sea Blues" for Ma Rainey and "Tight Like That" with Tampa Red. He also played piano in bands with jazz artists like Les Hite and Lionel Hampton. But with gospel he found his calling and his true genius took root and flourished. As director of the gospel choir at Pilgrim Baptist Church in Chicago, Dorsey helped a number of singers and had a forum for writing and experimenting with new songs he composed. These songs ushered in a new era for black gospel and other new songs emerged as the great singers—most of whom came out of choirs (often Dorsey's) as soloists—developed. As black gospel was recorded and released, these singers would establish national reputations and influence others who would never have seen or heard them otherwise. This served to unify black gospel and increasingly bring it to the attention of white churches and singers, who were influenced by the style and rhythms and often copied some of the songs and bought some of the records.

Thomas Andrew Dorsey was born in Villa Rica, Georgia in 1891, son of a Baptist minister, Reverend T.M. Dorsey and his wife, Etta. He was raised in Atlanta where he was influenced by early blues and jazz as well as the Isaac Watts hymns. Although his parents disapproved of show business, Dorsey was clearly attracted to it and mastered several instruments in his youth. In his teens he began playing blues and ragtime and throughout the 1920s was a prolific composer of blues songs. He was "saved" through a song, "I Do, Don't You" at a Baptist convention in 1921. During the following years, he kept a foot in both worlds—gospel and secular—and performed all kinds of music. But spiritually he never left the church, although musically he tried different roads. The problem was that gospel music, as it is known today, did not really exist then. There were no "gospel" songs; they were called "evangelistic songs."

Dorsey's first gospel song was "If You See My Savior, Tell Him That You Saw Me," written in 1928. According to author Tony Heilbut, Dorsey took five borrowed dollars and mailed five hundred copies to churches around the country. The first order did not come for three years. The breakthrough for Dorsey and his gospel songs, as noted earlier, occurred in 1930 at the National Baptist Convention for blacks in Chicago. The musical directors there, Lucie Campbell and E.W. Isaac, invited him to sell his music. That launched Thomas Dorsey as a gospel songwriter, and from 1929 on he only wrote gospel.

The 1930s were Dorsey's most prolific time as the Depression created a need for his optimistic, uplifting songs. He used the blues form in his melodies and his decidedly gospel lyrics were aimed at the poor and outcast. Part of genius is subconscious and Dorsey's use of blues and jazz musical forms was often not deliberate. Heilbut quotes him as saying, "You see, when a thing becomes a part of you, you don't know when it's gonna manifest itself. And it's not your business to know or my business to know" (64).

As the music became more accepted in the churches, Dorsey's stature as a songwriter grew until he was, in the words of Mahalia Jackson, "our Irving Berlin." The churches at this time—early twentieth century—had suffered from a musical lapse and did not supply the emotional support or physical outlet to allow the sermons to be effective. Dorsey, along with singers like Sallie Martin, ushered in the golden era for gospel, c. 1945-1960. The era was carried by Dorsey's Gospel Singer's convention, established by him and Sallie Martin in 1932 at the Pilgrim Baptist Church in Chicago. This convention attracted a number of fine singers and became an institution dedicated to advancing gospel as both an art form and a way of life.

Although Dorsey's songs were written first for the black congregations, they also struck responsive chords with whites. Two top publishers for white churches, Stamps-Baxter and R.E. Winsett, began anthologizing Dorsey tunes in the late 30s and his two biggest songs, "Peace in the Valley" and "Precious Lord, Take My Hand" were major hits in the white market, becoming million record sellers for Red Foley and Elvis Presley, respectively.

Precious Lord, Take My Hand
Precious Lord, take my hand, lead me on, let me stand
I am tired, I am weak, I am worn
Thru the storm, thru the night, lead me on to the light
Take my hand, precious Lord, lead me home.

When my way grows drear, precious Lord, linger near
When my life is almost gone
Hear my cry, hear my call, hold my hand lest I fall
Take my hand, precious Lord, lead me home.

When the darkness appears and the night draws near
And the day is past and gone
At the river I stand, guide my feet, hold my hand
Take my hand, precious Lord, lead me home.
(©1938 by Hill and Range)

This song came after a particularly traumatic time in Dorsey's life. He stated:

This song is very dear to me. I left my home one morning with another fellow driving to St. Louis to sing in a revival at a Baptist church. My wife was going to become a mother in a few days. We got 24 miles outside of Chicago, and I discovered I had left my briefcase with all my music in it. I turned around, drove back to Chicago and went home. My wife was sleeping and I didn't disturb her. When I got back in the car, the other fellow said he had changed his mind and decided not to go. As it was, Providence was trying to tell me not to go away. But I went on to St. Louis anyway. Next night, I was working in a revival, and I received a telegram: Your wife just died. Come home. Some fellows volunteered to drive me to Chicago, and when I got home the next day, I had the body moved. I had a bouncing boy baby. But that night, the baby died. That was double trouble. I felt like going back on God. He had mistreated me, I felt. About a week later, after we had put the baby and the wife away in the same casket, I was sitting with the late Theodore Frye, just drowsing. Just like water dropping from the crevice of a rock, the words dropped into the music, 'Take My Hand, Precious Lord.' (Horstman 57-58)

Peace in the Valley
Well, I'm tired and so weary, but I must go along
Till the Lord comes to call me away
Where the morning's so bright and the Lamb is the light
And the night, night is as fair as the day

There will be peace in the valley for me someday
There will be peace in the valley for me, Oh Lord I pray
There'll be no sadness, no sorrow, no trouble I'll see
There will be peace in the valley for me.

Well, the bear will be gentle and the wolf will be tame
And the lion will lay down by the lamb
And the beasts from the wild will be led by a little child
I'll be changed, changed from this creature I am.
(©1939 by Hill and Range)

Dorsey stated about this song:

It was just before Hitler sent his war chariots into Western Europe in the late thirties. I was on a train going through southern Indiana on the way to Cincinnati, and the country seemed to be upset about this coming that he was about to bring on. I passed through a valley on the train. Horses, cows, sheep, they were all grazing and together in this little valley. Kind of a little brook was running through the valley, and up the hill there I could see where the water was falling from. Everything seemed so peaceful with all the animals down there grazing together. It made me wonder what's the matter with humanity? What's the matter with mankind? Why couldn't man live in peace like the animals down there? So out of that came 'Peace in the Valley.' (Horstman 53-54)

Other songs Dorsey has written include "I Surely Know There's Been a Change in Me," "It's My Desire" (popularized by Guy Lombardo), "When I've Done the Best I Can," "How Many Times," "I'm Gonna Live the Life I Sing About in My Song," "Singing in My Soul," "Life Can Be Beautiful," and "The Lord Will Make a Way." Thomas Dorsey toured throughout America between 1932 and 1944, performing concerts of the new gospel music, called "Evenings with Dorsey." The singers included Sallie Martin, Mahalia Jackson, Roberta Martin, Theodore Frye and others he had trained. Admission was minimal and sheet music was sold at the concerts for a nickel a song. It proved to be an effective way of building a publishing company as well as promoting the songs, leaving copies at churches for others to perform wherever he went. In many ways this knack of self-promotion was as great a gift as the songs themselves. Dorsey sold himself and a movement as well.

Unlike many other forms of gospel music, black gospel has a distinctive, identifiable sound. Thomas Dorsey was a leader in introducing jazz rhythms and blues singing in the church, adding gospel lyrics to the blues tradition. According to Mahalia Jackson,

The basic thing is soul feeling...gospel music...is soul music. When they talk about jazz, the Holiness people had it before it came in. They would take a song like 'What a Friend We Have in Jesus' and give it personal expression. They gave it a joyful expression...expressed by things they couldn't speak. Some called it gospel music for years but it did not come into its own until way late...when the Holiness people helped to emphasize the beat (Ricks 139-140).

This "feeling" in music, which is uniquely black, comes from a deep felt emotionalism anchored in the black experience and a certain hopelessness in their earthly life that is balanced with a shining hopefulness in their life to come.

The inspiration of trouble, sorrow, thanksgiving and joy in addition to the highly individualistic style of the singers separates black gospel from white. The same song is rarely ever sung the same way twice, with an emphasis on improvisation within the song causing each performance to be a wholly different experience for both singer and audience. This inventiveness on the part of black singers renders it nearly impossible to transcribe this music in sheet form. Although it is put on sheet music, it is rarely sung by blacks exactly as it is written because the song essentially remains in the oral tradition. The sheet music serves as a source of lyrics for the singers and a guide for basic chords for piano players. While a white chorus will buy a number of copies of sheet music to learn a song—each member using a copy to sing from—the black choir will generally learn the song by ear and the only members with sheet music will be the director and piano player. For that reason, the sheet music for blacks will usually only include the lead melody line and piano accompaniment while sheet music for whites will have all the parts—soprano, alto, bass, tenor—written out.

Choirs perform most of the music during church services, serving as part of the worship. These choirs are comprised primarily of women while the small groups—quartets and quintets—are usually comprised of men whose music is most often presented in the context of religious entertainment outside the regular church service.

Most blacks belong to traditional denominational churches—Baptists and Methodists dominate—with the holiness churches having only a small portion of the gospel churchgoers. However, the significance of the holiness church is that its individualism has led to many innovations in black music. It has served as a leader and catalyst in bringing new forms of music into the black church, including the addition of music instruments, once considered "of the Devil" because it made the music sound "worldly" or like contemporary secular music.

Too, the holiness church has encouraged and inspired blacks to express their own culture, rather than be black versions of white churches. This has meant that the evolution of black churches to a mainstream church has been much different from their white counterparts. With churches so segregated this has served to divide Christianity and gospel music into two distinctive camps— black and white. While each may borrow songs and musical influences from the other, and the performers watch the opposite race to incorporate ideas into their own performances, the congregations remain separate, often unaware of the music of their counterparts.

Chapter 14
Southern Gospel

For many, southern religion means foot washing, snake handling, camp meetings, holy rollers, speaking in tongues, tent revivals, and intense emotionalism. It means a religion which stresses dramatic conversions and the baptism of the spirit, highly charged and fundamental in its beliefs. It is important to recognize that the unique character of the south in America's history has given rise and nurture to all of these facets of Christianity.

Southern religion is dominated by Protestantism and the two oldest religions—Catholicism and Judaism—have had little impact as religions. The dominant denominations in the south are Baptist, Methodist, Pentecostal, and Presbyterian.

It has been said that if you are southern, you are religious and indeed the South is often characterized by its religions. These religions are fiercely independent and characterized by revivals, in which charismatic evangelists reach large numbers of people with the "Word of God"; those who hear, in turn, experience conversion, salvation, regeneration, or spiritual rebirth. For those outside the church, the thrust is on conversion to the Christian faith while for those inside the church revivals seek to renew those already committed.

Preaching by revivalists is usually loud, long, dramatic, spontaneous, and earnest and the preacher is generally a charismatic figure. The conversion experience is intimate, personal, usually dramatic, and the key to the individual's salvation. This southern religion is generally conservative in its theology, committed to the unchanging truths of the faith, with an intense concern for the faith and morals of individuals as well as a strong commitment to evangelism.

Fundamentalism is not unique to any one denomination but cuts across all denominational borders and represents an effort to establish doctrines and propositions which are unchanging or absolutely "fundamental" to the Christian faith. Fundamentalists generally see any deviation from essential doctrines as a compromise of the truth, a weakness of the faith, and a betrayal of the gospel. They often have difficulty accepting someone as a Christian if the person does not affirm the truth of a wide variety of necessary articles of faith or accept a common dogma of biblical authority. These dogma include an insistence on the Genesis account of creation; the acceptance of Adam and Eve as parents of the race of man; Christ's virgin birth, sacrificial atonement, bodily resurrection, reality of his miracles, and a literal second coming. Fundamentalists are often rigid in their faith, speaking infallibly on matters of faith and morals with a tendency to judge those who are "true" Christians from those who they believe do not measure up because of ungenuine faith.

Southern religion is extremely personal and begins with the experience of conversion with a continuing encounter with God all through the life of the individual. This intimate communication with God through Jesus Christ is the essential rite of passage for the believer to be united with God in heaven as well as His church on earth. Although there are numerous doctrines of salvation—a process of nurture, growth and confirmation vs. a sudden, dramatic event—it always includes a deep recognition of sinfulness followed by a sorrowfulness and then a turning away from sin through the mercy of God and acceptance of Jesus Christ and his crucifixion as an atonement for sins. It includes a direct invitation for Christ to enter the human heart and serve as friend, savior, guide, and control. This initial religious experience must be followed by a series of experiences with God so that the person may "know" him. It usually culminates in a second decisive experience, the baptism of the Holy Ghost. Here, the individual may speak in tongues, prophesize, or feel the call to preach as he becomes sanctified for holiness in life.

These religious experiences serve as a common ground for Southerners and have cultural and social as well as religious significance. The isolation of the southern rural mountain people led to a conservatism in theology and a tendency to view their own unique experiences as closest to those of the New Testament. Unfettered by the pluralism of urban life, the rural Southerner shaped the south with his religion in social, cultural, and philosophical ways, making it different from the rest of the United States. One of those ways was through music and the religious function that singing schools, gospel sings, and shaped-note books held for Southerners.

One singing school which developed was the Ruebush-Kieffer school and publishing company, established in 1872 by Aldine Kieffer and Ephraim Ruebush in the Shenandoah Valley of Virginia. They began the Virginia Normal School in 1874, a singing school teaching the shaped-note system of reading and writing music. The singing school came about as an effort to preserve musical literacy during a time when most of the population was illiterate. It taught students the skill of reading a musical staff, singing by syllables, singing harmony parts and reading rhythm and led to the development of a whole industry of song publishing for books containing music to be used for lessons as well as a section on the "Rudiments of Music." The four basic shaped notes, fa, sol, la and me, were created by Philadelphians William Smith and William Little in the early 1800s. They assigned a right triangle for fa, an oval for sol, a square for la and a diamond for mi and put these shapes on the note heads correctly on the music staff with the notes retaining their original rhythm characteristics.

The earliest shaped-note books were *Southern-Harmony*, published by William Walker of South Carolina in 1835, and *Sacred-Harp*, first published by his brother-in-law, Benjamin Franklin White, who had moved to Georgia, in 1844. Other collections were published, including one by Joseph Funk, a Pennsylvanian, called *Harmonia-Sacra*. Locally, southerners nicknamed Funk's book "Hominy Soaker" but used it. Funk later switched from the four note system to the system of seven shapes, developed by Jesse Aiken in the middle of the nineteenth century and first published in his book, *Christian-Minstreal*.

Aldine Kieffer was the grandson of Joseph Funk and Funk's book was used at the Ruebush-Kieffer school. The significance of this school is that several people who attended would later play a major, direct role in the development of what later became known as southern gospel music. James D. Vaughan, who began the James D. Vaughan Music Company in Lawrenceburg, Tennessee, attended this school as did A.J. Showalter, another descendent of Funk, who later founded the A.J. Showalter Music Company in Dalton, Georgia. Both of these men were prolific songwriters as well as founders of singing schools.

In the early 1900s, V.O. Stamps, an east Texas native, was employed by the James D. Vaughan Music Company before establishing the V.O. Stamps Music Company in Jacksonville, Texas in 1924. He also began a singing school, the Stamps Music School, and was joined in 1926 by J.R. Baxter, who had studied under A.J. Showalter. These two men formed the Stamps-Baxter Company, which would come to dominate the field of southern gospel for several decades through the quartets they developed to sing and promote the songs they published. Frank Stamps, brother of V.O. Stamps, led a group of singers called the Stamps All-Star Quartet, which travelled extensively in the south in the late 1920s, selling songbooks published by the company and singing the Stamps-Baxter copyrights in churches and gatherings where gospel music was performed. This group later recorded for RCA. Frank Stamps headed the Stamps-Baxter organization after the death of his brother in 1940 and established the Stamps Quartet Music Company, which he headed until his death in 1962.

The term "southern gospel music" refers to the gospel music whose sound is akin to country music. It is, by and large, dominated by groups singing the traditional four-part harmonies and is, in reality, more national than southern, although it remains strongest in the south where it developed.

In his article, "Gospel Boogie: White Southern Gospel Music in Transition," Charles Wolfe briefly traces the history of modern southern gospel music. He states:

In the early 1920s, the publishers of gospel shaped-note songbooks began to hire quartets to travel throughout the country singing the new songs and popularizing the new songbooks. These quartets became so successful that several of them broke away from the publishers and began separate careers. Thus professional gospel music. (73)

Wolfe notes the breaking away of the quartets and groups from singing convention traditions was "the one basic, all important development" during this stage of southern gospel (74).

The singing convention was a social as well as religious event in countless rural, southern communities in the early twentieth century. Singers from an area would gather and sing songs from songbooks with shaped notes. While the Sacred Harp tradition used the same books and songs over and over, the singing conventions used new songs and new songbooks with competitions held to see how quickly and accurately members could sing a song they had never seen before. Representatives of the publishing companies (often quartets) would visit these conventions to promote these songbooks and the quartets would be featured on "specialty numbers" while the convention singers took a rest from singing.

Wolfe notes that as southern gospel developed professionally many singers could not read music, singing by ear instead; thus, the conventions provided moments of unease as groups would have to sit by idly while the people sang songs from the books. The professional quartets were commercially successful and gradually bought out the old singing convention giants (Vaughan, Henson, Winsett) and in some cases the new owner "simply stopped publishing convention books" ("Gospel Boogie" 81). This began a trend in this style of music from a participating audience to a passive one as the quartets did all the singing while the audience was expected to listen.

The year 1948 is cited as a crucial year in the development of southern gospel by Wolfe, who notes that it was during this time the Homeland Harmony Quartet of Atlanta had a national best-seller with their recording of a song titled "Gospel Boogie." The original Homeland Harmony quartet was made up of Connor Hall, Otis and James McCoy, B.C. Robinson and Hovie Lister; later, Lee Roy Abernathy replaced Lister. "Gospel Boogie," composed by Abernathy, used many innovative practices to further commercialize gospel music, often to the ire and alarm of the church leaders, many of whom viewed the commerciality of gospel music as blasphemy. Charles Wolfe quotes Rupert Cravens, who wrote an editorial in a magazine of one of the singing convention publishers. Craven states:

The cause of gospel singing is too sacred and universal for anyone conscientiously to take up some phase of it for personal economic, political or social purposes...it is a flimsy excuse when a godless, Sabbath desecrating quartet or singing group will say, after one of their typical Saturday night or Sunday shows, 'We are doing this for a living'...Why should people who love the Lord and clean Christian society have to listen to the music of the 'juke box' to find a medium of expression toward God?...Why should men who are supposed to love the Lord make for their most popular phonograph records and 'song-hits' a type of song that is too cheap in the light of God's holy purpose to deserve mention? Why should a so-called Christian audience go crazy over an all-night jamboree which is so often opened with a prayer but is thereafter carried on as if there were no God. ("Gospel Boogie" 80)

Although Cravens was reacting to the death of the singing conventions, there was a strong vein of truth in his editorial. Many modern southern gospel singers whose roots run back over twenty years recall that those times were marked by an emphasis on entertainment rather than "ministry" and often many of the singers were not true believers. They were boys who had been raised in the church and in Christian homes and loved to sing and looked at the quartets as a way to make a living doing something they enjoyed, feeling the lure of the spotlights much greater than a lure from the eternal light.

A factor that often entered into the acceptance by both audiences and performers for the entertainment aspects was that southern style religion preached that a person must serve either God or the Devil. Since the Devil was represented by secular music and the honky tonks, this was a road to be avoided; however, God was represented by gospel music and churches so if someone performed in church singing gospel music, it was "safe" for their souls as well as good entertainment. In the rural south, these gospel singings and gatherings served many needs—cultural, social, political, and personal—so they were deemed vital.

Too, the congregation heard preaching and received a heavy dose of the gospel on Sundays and weekday nights, so there was an aversion to a heavy dose of religion in these concerts by the audiences—they wanted safe, wholesome family entertainment and the gospel concerts provided it.

During the early years of field recordings, a number of gospel songs and performers were recorded. The dominant labels involved in field recording during the 1920s were Okeh, Paramount, Brunswick, Vocalion, Victor, Gennett and Columbia. These recordings, which provided the beginnings of the country music industry, were made primarily in the south—particularly in Atlanta but also in Johnson City, Tennessee, New Orleans, Dallas and Memphis—and most of the sales were in the south. In his article, "Columbia Records and Old-Time Music," Wolfe states that Columbia's recordings from 1925 to 1931 were electrically recorded and released on the 15000-D series. These recordings resulted in eleven million records containing twenty-two million songs (one on each side of the record) released in the south to a population just under 30 million. During these field sessions, over 300 different groups were recorded but only six accounted for half the releases. One of those six, the Smith Sacred Singers from north Georgia, was the top gospel group.

Gospel accounted for about 20 percent of the releases during this time, with the material consisting of "sacred harp material, quartet material, convention songs, and solos or duets of sacred material" (Wolfe, "Columbia" 121). The material included both pre-war and post-war material, some traditional songs as well as songs from the widely circulated paperback convention books.

Overall, the sales of the gospel releases accounted for about 15 percent of the total sales from the Columbia 15000-D series. An "average" sale was 15,600 per record, with fifteen records selling over 100,000 units each. However, the "smallest average sales" occurred with the gospel releases. An exception was the Smith Sacred Singer's record of "A Picture of Life's Other Side" which sold over 100,000 copies.

The gospel record industry really took hold after World War II with the proliferation of independent record companies. Gospel music had been released by the major labels prior to this, and a relative handful of gospel groups were recorded by these labels, but the independent labels—many specializing in gospel—allowed the market to be saturated with a variety of gospel music and gave this form of music an outlet and allowed it to develop its own market.

The independent labels permitted gospel groups to record the material they wanted in the manner they wanted. This allowed gospel to develop "naturally" instead of having to conform with record company preconceptions about commerciality. Too, the groups were encouraged to develop their own followings and a number of records were sold at concerts, making these recordings more accessible. The quartets also became businesses, producing and selling their own songbooks and, in some cases, forming their own record labels.

Radio also played a major role in the exposure of gospel music as a number of groups had their own radio programs in the 1930s and 1940s. This was the era of live radio and if a gospel group could find a sponsor, they would do a 15 or 30 minute program, obtain bookings and promote their recordings with these shows. They sang a great deal on radio, reaching people who would perhaps never hear them otherwise, thereby increasing their popularity.

As gospel music became a business, groups became increasingly aware of the commerciality of the songs and the influence of successful secular songs began to show itself in the songs of gospel songwriters. As country music grew, *Billboard* created a chart for country records and since many country artists came from gospel music, or at least had deep religious roots, they recorded gospel songs for the country market. It was in this manner that gospel songs first appeared in *Billboard* with artists like Hank Williams, Red Foley, Molly O'Day, the Biles Brothers and Johnny and Jack reaching the country charts with gospel songs. The first gospel song to sell a million copies was "Peace in the Valley" by Red Foley while Elvis Presley and Tennessee Ernie Ford later had million-selling gospel albums, proving the appeal of the songs. But the southern gospel groups, who often sang the same songs, were struggling to sell several thousand records; obviously the market for superstar artists was much larger than the market for gospel music itself.

As southern gospel music entered the 1960s, several significant developments occurred. First, there arose the popularity of the "all night sing," popularized by Wally Fowler. This consisted of a line-up of gospel groups who competed with each other in a sort of singing "contest" while the audience applauded their favorites. These were known for lasting all night long—from eight or nine at night until dawn—and proved very lucrative as audiences packed auditoriums. It was financially profitable for the groups, the best of whom could command good prices. It also provided a forum for exposure. A good showing on an all-night sing—or several of these sings—assured the success of a quartet and launched them into being full-time performers.

The all-night sings had actually begun in 1948 in Atlanta but their heyday was the 1950s and early 1960s as they spread all over the south. But by the end of the 60s they had run their course and it was no longer possible to draw large crowds with this format. Still, they allowed a professionalism to develop in southern gospel music as groups could now make a good living with this music and have a performance outlet that allowed them to be seen by large audiences. It also promoted the concept of a passive audience and the separation of performers and crowds. The singers were now slick, costumed professionals and the audience did not sing along; their role was to watch, listen and applaud. Again, it was the move from congregationalism to the choir, but this time it was outside of church in the concert setting.

At first gospel music helped shape country music as they both came out of the same tradition and had the same performers. The southern gospel world used the songs, styles, and commercial trends of country music in their own music to provide a gospel version of country music. They did not enjoy the popularity or success of country music during this period because they had to maintain a distinct difference—country music could sing about cheating, drinking, loving or any number of other things as well as God but gospel music performers could only sing about God. Too, the solo performer became the dominant country music artist while the quartet sound dominated the southern gospel world. Vocally, this was a major difference, although many of the songs sounded similar.

As the Jesus Movement took hold in the 1970s and contemporary Christian music came to dominate the gospel music world, southern gospel accounted for an increasingly smaller portion of the gospel music pie. Still, a large, loyal audience remained and the southern culture continued to be the major breeding ground for this kind of music. It continued to mimic the sounds of country music while also absorbing some of the sounds from the contemporary pop music world (which country music also did). Ironically, a major difference between southern gospel and the contemporary Christian music world remained outside the music itself. The buyers of southern gospel frequented secular record stores, often finding their favorite groups in the country section of the record bins, while contemporary Christian music found its buying audience frequenting the Christian bookstores. Because the Christian bookstore customer embraced contemporary Christian music, that music grew with the rapidly expanding bookstore market. Southern gospel was limited to its traditional audience and had to continue to depend on its exposure through radio airplay and artists' personal appearances. As record stores expanded in malls, which had limited space, southern gospel found it more and more difficult to be stocked in these retail outlets. It was inevitable that southern gospel would decline as a portion of total gospel, although the southern gospel fans remained among the most loyal and sales of this music remained steady during times when contemporary Christian music's sales fluctuated.

Chapter 15
The Speers and The Blackwoods

Southern gospel has long called itself a "family," presenting a "family" type of music, so it is not surprising that two of the most influential groups in southern gospel have been families—the Speers and the Blackwoods. These two families are influential because they have been so visible to audiences for so many years and because most fans of southern gospel know them. However, the most powerful families in southern gospel have been the Vaughans and the Stamps and these latter two families are most responsible for the success and visibility of the Speers and Blackwoods.

"Mom and Dad" Speer were Tom Speer and Lena Brock; he was born 1891 in Fayette County, Georgia, the fourth of eighteen children to J.J. and Emma Speer and she was born in 1900 in Shady Grove Hill, Alabama (in Cullman County). Soon after Lena's birth, the Brock family moved to Lawrence County, Tennessee, then again to Center Point, Tennessee.

The Speers were cotton farmers who knew the rigors of a hard, rural life. In 1902 young Tom's mother passed away and his father married Mary Estes Seymour, with whom he completed his family. Unable to attend school in his youth, Tom Speer entered the third grade when he was 23 and finished the seventh grade at 25; this would be the end of his formal schooling. Because of his love for gospel music, Tom felt God had called him to be a gospel singer. His mother often sang gospel songs at home and young Tom gave music lessons to his younger brothers and sisters. In World War I, he served in the Army in France and, after his return, met Lena Brock at a country church singing in Leoma, Tennessee. Lena's father taught singing schools and went to singing conventions all over Alabama and Tennessee; Tom Speer quickly became a pupil of Mr. Brock and courted Lena until February 27, 1920, when they were married in Athens, Alabama.

In December, 1920, their first child, Brock, was born, followed by Rosa Nell and Mary Tom and then, in 1930, Ben. They quickly became a singing family group with Lena playing the organ and Tom, or "Dad," leading. During these early years, Tom farmed to support his family in addition to his work as a singing school teacher.

As a teacher, Tom travelled all over Alabama, Georgia, Mississippi, and Tennessee and on weekends sang at conventions and in concerts. There were a number of "all day singings" which served as a social gathering, church picnic, and entertainment for poor rural Southerners and this is where the Speer family cut their teeth in gospel music. It was all centered on the church and these rural churches would usually sponsor a "homecoming" once a year as well as monthly gatherings in the summer where members would gather, play, socialize, eat, and sing. Later, these events would become larger and more organized and soon the county meetings grew into state conventions which attracted thousands of people to Birmingham, Nashville, and some of the other cities in the south. Some of the groups who formed in small southern churches later became professional quartets and were major drawing cards at the large singing conventions. These conventions attracted large crowds who demanded "special attractions." And, as the quartets became more well-known, they began to plan Saturday night programs where they could perform for a whole evening and make enough money to pay their travelling expenses.

In 1929—just after the Wall Street stock market crash—the Speer family moved to Lawrenceburg, Tennessee, home of the James D. Vaughan Music Company, which specialized in selling songbooks of gospel music and holding singing schools. At this time, "Dad" was selling insurance but the Depression soon took that business away. The singing schools also declined and Tom began collecting a bushel of beans or some other barter for his fees. However, things began looking up in the spring of 1934 when Tom got a job with the Vaughn Music Co. for $50 a month. Among the duties of "Dad" were editing music for the songbooks, writing lyrics, teaching harmony and sight singing and conducting the Vaughn Singing Schools, which regularly attracted a number of southern youth to Lawrenceburg in the summer. At the end of these two-week courses, a student would be able to read through and sing a song from one of the convention songbooks. The two-week courses were regularly offered in country churches and schoolrooms as well as at the Vaughn headquarters, but the major singing schools were those held twice a year (January and June) in Lawrenceburg at the Vaughn Music Co. These each lasted a month.

Tom Speer was a determined, ambitious man and in his desire to further himself as well as gospel music, saw radio as the chief medium. The family was used to hearing a Stamps-sponsored quartet on their car radio as they came from Sunday night singings. Since Lena Brock's brother, Dwight, worked as an executive for Stamps-Baxter, based in Dallas, they had connections there. So, after the death of James D. Vaughn in 1941, they joined the Stamps organization.

The family moved to Montgomery, Alabama where they began a gospel radio program. During this time, live entertainment was the major calling card for radio and numerous stations across the country featured local talent in 15, 30 and one-hour shows, A number of gospel groups received major exposure this way. The shows attracted advertisers, or sponsors, to the radio station who paid for the time. The groups advertised songbooks over the air and people sent in money—Stamps-Baxter, which published the books, received most of the money (the groups received a commission) and the books served to promote the songs written and published by these in-house organizations. In this way, the group developed a following and performed in concerts within the listening area. The major income for the groups came from ticket sales at their concerts, usually held in small churches or school houses. At WSFA in Montgomery, where the Speers performed a fifteen-minute program at 6 a.m. each weekday morning, they were followed by a young country singer, Hank Williams. In addition to the radio program and concerts, Tom Speer also wrote lyrics or music or both for the parent company for songs which would appear in the company's songbooks.

World War II saw the oldest son, Brock, go off to the army for four years. The War caused the demise of a number of these small groups, but the Speers managed to find replacements and continued singing gospel music throughout this time, adding a patriotic segment in honor of Brock during each of their shows. After the War, when Brock returned, the group moved to Nashville so Brock could attend college. Brock, who wanted to be a preacher, eventually received his divinity degree from Vanderbilt. He married Faye Ihrig in 1948. When "Dad" had his teeth pulled, Brock took over the emcee duties and thus found a way to combine his call for preaching with his love for gospel music.

The Speers had a radio show on WSIX in Nashville and in the 1950s appeared on television station WLAC. In 1964 they were regular performers on "Singing Time in Dixie," a popular syndicated TV show taped in Atlanta. They also appeared often with the LeFevres on another television show, "Gospel Caravan."

The first recordings by the Speers came in the late 1940s on Bullett Records; later they recorded for the Skylite Company, a gospel label formed by the Statesmen and Blackwood quartets. At this label, Brock began producing records, playing guitar on sessions, designing record jackets and writing liner notes.

As gospel publishers formed record companies, a number of new gospel labels emerged from companies whose source of revenue was shifting from the songbooks to the album sales. The John T. Benson Company, formed in Nashville during the early part of the twentieth century as a publisher, formed Heartwarming records in the early 1960s; the Speers signed with the company in 1965. Several generations have been included in the group at various times during the later years.

The career of the Blackwood Brothers parallels that of the Speer family, but the roots were planted about 20 years earlier, on Christmas Eve, 1900, when Roy Blackwood was born to William Emmett and Carrie Blackwood near Fentress, Mississippi. In 1905, daughter Lena was born while two other sons, Doyle and James, were born in 1911 and 1919, respectively.

The Blackwoods, like the Speers, were farmers but two of the sons, Doyle and James, wanted to become gospel singers, probably inspired by watching visiting groups perform in their local churches. Doyle learned to play a Russian balalaka and soon he and James formed a duet. In their biography, *Above All* (written with Kree Jack Racine), Doyle states that "My first and most lasting ambition was to learn everything possible about singing, and then to become a professional Gospel Singer" and he tells of early practices (31). He states:

(There were) many tree stumps in the fields my Dad worked, and these became my stages...I would go out in the fields, pick a stump to stand on, and pretending I was on the stage of a big hall, I would sing through every song I knew. Then I would run back to the house to get Mama's opinion of my voice projection and to see if my diction was remaining full and clear. As time passed I used stumps farther and farther away from the house, and the power of my stomach muscles, diaphragm, and vocal cords really did develop. I tried continually to widen my technical scope by listening to, and copying as closely as I could, the styles and techniques of well known performers of the day...like the Delmore

Bros. and Jimmie Rodgers...I was quite familiar with the guitar and soon had learned—
by ear—almost every song he had recorded complete with yodels. (32-33)

James was soon bitten by the gospel bug too and he and Doyle would often
discuss their future. In their biography, James states:

In discussions as to what we would do when we got out of school, our ambitions centered,
more and more, on Gospel Singing. I had attended several 'All Day Singing Conventions,'
and R.W. in his travels with Roy and Susan, had attended even more. We enjoyed immensely
the Christian fellowship and the programs at these Conventions. We greatly admired the
professional singers who we knew were making their living this way...As the years
progressed, R.W. and I became firmly set in our conviction that Gospel Singing should
become our life's work. We promised each other to learn everything possible about Gospel
Music and Gospel Singing until such time as we could set out on our own, and do our
very best to establish our name of Blackwood as a household word in gospel singing
circles. (49)

R.W. Blackwood was the son of Roy Blackwood, James' older brother. This
made R.W. the nephew of James, but the age difference—only two years—made
them more like brothers. Since Roy was a minister, the family moved around
quite a bit, from church to church as pastoring jobs ended or opened up. But
he always tried to make it home for Christmas and that holiday in 1933 was
particularly eventful for the Blackwood Brothers gospel act because Roy brought
back a Victrola—the first any of them had ever seen—and a number of records
by gospel groups. Doyle, James, and R.W. were soon studying those records.
James states:

We had learned a great deal from listening to these records and the various arrangement
of the songs. We found it was even better for us, technically, than listening to live
presentations, because we could play a record over and over, until we understood thoroughly
what was being done to achieve certain affects. (Racine 55)

It was during this holiday that the brothers and R.W. began a serious
discussion about a full-time family quartet which would go under the name
of "The Blackwood Brothers." The first step in that goal was realized when
they enrolled in a ten-night singing school at the Clear Springs Baptist Church
under the tutelage of a Mr. Ray. From that school came their first quartet, with
Doyle singing baritone, James alto harmony, Gene Catledge, a distant relative
singing bass, and Mr. Ray singing lead. Mr. Ray was apparently a demanding
taskmaster and required much practice and dedication from the Blackwoods and
they immersed themselves in singing. They state:

He (Mr. Ray) would require us to analyze the words until he was sure we understood
the song message thoroughly. Then, the melody would be analyzed, phrase by phrase.
Next, we would run through the parts until the intonation was exactly right. At this
point, we were ready to consider phrasing (the breathing points in the song), and the
word 'cutoffs.' When this was perfected we would select what we considered the best tempo
for presentation of our arrangement of the song. Lastly, came the dynamics (the 'softs'
and 'louds') and where and what extent they should be applied. (Racine 55)

After a number of practice sessions the group made their first appearance at the "All Day Singing" at the Concord Baptist Church, near Atkerman, Mississippi. Just before they sang they named themselves the "Chocktaw County Jubilee Singers." After this appearance, the group sang for a number of other engagements—including some that paid—for about a year and then broke up. The Blackwood Brothers had made their first big step into becoming professional gospel singers.

In September, 1934, Roy and his family moved back to Mississippi and a family quartet was soon formed with Roy singing lead, R.W. alto, James baritone, and Doyle bass. They sang together, pursuing their dream of making themselves a household name with a "Blackwood sound," until late 1935 when Roy was offered the pastorate of a church in Ft. Worth, Texas and Doyle was offered a position with the Homeland Harmony Quartet, a well known gospel group in Birmingham, Alabama. James, who was then 16, continued to sing with groups in the area. Two years later, the Blackwoods re-formed with James, now eighteen, singing lead (his voice had finally passed the "changing" period), R.W. (who was now sixteen) on baritone, Roy singing first tenor, and Doyle singing bass and providing musical accompaniment on guitar. The group decided to try for a radio program and auditioned at WHEF in Kosciusko, Mississippi.

James notes that, at this time on small, rural radio stations, "The broadcasting field was wide open to any one who could carry a tune, make a speech, scrape a fiddle, pick a banjo...or, for that matter...whistle! Most anybody who was willing and able to get the body to the station...was welcomed with open arms." Their audition came just 15 minutes after they walked through the station's front door and was broadcast live. The owner had herded them right to the mike and told them they had a 15-minute program to prove their stuff. According to James Blackwood, "Before we had finished our first number, the phones began to ring. Listeners were calling and congratulating the station on the program, and making requests for songs...instead of 15 minutes...our air time stretched out to an hour and 15 minutes" (Racine 71). The owner scheduled them to appear every Sunday morning for a 30-minute show. This led to personal appearances and the Blackwoods would announce their availability during the program as well as advertise where they would be appearing the coming week. During these appearances, the average income for the group was four to six dollars a night with admission priced at ten cents for children and 15 cents for adults. Their first big pot of gold came when they collected $27 one night at the high school in Noxapater, Mississippi and $55 another night in Houlka, Mississippi.

In 1938 the Blackwoods moved to WJDX in Jackson, Mississippi, where they had a daily broadcast. Always promoting themselves, they soon invested in a public address system that ran off the car battery with speakers attached to the top of their car. When they reached the area where they were to give a concert that evening, they always drove around—in town as well as on the rural back roads—announcing where they would be that night and the time of the concert. These speakers covered a mile wide radius and showed the Blackwoods to be both determined and innovative in their approach to promoting gospel singing. In fact, the key to the success of the Blackwoods seems to be that they "out-promoted" most other gospel quartets. This pursuit of publicity and promotion—which most others left to chance—as well as their ability to stay together over a long period of time, set them apart from other gospel groups and eventually made them a "household name" in gospel singing circles.

The Blackwoods' big success came when they moved to KWKH in Shreveport. They had two daily broadcasts for this station—at 6:15 a.m. and at noon—and by mid-afternoon would be travelling to an evening engagement. Since KWKH had 10,000 watts, the Blackwood's engagements carried them all over Louisiana, east Texas and southern Arkansas. It was also while they were in Shreveport that they became associated with the Stamps organization.

Roy Blackwood had first met V.O. Stamps in 1929 in Boaz, Alabama. Stamps has been described as having those "rare qualities of leadership that resulted in getting things done" (Racine 81). The Stamps organization had contacted the Blackwoods because of their success on the Shreveport station, which meant they were traveling enough to sell songbooks. The business arrangement was that Stamps would assist with the booking arrangements, securing bookings the Blackwoods would normally not get (such as large conventions), would provide a pianist and furnish a late model automobile. In return, the Stamps organization would receive a percentage of the gross income after a stipulated amount had been earned. The Blackwoods would take the Stamps name as part of their calling card; thus they changed their name to "The Blackwood Brothers Stamps Quartet" during this time to advertise their association with this organization, which was well-known and well-respected throughout gospel circles.

Since V.O. Stamps was adamant that the piano was the proper form of accompaniment for gospel singing, he required groups carrying his name to have a piano player and, to that end, provided piano players from the main office for the group. The first piano player for the Blackwoods was Joe Roper, who was replaced a few months later by Wallace Milligan, who remained with them until 1940.

Another prerogative of Mr. Stamps was that he would assign the quartets' territories. The Blackwoods had been successful in Shreveport, but V.O. wanted his younger brother, Frank, who was based in Shenandoah, Iowa, to be closer to the home office so he assigned Frank to Shreveport and sent the Blackwoods to Iowa. The Blackwoods took up their new chores on station KMA in mid-summer, 1940. At this station, they had three daily broadcasts—at 5:30 a.m., 7:30 a.m., and 12:30 p.m. The first was a transcription recorded the day before while the following two were live broadcasts. From their location in Iowa, the Blackwoods reached 27 states and Canada and their concert bookings took them to Iowa, Nebraska, Missouri, Kansas, Minnesota, and North and South Dakota. Their pianist during this time was Hilton Griswold.

The first major set-back for the Blackwoods occurred when World War II began. Since most of their income depended upon personal appearances, and since gas and tire rationing made this kind of travel impossible, the Blackwoods had to give up their career for awhile. Too, some of the members were draft age and knew that the Army was only a letter away.

During this time, the Blackwoods moved to San Diego, California, and took jobs working in defense plants. In the evenings, they continued to sing at nearby churches and schools and were active in the War Bond Drives. R.W. Blackwood was the first to be drafted and left in June, 1944. Doyle's health had begun to fail, so pianist Hilton Griswold took over the baritone part until he was drafted. He was replaced by A.T. Humphries, who was in the Navy at the time and stationed at San Diego, and his wife, LaVera, who served as pianist. James Blackwood was turned down by the draft while Roy Blackwood and his family returned home to Mississippi. Although this was a set-back of sorts for the Blackwoods at the time, it would prove to be a blessing in disguise in the long run. The Blackwoods made a small name for themselves on the west coast and were responsible for introducing their gospel quartet sound to that part of the country.

World War II itself would help southern gospel music because so many Southerners who grew up with this music were sent all over the country—and to foreign countries—and carried this love of quartet singing with them. These young men introduced others to this kind of singing and, when the war was over, there was an awareness of southern gospel music outside the south. This resulted in demands for appearances by southern gospel groups all over the country and led to a national awareness instead of just a regional appeal. However, the south certainly remained the stronghold for the quartet sound.

World War II ended August, 1945 and on October 1 of that year, the Blackwoods were back at KMA in Shenandoah, Iowa to resume their career. At this time, their line-up was Roy on first tenor, James on lead, Don Smith on bass, Hilton Griswold on baritone and piano. Doyle, who was an announcer on WAPO in Chattanooga, could not join them at this time but retained his full interest and share in the group. R.W. Blackwood joined them again in mid-December, 1945, after his discharge from the service.

It was during this time that the Blackwoods began their recording career. Ever alert to business and professional opportunities, James Blackwood calculated the group could sell albums at their personal appearances. They would thus generate more income as well as promote the Blackwood sound and name. Terry Moss, program director for KMA, had the equipment necessary for the actual recording as well as some contacts to get the pressings done. After the master was done and records were made available, the Blackwoods were in the record business. Soon they were selling records at the concerts and through the mail. This led them into the publishing business as they began finding songs to record whose copyrights would generate additional income.

During this time, Don Smith returned to California and was replaced by Bill Lyles and, in 1948, Doyle rejoined the group. The demand for concerts was so great that it was impossible to fill them all, so the Blackwoods decided to form two groups with the second group containing Roy and Doyle, along with Johnny Dixon on baritone and Warren Holmes on bass and Billy Grewin on piano. The first group was comprised of James and R.W. Blackwood, Bill Lyles, "Cat" Freeman on high tenor and Hilton Griswold handling the piano chores. Thus the Blackwoods doubled their income from personal appearances and added opportunities to sell records and songbooks.

By 1950, the mail order business had grown to the point that quartet number two was disbanded and Roy and Doyle devoted all their energies to record promotion and filling mail orders. It was also during this year that the Blackwoods left Shenandoah, Iowa, after ten years, and moved to Memphis, Tennessee. Here, they would establish their permanent headquarters.

In Memphis, they appeared on WMPS. The line-up was James on lead, R.W. on baritone, Aldon Toney first tenor, Bill Lyles bass and Jack Marshall on piano. Marshall replaced Hilton Grishom, who had decided to remain in Iowa. In 1951, they were signed to RCA Victor by Steve Shoals, the legendary A & R man, who contracted them to record singles. There was some conflict here as the Blackwoods kept their own record label and insisted on putting out albums under that label while also recording for RCA, which offered them national distribution.

Perhaps the biggest break for the Blackwoods came in 1954 when they appeared on the Arthur Godfrey Talent Show on CBS (TV and radio). Singing "Have You Talked To The Man Upstairs," on June 12, 1954, they won the contest (judged by audience applause) and appeared throughout that week on the network on the Godfrey Show. This was their biggest exposure to date and was followed by their greatest tragedy a couple of weeks later.

On June 30, 1954, the Blackwoods were appearing in Clanton, Alabama. R.W. Blackwood and Bill Lyles, who had been flying the plane the Blackwoods were then travelling in, took the plane up during the afternoon. Something went wrong during the landing and the plane crashed, killing R.W. and Lyles. A huge memorial service and funeral was held on July 2 at Ellis Auditorium in Memphis and news of the tragedy was broadcast nationally, made pertinent by the Blackwood's recent network appearances.

The ever-opportunistic Blackwoods resumed their concert schedule two days after the funeral with an engagement in Fort Worth, Texas and on July 10 began a series of "Memorial Sings" in Tupelo, Mississippi with Cecil Blackwood, R.W.'s brother, joining the quartet on baritone, and J.D. Sumner taking on the bass chores (he had formerly been with the Sunshine Boys Quartet). One month after the tragedy, on August 4, 1954, the Blackwoods appeared at a Memorial Sing in Clanton, Alabama, where the crash had occurred. During this time, RCA released "Have You Talked To The Man Upstairs" and it became a best seller.

Another change came out of this tragedy: the Blackwoods gave up travel by airplane and went back to cars. In 1955, they bought a bus and refurbished the interior for travel and sleeping. They were the first southern gospel quartet to utilize this mode of travel, which soon became the major means of transportation for gospel, country and rock music stars who were on long tours.

Part 3

Chapter 16
Spirit in the Sky:
Gospel Music on Pop Radio

As radio gave up live entertainment in favor of records in the 1950s because of economics, recordings achieved a new significance. And, as records achieved popularity, the importance of trade charts began to rise and affirm the popularity of particular recordings. These charts surveyed the sales and airplay of certain records and each week listed them in numerical order of their popularity.

Two single records, which each reached number one on the music trade charts, reflected large social movements which began in the 1950s. In 1955 Bill Haley and the Comets had a number one hit with "Rock Around the Clock," marking the official beginning of the rock 'n' roll era; in 1958 the Kingston Trio had a number one song with "Tom Dooley" ushering in the folk music movement. These two musical moments would become musical movements which would dominate popular music in the early 1960s and ultimately influence the Jesus Movement at the end of the 1960s. It is noteworthy that these two major social movements were as much created by radio and records as the records reflected a social undercurrent of the time.

Rock 'n' roll separated the kids from the parents; folk music gave them a social conscience. Rock 'n' roll was divisive between the generations because of the music while folk was divisive because of the lyrics. As the Jesus Movement developed and spread, it was heavily influenced by both of these musics—rock 'n' roll moved the body, folk moved the mind.

Tracing the roots of most religious movements in America, one finds they make their biggest impact when they affect the secular culture as the secular culture affects them. Musically, religious movements tend to take their lead from the secular music of the day. The music of the Jesus Revolution came from the pop music world, beginning with rock 'n' roll, encompassing the folk movement and on through the acid rock of the latter part of the 1960s.

The 1960s were characterized by intense social turmoil in the midst of the search for love, peace, and brotherhood. In many ways—and for many people— the social revolution of the 60s began as a spiritual quest. Youth rebelled against an increasingly technocratic and bureaucratic society, as well as against the hypocrisy and materialism of their parent's generation. They sought "truth" and a higher calling for life, a calling that would bring meaning and purpose and would be deeper than the selfish pursuit of materialism and blind acceptance of the status quo.

The spiritual search of the '60s led some to experiment extensively with drugs, others to seek out the Eastern religions and still others to turn to Jesus. Through it all, the common denominator was music. The irony of the anti-materialism in the '60s generation was that a good stereo system and large collection of the right albums was essential and as much a part of their life as breathing. On these records were the voices of their generation, singing messages to this whole counter-culture. It was the form of expression for those times, a natural outlet to express whatever they were thinking and doing. It is only natural that those who became "Jesus people" during that time would still look at music as a very vital and important part of their life.

In *The Greening of America*, a book which captured the shift in consciousness perhaps better than any book of that era, author Charles Reich discusses the importance of music to that generation. He states: "Music has become the deepest means of communication and expression for an entire culture...For the new consciousness, this music is not a pastime, but a necessity, on a par with food and water...(it) is a daily companion to share, interpret, and transfigure every experience and emotion" (260, 262). Thus music became the major means of communication for the youth in the Jesus Movement via radio and records.

It is one thing to look at the popularity of airplay of songs and artists on the radio, it is a bit different to look at sales. Sales can offer a "true" picture of the popularity of music because this is the music people consider important enough to buy and keep. It is also significant because top-selling albums sometimes do not include a single that gets radio airplay. This means that radio acceptance and popularity do not necessarily tell the whole story about the success of a particular kind of music. This is particularly true of gospel music.

The Recording Industry Association of America (RIAA) is the organization which monitors record sales and awards "Gold" and "Platinum" records. When they have officially proclaimed a record gold, it means that one million copies of the single or 500,000 copies of an album has been sold. It is the only thoroughly reliable yardstick to measure the success of record sales.

The RIAA began awarding gold records in 1958 and in that year "He's Got the Whole World In His Hands" by Laurie London achieved gold status. It also reached the number one position on the charts in April of that year, about six months before "Tom Dooley." This was Laurie London's only success in the charts; ironically, Mahalia Jackson also recorded this old gospel song and released it at the same time. However, Mahalia's version only reached number 60 on the charts.

In 1959, Tennessee Ernie Ford's album, *Hymns* was awarded gold status and in 1961 his *Spirituals* album achieved that plateau. He had two other gold albums in 1962, *Nearer the Cross* and a Christmas album, *Star Carol*. However, Ford, who hosted a popular weekly television show during this time, saw none of his gospel singles on the pop charts during this time and was better known to radio listeners for his hit "Sixteen Tons."

It is perhaps unfair to consider Christmas albums as gospel albums—although in a sense they are—but it must be noted that 18 Christmas albums achieved gold status between 1958 and 1970. Among them were releases by Johnny Mathis, Mantovani, Ernie Ford, Eugene Ormandy and the Philadelphia Orchestra, Perry Como, Ray Conniff, Robert Shaw, Andy Williams, Dean Martin, Herb

Alpert and the Tijuana Brass, Nat King Cole, Harry Simeone, Jim Nabors, and Bing Crosby.

There has always been a market for gospel songs on the radio and for gospel albums. For example, in 1955, "Angels in the Sky" by the Crew Cuts, "The Bible Tells Me So" by Don Cornell, and two recordings of "He," one by Al Hibbler and the other by the McGuire Sisters all reached the top 15 in *Billboard's* pop charts; in 1956 "Every Time (I Feel His Spirit)" by Patti Page, "Give Us This Day" by Joni James, "The Good Book" by Kay Starr, and "Sinner Man" by Les Baxter all reached the charts; in 1957, "Peace in the Valley" by Elvis Presley and "There's a Gold Mine in the Sky" by Pat Boone charted; in 1958, "A Wonderful Time Up There" by Pat Boone as well as the two versions of "He's Got The Whole World in His Hands" were on the charts; "Battle Hymn of the Republic" by the Mormon Tabernacle Choir, "Deck of Cards" by Wink Martindale, and "When The Saints Go Marching In" by Fats Domino all charted in 1959.

The 1960s began with Ferlin Huskey's "Wings of a Dove" reaching the number 12 position; in 1961 there was chart activity for "Child of God" by Bobby Darin. "Michael" by The Highwaymen was a number one song. In 1963 The Singing Nun had a number one song with "Dominique" and Steve Alaimo reached the charts with his version of "Michael"; in 1964, "All My Trials" by Dick & Deedee, "Amen" by the Impressions, "I Believe" by the Bachelors, "Oh Rock My Soul" by Peter, Paul and Mary, "Michael" by Trini Lopez, "Tell It on the Mountain" by Peter, Paul and Mary and "You'll Never Walk Alone" by Patti LaBelle & the Blue Belles all reached the charts. In 1963, *The Lord's Prayer* by the Mormon Tabernacle Choir was awarded a gold album.

The success of gospel songs on the pop charts in the late fifties and early sixties is an early indication of the spiritual revival that was to take place in the mid to late 60s. Indeed, it seems there was a spiritual revival before the Christian revival which took place at the end of that decade. In some ways, this spiritual movement paralleled the career of Peter, Paul and Mary, who came to national attention in 1962 with "Lemon Tree" and "If I Had a Hammer." In August 1963 they reached the number two spot on the charts with "Blowin' in the Wind," a song which defined this spiritual movement for many. The folk movement was filled with old, traditional gospel songs and Peter, Paul and Mary were on the charts with some of these numbers. They provided political activism with spiritual overtones (or undercurrents) during this period.

In 1965 "Turn, Turn, Turn," a rewriting of the biblical Ecclesiastes, was a number one song by the Byrds and "Eve of Destruction" by Barry McGuire also reached that spot. "People Get Ready" by the Impressions was also a hit that year. "I'm a Believer" was not a song about Christianity but that title reflected the religious undercurrent in 1966 when it became number one. "Crying in the Chapel" by Elvis reached number three in 1965 and "Blowin' in the Wind" became a top ten song for Stevie Wonder in 1966.

At the end of 1967, the Beatles reached number one with "All You Need is Love," which also achieved gold status and ushered in 1968, the Year of Love, capped by the Summer of Love. In 1968, Elvis Presley was awarded a gold record for his gospel album, *How Great Thou Art* while Simon and Garfunkle broke the invisible barrier pop radio had put up against the word "Jesus." That was the year of *The Graduate* soundtrack and the number one single, "Mrs. Robinson" featured the line, "Jesus loves you more than you will know" in the chorus.

In addition to *The Graduate* at movie theaters, there was *Hair* on the Broadway stage and Woodstock, the ultimate concert. And all of these were somehow "spiritual" experiences as well as entertainment to this generation. Perhaps this "spiritualness" was best expressed in another hit song, "Abraham, Martin, and John" by Dion DiMucci.

In May 1969, "Oh Happy Day" reached the number four position on *Billboard's* chart. The song was an old spiritual and was recorded by the Edwin Hawkins Singers, a black youth choir and their leader from Oakland. Other than Mahalia Jackson, who reached the charts several times but never had a top ten single, The Edwin Hawkins Singers were the only genuine gospel artists to have a hit single on secular radio. All through this period of the late 60s, a number of spiritual and gospel-flavored songs were hits but were recorded by secular artists. This was basically because the marketing and promotion network at major labels was geared to get pop radio airplay and sell big numbers while the gospel labels weren't.

In 1969 came the anthem "Get Together" by The Youngbloods, a rock song ready-made for campfire gatherings, as well as "Jesus is a Soul Man" by Lawrence Reynolds. This put Jesus in the middle of the Black Movement in this country.

A crucial year in tracing the roots of contemporary Christian music is 1969. "Crystal Blue Persuasion" and "Sweet Cherry Wine," both by Tommy James and the Shondells, "Dammit Isn't God's Last Name" by Frankie Lane, "Kum Ba Ya" by Tommy Leonetti, "That's the Way God Planned It" by Billy Preston, "Turn! Turn! Turn!" by Judy Collins and "You'll Never Walk Alone" by the Brooklyn Bridge, all with a Christian message in the lyrics, reached the charts.

Writers Andrew Lloyd Webber and Tim Rice had written a fifteen-minute operetta titled *Joseph and the Amazing Technicolor Dreamcoat* in 1968 about the Joseph in Genesis. It was written for the schoolboy choir at Celet Court School in London and, when presented, was well-received. The two decided to do another more elaborate rock operetta. The result was *Jesus Christ Superstar.* The recording was financed by MCA Records and the Broadway play and subsequent movie had a profound effect on America, producing several hit singles for pop radio as well as giving the public a new version of Jesus—one of a "superstar" who was a questioning man. The church (by and large) attacked the play and music because they did not like this new version of Jesus. The writers left Jesus in the grave at the end—there was no resurrection—so the result was Jesus portrayed as a man, not Divine. Theologically, it was on shaky ground but it brought a widespread awareness of Jesus and rock music to the American public when it premiered on October 27, 1970.

Two songs from the rock opera *Jesus Christ Superstar* became hit singles— "I Don't Know How To Love Him," recorded originally by Yvonne Elliman as well as Helen Reddy and "Superstar," with its chorus of "Jesus Christ, Jesus Christ/Do you think You're what they say You are" which provided this generation with more questions that began with "How many roads must a man walk down?"

In addition to the songs previously mentioned, there was "Amazing Grace" by Judy Collins, "Are You Ready" by the Pacific Gas & Electric, "Church Street Soul Revival" by Tommy James, "Holy Man" by Diane Kolby, "I Heard the Voice of Jesus" by Turley Richards, "Oh Happy Day" by Glen Campbell, "Spirit in the Sky" by Dorothy Morrison, "Stealing in the Name of the Lord" by Paul Kelly, "Stoned Love" by the Supremes, and versions of "Fire and Rain" by James Taylor, R.B. Greaves and Johnny Rivers, which all reached the charts in 1970.

In 1971 there were two more gospel songs that were hits—"Put Your Hand in the Hand" by Ocean and "Amazing Grace" by Aretha Franklin. Both achieved gold status. Also on the charts in 1971 were "All My Trials" by Ray Stevens, "Come Back Home" by Bobby Goldsboro, "Deep Enough For Me" by Ocean, "Mighty Clouds of Joy" by B.J. Thomas, "My Sweet Lord" by Billy Preston, "Take My Hand," by Kenny Rogers and the First Edition, "Life" by Elvis Presley, "Grandma's Hands" by Bill Withers, "Think His Name" by Johnny Rivers, "Top 40 of the Lordy" by Sha Na Na, "Turn Your Radio On" by Ray Stevens and "Wedding Song (There is Love)" by Noel Paul Stookey.

Godspell, another rock opera based on Jesus, appeared in 1972 and was also awarded gold status. The play, which pictured Jesus as a gentle clown, again offended the religious establishment but caused the youth to take another look at Christianity. The movie was not as big a hit as the play but one of the songs, "Day by Day," did become a hit single. Also in 1972 "I'd Like To Teach The World To Sing," which began as a commercial for Coca Cola, became another spiritual anthem for brotherhood. A country hit also reached the pop charts. "Me and Jesus" by Tom T. Hall provided the chorus which articulated the defiant stand many were making about Christianity:

> Me and Jesus got our own thing going
> Me and Jesus got it all worked out
> Me and Jesus got our own thing going
> And we don't need anybody to tell us what it's all about.
> (©Hallnote Publishing. Used with permission)

Concert for Bangla Desh by George Harrison and Friends came in 1972 and provided one of the first attempts of rock artists to put their social conscience into action. Featuring appearances by Harrison, Eric Clapton, Bob Dylan and others, it served as a model of how not to raise money for a worthy cause as much of the proceeds somehow disappeared or were eaten up by extravagant overheads.

Other gospel related songs which reached the charts in 1972 were "Amazing Grace" by the Royal Scots Dragoon Guards, "I'll Take You There" by the Staple Singers, "Joy" by Apollo 100, "Jesus is Just Alright" by the Doobie Brothers, "Jubilation" by Paul Anka, "Morning Has Broken" by Cat Stevens, "Speak to the Sky" by Rick Springfield, "That's The Way God Planned It" by Billy Preston, "Wedding Song (There is Love)" by Petula Clark, and "Wholly Holy" by Aretha Franklin.

The year 1973 brought a platinum album for the movie soundtrack of *Jesus Christ Superstar* as well as an answer from Glen Campbell, "I Knew Jesus Before He Was a Superstar." Also in 1973 was the gold album by Kris Kristofferson, *Jesus Was a Capricorn* that featured the single "Why Me, Lord," one of the most overt Christian songs to ever be a major hit. "Jesus is Just Alright," which was a top ten single for the Doobie Brothers, furthered the cause.

There was less gospel activity on the pop charts in 1974 through 1976, although gold records were awarded for *The Lord's Prayer* by Jim Nabors as well as another version of that song by Sister Janet Meade. "I Don't Know How to Love Him" by Helen Reddy and *Did You Think to Pray* by Charley Pride also went gold. But 1977 was a different story as Debbie Boone had a number one single and a platinum album with *You Light Up My Life*, which was not really a Christian song but could be interpreted that way. Daughter of former pop star Pat Boone, who had gone from the pop world to become a Christian celebrity, she soon followed her father's footsteps after a few more attempts in the secular market.

Perhaps the most significant musical event in 1977 was the gold record given to *Alleluia—Praise Gathering for Believers*. This was a Christian musical released on Benson, a gospel label, and marked the first time a gospel label had ever achieved this sales success. Also in 1977 the first President to publicly declare himself "born again" took office. After Jimmy Carter, the Jesus Movement ceased being an underground phenomena and took its place in the mainstream of American life. At least it ceased being viewed as a radical element and became comfortable with middle America.

Musically, the Jesus Revolution paralleled the career of Bob Dylan, who began in the '60s singing and writing folk songs including "Blowin' in the Wind," then went into rock. He released *John Wesley Harding*, a haunting album full of biblical allusions in 1968 before returning to rock. By the end of the 1970s, Dylan was releasing gospel albums as "The Voice of a Generation" continued to stay a little ahead of musical trends and produce culturally definitive works.

Chapter 17
Elvis and Gospel

Americans have always shown an affinity for gospel songs done by non-religious artists. This is best exemplified by Tennessee Ernie Ford's success recording gospel music in the late 1950s, and with Elvis Presley, who consistently recorded gospel albums and sang gospel songs in his performances throughout his career. All of Presley's gospel albums sold well—even the one recorded in 1957 when he was at the height of his notoriety as a rock 'n' roller, dangerous to youth's morals and the perceived enemy of preachers who openly accused rock 'n' roll as being the Devil's music and Elvis as being the Devil himself.

Presley looked at gospel music as his heritage and he turned to it for spiritual strength. It was his boyhood, his cherished memories of childhood, his mother's favorite music, and a tradition too deeply ingrained for him to ever let go. It was a faith taken to the point of superstition, but in the beginning it was a child-like faith in the confusing and complex world that rock 'n' roll was inhabiting in the 1950s. When he sang gospel, Elvis was not only fulfilling a spiritual obligation (self imposed) but also bringing back pleasant memories of his childhood. He was showing his mama he loved her, showing himself that he had not forsaken his roots or his God and perhaps showing God—in the best way he could—that he was still a good boy, still God-fearing, and that he wanted salvation.

The first gospel quartet Elvis is professionally associated with is the Jordanaires, who recorded with him on his earliest RCA recordings. Elvis met the Jordanaires at the Grand Ole Opry when he performed there in 1955. The Jordanaires formed in 1948 in Missouri but Gordon Stoker, first tenor, was the only original member left at this time. Hoyt Hawkins, baritone, had joined in 1950 and in 1953 Neal Matthews, second tenor, joined and Hugh Jarrett was added on bass. All had studied music in college and sang spirituals as well as barbershop quartet songs. Their performance of spirituals was the reason they were on the Opry and the reason Elvis asked them to record with him.

On January 5, 1956, Elvis did his first session for RCA. The session was held at 1525 McGavock Street in the studio owned by the Methodist TV, Radio and Film Commission. The producer of the session was Steve Shoals, who had negotiated the purchase of Elvis' contract and all masters previously recorded by Sun in Memphis. He paid Sam Phillips $35,000 plus a $5000 bonus to Elvis. Also at this session were Colonel Tom Parker, who was not Presley's full-time manager yet (Bob Neal had been managing Elvis in Memphis and was still performing that duty part-time), guitarist Chet Atkins, Elvis' road musicians Scotty Moore, D.J. Fontana, Bill Black, and the Jordanaires.

116

During the three hour session, Elvis recorded three songs: "Heartbreak Hotel" was the first finished, then "I Want You, I Need You, I Love You," which would be his second single from RCA, and "I Was The One," which was issued on the "B" side of "Heartbreak Hotel." According to Jerry Hopkins in his 1971 book *Elvis: A Biography*, the young singer told his back-up group that "if any of the songs went big, he wanted to record all his stuff" with them. Gordon Stoker notes that "We didn't think they'd go big. We didn't think much about it at all. We didn't even remember Elvis' name, really. It was just another job for us."

In 1956 Elvis exploded, selling ten million records and making appearances on television shows with Jackie Gleason, Milton Bearle, Steve Allen, and Ed Sullivan. These appearances launched him as a teen idol and cultural icon. The remaining songs on Elvis' first album were recorded in New York at the RCA studio there with three songs from the Sun tapes added to round out the release. As Elvis continued to come back to Nashville to record, the Jordanaires were on the sessions, singing with him.

The success stuck and Elvis ended up with Colonel Tom Parker and RCA where, as they say, the rest is history. Presley's first gospel recording came soon after he joined RCA, at the height of his rock 'n' roll popularity—after he had sold ten million records in one year (1956) and appeared on the major network television shows of the day. It came at a time when the younger generation was increasingly turning their backs on the religious heritage of their parents, shaking off all the inhibitions that religion had instilled in order to pursue rock 'n' roll, a music that released rather than restrained them, a music that fueled their mood for rebellion.

The first gospel album from Elvis was *His Hand in Mine* and the cover shows a carefully groomed young man, albeit with hair a little long for the era, dressed in a tuxedo and seated at a piano. Except for the fact that it is Elvis, it is not untypical of gospel record covers of the day. Inside, the songs were primarily old gospel standards done with a beat. Elvis, though respectful of gospel music, still made it exciting.

Calling Elvis Presley the most important figure in the history of rock 'n' roll is not an original thought, nor is the notion that he is the most important figure on shaping the American popular culture in music in the latter half of the twentieth century. These ideas may not be totally accurate—musical movements and social changes hinge on more than just one person, even a performer as dominant as Elvis Presley. But it is interesting to note that many of the things which attracted so much initial attention to Elvis—his long hair, flashy clothes and flair for showmanship—came from the southern gospel world. J.D. Sumner, a former member of the Blackwood Brothers in Memphis and later with the Stamps Quartet when they performed with Elvis during his final years, states that "southern gospel singers always wore flashy clothes, even back in the early '50s. And we had real long hair combed back before long hair ever came in style" (See "Notes" re: quotes from Sumner). Sumner also notes that during the early days of Elvis, the singer "lost jobs because he was trying to wear his clothes and hair like gospel singers."

Elvis admitted to copying the singing style of Jake Hess, telling Johnny Rivers once as one of the Statesmen's records was playing (Hess was lead singer for this group) "Now you know where I got my style from." It is ironic that the source for so much of Elvis Presley's music and personal style came from the southern gospel world. These attitudes, tastes, and style in his dress and performances were then passed on to a whole generation of teenagers who had never heard of southern gospel or, if they did, despised it. Meanwhile, the man who stood alone at the top of the rock world, inspiring countless others to pick up a guitar, gyrate and sing, always had a yearning in his heart to be a member of a gospel group.

Elvis came from a Pentecostal background and this Bible belt religion was infused in him from earliest childhood by his mother. His attraction to gospel music came naturally—he loved singing and was deeply religious so the notion of being a gospel singer seemed to be the best way of reconciling those two drives. He heard a number of gospel groups in Memphis and tried out for at least one of them.

Jim Hamill and Cecil Blackwood had a quartet, The Songfellows, which they began while in high school in Memphis in 1952. When Elvis was a teenager driving a truck for an electrical company, he auditioned for the group. According to some versions of this story, Hamill put his arm around Elvis' shoulder and said, "Son, you better stick to driving that truck. You can't sing a lick!"

But, according to Hamill, the story is a bit different. Hamill said:

I did not tell Elvis he couldn't sing. I told him he couldn't hear harmony—and he couldn't. As long as he was singing lead, he was fine, but when the baritone or the tenor took the lead, then someone had to sing harmony, and he could not harmonize. He'd sing baritone a line or two, then switch off to tenor for a couple of lines, and wind up singing the lead part. That was the reason we didn't take him into the quartet with us. (Terrell "Three chords..." 24)

A few months after being turned down by the Songfellows, Elvis signed with Sam Phillips and Sun Records. Around this same time, Elvis was hearing harmony better and so Hamill and Cecil Blackwood asked if he'd like to join the quartet. The offer came because Cecil was leaving The Songfellows to join the Blackwood Brothers after two members of that original group had been killed in a plane crash. According to Hamill, Elvis talked to Phillips about getting out of the Sun contract to sing gospel. He was unable to, but this was certainly not the end of Elvis' involvement with gospel music. Until his death Elvis continued to sing gospel, follow the careers of gospel quartets, and featured some of those quartets on his records and shows.

The Imperials, a southern gospel quartet begun by Jake Hess, were hired by Mary Lynch, secretary to Chet Atkins, for Elvis' gospel album *How Great Thou Art*. RCA wanted the sound of a choir so the Imperials were hired in addition to the Jordanaires and some female singers. The Imperials had an office in the RCA Building and had become friends with Mary Lynch.

Elvis went from being a teen heart throb to a member of Uncle Sam's Army. When he was discharged from the Army in 1960, he went to Hollywood to make movies. As a result, Elvis had not performed before live audiences—except on movie sets—for eight years when he decided to return to the stage. This was in 1969 and he hired the Imperials to perform with him. The offer to the Imperials came after the Jordanaires had turned down his invitation to play Vegas and tour because, as studio singers, they did not feel they could afford to be away from Nashville so much.

After the Imperials left, Elvis instructed Charlie Hodge, one of his "Memphis mafia," to call Sumar Talent for another gospel group. Heading the agency at the time was J.D. Sumner, and he suggested the Stamps Quartet, who had been re-formed and were coming along well as a group. Sumner had gotten off the road and gone into management and booking. He had hired another bass singer, Richard Sterban (now with the Oak Ridge Boys) to sing with the Stamps. The rest of the line-up included Bill Baize, Ed Enoch and Donnie Sumner, J.D.'s son.

J.D. saw this booking as a short-term replacement for the Imperials, which Sumar also booked. In short, he felt he was protecting his client, the Imperials, who were facing the double booking problem. He expected the Imperials to re-join Elvis at some future time.

J.D. Sumner had met Elvis around 1949 when Elvis was 14 and J.D. was a member of the Sunshine Quartet. Elvis had always been a fan of gospel music and Memphis was a hotbed for this activity, being the home and headquarters for the Blackwood Brothers, the leading quartet in southern gospel at the time. When J.D. joined the Blackwoods, he continued to see Elvis at concerts, letting him in the back door at the Memphis Coliseum occasionally so he would not have to pay. For the young Elvis, people like J.D., the Blackwoods and other gospel quartets were idols and he set his sights on someday singing gospel with them. Thus, when Elvis saw Sumner sitting down while the Stamps assembled on stage to rehearse, he promptly asked, "Why aren't you up here?"

J.D. replied that he had just come as a manager and booker looking out for his group. Elvis told him in no uncertain terms to get himself on stage and pointed out that J.D. had his own microphone set apart to sing in and Elvis wanted some of those deep bass drops that Sumner was noted for.

Later, Elvis told the Stamps he wanted them to open his show with a 20-minute performance. The Stamps gathered and began naming songs they could do—secular tunes—but Sumner made the decision to stick with gospel. Their first solo performance was in Greenville, South Carolina and the group received two standing ovations. Later that night, Elvis called J.D. to his room and thanked him for the gospel performance, then gave him a check for $10,000 and asked if the Stamps would continue to sing gospel to open the show. J.D. looked at the check and replied, "Why certainly, boss."

A three girl line-up, The Sweet Inspirations, also sang with Elvis, joining him just before the Imperials did. These three black women had gospel roots and contributed to the big sound Elvis liked on his shows. However, they did not record with him (except on his live albums).

J.D. Sumner has often told about touring with Elvis, how after almost every show Elvis would gather the singers together to sing gospel songs. Sumner spent a good deal of time at Elvis' home and was always amazed at how many gospel albums Presley owned. "All he listened to was gospel," said J.D. "He didn't even listen to his own records." Sumner relates a story that occurred when a whole group was at Elvis' home in Memphis to record. Elvis would only record when he felt like it and on this particular Saturday evening he apparently did not feel like it, although RCA had set up a whole studio in his home. Finally, just before eight on Sunday morning Elvis came down and told the group he did not want to record and that he was going to watch the Florida Boys, whose show was coming on television in a few minutes.

Sumner was surprised and rushed back to his hotel room to watch the show too. He told the Florida Boys about the incident, and they were pleased and surprised, but they would never have known that Elvis was a fan unless Sumner had told them. This underscores a unique situation: although Elvis was a big fan of southern gospel, and many in southern gospel were fans of him, there was no communication between the two. Part of this was because of the isolation of Elvis, but part of it was because the rock world and the southern gospel world are literally worlds apart. They only came together because of Elvis Presley using southern gospel groups on his show.

Much more could be said about Elvis' affection for gospel music but it can all be summed up by noting that at his funeral in Memphis in August, 1977, Kathy Westmoreland—who sang with Elvis on his shows and records— sang "My Heavenly Father Watches Over Me," Jake Hess and two members of the Statesmen sang "Known Only To Him," James Blackwood with the Stamps sang "How Great Thou Art," and, finally, the Stamps sang "Sweet Sweet Spirit."

It is difficult to gauge Presley's affect on gospel except to note that by influencing popular music in general, he certainly had an affect on gospel, which often incorporates popular musical trends in songs and reflects those trends in recordings. The effect gospel music had on Presley is also difficult to ascertain but at the end of his life, it is obvious that Presley kept in touch with his strong religious roots through gospel music. Indeed, it may be argued that after 1956 gospel music was Christianity for Elvis. He seemed to find spiritual nourishment there and used the music as a way to keep in touch with his earlier days before he became a rich and famous rock 'n' roll star.

In many ways Elvis can be seen as a tragic figure because he could only sing the message, he could not live it. He remained haunted by gospel music and the gospel itself all his life but somehow could not reconcile his later life with his boyhood beliefs. Still, it is through Elvis that so many rockers and rock writers know about the gospel roots of early rock 'n' roll. The music has moved far away from those roots through the years, especially with the British influence and their lack of religious roots in rock, but the emotional fervor and dramatic intensity so prevalent in southern religion is still encased in the best of rock 'n' roll.

In the end, the biggest contribution of Elvis to gospel is that he made the rock 'n' roll world aware of the music and gave it a platform on his shows and a sense of respectability in the rock world. He showed his audiences that at the heart of his own music was gospel as he shared the songs and influences which formed the core of his being.

Chapter 18
Mahalia Jackson and Sam Cooke

In the 1950s and into the early 1960s the most important artists in black gospel music were Mahalia Jackson and Sam Cooke. Both appealed first to the black church audience, then crossed over to the white audience—Mahalia in the gospel field while Sam Cooke made his greatest impact on the white audience in the pop music world.

Mahalia Jackson, gospel music's superstar, began singing gospel in Chicago churches after she had moved there from New Orleans, where she was born in 1911. Daughter of devout Baptist parents, Mahalia idolized Bessie Smith and the blues-influence carried over to her own style, although she never left the gospel field. Initially, her repertoire was the Baptist hymns and it was the hymn that held her heart at the end; here, she could pour out her soul best, using elements of the blues delivery to make each song a personal statement.

Mahalia moved to Chicago in 1927 after quitting school and was soon singing with the Greater Salem Baptist Church choir, often doing the lead vocal. She supported herself during this time as a domestic, doing laundry and serving as a maid. Soon, she was singing with the Johnson Gospel Singers, organized by Robert Johnson, son of the pastor of the church where she attended. Along with Robert's brothers, Prince and Wilbur, and Louise Barry Lemon, the five-member group became professional—one of the first in black gospel—earning their living with gospel music. According to black gospel historian Tony Heilbut, their style was "advanced and free" and Johnson played a "distinctive boogie-woogie piano geared to the Dorsey bounce" (92). They also performed a series of plays Robert wrote, with Mahalia and Robert usually singing lead in these church dramas. In the early 1930s the group played a number of local churches, but by the end of the decade the group had split and each member was singing solo.

During her career, a number of people wanted Mahalia to use her rich and powerful vocal talents to sing music other than gospel. One of these was her first husband, Isaac Hackenhull, whom she married in 1936. Hackenhull wanted her to sing classic pop songs and jazz and Mahalia made some attempts. However, the church was embedded in her too deeply and, wracked by guilt, she abandoned this music after only a few attempts and returned to gospel, where she was clearly most comfortable musically, spiritually, and emotionally.

Always a good businesswoman, Mahalia opened a beauty salon and then a florist shop; both succeeded for a short time. Like a number of other gospel pioneers who survived, it was her business acumen, as much as her talent, that was a key to her success. She was not the only one—Thomas Dorsey, Sallie

Martin, and Sam Cooke also made smart business moves which assured them of financial success.

Mahalia's first recording was "God's Gonna Separate the Wheat from the Tares" in 1937 b/w "Keep Me Every Day." The first song was one Mahalia had adapted from the wakes she had attended as a child in New Orleans and the second was an old Baptist hymn. This first record brought her national recognition and made her name equal with the other great soloists in Chicago during that time: Willie Mae Ford Smith, Sallie Martin, Madame Lula Mae Hurst, Mary Johnson Davies, Roberta Martin and Louise Lemon. It was a rich time for female soloists and Mahalia was just one of a number, but her strong southern influence, which manifested itself in the moaning, growling, strutting, and skipping stage performances, soon brought her to the forefront.

Mahalia joined forces with Thomas Dorsey in the early 1940s, creating more national attention as Dorsey toured the nation. She sang his songs like "Precious Lord" and "If You See My Savior" in a way that was distinctively hers, changing the melody and meter, stretching out the song, slurring her words, and projecting herself to the audience in a way that was both spirit-filled and sexy at the same time. This caused Dorsey much consternation as he tried to coach Mahalia to sing his songs in the manner written. Mahalia's fiery spirit soon made Dorsey's attempts futile and finally he resigned himself to her individuality. By 1945, she was famous in the black churches.

In 1946, Mrs. Bess Berman signed Mahalia to Apollo Records, a small firm based in New York. Although the relationship with Berman was at times volatile and argumentative, Mahalia produced a string of recordings over the next eight years which were both brilliant and definitive. Her third release, "Move On Up a Little Higher" reportedly sold over a million copies. Her concerts during this time were equally memorable and sometimes she would spend almost half an hour on "Move On Up" or some other hymn. As author Heilbut observes, "her most powerful performances were reserved for 'going to heaven' tunes" (95).

In 1950 another career breakthrough occurred when Chicago journalist Studs Terkel began featuring Mahalia Jackson on his television show. The show was centered on jazz and the resemblance to Bessie Smith and natural jazz vocalizing was inherent in Mahalia's style. International acclaim came in 1952 with her recording as a duet with James Lee of "I Can Put My Trust in Jesus," which won a prize from the French Academy. Her first European tour followed and the international attention increased when her recording of "Silent Night" became a top seller in Norway.

Back in America, booked by her nephew Alan Clark, Mahalia played churches. She was accompanied by young singers and musicians. Soon, she became famous to white American audiences and began to embody the quintessential gospel singer—a black Kate Smith who was saintly, stately, and who sang with incredible power. She had her own radio and television programs beginning in 1954, the same year Columbia Records signed her and instigated a tremendous national publicity campaign on her behalf. A special feature in *Life* followed as commercial success on Columbia catapulted her to greater fame.

By this time, Mahalia was singing almost exclusively to white audiences because the black churches could no longer afford her. Accompanied by pianist Mildred Falls, Mahalia presented a program of pop-gospel type songs, leaving her sanctified roots resting off stage. In 1958 she sang at the Newport Jazz Festival and an album recorded with Percy Faith became a national best-seller. She was now clearly the Queen of Gospel Music, known better than any other gospel singer in America to white audiences as well as black.

In the 1960s she championed the cause of Civil Rights with Martin Luther King, whom she befriended, and sang at John Kennedy's inauguration in 1961. When King was assassinated, she sang "Precious Lord" at his funeral. The final years were stormy times for Mahalia and her image was tarnished after her marriage and divorce from musician Sigmund Galloway. Still, she continued to record and tour—both internationally and in the United States—until her death at the beginning of 1972. By this time, her name had become synonymous with "Gospel Music" and she was an international celebrity.

The story of Sam Cooke is one that bears telling because Cooke was the first gospel artist to cross over into the pop world. Marred by a tragic ending, it is nevertheless a lesson in the appeal of gospel music to a young audience and, ultimately, to the secular world.

Born in Mississippi in 1931, Sam Cook (no 'e') grew up in Chicago, where his father was a Church of Christ Holiness minister. He joined his two sisters and brother in a group called "The Singing Children" when he was nine and became a member of the Highway QC's a few years later. This latter group was an offshoot of the Soul Stirrers, perhaps the most popular black gospel quartet of the day, who wanted to form a group of young singers as a sort of "farm club" for the parent organization. Here, Cooke was coached by Soul Stirrer member R.B. Robinson, who brought him into the Soul Stirrers when lead singer R.H. Harris left in late 1950.

The Soul Stirrers formed in Trinity, Texas in 1934. Jesse Farley, who has remained with them longer than any other original member, joined in 1935. Almost from the very beginning, the Soul Stirrers stood apart from most other quartets, who sang spirituals and jubilee songs, by singing newer "gospel" or original compositions. They were innovative in their use of lead singers, employing two and bringing the lead vocalist out front. Through Harris, their first lead singer, they virtually created the gospel quartet tradition. Among Harris's innovations were the technique of ad-libbing within a song, singing delayed time—off the regular meter from the rest of the key lyrics. The group was among the first traveling quartets who were full-time performers and their early success from concerts caused many other quartets to adapt the newer "gospel" songs instead of the more traditional spiritual and jubilee songs.

When Sam Cooke joined the Soul Stirrers they were already the biggest name in black gospel quartet circles. Their sex appeal was also known—it was the reason Harris, a devout man, quit—and their reputation as musical innovators was established. But it was Sam Cooke who brought the young people in droves to gospel concerts and who became the first "sex symbol" in the music, which he used as a launching pad into pop stardom. Along the way he created a distinguishable style characterized by his semi-yodel. He developed into a first rate songwriter in both the gospel and pop fields, and created the pattern of success which so many others—from David Ruffin to Jerry Butler to Lou Rawls to Johnny Taylor—sought to emulate. In other words, it wasn't just his vocal style that made Cooke so influential, it was his lifestyle as well.

Cooke had just passed his twentieth birthday when he sang on his first recordings with the Soul Stirrers in 1951. Included in the session was the Cooke-penned hit, "Jesus Gave Me Water." His singing style, which imitated Harris and included some attempts at "shouting" like other popular lead singers of the day, was quickly settling into his own trademark of sophisticated sanctification. His effortless emotions somehow still touched the depths of passion. Soon, he became the rage of the gospel world as young girls lined up outside venues to wait for him. Cooke, with his movie-star good looks, was the perfect male symbol—young and pretty, with a voice that could send chills up any spine. His charisma during performances brought the youth down front to the stage where they would stand all performance long—and the result was that the covert sexuality of gospel suddenly became quite overt with Mr. Cooke.

Cooke had flirted with the idea of crossing over to pop a number of years before he actually did so. He wanted to appeal to the white audience—there was more money, prestige, and fame there—and he knew he could do it best through pop music. Still, he was reluctant to take the step because of the usual inhibitions gospel singers feel when singing for "the world." It would not be until 1957 that he did take that step, and even then he tried to step back into gospel music and have his feet in both worlds. But it could not work that way.

Cooke was not the first singer to leave gospel for pop music. Dinah Washington had done it years before and Ray Charles, only a year older than Cooke but more a veteran in the recording studio (he had begun recording in 1948 when he was 18), had shown the powerful appeal inherent in gospel music when he took a traditional gospel song, put some secular lyrics to it, and delivered it with the gusto and delivery of a sanctified holiness preacher. This resulted in the hit, "I Got A Woman" in 1953. This began the rhythm and blues explosion of 1953 and 1954 when a number of white teenagers discovered black music and modified it into the rock 'n' roll revolution. The revolution accelerated in 1955 with Bill Haley and the Comets' "Rock Around the Clock" and culminated with Sam Phillips' answer to his quest for a white man who could sing like a black, Elvis Presley.

Other precedents for black success in the white market were the quartets like the Mills Brothers, Ink Spots and Orioles, who presented a supper-club type harmony on songs like "Crying in the Chapel." The key year is 1954. This is the year Elvis made his first recordings in Memphis for Sun Records, Roy Hamilton had a pop hit with the gospel song, "You'll Never Walk Alone," and Ray Charles had a pop hit with a gospel-influenced performance of the bawdy "I Got A Woman." Then in 1955 and 1956, a succession of black acts, beginning with Little Richard, Chuck Berry, Fats Domino, the Coasters, and the Platters opened up the musical world for black artists to appeal to white audiences. It was a world ripe for Sam Cooke, but he was hesitant and did not make his move until 1957. Perhaps it is because he had more to lose than the others that caused him to defer his decision, but more likely it was his own inner religious convictions and the sermons he must have heard from black preachers who were admonishing their people to refuse the temptation of the sinful world and be assured of their salvation by staying with the church.

Since 1949 the Soul Stirrers had been recording for the Specialty label, an independent Los Angeles-based firm. The label had begun recording another top black gospel quartet, the Pilgrim Travelers, a year before. The Soul Stirrers were brought to label owner Art Rupe by the head a&r man, J.W. Alexander. Producer Bumps Blackwell, who produced the group, wanted to cut Cooke on some pop songs. Rupe was against the move since he had been having success with gospel and did not want that jeopardized. The first pop single from Cooke, titled "Loveable" and released under the name Dale Cook in 1957, sold about 25,000 copies and angered Rupe to the point that it ended Cooke's and Blackwell's career with the label. Since Rupe owed Blackwell money, there was a deal settled where the producer would get the unreleased tapes from the pop session he had cut with Cooke. He took these over to another small label, Keen Records, which put out the record.

That record, released in the fall of 1957, was "You Send Me." It quickly went to the number one position on both the r&b and pop charts. That began Sam Cooke's pop career and songs like "Wonderful World," "Only Sixteen" and "Everybody Loves To Cha Cha Cha," which he either wrote or co-wrote, followed before he went with RCA. There, his career continued to thrive with the release of his single, "Chain Gang" and it culminated with perhaps his finest song, "A Change Is Gonna Come," written after he had heard "Blowin' in the Wind" for the first time. This became a hit after his death in 1964.

Cooke's death, both tragic and grisly—he was shot to death by a prostitute after allegedly threatening her and roughing her up—was gist for sermons. Those in the gospel world saw it as just reward for someone who had turned his back on his gospel roots while others saw it as perhaps the logical conclusion of what had been thinly disguised in the past—Church folk dabbling with loose women.

Still, this does not dim Sam Cooke's considerable achievements in the gospel field in the early fifties: he was the first sex symbol and brought young people by the droves into gospel concerts, proving that the music could have an appeal for the young as well as the old. Too, he showed that a performer with gospel roots could have a major affect on the pop world, that the talent of gospel performers was first rate and the church—via musicians and singers who received their early training and experience there—would be a major influence on pop music in the rock'n roll revolution from the mid-fifties through the sixties. Since the rise of soul music paralleled the rise of the Civil Rights Movement (as noted by Peter Guralnick), this places the career of Sam Cooke in the strategic center where gospel, soul, and social activism all fused to bring about a major social revolution.

Chapter 19
The Jesus Revolution

In the 1940s and '50s in America, Christ was awesome; in the 60s he became accessible. The youth who had moved away from the stern God of their parent's church readily embraced the warm, loving God of the '60s who was concerned with peace, love, social justice, and most importantly, each individual's life. As kids rejected the values and culture of their parents, they discarded the old Christianity as well. But somewhere they found a new Jesus, one they could relate to and one their parents were often repelled by. In the '40s and '50s, Jesus was a safe, middle-class figure, comfortable in country clubs; in the '60s He had gone to the streets and become a radical. At least that was the two versions of Jesus at odds with each other at the beginning of the Jesus Revolution.

Just as there was a spiritual revolution going on outside the church in the 1960s, there was also one going on inside the churches. Perhaps this was first reflected in the career of Bill Gaither, whose songs became anthems for churchgoers and whose career paralleled the rise of renewal within the Christian world. Gaither, his wife Gloria, and brother Danny were all from Anderson, Indiana and, like so many others, had a gospel group that sang whenever they could. They recorded their first commercial album in 1964 and its success soon surpassed everyone's expectations. Nearly 300,000 copies of that first album were sold—an unheard of number in the Christian market—and their following albums did as well. The key was the songs that Bill and Gloria Gaither composed. They were quickly adapted by church congregations. One of their first successes was "The King is Coming."

The lyrics are picturesque and theatrical and reflect the strong belief in the Second Coming. Most of the Christian revivals in America have keyed in on the end of the earth and Second Coming to impress upon believers the urgency of the message. It is a Biblical prophecy and fundamental Christian movements require the Bible to be taken literally as the word of God. This fact lends itself to "second coming" songs being popular in the Christian revivals.

In his book *Why Should the Devil Have all the Good Music*, author Paul Baker traces the beginning of the Jesus Movement in America to 1967 when the Christian World Liberation Front opened the first Christian coffeehouse in the Haight-Ashbury district of San Francisco. It was headed by "Holy Hubert" Lindsey, who had preached in Berkeley at the University of California in 1965 when that school came to national fame from anti-war riots. There were other seeds as well—a number of other small coffee houses and small underground newspapers. These paralleled the rise of "head" shops in the secular culture, small gathering places where drug paraphernalia and underground rock albums

126

were sold. In the Christian world, there was the same funky decor, the same ambiance, but no drugs.

The folk movement of the early '60s spawned hootenannys which influenced countless youths who sat around campfires and gathered at Bible camps and youth meetings to sing songs such as "Kumbaya," "Amen," "I've Got the Joy, Joy, Joy," "Give Me Oil in My Lamp," "When the Saints Go Marching In," "Do Lord," and a number of other sing-a-long type songs. Although many of the youths attending church knew these songs, the music never made it inside the church sanctuary; the religious leaders preferred 200-year old hymns instead. However, there were several travelling groups from evangelistic organizations like Youth For Christ which began appearing at churches and schools. These groups were well-scrubbed, wholesome and had All-American looks and smiles— models of youth—so the adults could easily accept them.

Billy Graham's organization had produced a number of Christian films before *The Restless Ones* in 1965 but this one was different because of the music, which was contemporary and aimed at the '60s protest audience. The music, scored by Ralph Carmichael, was tame by later standards, but contained the song "He's Everything to Me," which immediately proved popular. The fact that it came from a Billy Graham film, however, made it acceptable to the church audiences who viewed the film.

1965 was also the year for *Good News*, the first Christian folk musical. *Good News* was composed by Bob Oldenburg, Billy Ray Hearn, Cecil McGee and a few others. The idea was sparked by large road shows like *Up With People*. The second major Christian musical, *Tell It Like It Is*, by Ralph Carmichael and Kurt Kaiser, proved to be even more popular with church youth as the Jesus Movement ignited within the Christian world.

The first commercially released Jesus rock album was *Upon This Rock* by Larry Norman, released on Capitol in 1969. Norman had been a member of the group, People, whose recording of "I Love You (But the Words Won't Come)" reached number 14 on the pop charts in 1968. Norman wanted to title the follow-up album *We Need a Whole Lot More of Jesus and A Lot Less Rock 'n' Roll* and put a picture of Jesus on the cover but the company balked and the day the album was released Larry broke with the band. A year later he was invited by Capitol to record a solo album and the result was *Upon This Rock* which included the song "I Wish We'd All Been Ready." This song was recorded by some secular acts as well and quickly became an underground classic in Christian circles.

Norman also provided another anthem to the Jesus Revolution, "Why Should the Devil Have All the Good Music" that answered the question of why rock and religion should mix as well as articulating the important role music held in the lives of young believers.

Norman had a profound influence on the Jesus movement and his "one way" sign (one finger pointed heavenward) and songs provided a rallying cry for the movement. With his incisive lyrics, long blonde hair, sharp wit and controversial stage appearances, Norman shook the foundations of many traditional churchgoers but ignited a number of young people, Christians and non-Christians alike, who realized Jesus could be hip and contemporary and the Bible could apply to the current world.

Another early Jesus music album was *Mylon* by Mylon LeFevre on Cotillion Records in 1970. Mylon had grown up in southern gospel, a member of the famed LeFevre Singers and had been performing gospel with his family since he was five. He had also written a number of gospel songs, including "Without Him" recorded by Elvis Presley. The album was an underground classic but LeFevre's own life led him away from his Christian roots and into rock 'n' roll where he "backslid" into drugs before recommitting his life in the late '70s and recording albums for gospel labels.

The Everlastin' Living Jesus Concert was the first album released by Maranatha! Music. It came in 1971 at a time when Calvary Chapel in Costa Mesa, California was drawing thousands of youths to their services. Calvary Chapel was headed by Chuck Smith and featured a "hippie" preacher named Lonnie Frisbee as well as music that was performed by some of those attending the church services. Because so many talented musicians attended the church and because so much music originated there—as well as the fact that Calvary Chapel appealed to the contemporary young person whose music was so much a part of their life—Maranatha! Music was formed. The label became a leader in "praise" or "worship" music but their first release (later titled simple "Maranatha! 1") was a live recording of a contemporary Christian concert.

Although this first album was important and influential, it was not as influential as Calvary Chapel. The Chapel was the spiritual home of a number of early contemporary Christian musicians. Some of those who attended were Debby Kerner, Ernie Rettino, Children of the Day, The Way, Country Faith, Karen Lafferty, Good News, Mustard Seed Faith, Blessed Hope, Gentle Faith, Selah, Kenn Gulliksen, and others. The first group to emerge from Calvary Chapel was Love Song, comprised of Chuck Girard, Jay Truax, Tom Coombs and Fred Field.

Love Song's first album was released on Good News Records in 1972 and proved to be an immediate success in both the gospel and secular worlds, where it was distributed by Liberty Records. It is significant because it was the first "hit" album to emerge from the Jesus Movement. The group never again attained the commercial success of their first album but they were still a very significant and influential group in the early 1970s.

Other early albums of Jesus music included *Truth of Truths*, a rock opera; *The Armageddon Experience* from Campus Crusade's contemporary group; *Born Twice* by Randy Stonehill; *Songs From the Savior* by Paul Clark; and *Agape* from the first hard-rock Christian group by the same name.

Another early group in contemporary Christian music was Andrae Crouch and the Disciples, first formed in Los Angeles in 1965. Crouch, whose father was a preacher, worked with Teen Challenge, helping alcoholics and drug addicts. He played part-time until 1970, when he gave up his job and began performing full-time. His first single, "Christian People" was on Liberty Records and when he appeared in the early '70s on Johnny Carson's "Tonight Show" it was a real coup for a Jesus group. On the show he was backed by "Sonlight," a group consisting of Fletch Wiley, Bill Maxwell, Harlan Rogers and Hadley Hockensmith—all of whom would become top studio musicians for contemporary Christian acts.

Most of the early Christian music came out on secular labels—Norman's album on Capitol, LeFevre's on Cotillion—or brand new labels formed for contemporary music—Maranatha! for the Calvary Chapel artists and Good News for Love Song's initial recordings. The established gospel labels, primarily Word and Benson, were apprehensive, wondering whether rock was the devil's music or not. The church also questioned whether the Jesus Movement was indeed really Christian. However, as the movement spread and the major Christian labels saw more and more young people attracted to the music, they began signing acts like Randy Matthews, who was the first Jesus rock artist for Word Records.

Chapter 20
The Catholics in America

The Catholics have long been a "breed apart" from mainline American Protestantism and have generally had little if any affect on the Christian revivals in America. Their rigid structure and control by the Pope left their faith basically unchanged while American Protestant religions were changing dramatically. However, major changes brought about by Vatican II introduced contemporary music into their religion through the "folk masses" of the mid-60s. The introduction of folk music into the Catholic church service preceded the introduction of contemporary music into Protestant churches. With this move—and their overtures to Protestants to unite under the banner of Christianity—the American Catholic church for the first time affected a major Christian revival—the Jesus Revolution of the late 60s and early 70s. And when John Kennedy became the first U.S. Catholic president, many of the traditional fears and superstitions held by American Protestants against Catholics were ended.

The split in 1054 led to Europe coming under the Roman Catholic Church as Christianity spread westward. The next major split in the Roman Catholic Church occurred in the sixteenth century with Martin Luther's Protestant Reformation, which began in Germany and soon encompassed most of Europe. England's split with Catholicism in Great Britain during this time created a schism between Anglicans, Protestant puritans and reformers, and Catholics, which led to the first Catholic settlement in America by Lord Baltimore (George Calvert) in Maryland in 1634.

The Calverts were a genteel family who had converted back to Catholicism in Protestant England—not a popular move—but remained in favor with King James I and later Charles I. George Calvert's son Cecil, received a charter for the colony in 1632 and the settlers first landed in the spring of 1634. The colony soon found itself in the midst of strong anti-Catholic sentiment in the new country as most of America was settled by Protestants. This led the Marylanders to pass a religious tolerance act which forbade religious dissension and eventually served as a model for the rest of the colonies in religious toleration.

The major problem with Catholicism during the Protestant Movement was that Catholics continued to hold an allegiance to Rome and the Pope while the Protestants could be aligned with a particular nation and its leaders without compromising their faith. Thus, Catholicism was always considered a threat to religion in the Protestant era and many saw Catholicism as denying God's ability to speak to each and every individual. The highly structured, ritualistic service did not seem to fit the new country whose religions were increasingly individualistic and whose new beginnings sought to cut old ties and leave the past behind. In a land where religion came from the people, the Catholic style of clergy-oriented religion was a bit impractical as well as undesirable—the laity wanted to be active, not passive and Catholicism tended to snuff out sparks of the individualistic and pioneering spirit inherent in the young country.

Catholicism spread slowly in America because the Catholic missionaries did not do well against the zealous Protestant missionaries from such sects as the Baptists, Methodists, Lutherans, and other Protestant offshoots. Still, Catholicism did grow and become a dominant religion in the United States, centered primarily in the large metropolitan cities where immigrants from Catholic countries in Europe settled.

Since Catholicism is a universal church, the same mass with the same music is used all over the world. This meant the masses in Rome or Rio de Janiero were no different from those of Detroit or Cleveland and these Masses are basically the same in the twentieth century as they were in the sixteenth century, which was basically the same mass that had been performed for centuries before that. The music did not change either and so the chant-song still predominated until the mid-twentieth century.

To a large extent the Catholic Church became a universal church by adopting a universal language—Latin—for the services. This meant a believer could go into a Catholic church anywhere in the world and hear the same Mass. Also, it could be assured that believers everywhere were of one mind and one allegiance to the church—subjugating differences and denying individuality—through the hierarchy of Pope, Cardinals, Bishops, and Priests, who spoke for and controlled the silent laity. This changed significantly with Vatican II.

Vatican II was convened in 1962 by Pope John XXIII and completed under his successor, Pope Paul VI in 1965. The most significant results of this church council, held in three different sessions, were that the old Latin in the Mass was discarded and replaced by the vernacular or local language and the laity was encouraged to participate more fully in the Mass and use initiative in both religious and temporal affairs. These sessions also sought to end the isolationism of Catholicism as they embraced all of Christianity and, indeed, all the peoples of the earth as God's creatures.

Musically, Vatican II meant the introduction of a whole new set of songs in the Mass and the encouragement of individuals to write songs for the services. Thus was born the "folk mass" as the antiquated faith renewed itself with modernization. This modernization led to a musical movement in the Catholic Church which embraced the popular music of the day. The Jesus Movement in the late 1960s, also took popular music and used it to celebrate faith, making it relevant to contemporary youth. In a certain sense, the Catholic folk mass paved the way for Jesus Rock as Vatican II proved to be the forerunner of the non-Catholic Jesus Revolution. This first folk mass, "Mass for Young Americans" was produced by Ray Repp in 1964.

The result of these movements within the Catholic organization was a charismatic renewal in which many individual Catholics developed a direct personal relationship with Christ. The mass became more "people" oriented and this, in turn, resulted in a great demand for liturgical music. Almost overnight every Catholic church in America had to have songbooks, songs, and books of readings to accompany the new mass. This led to the formation of Catholic groups and songwriters who could write this material for the mass. Perhaps the most influential of these groups is the St. Louis Jesuits.

The St. Louis Jesuits are called by that name because they are all Jesuit priests who studied at St. Louis University. Individually, they are known as Bob Dufford, Dan Schutte, John Foley, Roc O'Connor and Tim Manion and they began composing and developing their music in the early 1970s. The first among the group to begin composing music for liturgical use was John Foley. Foley and John Davanaugh met at the Jesuit novitiate in Florissent, Missouri, in the '60s and inspired each other with their folk-guitar compositions for the liturgy. Both arrived in St. Louis in the mid-60s for philosophical studies and wrote numerous compositions. Foley's music and reputation soon spread and by the time he left St. Louis for a teaching position in Denver in 1967 his music had already become popular within Jesuit circles.

Bob Dufford was familiar with Foley and his music because he, too, had studied in St. Louis and been involved with the choir there. When Dufford left for Omaha, Nebraska, to teach high school, he too began to compose songs. Dufford met Dan Schutte when he visited the Jesuit Novitiate in St. Bonifacius, Minnesota, in the spring of 1968. Schutte had written several songs for the guitar for the congregation there and John Foley's songs had begun to filter into the novitiate. Roc O'Connor was in the same novitiate in Minnesota with Schutte and offered his skills as an accomplished guitarist to the choral groups that Schutte and others organized for their community liturgies.

Dufford and Schutte arrived in St. Louis in 1970 and they began working with Roc O'Connor and John Foley to provide music for the group that worshipped on Sundays at Fusz Memorial, the Jesuit house of studies. Word of their music soon spread and they were besieged with requests to perform. Meanwhile, Tim Manion arrived in St. Louis in 1971 from the novitiate in Florissant, Missouri. Tim had been a part of the liturgy music in Missouri and was familiar with the music of Dufford, Schutte, and Foley.

During the next two years, this group began to explore ways for the publication of their music. Discouraged and disheartened after their contact with religious music publishers, they decided to produce and publish a collection of 57 songs on their own and to record a set of albums. However, in the midst of this project, they were approached by a relative newcomer in the field of Catholic publishing, North American Liturgy Resources, who made them an offer to record and publish their music. Impressed that NALR could do far more than they could on their own, and flattered by NALR's interest and desire to work with them, the group agreed to the agreement. Their first project, *Neither Silver Nor Gold*, was issued in June 1974.

In 1975 the Jesuits (except for Tim Manion) scattered to Omaha, Berkeley, California, and Toronto. They continued to collaborate, though, and spent a summer together in Berkeley composing new music for their second collection. The result was *Earthen Vessels*, released in December, 1975, which sold over half a million units.

The success of the St. Louis Jesuits parallels the success of Catholic music. The fact that it has grown tremendously since the mid-60s is well documented; however, for those not in the Catholic circles, this growth, music and influence has been largely unknown. In fact, most of those involved in the contemporary

Christian music world are not even aware of Catholic music, although an occasional act appears on the charts. Perhaps the best known of the Catholic musicians is John Michael Talbot, a contemporary Christian musician who has become a third order Franciscan monk and whose albums reach both the Catholic and contemporary Christian markets, giving the gospel mainstream a taste of liturgy music.

There are almost 19,000 Catholic parishes in the United States administered by nearly 200 dioceses. All of these parishes, or churches, have needed hymn books, song sheets and chorus scores since the Mass was changed into English. This fact, along with the spiritual renewal in the Catholic charismatic movement—paralleling the charismatic and evangelical Christian movement in America since the Jesus Revolution of the late 60s—has been responsible for the tremendous growth in the Catholic music market.

Chapter 21
The Major Labels:
Word and Benson

Of all the independent labels in gospel music, Word Records has come to dominate the industry like no other, becoming a total Christian communications company with book publishing, video tapes, and audio teaching cassettes in addition to their record labels. Word owns several labels and has distributed a number of other labels in Christian bookstores as well as in the secular marketplace. Musically, they are diverse, recording and presenting southern gospel, inspirational choirs, black gospel, Jesus rock, contemporary Christian music and great soloists to the Christian community.

Word Records was begun by a Baylor college student, Jarrell McCracken, in the fall of 1950 when he recorded a spoken word allegory of Christianity and a football game. The recording was "The Game of Life" and this improbable beginning launched the largest gospel record label in the world.

The idea originated with Ted Nichols, a minister of music at the First Baptist Church in Hearn, Texas and came from an article written by Jimmy Allen, a student at Howard Payne University. The article was an imaginary play-by-play broadcast of the struggle between Christianity and the forces of evil, broadcast over a station with the call letters WORD.

At that time, McCracken was working his way through Baylor as a sports announcer. Nichols was setting up a program for a local youth rally and approached McCracken to give a talk before the rally comparing Christian life with a football game.

After reading the magazine article, and with the help of two station engineers, McCracken wrote a complete script. McCracken added the sound effects of a football game and recorded "The Game of Life" on two 78 rpm transcriptions. Nichols played "The Game of Life" at the youth rally and the recording was so popular that about a dozen people requested copies. In December 1950, McCracken placed an order for 100 copies of the two-record set. This cost him $70. One of his friends suggested those first labels bear the name of the mythical radio station, WORD, that broadcast "The Game of Life." That record, the first for Word, is still available.

Although it sounds like a Cinderella story, young Baylor student Jarrell Franklin McCracken discovered in the two phonograph records the basic elements that would change not only his own life, but also Christian music's developing industry. Reflecting on that time, McCracken stated,

I really didn't envision much of anything specifically. I felt an inspiration after getting out the first record, which was really not meant to be anything other than a speech, but people started asking me what I was going to do next. I really didn't know, but I wanted to share with people some of the beautiful, inspirational, religious experiences we had on the campus. I kept thinking how great it would be to put these great services on record. That's about as far as my vision went. (See "Notes" re: quotes from McCracken)

Word's first artist was Frank Boggs, a baritone and friend of McCracken's, who was studying at Southwestern Baptist Theological Seminary. Boggs first recorded for Word in 1951. McCracken incorporated the organization with the offices in the kitchen of his apartment; he was single at the time. During this time McCracken recorded Richard Baker, a song director from Ft. Worth, Billy Pearce, Dick Anthony, the White Sisters, the Melody Four Quartet, J.T. Adams and some of the choirs at Baylor. The only real financial successes were "The Game of Life" and Boggs, who went on to establish a prominent name for himself as a male soloist. (This was the era of the male soloist in gospel music with George Beverly Shea the most prominent.)

Financially, the company was helped along by various friends of McCracken's, who would contribute some cash to the enterprise from time to time. McCracken was supporting himself by teaching some courses at Baylor.

It was during this time (the early '50s) that the long-play record, a breakthrough in technology, became a reality. No longer limited to the 78, companies could now record entire albums. Consumers responded by demanding the new product.

Discussing the advantages and disadvantages of establishing a base in Waco, Texas instead of New York, Los Angeles, or Nashville, McCracken stated, "There wasn't anyone around to say 'You can't do that' or 'It won't work.' We just went ahead and did it." McCracken contends that the innovative, pioneering spirit prevalent at the start of Word helped overcome the lack of expertise in the record business. Too, while the company did make and sell records, it was not in the record business as it is known in secular terms but rather an extension of the church and the religious world.

In May 1952, Marvin Norcross, a young accountant from Dallas, was introduced to McCracken by Ted Snider, one of McCracken's partners at Word and the best man at Norcross' wedding. The two young men (McCracken 24 and Norcross 23) talked for about three hours and at the end of the conversation McCracken asked if he'd like to be a partner in the organization. Norcross agreed. "I wanted to be in business for myself and I wanted to do something to help further the gospel," he said. "Since I'm not a preacher, I thought this was a good opportunity to help further the gospel." (See "Notes" re: quotes from Norcross). On the question of how much it would cost to buy into the operation, McCracken added up Word's unpaid bills and came up with the sum of $962. Norcross offered $1,000 instead so that the new organization would have $38 in working capital for a fresh start.

In 1954, McCracken realized the company could not survive on the sale of Word's records alone and decided to enter into the wholesale distribution of records. Among the products the company took were a progressive jazz label; classical product from Westminister Records; Cricket Records—a line of twenty-five cent children's records from Pickwick; and Angel Records, a division of EMI. Word was in the wholesale distribution business for four years, until 1957 when, according to Norcross, "The distribution business went sour." By that time, because of McCracken's foresight, Word had begun the Family Record Club with a record-of-the-month plan. This was started in 1957 with the profits from the wholesale distribution business.

The wholesale distribution business taught the Word organization valuable lessons about selling records to stores. The Family Record Club taught them about direct mail and they continue to sell by direct mail with approximately 100,000 members in their record club. In 1958, a direct sales division was established to sell the Word Audio Library door-to-door. This library consisted of records, tapes of talks, Bible lessons and songs and its success lasted about four years, or until around 1962, when it was discontinued.

In 1957, Kurt Kaiser, a brilliant young pianist, composer, arranger and conductor, joined Word as vice-president and director of artists and repertoire. He soon became one of the most influential people in sacred music. By 1960, the sale of Word Records was approximately $4 million annually.

The '60s began for Word with the purchase of Sacred Records, a move which brought Ralph Carmichael into the organization. Carmichael was and is a noted west coast writer, arranger, and producer who had been a pioneer innovator in the Christian music field since the late '40s when he recorded religious music with the popular sound of the day. He raised more than a few eyebrows in church circles, which were used to hearing religious music recorded with an organ or piano only.

The purchase of Sacred Records also involved the purchase of half of Lexicon Music, a publishing operation owned and run by Carmichael. This involved Word in a total music publishing operation for the first time. In 1957 Marvin Norcross conceived the idea of Canaan Records, a label that would feature southern or country style gospel music, consisting primarily of male quartets. The idea was premature at that time, but in 1963 the label got underway with Norcross signing the Florida Boys as the first act. Norcross had gotten the idea from John T. Benson, whose Benson Company, based in Nashville, was already recording some southern gospel groups, beginning with the Speer Family.

In the summer of 1965, Word announced it was starting a book publishing division. The first book, entitled *The Taste of New Wine*, was by an obscure Episcopalian layman named Keith Miller. It was an immediate best-seller and remains popular in Christian literature.

In the mid-1960s American culture was dominated by turmoil, unrest and Vietnam. There was also the Jesus Revolution, a movement where large numbers of young people became Christians. At Word, Billy Ray Hearn had been hired in the A & R department. Because of his interest and involvement in contemporary Christian music, he was given the nod to begin Myrrh Records, a division of Word, which would be their contemporary label while the more traditional artists remained on Word.

The first album on Myrrh was by Ray Hildebrand, who had two albums released on Word before his Myrrh release. Hildebrand was known for being the "Paul" of Paul and Paula, whose recording in 1962 of "Hey, Hey Paula" sold close to three million records. The second album released by Myrrh was by an artist who had also had an album on Word. But Randy Matthews was different; his album on Word, *Wish We'd All Been Ready* was the first contemporary Christian release (i.e. combining rock 'n' roll and gospel) for that label and he became the first Jesus rock artist to record for Word as that organization entered the contemporary field.

A major reason for the success of Word and these different labels was a move it made in 1960. The company decided to discontinue its association with wholesale distributors who were handling its product and assume its own distribution. This meant that beginning in 1960 Word sold directly to record outlets and Christian bookstores instead of having their product serviced by wholesale distributors. The reason for the move, according to Norcross, was because Word felt they could more properly promote their own product and could offer special price deals they could not do through distributors. Whenever they had tried a special sales program previously, they found the distributor generally benefited with higher profit margins while the individual stores and customers paid the same price.

In 1969 Word purchased the Rodeheaver Company in Winona Lake, Indiana, one of the nation's oldest publishers of sacred music. That same year Canaanland Music, a publishing division of Canaan Records, was begun in Nashville by Aaron Brown, giving Word its first offices outside of Waco, Texas.

A Christian musical, "Tell It Like It Is" written by Kurt Kaiser and Ralph Carmichael in 1969 proved to be a landmark musical in the Christian world. Also at Word, a minister's taped digest was introduced, later evolving into "Catalyst" and "Focus"—a series of teaching cassettes. Word also assumed the publication of *Faith/At/Word* magazine. The introduction of Creative Resources saw a whole new line of mixed-media teaching and discussion aids become available for use in churches, homes and small groups. Also in 1969, Word, Inc. had its first million selling record. Oddly, it was a comedy record by southern gospel artist Wendy Bagwell entitled "The Rattlesnake Remedy," a satirical take-off on those who used poison snakes in church services—a practice foreign and undesirable to the narrator of the record.

The seventies brought more growth to Word as the Myrrh label grew with the contemporary Christian music field. In fact, sales in all the music fields increased to the point that by the end of 1979 Word, Inc. was grossing approximately $40 million in sales a year and employing 400 people—still based in Waco but with offices established in Nashville and Los Angeles.

In the mid-seventies, Word began to distribute labels again, only this time it was small Christian labels such as Good News, Paragon, Solid Rock, Maranatha, Jim, Lamb and Lion, New Pax, and Image as well as Canaan, Myrrh and Dayspring, which they owned and Light, owned in partnership with Ralph Carmichael. This move to distribute other labels was made for several reasons. First, the contemporary Christian music field was growing at a phenomenal pace, and, second, it increased business for Word and its salesmen, making the organization more profitable and able to employ more salesmen.

Perhaps the biggest move that happened to Word occurred in 1976 when they were purchased by ABC Entertainment Corp., making McCracken one of the principal stockholders in the corporation, which owned the ABC television network. With this move, Myrrh was distributed for a short while by ABC Records with the belief that sales would increase. However, the opposite occurred as they found a secular label did not understand Christian product well enough to sell it well. After that lesson, Word retained its autonomy within the ABC organization and when ABC Records was sold in 1979 to MCA, Word remained with ABC, existing as a separate entity under the corporate umbrella.

As Word entered the 1980s, it expanded into black gospel, the only field it had not successfully marketed in the past. Word quickly took black gospel to Christian bookstores and helped it cross over into the white market, breaking down some of the racial boundaries in Christian music. However, the black gospel they marketed was contemporary, part of the pop sound. They generally avoided the choirs and soloists, leaving that market to the traditional black companies.

Since the 1960s, Word has dominated gospel music and by the 1980s their records accounted for 60-70 percent of all gospel music sold in America. But, as Word increased its dominance of the gospel music industry in the 1980s, some problems developed within the organization. In March, 1986, ABC merged with Capital Cities, Inc. and the new organization sought a stronger say in the running of Word. Finally, in September, 1986, Jarrell McCracken, after 35 years at the helm, left the company. Although official reports stated he left to "pursue other interests," it soon became obvious that he did not leave of his own accord. Still, the company, organized under three divisions—Word Records and Music, Word Publishing, and Word Direct Marketing Services—remains the major Christian company marketing gospel music with music accounting for about 50-60 percent of their $80 million annual income.

The other major Christian label for contemporary Christian music in the early 1970s was the Benson Company with their two record divisions, HeartWarming and Impact. They added Greentree in 1976 just for contemporary music. Founded in 1902 by John T. Benson, his wife Eva, and Rev. J.O. McClurkan as a publishing company, the organization was originally formed to distribute religious pamphlets in the Nashville area. It published its first songbook, *Living Water Songs,* in 1904 but remained a small, local company until 1935 when John T. Benson, Jr. took over the company. The younger Benson expanded the company dramatically and between 1948 and 1951 the company went from $12,000 a year in gross revenues to $100,000 a year.

Bob Benson, the second son of John T. Benson, Jr. and the third generation of Bensons involved with the company, joined the organization in 1960 and soon the company's revenues were over half a million dollars a year and the company made its first venture into the record business when HeartWarming Records was created. John T. Benson, III joined the organization in 1969 after the company had been successful with its first artists, which included the Speer Family, the Rambos, and the Bill Gaither Trio, and the company expanded into contemporary Christian music in the 1970s and moved away from the southern gospel quartet music they had begun with.

The company has remained in Nashville since its inception but was sold to the Zondervan Corporation, a Christian company known for its Bible publishing and chain of Family Bookstores, 1980.

Chapter 22
Bill Gaither

I was first asked if gospel was going to be the 'next big thing' in 1965 by a reporter. My answer then is the same as my answer now: No. It will never become an alternative to pop music because the lyric is a limiting lyric. The lyric is talking about discipline, what it's going to require you to give up as opposed to the secular lyric which is saying, 'help me make it through the night' or 'how could this be bad and feel so good.' The gospel lyric is the opposite. It's saying, 'I'm going to tell you that this is going to cost you something.' I don't think the whole world wants to hear that. (See "Notes" re: quotes from Bill Gaither)

That statement was made by Bill Gaither, who may be considered the godfather of contemporary Christian music. He dominated the field of gospel music from the mid-60s through the 70s. Along the way he captured the first gold album by a gospel artist on a gospel label for his musical, *Alleluia*. He also won the Dove award for "Songwriter of the Year" eight consecutive years and collected seven Grammies and a total of thirteen Dove awards, becoming a performer who could regularly fill 10,000-seat auditoriums with his group, the Bill Gaither Trio. He did all this before the explosion of contemporary Christian music brought gospel music to the attention of the secular world. For Gaither and his group, however, there was little secular recognition because he was firmly entrenched in the Christian world, playing for Christians. To them, he was a major star; to those not in this world, he was an unknown.

Bill Gaither had grown up in Anderson, Indiana and attended Anderson College, where he graduated in 1959. While in college, he met Gloria Sickle, whom he married after her graduation in 1963. The couple began teaching at Alexandria High School; he taught English while she taught French.

As a child, Bill learned to play piano and organ and performed whenever he could throughout school, in recitals and as an accompanist. After his college graduation, Bill taught high school for seven years, acquiring a Masters degree in Music at Ball State in Muncie along the way. He formed his Trio in the mid-1950s, playing for civic clubs, Farm Bureau meetings and in churches. In 1967 Gaither quit teaching school to devote all of his time to gospel music.

Along with his wife, Gloria, Bill Gaither began as a songwriter and that's where their major contributions to gospel are—through compositions lik⌐ "He Touched Me," "Because He Lives," "The King is Coming," "There's Just Something About That Name," "I Am A Promise," "I Am Loved" and countless others that have made their way into churches where congregations sing them regularly. Their early songs brought him to the attention of Bob Benson and the Benson Company, a Christian record and publishing company. Bob Benson was in Anderson, Indiana, the Gaither's hometown, to watch the Imperials perform in the early '60s. Gaither, who had booked the show, opened as a warm-up act with his trio.

The Trio had pressed a custom album; Benson asked if they could sell a couple thousand on their own and Gaither said he'd give it a shot. The agreement was that Gaither would be responsible for the sale of several thousand—guaranteeing that many sold—and the Benson Company would distribute it to Christian bookstores, trying to garner additional sales.

Gaither had had songs recorded by the Imperials, Doug Oldham, Elvis, George Beverly Shea and countless others as well. Those songs have been described by Gaither as "like a brush fire that kept getting out of control." At this early stage, the Bill Gaither Trio was a family affair consisting of Bill, his brother Danny, and sister Mary Ann. His sister decided to leave to get married and there was the problem of replacing her; the solution would determine the future of the Trio as a recording act. "The real factor in us becoming a major recording group came when my wife joined us," said Gaither. "When my sister left to get married, we tried several other singers who were great singers but, for whatever reason, the people didn't really accept them. So finally I said, 'Honey, you've got to help us.' She said, 'I can't sing.' I said, 'I know you're not a great singer, but you're my wife and you helped write these things and spiritually we are in this thing together and I think God will bless.' I think we're a good example of 'It's not by might, it's not by power, it's by my spirit saith the Lord' because Lord knows we were not great singers." The group did always have a great singer for lead though; first Bill's brother, Danny, and then after Danny left the group in the mid-1970s, Gary McSpadden.

Gloria joined the Trio singing harmony in the early 1960s and in 1968 the group recorded their album with "The King is Coming" and "Jesus, There's Just Something About That Name" on it and the singers who couldn't sing suddenly had a hit on their hands. Gaither said:

My wife is a great communicator. On that album, she did a narration on two songs that became big songs on that album. She communicates with power and when she says something she says it with authority. It was a special moment.

The album was a landmark for the Gaithers and for gospel music. Said Gaither:

Back then, 25-30,000 was a great number to sell and for us 5,000 was a big number. And I'll never forget when we made that record, it went 10,000, then 20, then 30, then 50,000 and we couldn't believe those kinds of figures. Then it went 100,000, then 150, then 200, then it went 250,000 and in our field that was totally unheard of.

News of the album had spread through word of mouth, through the Benson company learning how to market to the Christian bookstores, and through the Gaither's own personal appearances and the extensive mailing list they had compiled. Songs like "The King is Coming," "Jesus, There's Just Something About That Name," "The Family of God" and others which would become standards and establish the Gaither songwriting talent in gospel music.

When Graham returned to the States, he contacted Shea about singing for some gospel meetings in Charlotte, North Carolina, which became the unofficial launching of his Crusades. The year was 1948 and Billy Graham had to overcome a number of obstacles, mostly connected with the bad reputation itinerant evangelists had received who attempted to follow the success of Billy Sunday in the 1920s and 1930s. The big break came in September, 1949, when the troupe brought their "city-wide" campaign to Los Angeles. The campaign received international coverage from the Hearst newspapers after the conversion of several Hollywood celebrities. Chief among these was Stuart Hamblen, a popular radio entertainer who later wrote "It Is No Secret" and a number of other gospel classics. Other celebrities who were converted were 1936 Olympic star Louis Zamperini and underworld figure Jim Vaus.

In 1951, Shea signed with RCA, where he would enjoy major record success in the latter part of the decade. Paul Barkmeyer originally approached Shea and the contract was drawn up by Sam Wallace and Elmer Eades. The first session was produced by Stephen H. Shoals and featured Shea backed by the Hugo Winterhalter Orchestra on an album titled *Inspirational Songs*. Among the songs included on this first RCA album were "Ivory Palaces," "Known Only To Him," "Tenderly He Watches," "If You Know The Lord," and "It Is No Secret."

During the first four years with RCA, Shea's records did not sell enough to pay for the cost of recording and pressing. Still, the label believed in him and continued to release recordings, produced first by Shoals and later by Brad McCuen and Darol Rice.

Shea was the beneficiary of big breaks received by Billy Graham when Henry Luce featured the evangelist in *Life*, which led to a White House visit with Harry Truman. The "Hour of Decision" radio broadcasts began on December 5, 1950 from Atlanta with the first program broadcast over 150 stations. By the fifth week, it had the largest audience of any religious program in history. By 1952, Shea was singing regularly on "The Hour of Decision" broadcasts (many of his performances were taped), and "Club Time," both national programs broadcast weekly, as well as "Songs in the Night," also a weekly program broadcast over WCFL in Chicago. In that year, "Club Time" ended and, after eight years on "Songs in the Night," Shea turned over his duties to Glen Jordan so he could devote all his energies to the Billy Graham Evangelistic Association (BGEA).

During the first Crusade abroad in 1954, Shea found a song which would be linked with him throughout his career—and the success of each owed a great deal to this connection. The song was "How Great Thou Art." The sheet music was given to Shea by George Gray, who worked with the publishing firm of Pikering and Inglis, Ltd. after a chance encounter in London on Oxford Street. Several months after his return to the US, Shea was going through his notes and found the leaflet and sang it to himself. He liked the song, as did Cliff Barrows, music director for Graham who had also received a copy. Shea performed it first at the Toronto Crusade in 1955 at the Maple Leaf Garden. The song had an immediate success.

The song was originally written in 1885 or '86 in Sweden by Reverend Carl Robert and titled "O Store Gud" (O Great God). Robert was a preacher and religious editor who died, never knowing the impact the song would have on

Bill Gaither's audiences are comprised mostly of Christians, churchgoers who come for an evening of music and worship. He does not have to convince them of the Christian way of life or defend his faith before them. They believe together. Gaither said:

I don't feel I've been called to be a mass evangelist like Billy Graham. I certainly believe in personal evangelism but in our music and concerts my main motive has been to minister to the body of Christ. I don't think there are a lot of non-Christian people coming to our concerts.

Gaither chaffs at the notion that gospel writers are more limited than secular writers because of the topic. He said:

We don't have as many limitations as secular writers, because most of the topics of secular songs have something to do about love. I believe 80 percent have something to do about loving or relationships if they're going to get popular. But in all fairness, from the Christian perspective there are a number of topics on which we write. One is the sovereignty of God, how God leads us, all the various characters of the Old Testament, the birth of Christ and the life of Christ, the death of Christ, the resurrection of Christ and how that applies to our lives on a day-to-day basis. We have the whole area of praise to God and Christ, the whole area of the body of Christ, the family of God, and the church. Also the whole testimonial area of how this has affected my life, i.e. 'amazing grace, how sweet the sound that saved a wretch like me.' That has been a recurring theme down through the years. The whole theme of teaching ideas, about how to live. Then the whole servanthood concept of Christ washing the feet of the disciples and how that works on a daily basis. That's just a few of the topics. There are a lot of topics in the gospel world and the people who listen to gospel music like to hear from those topics. I say again we have more topics about which to write than I hear in pop music because to get a hit in pop music, you usually have to write about the romantic love relationship.

Bill Gaither is not just a successful songwriter and artist, he is a successful businessman as well, owning the publishing of his songs and operating Spring House, which books concerts for artists and markets material to the churches. Except for the distribution company, which is based in Nashville, all his other ventures are based in the small town of Anderson, Indiana. It is where Bill and Gloria Gaither grew up and where they still live. It is from this town in Indiana that the music of Bill Gaither was born and developed. Gaither has said "you can't keep a good song down" no matter where it comes from. You can't keep a good man down either, no matter if he lives in Anderson, Indiana, or one of the music capitols of the world.

Chapter 23
Fanny Lou Hamer and James Cleveland

The black church and politics have often been linked, with preachers often serving as a lightning rod for political issues. It was Martin Luther King, Jr., a preacher from Atlanta and Montgomery, Alabama who led the Civil Rights Movement in the 1950s and 1960s. A number of other black politicians have come from churches and the Civil Rights Movement itself owes the major portion of its victory to the grassroots support of church members. Since music is a key focal point for the black church, it is logical that black gospel music would play a pivotal role in the Civil Rights Movement. Although there are a number of television clips of people singing "We Shall Overcome," "Blowin' in the Wind," and other songs while their arms are locked together, it was the old black gospel standards which provided the foundation for that movement. And it was people like Fanny Lou Hamer who had the courage to become leaders in that movement, using music at the grassroots level.

If you were black, rural Mississippi in 1964 was not the most comfortable place to live. The public bathrooms were marked "Men," "Women," and "Colored." There were "White" water fountains and there were "Colored" water fountains. All public places, including restaurants, movie theaters, and bus stations, were either segregated with special places for blacks or reserved for whites only.

In the summer of 1962, the Student Non-Violent Coordinating Committee (SNCC) came to Ruleville, Mississippi to work on a voter registration drive. At that time blacks had to pass a literacy test in order to vote—a requirement not applied to white voters. This literacy test required them to copy and interpret, to the satisfaction of the county examiner, an arcane section of the Mississippi state constitution. The SNCC volunteers knocked on doors to get blacks to go to the courthouse in Indianola, about 26 miles away. After a week, they held a big mass rally to stimulate some community interest. Finally, registration day arrived and 18 people boarded a bus for the trip to the courthouse.

According to Charles McLauring, who was in this group of volunteers, a "short, stocky lady" was the first to step off the bus and go in to register. The others followed—all taking the literacy test and all failing.

That lady was Fanny Lou Hamer and she lived on a plantation in the area. After the group had taken the test they boarded the bus to return home. A police car stopped them on their way out of town and informed the driver he was under arrest for driving a bus the color of a school bus. They took him to jail and everyone was "shaking with fear," according to McLaurin (12). No one knew if they would all be put in jail or whether they would just be left there on the road.

Then a voice was heard singing some old hymns and spirituals. It was Fanny Lou Hamer. Somebody on the bus said, "That's Fanny Lou, she know how to sing." (McLaurin 13). And she did know how to sing as she sang with a power in her voice that calmed and comforted the others on the bus. It was a voice that carried the power of Jesus as she sang the gospel songs that expressed a faith that was like a rock in her life.

When the police came back to the bus, they informed everyone that the driver needed $52 to pay his fine. A collection was taken, the money was raised and they all went home. But there were problems waiting for Fanny Lou. The plantation owner had been told that she had tried to register and he informed her husband, Pap Hamer, that Fanny Lou had to go back to the courthouse and withdraw her name or she would have to move. With that, Fanny Lou packed her belongings and moved into Ruleville, where she stayed with a friend. That night nightriders shot up the home where she was staying. They also fired into the homes where other SNCC members were staying.

Several weeks later Fanny Lou went to Nashville for an SNCC conference where she was asked to sing. She sang "This Little Light of Mine," "Ain't Gonna Let Nobody Turn Me Around" and other songs that became part of the spirit which motivated people in the Civil Rights Movement. The "Freedom Singers" were born that night and this group from SNCC toured college campuses in the north to raise money for SNCC. They also made several albums.

Fanny Lou Hamer and many other blacks proved during the Civil Rights Movement in the 1960s that living the Christian life is risky business and carrying the message of the gospel is dangerous. Fanny Lou performed some of her gospel music while she was in her 40s in a concert setting before warm, appreciative audiences, but most of Hamer's life was spent singing gospel music because that was where she found her strength.

Fanny Lou Hamer demonstrated to people the power of gospel music and the power of love. She and other SNCC workers faced constant threats and beatings by southern police. Once in Charleston, South Carolina, Hamer and a group of workers were held for three days in a jail and brutally beaten. She suffered kidney damage and developed a blood clot in her left eye that permanently impaired her vision from that incident. Still, she refused to consider hate or revenge. "It wouldn't solve any problem for me to hate whites just because they hate me," she once said. "There's so much hate. Only God has kept the Negro sane" (Collum, "Stepping Out" 13).

In a world that places such a high priority on keeping a job and protecting loved ones, Fanny Lou Hamer chose instead to stand up for her rights and believe God created blacks equal to whites. When her husband and two daughters left the plantation to join her in town, the plantation owner confiscated all their belongings, claiming they owed him money. The day after Hamer attended a Mississippi Freedom Democratic Party meeting, her husband was fired from his job.

Hamer, her husband and their two adopted daughters had lived in grinding poverty as sharecroppers on a plantation for 20 years before she stepped out, at the age of 43, to become involved in the Civil Rights Movement. The sharecropper's life was tough—they were provided with a house and food, seed, fertilizer and farm equipment on credit from a company store owned by the plantation owner. After the crops were harvested, the owner would receive half the income and the sharecropper the other half. However, the bill at the company store always managed to exceed what sharecroppers got for their crops.

Hamer's politics were linked directly to the gospel. She wrote in 1968, "I think the sixth chapter of Ephesians, the eleventh and twelfth verses helps us to know...what it is we are up against. It says, 'Put on the whole armor of God, that ye may be able to stand against the wiles of the devil. For we wrestle not against flesh and blood but against principalities, against powers, against the rulers of darkness of this world, against spiritual wickedness in high places.' This is what I think about when I think of my own work in the fight for freedom" (Collum "Stepping Out" 15).

Fanny Lou once stood up in a meeting and said, "I've been sick and tired for so long that I'm sick and tired of being sick and tired" (Collum, "Prophet" 4). That phrase—"sick and tired of being sick and tired"—stuck with her during the Civil Rights Movement and is now etched on her tombstone in Ruleville, Mississippi. She died in 1977 and is buried on land purchased by the Freedom Farm Cooperative.

In the 1970s, James Cleveland became arguably the most important individual in traditional black gospel. He was important because of his influence on other singers, for his help and support of other acts, as an artist whose records had an impact in gospel, and as the founder and president of the Gospel Music Workshop of America. During a period in the late '60s and early '70s, when blacks struggled for self-respect as well as respect from society, Cleveland helped to provide that respect for those who were involved as singers in churches and who attended his convention. With the slogan "Where Everybody is Somebody" and the underlying theology that everyone is someone important in the eyes of God, Cleveland's convention not only helped singers and musicians with their music, it also lifted their hearts, minds, and spirits.

Thomas Dorsey was the first to gather black choir members together for a convention in 1932, but there were a number of singers Dorsey did not reach. Cleveland's first convention was held in Detroit in 1968 and attracted over 3000 registrants. The next year almost 5000 attended the convention in Philadelphia and in 1970 over 5000 came to St. Louis for the gathering. From there, they held conventions in Dallas, Chicago, Los Angeles, Washington, Kansas City, and New York. At each of the conventions, more classes and seminars were added to help choir members and musicians as well as radio announcers and choir directors. Each night choirs from numerous churches performed and Cleveland often dropped in to perform with a choir or sometimes solo with just a keyboard player (often Billy Preston). He was clearly the center of attention and the magnet that pulled all the disparate forces together. Cleveland's convention managed to speak to the black experience and gratified a desire for significance in a world that often treated blacks as second-class citizens. It made Cleveland more than just another gospel singer.

Cleveland said of his workshop:

It was a dream I had. There are a lot of good gospel musicians that need help, you know, like there are a lot of people that play by ear. They don't know where to go to get someone to help them. There are no colleges or schools that actually teach gospel; therefore, the man that has a little knowledge that wants to increase his knowledge doesn't have any place to go. Directors, songwriters, organists, soloists, people who want to learn how to effectively be a lead singer, etc., every phase of gospel music—there is no place they can turn other than to people in the business—so I've asked these people to donate a portion of their time each year to help other musicians. (See "Notes" regarding quotes from Cleveland)

Born in 1932, James Cleveland was raised in Chicago and, as a boy soprano, sang in the church where Thomas Dorsey was minister of music. He heard the piano playing of Roberta Martin and was captivated. Since his family could not afford to buy a piano, he used to practice each night on the window sill where he took the wedges and crevices and made them into black and white keys.

Before he made his mark as a singer, Cleveland made his mark as a piano player, developing a hard, driving style when he played behind Roberta Martin. As a singer he was influenced by Myrtle Scott and Eugene Smith of the Roberta Martin Singers. The flamboyance of Smith was combined with the influences of ballad singer Robert Anderson, jazzman Louis Armstrong and blues singer Dinah Washington, once the lead singer for Sallie Martin. Washington showed Cleveland the fusion between gospel and the blues and he wove those two musical forms together.

James Cleveland was energetic, bright, and ambitious. He would go anywhere and ask anyone for a chance to sing and play. In the mid-fifties, Cleveland's arrangements caught the ears of the gospel world as he fused some secular blues and jazz influences into black gospel. He was a member of Albertina Walker's legendary Caravans and he worked with such greats as Dorothy Norwood, Inez Andrews, Imogene Green and Norsalus McKissick. He was the architect of the strong, pushing gospel sound, a sound that drove a song.

Cleveland's gruff vocal style came after his voice changed from soprano and, as he drove himself to sing more and more—fractured his once beautiful voice into a deep growl. He is not a pretty singer by anyone's standards, but he is one of the most effective in bringing across a gospel song and pulling emotions from a crowd.

After recording for several labels with various groups, Cleveland signed with Savoy Records and released records with the Cleveland All-Stars (featuring Billy Preston on keyboards) and the Gospel Chimes (which featured Jessy Dixon). Finally, Fred Mendelsohn, head of Savoy, teamed Cleveland with the Angelic Choir of Nutley, New Jersey, and that's where he found his niche. Working with this choir, as well as a number of others across the country, Cleveland put out records that featured the choirs as a background and on the choruses while he worked with the verses, molding them to his own style.

The 1980s saw Cleveland fall out of vogue with some of the younger black gospel performers and fans. While they moved into the slick, smooth sound influenced by R&B and disco, Cleveland remained with his raw, gutsy, blues-based soul sound. The result has been a bit of a split in black gospel which has resulted in two overlapping factions, usually referred to as contemporary and traditional.

Cleveland spoke of the importance of music in the gospel world as well as the gulf that often exists between a singer's own spiritual life and the one he/she sings about. He stated:

There are a lot of people who have the ability to expound that are not necessarily heavily religious. There are a lot of people who can sing and bring tears to your eyes but are not deeply religious. But there are people with the ability to sing gospel. It comes natural to black folks because it's so kin to the other types of black music and we have people who can stand up and sing gospel and they have fantastic voices that would impress you if you didn't know anything about their lives. Then there are folks who don't really care about church and don't really care about the cause but they can still do the job. What we're trying to do is see that person become dedicated to the music, not just be in business for a dollar—see that person becomes dedicated and sing music so its inspiring to others to come to Christ and the church. More people are drawn to the church through music than what you are preaching. Over the years people have been turned off to preaching so much that they don't want to come to church. But music is one of the most perfect magnets you can use to draw people to church...I think that any minister of any church of a denomination believing in music should have a well rounded music department because music softens the heart of the people and the minister can deliver the sermons and effectively a team is going to win souls for Christ.

Cleveland was acutely aware of the problems gospel music—particularly black gospel—has had to face in order to be heard by the public. He states,

I would certainly like to reach a wider audience, because I find people like gospel as well as anything else, when they get a chance to hear it. My problem, or the problem of most of these singers, is we can't become as big name—wise as the pop singers only because we don't have the exposure. You see, they hear pop 20 hours a day and they hear gospel one hour, and that's usually five or six o'clock in the morning on most radio stations when nobody gets a chance really to hear it. Therefore, the artist can never really be known because they're never exposed at the right time when people can connect with them. But if we had a decent amount of radio time dedicated for gospel time in major cities, the artists would become bigger because their popularity would grow as people know who they are. Then record sales would grow and so would public appearances.

There have been big changes and progress in black gospel and this has brought it closer to mainstream music and allowed gospel groups to sound more like those on the radio. He stated, in 1978,

I see it growing. I remember when quartet singers didn't have any instruments at all, and now they just about all have rhythm sections. Quartet singers used to stand on the floor and sing with no music—now they have guitars, basses, organs, drums, piano, etc. I've seen it come of age with using the instruments. I've also seen the church choirs who were frowned on for bringing instruments in the church at first because folks thought instruments could only be used for worldly music. So I've seen churches accept new trends in gospel music. There was a time when it was unheard of to have a drum in church, but now churches have an organ, piano, drums, bass, and some have horns and other instruments. I've seen them accept the music for music's value and not claim that a tune is sinful because a tune is not sinful. It's the words that you put to a tune that makes it sinful. People like music; even if they hear a song with no words they'll get into the music.

The economic panacea of selling black music to white buyers has long been a part of the music industry and now permeates black gospel. Black gospel now reaches an audience. It has been watered down from a raw sound and made more palatable for commercial tastes. Cleveland has been aware of this and stated:

Andrae Crouch has bridged the gap between black and white audiences and done a very good job. The white artists are very interested in the more soulful type of gospel music. Also, in the contemporary sound of gospel music, many black musicians are now embracing the contemporary sound. There is a great upsurge of white choirs that sing like black choirs and the blacks have always tried to excel and perfect their performances relating to sound, arrangements, and instrumentation. Orchestrations and the like bring us closer to what the white man has been doing all the time. Then the white man is coming more to the soulful side, trying to deal more with the spiritual than the technical aspect. So they're coming our way, and we're going their way. Somewhere in the middle of the road we're bound to run into one another!

Indeed, in many ways they have already run into one another; black gospel has influenced white gospel musically while the white gospel field has influenced black gospel from a marketing perspective. Still, black gospel does not have the network or organization for its music that white gospel does. While contemporary Christian music has a network of Christian bookstores to carry its product and a number of gospel radio stations, as well as TV programs and print media, to showcase the talent, black gospel is generally sold in independently owned record stores (called Mom and Pop stores) in the black sections of town and heard on black radio stations as a one-hour program. Christian bookstores have been reluctant to stock black gospel, perhaps not trusting black American Christianity as well as not finding a great demand for the distinctive black gospel record. There are, however, a number of blacks who have become increasingly acceptable to this white market. Unfortunately, the gospel performer has to choose his audience and those black performers who have whites buying their albums often find they have lost their black audience. Cleveland has kept his black audience and, as a result, few whites buy his recordings. However, that is probably because Cleveland is a voice for the black person in America—he speaks to the black experience through his music and preaching—and the white audience has trouble relating.

This dichotomy between black and white gospel has caused some blacks to disown their heritage, to step away from traditional black gospel as they moved toward the commercial market. One of James Cleveland's greatest attributes is that he has never stepped away, preferring to give a dignity to the music that comprises the very roots of the black church and its music.

Chapter 24
Cathedrals, Florida Boys and Kingsmen

Southern gospel music is a mixture of barbershop harmonies and country music. Characterized for years by the four man group singing with a piano, it now includes mixed groups—male and female singers—as well as solo acts, family acts, duets and trios, all supported with full productions of guitar, bass, drums, keyboards and other instruments on their recordings. Although it is not limited to the south, this is where its roots are and where it is strongest. It is a rural-based music, appealing to those whose taste in life and religion is simple and down-to-earth. Shunning pretense, it is "people" music, and the performers and audiences often mingle before and after the shows, with members of the audience often being singers themselves with their own groups. But underlying the outward veneer of simplicity there is a complexity in the four-part harmonies and the nuances of the lead singers which makes one group sound unlike numerous others.

The Cathedrals are a part of this world and have been for over 20 years. They are full-time musicians and ministers, meaning that nearly every week they leave their homes and climb aboard a custom bus where they will eat, sleep and travel thousands of miles to hundreds of concerts to perform in churches, civic centers, auditoriums, schools and at events such as revivals and homecomings where people gather for several days and enjoy a festival type outdoor picnic whose main attraction is gospel groups.

The Cathedrals began as a trio with Rex Humbard in 1963. At that time, the group was comprised of Glen Payne, Bobby Clark, and Danny Koker. George Younce had been in the Blue Ridge Quartet with Jim Hamill (now of the Kingsmen) when Rex Humbard called and asked him to come to the Cathedral of Tomorrow—the church Humbard had established in Akron, Ohio, with his national television ministry—and sing. He did and the Cathedral Trio became the Cathedral Quartet in November, 1964.

Glen Payne and George Younce, the two cornerstones for The Cathedrals, met for the first time in Stow, Ohio, when George came to join Glen's group. "I knew of Glen before then, but that's the first time I actually met him," said Younce. Both had been in the Weatherford Quartet, but at different times.

The first time George met Glen was not the first time George met Rex Humbard. Their relationship went back 13 years earlier when the Weatherfords were part of the Humbard team. That was in 1956, but later that year George, along with Jim Hamill, Danny Koker, and Tallmadge Martin, moved to Milwaukee to re-form the Watchmen Quartet. "I'll never forget what Rex said when I left there," said George. "He said, 'Go ahead and get this out of your system. But one day you'll be back.' I never did think I would but 14 years later the Lord spoke to me and then Rex called and I came back."

The beginning of the Cathedral Quartet was not the beginning of singing gospel music for either Glen Payne or George Younce. Glen had first wanted to be a gospel singer "around six or seven when I sang with my Granddad," he said. "I was raised in a Christian home and our type of music had always been gospel. I had heard quartets since I was knee high and that's what I wanted to do."

The big turning point came when he was 17 and Frank Stamps called to give him a job with the Stamps Quartet. The Stamps had formed quartets during the early part of the twentieth century to promote their songs and songbooks. These groups would travel around to various churches and gatherings, singing new songs and selling books, hoping the tunes would catch on and the audiences would want to purchase the new material to sing for themselves in churches. Additionally, the Stamps and others operated "singing schools" where singers would come for several weeks and learn the rudiments of four-part singing and reading in the "shaped note" style where the musical notes are written in shapes (triangles, squares, ellipses) so that a singer can quickly grasp the melody by knowing which note goes with which shape. This method made the musically literate musically proficient without dragging them down with music theory. It became a shorthand way of sight reading music.

And what did Glen's parents say when their 17 year-old son decided to hit the road and sing? He replies,

They were thrilled to death. It was like I'd gotten into the President's office because it's like something they always wanted to do. I had sung with my mother and daddy when I was a kid. And then to think I was going full-time with the Stamps Quartet! They were tickled to death. They only lived about 30 miles away so they used to come and hear us sing.

Later, Glen would be drafted into the service. When he returned, he returned to gospel singing, joining the Lester Stamps Quartet and then the Stamps-Ozark Quartet until he joined the Weatherfords in 1957. That was the year Glen moved from his native state of Texas to Ohio. Glen stayed with the Weatherfords until 1963, when he started the Cathedral Trio.

George Younce was bitten by the gospel singing bug in Lenoir, North Carolina. "I went to hear a group called the Harmoneers," he said. "And I was just a teenager. They were playing in Gainesville, North Carolina, at a high school there and when I heard them that night, I'll never forget it, I knew that's what I wanted to do."

George, too, had come from a Christian home where gospel singing was part of everyday life. His father was a bass singer and sang in the choir and in the Sunday afternoon singing conventions. "Back then, I wanted to sing like my dad," said George, "but I didn't think I ever would 'cause when I was in the fifth grade I won a prize for having the highest voice in our room."

The first group George was in was called the Spiritualaires and what changed him from a lead singer to a bass singer was an experience he'll never forget. He states,

Some of us boys around home formed a quartet and I was the lead singer. One morning we got up to sing in church and, I'll never forget it, my voice was changing but I didn't know it. I had the lead to start out on a song. I hadn't tried to sing that morning and when I started my voice broke so I backed up and coughed and tried again and then backed up again and kicked the piano and tried again. I never did get it out that morning and we never did sing. I think I was 15 years old and I waited about a year before I sung again and when I did one of the boys said, 'Why don't you try bass,' and that's when I started.

George became a full-time gospel singer through an odd set of circumstances. He states,

I was in the service with a boy from West Virginia and he got killed. I went to visit his parents—I didn't know them but I knew Bill—and when I was there I met a quartet who was there that day and their bass singer had just moved to California. So we rehearsed a little bit and they said, 'Move on up here.' I wanted to sing so bad that I moved on up there and lived with one of the boys and we sang on weekends. Whatever they made they took out for the gas and the car—they all had jobs—and they'd give me what money was left over because I didn't have a job at the time. Of course, living with them it didn't take anything.

That was 1954 in Beckley, West Virginia, and the group was the Watchmen Quartet, who teamed with Rex Humbard in 1956. From there, George re-formed the Watchmen Quartet before joining the Blue Ridge Quartet in 1957 where he stayed until he joined the Cathedrals in November, 1964.

Since that time, there have been a number of Cathedral members, including Bobby Clark, Danny Koker, Mack Taunton, George Amon Webster, Lorne Matthews, Roger Horne, Roy Tremble, Bill Dykes, Jim Garstain, and Haskell Cooley. In 1979, a big change occurred for the Cathedrals. Three members— Roy Tremble, George Amon Webster and Lorne Matthews—all decided to leave the group. That left the two cornerstones, Glen and George, standing alone. George states,

Glen and I were talking one day over at my home, and I said, Maybe this is the Lord's way of saying He wants us to retire or something. So we prayed, Lord, if this is it, then make it impossible for us to get anybody we can sing with and want to be with. And the Lord proved to us from the first member that he wasn't through with us yet. That was when Kirk Talley called. I'm glad we didn't have to pick the members—the Lord sent them. He sent the members so we could keep our own style and sound and that was really unreal to us to have three new men come in and still have your own sound. You can replace one man and still have your own sound—but three?

Gospel music takes its toll on the singers and their families through the incessant travelling. It is not easy to constantly have to leave home, a wife and growing children, and climb aboard a bus to go to distant places and sing. Those who leave this gospel world generally do so because they tire of this life week after week, year in and year out. For that reason those who continue to travel and sing must feel a special call, a special mission to do what they do. Glen reflected on this when he stated:

After years of travelling I think you realize your days are numbered when you travel as much as we do on the road. I think you realize it's more a ministry. When you first start out, the glamour of it all is important to you. As you get a little older you realize to sing the gospel means seeing somebody saved. Blessing people's hearts becomes more important to you. I get tired of riding the bus but I don't get tired of singing. And the gospel is still a thrill to me. I still enjoy every time I walk out on that platform. But after 40 years the road life is harder. It don't get any easier—the older you get it gets harder. But we feel that God called us to sing and that's what we're going to do as long as we can.

Glen admits that the biggest change through the years has been "my heart."

When I first started singing I sang from the head up. But the Lord has really overhauled me and now I sing from the heart. I feel like I'm more dedicated to the cause now than I was. I'm proud to say I'm a gospel singer but I'm also proud to say that I'm a Christian. I'm a family man and I love what I do. But I also love to see people find Jesus and give their lives to the Lord. That's what it's all about.

George echoes Glen's sentiments to a large extent. He states:

I'm probably more excited about what God is doing right now than I ever have been. After 36 years I know that God is blessing and that he is the strength. It's exciting. Sometimes I feel a little guilty because I see some groups struggling and I know they're wanting to do well. But it's just thrilling to see how the Lord's working.

George, too, has seen some big changes in himself.

I like to think of myself as still being the same as I was when I started out. But, of course, I'm not. I thank the Lord I've been able to adapt myself to the different styles of music but I guess the biggest change in me has been wrought by the Lord Jesus Christ because when I started singing, I loved to sing but I really didn't know the one I was singing about. I wasn't a Christian. I loved music but I really wasn't a Christian and now, to sing the songs I knew back then when I just liked the beat and the syncopation, and to know the message is probably the biggest change.

Glen and George have been on the circuit a long time and both admit they get tired of travelling. Still, they push on because they feel it is "God's will" they sing the gospel. The road has been long and rough but it's been made a lot easier by their families, something George and Glen constantly stress. "We've always been so grateful that our families have always been behind us," said Glen. "They've been our greatest support. They pray for us. Naturally, our wives would like for us to be home more but we're home more than a lot of people think. Most of the time we have Monday, Tuesday and Wednesday at home."

George echoed Glen's feelings.

If it hadn't been for my family believing in me, I wouldn't have been able to travel and do what I'm doing with the freedom I'm able to. If my wife didn't want me to or my children wanted me at home, it would be hard to stay on the road. But she has given her utmost support to me through the years. I've got four girls and one boy and they've all said, at one time or another, 'Daddy, we believe you're doing what God wants you to do and as long as you're doing what God wants you to do, we're happy.'

The Florida Boys have also been a major force in southern gospel music for a number of years. They have staying power because of their talent, persistence, dedication, and some just plain ole stubbornness which says that no matter what the obstacles or problems, the most important thing is to keep doing what you're doing and singing what you're singing.

The group began in 1947 when J.G. Whitfield and Roy Howard formed the Gospel Melody Quartet in Pensacola, Florida. Whitfield had always wanted to sing and before World War II had sung with a group called the Happy Hitters. After the war, Whitfield and Howard put together a group that included Guy Dodd on tenor, Edward Singletary on baritone, and Tiny Merrell at the piano with Howard singing lead and Whitfield singing bass. Generally, they sang at conventions, churches, schools, and wherever else they could around Pensacola.

Tragedy struck the quartet in 1951 when, after singing at a Pensacola radio station, Roy Howard died suddenly of a heart attack. But the group kept going and in September, 1952 Glen Allred joined, playing guitar and singing baritone, while Les Beasley, singing lead, was added in the spring of 1953.

The name of the group changed to The Florida Boys around 1954. The change came because the group—still calling itself the Gospel Melody Quartet— was being promoted by Wally Fowler, who had earlier popularized the all-night sings in southern gospel. Fowler insisted the group's name was not distinctive enough and so on posters that advertised their concerts would put "The Boys From Florida." According to Les Beasley, "Wally is really the one who made us change our name. He was the biggest guy in our life as far as promotion was concerned so we went on with the change."

According to one story, the "official" name change took place one morning when Whitfield walked into a rehearsal. "Fellows," he reportedly said. "As of today, we're the Florida Boys." Les Beasley asked, "Just like that?" Whitfield replied, "Just like that. That's the only way we can do it." Nobody argued with his reasoning and from that time on the group was The Florida Boys. At this time, the group members included Beasley, Allred, Whitfield, Buddy Mears on tenor and Emory Parker on piano.

J.G. Whitfield quit the group in 1958. He had already gotten involved in promoting concerts and saw that his interest was heading more in the direction of business. So after his marriage in 1957, Whitfield turned the group over to Beasley, Allred, and Derrell Stewart, who had joined as the piano player, and settled in Pensacola with a local business.

Although Whitfield continued to sing off-and-on through the years, as well as promote concerts, his biggest contribution to southern gospel came with the introduction of *The Singing News*, the periodical for southern gospel which he began in 1969 after getting a list of 100,000 possible subscribers from his own mailing lists (for promoting concerts) and the lists of two other gospel promoters, W.B. Nowlin and Lloyd Orrell. The idea came from *Good News,* a newsletter published by the Gospel Music Association, which was then headed by J.D. Sumner.

After Whitfield left the group, there were several slow years. But in 1959 the group received a big break nationally with their 30-minute television show, "The Gospel Songshop." The group had been on local television—they had appeared on the first commercial telecast in Pensacola, Florida when that station went on the air, sponsored by Dave Trent's Used Car Lot and other local sponsors.

The Chattanooga Medicine Company had been sponsoring gospel music on radio with the LeFevres in the 1930s and 1940s and wanted to get involved in television. But the company could not get the LeFevres because this group was doing a show, "Gospel Music Caravan," sponsored by Martha White. Since the account representative for the company knew Whitfield, he approached him about doing a television show. The show played in a test market in Greenville, South Carolina on a Saturday in the late afternoon and was a huge success. So they cleaned up the show a bit—made it a little smoother—and took it national.

A deal was worked out so the Chattanooga Medicine Company purchased 31 weeks of air time a year and the rest of the year local sponsors purchased ads. This ran for several years before the Chattanooga Medicine Company quit sponsoring the show. That's when Noble Dury and Associates stepped in. Jane Doughten, a vice-president with the company, and Les Beasley came up with the concept of the Gospel Singing Jubilee, which would feature several groups on an hour-long program. They sold 15 minutes to the Chattanooga Medicine Company, and let 30 minutes be given to each local station to sell time and the show was off and running.

Later, the agency ran up against an anti-trust ruling that said you could not be a producer and an agent too so they formed a separate company, Show Biz, headed by Bill Graham, which continued to produce the show.

"The Gospel Singing Jubilee" was one of the first Sunday morning gospel singing programs and opened up Sunday morning television, which had been a dead time. The show began in 1964 and at one time was on in virtually every major television market in the United States. The show ran for twenty-five years and closed after winning a number of Dove Awards (for "Best Television Program").

The first recordings by the Florida Boys were on their own label, which was a subsidiary of King Records out of Cincinnati. The recordings were on 78s and were sold over their radio show and at personal appearances. There were also a number of transcriptions made from their local radio programs— there would be three or four fifteen-minute shows each day in Pensacola—and then they would make shows to be aired on other stations.

The first big "break" in recordings came through Bill Beasley, from Cincinnati, who had a label that recorded a number of sound-a-likes, which he sold for 33 cents apiece. The Florida Boys made some of these sound-a-likes. Then Beasley formed a gospel label called Faith and offered the Florida Boys $1000 advance per album to record. Since the group had never really gotten any money from their records before, this seemed like the big time. This was in 1959 and the group made three or four albums which were beginning to sell well.

In 1963, Jarrell McCracken, president of the fledgling Word Records in Waco, called Les Beasley to ask if the group would consider recording for Word. McCracken had seen the group on television and wanted to start a southern gospel division. And that's how the Florida Boys became the first artists signed to Canaan Records, headed by Marvin Norcross, which began Word's involvement in southern gospel.

The first big hit for the group was "There's a Leak in This Old Building," which received additional fame when Elvis Presley sang it in the movie *Love Me Tender*. That first hit happened around 1954 and their next big hit was "Surely I Will." The first album came out in 1958 and was called *The Eleventh Anniversary*. That was the first time the group had ever recorded an album's worth of material on a 33 rpm vinyl record—prior to that they had recorded single songs on 33's after recording single songs on 78's.

The gospel heritage runs deep for the Florida Boys—deeper than all the years they have been together. For Les Beasley, those roots go back to the 1930s and 1940s in the Texas and Louisiana area where he first heard the Stamps-Baxter gospel singers on radio. He soon developed a love of gospel music growing up in his father's church and always felt pulled to the male quartet sound. In 1946 he began singing with the McManus Trio in New Orleans. This husband-wife team, along with Les, did a number of Youth For Christ rallies and one-nighters all over Louisiana. After a stint with the Marines in Korea, Beasley returned to this group to continue singing gospel music.

Glen Allred began playing his guitar in 1948 with the Dixie Drifters, a country band in his hometown of Monterey, Tennessee. Later he played for the Monterey Quartet before playing guitar with the Oak Ridge Boys.

For Derrell Stewart, the summer of 1952 was a big turning point. That's when he studied piano for six weeks with James D. Walbert, whose father was an executive with the Vaughan Music Company. His first professional job was playing for the Dixie Rhythm Quartet in Dothan, Alabama before being hired by Whitfield for the Gospel Melody Boys.

The Florida Boys are among a select few—along with the Blackwood Brothers, Speers, and LeFevres (now the Rex Nelon Singers)—of groups who have survived over the long haul. Indeed, in the southern gospel world, only the Blackwoods have survived longer with their same basic sound and line-up. But the Florida Boys have shown a durability that surpasses even this group because their core members—Beasley, Stewart and Allred—have been intact since the early 1950s. That's no small achievement in a world as volatile as the music world.

Ironically, although the Florida Boys have been around a long time and made a number of significant contributions to gospel—especially in the area of television—their success has been the least acknowledged of all the early groups. They've never been as good at promoting themselves as the Blackwoods and never had a figure to rival a Dad Speer in their group. Still, their success is genuine and lasting.

A third major group in southern gospel is The Kingsmen. In an era when southern gospel, like other forms of gospel, has sought to upgrade itself and cut the ties from its rural southern heritage, the Kingsmen are unique because they cling to that heritage. Lead singer Jim Hamill refers to their music as "three chords and a cloud of dust" and it is this decision to shun pretenses and stay close to their roots that has ensured the Kingsmen of a continuing appeal.

The leader of the Kingsmen is Eldridge Fox, who decided he wanted to be in southern gospel when he was a youngster in the first grade. That was when he went to his first concert and, according to Fox, "From that moment on, my dream and my goal was to be a gospel singer and have a gospel quartet" (Coffman).

While in high school in Ashville, North Carolina, Fox formed a quartet called The Silvertones with Frank Cutshall, Charles Stoll, Jim Kirby, and Lena Elliot. In their junior and senior years they sang on weekends. After graduation in 1954 most of the members entered the armed forces, which put a halt to their gospel singing careers. Fox joined The Ambassadors, playing piano and singing lead in 1955 and 1956 before spending time in the Army in 1956 and 1957. He managed to sing with the quartet on weekends in Atlanta where they backed Wally Fowler. He also worked for Hovie Lister and the Statesmen, running their Faith, Henson, and Vep Ellis music companies.

After the Silvertones disbanded, another group formed in Ashville. Comprised of Charles Collier, Louis McKinney, Raymond McKinney, Reese McKinney and pianist Charles Mathews, the group was named The Kingsmen. Mathews, who named the group, died and was replaced by Martin Cook—later with the Inspirations—on piano.

In 1957, Charles Cutshall returned to Ashville from the Air Force and joined the Kingsmen, replacing Louis McKinney, who had been killed in an automobile accident. In 1958, Fox moved back to Ashville from Atlanta and replaced Martin Cook as pianist.

At this time the Kingsmen were weekend singers, holding down regular jobs during the week, but the group soon disbanded because of conflicts between their jobs and singing. Fox, who still dreamed of owning a quartet, bought out the other members of the group and retained the name "Kingsmen."

In July, 1970, Eldridge Fox set about putting his dream in motion, hiring Jim Hamill to sing lead, Jerry Redd to sing tenor, Ray Dean Reese to sing bass, and Charles Abee to play piano, with himself singing baritone. Fox soon proved adept at managing until he reached the point that managing the group took most of his time and he became a part-time singer, only singing with the group occasionally while handling the business the rest of the time. The group thrived, but as Fox moved out of the spotlight another figure became known as the personification of the Kingsmen on stage. That man was Jim Hamill.

Hamill was born in Big Stone Gap, Virginia and began singing lead in church when he was seven. At twelve he sang with his grandfather, aunt, and grandmother at the Tri-State Singing Convention. Then his father moved to Memphis where he pastored the First Assembly of God Church where the Blackwoods attended. Hamill got to know the Blackwoods and in 1952, while in high school, he formed a quartet with Cecil Blackwood. This group, The Songfellows, is the group Elvis Presley auditioned for and was turned down.

When Cecil left the Songfellows to join the Blackwoods in 1954 after the deaths of R.W. and Bill Lyles, Hamill attended Bible College, but soon grew dissatisfied because he was not singing. He was offered a job with a group— also called The Songfellows—in Shenandoah, Iowa and went to work for them, broadcasting over KMA. At this time Hamill was making $50 a week, performing nearly every night, as well as broadcasting two shows live on the radio each morning.

After the Songfellows, Hamill joined the Melodymen, then the Weatherford Quartet before singing with The Foggy River Boys on Red Foley's "Ozark Jubilee." After this, Hamill sang with the Blue Ridge Quartet, the Rebels, the Oak Ridge Boys and then the Rebels again until 1971, when he joined the Kingsmen.

The big change in the Kingsmen occurred when Fox decided to concentrate on the business side of the industry and asked Hamill to take over the songs and stage shows. Hamill elected to mold the quartet into an emotional, rough-edged group with a strong backbone of fundamentalism. He told the group when he was making the change that "as long as there were fundamental, Bible-believing churches we'd always have a place to sing the old-time Gospel" (Terrell 33).

Jim Hamill is a big man, larger than life with a legendary love for golf and laughter. He is proud to be "down-home" and "country folk" and that is the image he has created for the Kingsmen. It is this image, which emerges from the genuine nature of Jim Hamill, that has created a lasting appeal in southern gospel for the Kingsmen. Southern gospel's roots are in the rural south and that's where Hamill and the Kingsmen remain, ignoring the trappings of slick productions and uptown lifestyles to provide their fans with a vision of the past when quartet singing was four men on stage from the backwoods singing straight from their hearts.

Chapter 25
Sparrow Records and Keith Green

The first major contemporary Christian music label was Myrrh, begun by Billy Ray Hearn while he was at Word Records. Myrrh, a division of Word, signed acts like Barry McGuire (who had hit the pop charts with "Eve of Destruction" some years before), the Second Chapter of Acts, and others who were appealing to the youth with the gospel message. This was significant because the major gospel labels had traditionally sought to sell records to consumers in the church world—and those consumers were usually over 25. When Word put its muscle behind Myrrh and contemporary Christian music, this lent a respectability to that music and assured it shelf space in Christian bookstores, which is where consumers buy most gospel music.

After Myrrh had been launched, Billy Ray Hearn received a phone call from Los Angeles wanting to know if he would be interested in starting a new label. A number of sleepless nights later, Hearn moved to Los Angeles and began Sparrow Records. That was January, 1976 and during the ensuing years, Sparrow became a leader in contemporary Christian music through their philosophy of signing acts who were committed to ministry and who used their music as part of that ministry to reach people—young people—with the gospel.

Hearn grew up in Beaumont, Texas where he received music lessons in both the church and school (he played violin at five). He spent two years in the Navy at Pensacola, Florida after graduation and while in the service also worked in the music program of a local church. Later, he attended Baylor University in Waco, Texas, where he received a Bachelor of Music degree with a major in church music. He joined Trinity Baptist Church in San Antonio as youth and music director after graduation and stayed there four years, until he joined the Baptist Seminary in Fort Worth, where he taught music ministry and conducting. Hearn became minister of music at the First Baptist Church of Thomasville, Georgia in 1960 and stayed there for eight years, developing a large music program as well as booking contemporary music groups into his church who were touring in the southeast. Working with young people and contemporary music, he developed the musical, *Good News*, which debuted in 1968. He came to the attention of Word when the musical, a major success, toured throughout the U.S. and Europe. This led Word to invite Hearn to join their staff to help promote some musicals the company had developed, including *Tell It Like It Is* by Kurt Kaiser and Ralph Carmichael.

After three years as a contemporary label, Myrrh was coming under increasing fire by Word executives, who did not feel there was any future with contemporary Christian music and the new label was costing too much money while not generating enough income. But Jarrell McCracken, head of Word, stood behind

Hearn and the label continued. However, Hearn grew increasingly frustrated and by 1975 was looking for ways to begin his own label. That "way" jelled when he received a phone call from Seth Baker, head of the CHC Corporation in Los Angeles.

The CHC Corporation owned *Los Angeles* magazine and had begun a book publishing company, Acton House. The call to Hearn was made because they wanted to begin a record label too, and felt Hearn was the man to head it. So Sparrow opened its doors January 1, 1976 in Los Angeles with no artists.

The first artist signed was Barry McGuire, whose contract was up with Myrrh and who wanted to go with Hearn. Then the Talbot brothers—John Michael and Terry—each signed for an album, as did Janny Grein. Second Chapter of Acts—a group Hearn had signed to Myrrh and worked with extensively there—felt they should stay with the Word organization for one more album but one of their members, Annie Herring, signed with Sparrow for a solo project. These first albums were released in May, 1976.

That first year, Sparrow sold about $700,000 worth of albums, but their big break came when they signed Candle, a group organized by Tony Salerno, who produced children's albums. Hearn was reluctant to sign the group—he did not feel this music fit with Sparrow—but was finally convinced after hearing some of the material. He then created a separate label, Birdwing, just for the group. Their first album, *Chief Musician*, sold reasonably well but the first hit album, *The Music Machine*, came out the following year, 1977, after it was previewed at the Christian Bookseller's Convention in July. That album was the top seller for Sparrow during their first five years in business and instigated an avalanche of childrens' records from Christian labels.

Sparrow became an independent company in August, 1977, after the CHC Corporation had been sold to ABC. CHC offered to sell the stock to Hearn. He organized a group of investors who purchased the Sparrow stock on August 31, 1977.

Hearn's philosophy has always been "We don't sell records—we support artists" and further that "We don't sign artists unless they can become part of the family—that's a very close knit fellowship of all our artists, who support each other, who love each other, believe in each other" (See "Notes" re: quotes from Hearn).

Sparrow started small but this was an advantage because it was the one-to-one relationship they established with Christian bookstores and distributors in the early days that assured their success. In a 1978 interview, Hearn stated:

There are four or five thousand bookstores but three thousand of them aren't anything at all active in selling records and only about 500 of those sell 80 percent of our product...so we hired two kids to get on the phones and we called every store and in about three months we had 1800 accounts direct to stores on the phones and we told them the story...(the kids) were really into what we are and knew exactly what to say to the bookstore people. I've always hired very dedicated Christian people...they lived the music we were into...It's better to sell direct and make sure all of your product is in the stores...and you control your own promotion campaigns, your own in-store advertising dollars.

Hearn also knew how to control costs. He didn't spend any more in production than anyone else was spending, but noted,

I had learned how to be very tight with our budgets and I put a lot of the burden of the company on the shoulders of the artists. I was not a big fat company that had money in their eyes, I was the young no-money company that the artist wanted to succeed and so I would give them a very tight budget and they would do everything they could to produce fantastic records with very little money.

Still, Sparrow was very attentive to quality and Hearn states:

(We) gave the illusion that we spent a lot of money, but really didn't...it was very close attention to quality. I also believed in the spiritual qualities of the artist. We are very dedicated to spiritual qualities because we feel like people who buy religious records want the spiritual quality, or they wouldn't be into religious records. It takes a person who is totally involved in religious activities to buy religious records. So they need to feel tremendous spiritual quality in the record as well as technical quality.

Perhaps the artist who exemplified the Sparrow philosophy best was Keith Green, who, with his early success, put Sparrow into the major leagues of gospel music. When his first album, *For Those Who Have Ears* was released in 1977, it marked the introduction of an artist who would have a profound affect on contemporary Christian music for the next several years. More than any other artist, it was Keith Green who provided the example of ministry over everything else in his career and who inspired, encouraged, frustrated and questioned record executives and recording artists in the field of gospel music.

The lesson of Jesus, as told in the gospels, is that Christianity is a dangerous way of life. Jesus was killed, so was the apostle Paul and many other early believers. Yet, in contemporary America, Christians are in no life-threatening danger. Although some claim persecution for their faith from those who don't believe, the fact remains that, by and large, they have a very easy life and ostracism is more likely to come from within the church, not from outside in this subculture. Still, the gospel remains a loaded gun, and those who truly believe and live out their beliefs do stand apart, do face trials and tribulations, and, even in apathetic American culture where anyone can pretty much believe what they want and not face any dire consequences, have their lives threatened in a very real sense.

Keith Green was not crucified or assassinated for his beliefs—he died in a plane crash—but he personified this radical Christianity. It is almost appropriate that he died young because he seemed to put his life on the line for his faith. Keith Green did stand out for his beliefs, even within the Christian culture, and became a light to follow, an inspiration for others involved in gospel music, an example of the Christian as radical. He represented that side of the gospel music industry that says "No time for entertainment—that is frivolity. Here is The Truth! Accept it. Proclaim it. Live it."

A Keith Green concert was really a misnomer; it could hardly be called a "concert" at all. He did perform at his concerts, though it sometimes seemed it was out of a sense of obligation, a drawing card, a warm-up for the audience. In most travelling religious services, it has traditionally been customary to have some singing to start the evening. That is why Dwight Moody had Ira Sankey, why Billy Graham has George Beverly Shea. But Green was Moody and Sankey, Graham and Shea, with the emphasis on preacher, not singer. In a two and a half hour evening, Green would probably perform ten songs or less.

In one concert, Green took the stage after a few opening remarks by Winkie Pratney, a minister who was part of Green's community. When he came on stage and sat at the piano, Keith announced in a tone of urgency, "I'm here because of the broken heart of God and I hope at the end of this evening His heart will be a little less broken" before playing "How Could They Live Without Jesus." He played several more songs before stopping to talk a while from the piano. The stage held only a grand piano and a lectern. There was no band, no fancy lighting, no wall of speakers. Following a few more songs, Green sang "There Is A Redeemer" and then said, "That is the crux of the whole night."

When "There Is A Redeemer" was finished, Green left the piano bench and walked over to the lectern, opened his Bible, and delivered a full-scale sermon. He spoke from Isaiah 53, a prophetic chapter in the Old Testament which speaks in descriptive detail about the coming Messiah for Israel. It was a long, passionate talk, full of warning, rebuke, and exhortation.

There is a story that Green once came out to start a concert and, after beginning the concert, abruptly stopped in the middle of the first song and went backstage, where he lay face down on the floor praying. He would not get up and play again until he had communicated with God and felt he was ready to proclaim His message. Such was Green's dedication and commitment that he had to feel at one with God before he would go out in front of an auditorium full of people.

In revivals, it is customary to invite people to come forward after the sermon, to allow people the chance to commit their faith publicly. It is a moving scene for those who don't go forward, a life-changing experience for those who do. Keith Green invited people to come forward in his altar calls and a number did come forth. Green had established counselors ahead of time—the evening had been planned months in advance and there were training sessions for those enlisted to help—and as the people moved forward, they were directed to rooms behind the stage set aside for this purpose. There would be 10 weeks of Bible studies in homes and churches for those who came forward. Green also took up a "love offering," saying that "It didn't cost you anything to get out" but making the point, "I am not ashamed to admit we need the money and if the Lord leads you to give, please do so." At other concerts, Green made an impassioned call for missions, moving many youth to join a missionary group and serve overseas. It was a direction Green was heading when he died.

Keith Green had come through a long spiritual odyssey in his life. It has been said that he "always had a thirst for God." He was born Jewish but raised in Christian Science. He came from a musical family—his mother sang with the Dorsey bands and his grandfather with Eddie Canton—and Keith showed musical precociousness early. Beginning with the ukulele when he was three, he advanced to the guitar at five and the piano at six, writing his first song at eight and making his first record at ten. He signed a recording contract with Decca when he was eleven.

Green had an early desire to be a star in the record business, and actively pursued that goal during his early years. However, on his nineteenth birthday, after a bad LSD trip, Keith Green confronted Jesus and stated he finally saw himself as God saw him, "filthy dirty." Later that year, he met Melody Steiner, an orthodox Jew, and the two were married on Christmas day, 1973. Together they embarked on a spiritual journey, as well as music stardom, signing as writers with CBS in 1974. But in 1975, Green deepened his Christian faith with a commitment, or "surrender," as he put it, saying "Lord, I'll never play music again unless You give me the words to sing, and You give me the places to play."

It was at this point the Greens opened their home for anyone in need and began to witness "compulsively." Living in the Los Angeles area, they eventually had six houses with over 70 people involved, the beginning of their organization called "Last Days Ministries." A few years later, they reduced their number to 25 and moved to Lindale, Texas, where they established a complex that included a division for record sales as well as one for printing tracts and newsletters. The *Last Days Newsletter* was sent to over 100,000 every six weeks during the time Green was alive.

Keith Green signed a recording contract with Sparrow Records and released his debut album, *For Him Who Has Ears*, in 1977. It was an immediate, overwhelming success. In the gospel industry most acts begin with custom records, where they pay for the recording and distribute the records themselves, hoping to land a deal with a major label. Given the choice, the great majority of artists want to be on a major label. Keith Green proved here that he was not the average gospel artist.

After his initial success, Green went to his label and told them he did not want to be on the label and in the Christian bookstores—he wanted to distribute the records himself. The major reason is that he wanted to make his records available direct to consumers, free if they could not afford to pay. He felt the marketing system did not allow people to receive a free album and wanted his message available to all. This startled the gospel industry and some branded Green a "kook" for this attitude. However, his records continued to sell by direct mail in great numbers and he did indeed give away a number of the albums free. He also paid for recording costs out of his own pocket. The result was that Green went from rising young star to major influence—a man who practiced what he preached, who had the courage of his convictions, who lived what he sang. If the gospel—and salvation—are free, you cannot charge $8.98; at least Keith Green could not.

Throughout his career as a gospel artist, Green was concerned and often repulsed by the gospel music industry. He wrote, "The only music ministers to whom the Lord will say, 'Well done, thou good and faithful servant,' are the ones whose lives prove what their lyrics are saying, and the ones to whom music is the least important part of their life—glorifying the only worthy One has to be the most important!" Green recognized that many gospel artists are shallow and did not want to be like that. He also realized the audiences were often not challenged and wanted to change that. Dedicated to proclaiming "truth," it was not unusual for him to lecture an audience, reprimand them, call them "a brood of vipers" and antagonize them. But he convinced many to stop taking

Christianity lightly. This was life and death stuff and he was on a life and death mission—the gospel was the fire escape and you better get on it.

Towards his last days, Keith was beginning to mellow, trying to inject more compassion and "love" in his message and music. He was seeing the limitations of being harsh and the danger of being rash and compulsive. Though headstrong and impetuous in his manner, he was slowly changing and tempering himself.

Keith Green died on July 28, 1982. He was taking some friends on a plane ride to see the Last Days complex from the air. The twin engine Cessna 414 took off just before 7:30 p.m. with a young couple and their six children, a pilot, and Keith with two of his small children, ages three and two. The plane was overloaded and never got more than 100 feet off the ground on its thirty second flight before crashing and burning in a wooded area about a quarter of a mile from where it took off. Keith left behind his wife, who was pregnant, and a one-year-old daughter. The man who had made such an impact on gospel music by being a man of God first and a musician second died when he was twenty-eight.

Chapter 26
Music in the Church:
George Beverly Shea and Sandi Patti

The church is the cornerstone for Christianity and church music is the lasting music of Christianity; it is the songs adopted in hymnals, sung by choirs and congregations, and passed from generation to generation. The church audience is a unique audience in American music because the performances are isolated from American secular entertainment by the belief that the purpose of music is ministry, not entertainment, and that songs should change lives and be part of the Christian experience, conveying a message that will ultimately help a life and save a soul.

Singers who have appeared on evangelistic crusades with famous evangelists—like Rodeheaver and Sankey—have been major "stars" in their own right. They brought the church to the public arena and, with their singing, put the crowd in the right spirit. They were great soloists and great song leaders who delivered songs of faith to audiences comprised of both believers and non-believers. However, it was the believers who were the controlling force.

George Beverly Shea was the first international singing "star" in the church world. He achieved this position from his solos on the Billy Graham Crusades and his exposure on television, radio, and records. His songs, delivered with a reserved emotion, a controlled passion, have been assimilated into hymnals and choir books. Musically, he blazed no new paths but rather achieved his fame and position of respect by providing the church audience with traditional messages carefully encased in the tradition of American Protestant Christianity.

The son of a minister, Shea was born February 1, 1909, the fourth of eight children. He spent his teenage years in Ottawa, Canada and sang with a quartet at Houghton College, which he attended briefly before having to drop out because of lack of money during the Depression years. Shea moved to New York with his family in 1936 when his father was offered the pastorate at the First Wesleyan Methodist Church in Jersey City, across the Hudson River from Manhattan. He obtained a job as a medical secretary with the Mutual Life Insurance Company, where he worked for nine years. But he also had his foot in the door of a singing career at this time, doing 30-minute programs from 7-7:30 a.m. on WKBO in Jersey City, singing on Erling C. Olsen's program "Meditations in the Psalms" on WMCA, and taking voice lessons after work.

During his years with the life insurance company, Shea sang at weddings, in church during tent meetings conducted by Jack Wyrtzen, on radio, and wherever else he could. He also wrote the music to "I'd Rather Have Jesus" from the poem by Mrs. Rhea Miller and began singing this in services. His first recording was for Decca after talking with A & R man Jack Kapp, who offered him the proposition that "If you do better than the singer we have in mind, we will give you a contract. If not, you'll have to take the records on yourself" (Shea *Then Sings* 59). He recorded "Jesus Whispers Peace," "Lead Me Gently Home, Father," "I'd Rather Have Jesus," and "God Understands," accompanied by Mrs. Percy (Ruth) Crawford on organ. There were 500 records pressed initially and eventually 7000 were sold.

Shea's major break came when Dr. Will Houghton, president of Moody Bible Institute of Chicago offered him a job with the radio station at the school. Shea sang each week on Houghton's program, "Let's Go Back To the Bible" on WMBI and in 1939 became a staff announcer with duties that included emceeing, interviewing, newscasting, continuity writing, programming, administration, auditioning, and singing.

At that time Billy Graham was a student at nearby Wheaton College. One day he stopped by the station and told Shea how much he enjoyed hearing him sing on the program "Hymns From the Chapel" each morning at 8:15. This relationship would become valuable in the future as Graham became a major figure in American religion in the 1950s. But for the time, Shea continued doing weekend concerts around the Chicago area.

In 1942, Shea took a leave of absence to join Jack Wyrtzen for a summer of crusades in the New York area. He spent the time travelling throughout New Jersey, New York and Connecticut singing for youth rallies while also singing on WHN on Sunday mornings. When Shea returned to Chicago in September, he talked with Torrey Johnson about conducting youth meetings in that area and soon "Chicagoland Youth For Christ" was held in Orchestra hall on Michigan Avenue with Shea singing and young Billy Graham speaking. From that initial concert came the organization, "Youth For Christ International" which Torrey Johnson was to head.

Shea resigned from WMBI in 1944 to accept a position with "Club Time," a fifteen-minute radio program sponsored by Club Aluminum and broadcast weekdays over WCFL. "Club Time," which initially had a 13-week contract, continued to be renewed and was eventually put on the ABC network. It began in September, 1945 and lasted seven years. Shea's job was to host the program and sing several songs, including the favorite hymn of some famous person. It was on "Club Time" that Beverly Shea became George Beverly Shea at the insistence of the advertising agency; it seems they felt listeners were confused that a man could be named "Beverly."

When Billy Graham, then a young pastor at The Village Church in Western Springs, Illinois, took over the WCFL program, "Songs in the Night" from Torrey Johnson in 1944, he persuaded Shea to sing on the program. This lead to a lifelong friendship and working relationship that was interrupted temporarily by World War II when Graham joined the Army for a year before being released (he contacted a severe case of mumps) while Shea continued to sing on "Songs in the Night" and "Club Time." After Graham was discharged from the Army, the young preacher began preaching for "Youth for Christ" and travelled to Great Britain where he held meetings for six months all over the British Isles.

When Graham returned to the States, he contacted Shea about singing for some gospel meetings in Charlotte, North Carolina, which became the unofficial launching of his Crusades. The year was 1948 and Billy Graham had to overcome a number of obstacles, mostly connected with the bad reputation itinerant evangelists had received who attempted to follow the success of Billy Sunday in the 1920s and 1930s. The big break came in September, 1949, when the troupe brought their "city-wide" campaign to Los Angeles. The campaign received international coverage from the Hearst newspapers after the conversion of several Hollywood celebrities. Chief among these was Stuart Hamblen, a popular radio entertainer who later wrote "It Is No Secret" and a number of other gospel classics. Other celebrities who were converted were 1936 Olympic star Louis Zamperini and underworld figure Jim Vaus.

In 1951, Shea signed with RCA, where he would enjoy major record success in the latter part of the decade. Paul Barkmeyer originally approached Shea and the contract was drawn up by Sam Wallace and Elmer Eades. The first session was produced by Stephen H. Shoals and featured Shea backed by the Hugo Winterhalter Orchestra on an album titled *Inspirational Songs.* Among the songs included on this first RCA album were "Ivory Palaces," "Known Only To Him," "Tenderly He Watches," "If You Know The Lord," and "It Is No Secret."

During the first four years with RCA, Shea's records did not sell enough to pay for the cost of recording and pressing. Still, the label believed in him and continued to release recordings, produced first by Shoals and later by Brad McCuen and Darol Rice.

Shea was the beneficiary of big breaks received by Billy Graham when Henry Luce featured the evangelist in *Life,* which led to a White House visit with Harry Truman. The "Hour of Decision" radio broadcasts began on December 5, 1950 from Atlanta with the first program broadcast over 150 stations. By the fifth week, it had the largest audience of any religious program in history. By 1952, Shea was singing regularly on "The Hour of Decision" broadcasts (many of his performances were taped), and "Club Time," both national programs broadcast weekly, as well as "Songs in the Night," also a weekly program broadcast over WCFL in Chicago. In that year, "Club Time" ended and, after eight years on "Songs in the Night," Shea turned over his duties to Glen Jordan so he could devote all his energies to the Billy Graham Evangelistic Association (BGEA).

During the first Crusade abroad in 1954, Shea found a song which would be linked with him throughout his career—and the success of each owed a great deal to this connection. The song was "How Great Thou Art." The sheet music was given to Shea by George Gray, who worked with the publishing firm of Pikering and Inglis, Ltd. after a chance encounter in London on Oxford Street. Several months after his return to the US, Shea was going through his notes and found the leaflet and sang it to himself. He liked the song, as did Cliff Barrows, music director for Graham who had also received a copy. Shea performed it first at the Toronto Crusade in 1955 at the Maple Leaf Garden. The song had an immediate success.

The song was originally written in 1885 or '86 in Sweden by Reverend Carl Robert and titled "O Store Gud" (O Great God). Robert was a preacher and religious editor who died, never knowing the impact the song would have on the world. The first translation from Swedish to German had been done in 1907 by Manfred von Glehn and it had been translated into Russian in 1912 by Reverend Ivan S. Prokhanoff. It was included in a book of Prokhanoff's hymns published in 1922 (in Russian) by the American Bible Society as well as in a second book of hymns, published five years later. This second book came into the possession of Mr. and Mrs. Stuart K. Hine, a missionary couple who used the song in their woだ in the Ukraine. Hine translated the first three verses into English and added a fourth stanza in 1948; this was printed in a Russian gospel magazine published by Hine in 1949. Other missionaries saw the song and requested copies, so Hine had some leaflets printed; it was one of these leaflets which Shea received from Gray in 1954.

"How Great Thou Art" became a standard during the 1957 Crusade in Madison Square Garden, where Shea performed it with the choir 99 times during the 16-week Crusade. The average attendance for this Crusade was 19,000 per night and resulted in 14 Saturday night television programs. In the ensuing years, Shea won a Grammy and was given an award by RCA for selling over a million albums. He recorded the song three times with RCA and several times with other labels in addition to performing it countless times live. The tall, genial man became a major "star" in the gospel world through singing this and other songs in this rich bass voice. The songs he sang fit perfectly in church— a key to their success—and Shea's voice is the epitome of the great choir soloist. His exposure on the Billy Graham Crusades and in the electronic media have made him a household name in gospel circles and he became the first major singing "star" to emerge in the second half of the twentieth century, preceding (and laying much groundwork for) the boom in gospel music during the latter half of the twentieth century. It was Shea who first proved that a religious artist could reach a sizeable market recording only gospel music directed at the Christian audience whose focal point is the church.

The artist who has emerged as the leading artist in the church world in the 1980s is Sandi Patti. Like Shea, she has proven the commercial viability of someone whose music is aimed directly at the church audience rather than the pop audience, whose taste in music is governed by radio instead of the church. Along the way, Miss Patti has achieved a level of success which would rival any pop act—numerous awards, gold and platinum albums, and packed concert halls where she headlines before crowds of 6-10,000 people regularly.

Sandi Patti was actually Sandi Patty until her first album appeared. It was a custom album (she paid all the production and manufacturing costs herself), entitled *For My Friends*, and the manufacturer made a mistake and printed "Patti" instead of "Patty." Sandi decided to change her name rather than change the album cover or try to explain the mistake.

Shortly after this album was released, a record company executive called Sandi and wanted to talk with her about recording an album for a major label. It was only a few days before Sandi's wedding so she politely told him she'd rather think about the wedding and the marriage. The executive called several months later as Sandi and John Helvering were settling into their new life. In 1979, her debut album for the Benson company, *Sandi's Songs*, was released.

Sandi had her first music lessons from her mother, who was a piano teacher, and her father, Ron Patty, who was a minister of music. She made her singing debut at the age of two and a half in an Oklahoma City church choir, doing a squeaky version of "Jesus Loves Me." Later, she toured with her parents and two brothers as "The Ron Patty Family," singing in churches. At Anderson College, she was preparing to become a music teacher; however, people continued to request concerts and she obliged until she had to choose between teaching and a music ministry. She chose to sing, managed by her husband, and her music ministry took off.

Sandi's professional singing career actually began in college as a studio singer, recording commercials for Juicy Fruit gum, Steak 'n' Ale restaurants, and other accounts. Her next big progressional step was joining the Bill Gaither Trio as a back-up singer. Later, she stepped out into the spotlight as a featured solo performer during the Gaither's tours, doing "We Shall Behold Him." That song soon proved immensely popular, winning a Dove for "Song of the Year" honors (for songwriter Dottie Rambo) while Sandi captured the "Female Vocalist" award. She also toured with the Gaither Vocal Band, the Imperials, Doug Oldham, Larnelle Harris and Dino before headlining her own concerts.

Sandi became a Christian on her eighth birthday and grew up as a believer. There are no stories of intense soul searching or rebellion in her past; she accepted the Christian faith and began growing in it and that was that. This is the life she is comfortable with and those are the kind of people who comprise the audience at her concerts. Indeed, an artist like Sandi Patti is uncomfortable outside the church world, which is a major reason she could never cross over into the pop market and be either successful or comfortable.

As a singer, Sandi personifies the great church choir soloist more than the great stylist. Her voice is clear and straightforward. And it is in a church where her voice fits most comfortably, singing the songs of worship and praise that can be heard from any church choir on a Sunday morning.

It is an often overlooked fact that the music sung by church choirs on Sundays and special programs during the week reaches more people directly than any other outlet for gospel music. The publishing of this music has long been a major source of income for the industry, accounting for about a fourth of the total income of the gospel music world. This publishing industry includes not only the publishing of songs on records and the spin-off songbooks but a whole portfolio of material aimed directly at churches and their choirs. This takes the form of octavos, cantatas, musicals, collected works, compilations, instrumental sheet music and hymnals.

Gospel publishers promote and sell their music primarily through music ministers of churches—a person whose job it is to take care of all music in a church. This is a staff position and this person is responsible for the regular choir as well as specialized choirs—such as children's—and special musical programs at Christmas, Easter, and other times of the year. The minister of music is also responsible for booking outside musical groups into the church for concerts. For this he often works with a Youth Minister, whose main function is to involve the church youth with various activities and programs.

The music ministers of churches are reached primarily through workshops staged by the different publishing companies for choral readings and demonstrations of new material. At these workshops, the music ministers are usually given a sample kit of music as they gather together to sing through some of the works. From this experience they decide whether they would like to purchase this music for their church. Since these ministers purchase large quantities of each work for their choirs, these seminars and workshops are an extremely important link between the music minister and the publisher.

Publishing company representatives also regularly call on music ministers of large churches to keep them informed of their latest musical offerings. They can also contact the youth minister about new albums for listening parties or artist videos and movies.

Still, the church publishing industry and the gospel music industry are two different worlds. There is some overlapping—choirs may want to perform a hit song from an album or a musical may be a successful record as well as sheet music collection—but they remain two distinct camps. However, since the church remains the basic foundation for the Christian culture, reaching that audience has been essential for the gospel music industry. Since the beginning of the 1980s the industry has turned inward and directed its music more towards the church because the Christian record buying consumers are here.

Throughout the history of Christianity the church has remained the center of Christian life and gospel music. Although many contemporary gospel artists play in concert auditoriums, will play music that the church will be uncomfortable with, or will embrace the glitter and gleam of show biz, the bedrock of gospel music remains the church, particularly the choir. Many young Christians artists flee from the church because they want to reach a different audience, because the church does not accept their music, or because they are simply uncomfortable there. Not so with Sandi Patti; the church is her home.

The church has openly embraced Sandi, as evidenced by the number of Dove Awards she has received. She is their kind of person and their kind of singer—evidenced by the fact that, although Amy Grant has received the most attention from the secular world for gospel music, Sandi Patti has been the artist most honored within the gospel world. Her concerts (often at large churches) seem like worship services as she stands on stage, leading the service, accepting that each member of the audience believes what she believes, accepts what she accepts. She does nothing to challenge their faith; she accepts and encourages it.

Both George Beverly Shea and Sandi Patti exemplify the traditional church singer: someone who does not rock the boat musically, whose faith is traditionally Christian, and whose personality and lifestyle are conservative and harmonious with the great mass of Americans who fill the church pews each Sunday.

Chapter 27
Jimmy Swaggart

There have been preachers on television since the 1950s. But from the mid-1970s on, the big news in the Christian world was the TV preachers, who had always been the most visible part of that culture. Those preachers were, in a sense, an aberration from that culture. They were highly emotional, very dramatic, and the money they brought in and the lifestyles they lived were not the same as the typical everyday Christian. The world of TV evangelists has always been dominated by a handful of men, eight to ten at the most at any given time.

Musically, these preachers rarely break any new ground, seeing music in the traditional role of "preparing the way" for the message. As the shows got slicker in the '70s and '80s and began adopting talk-show type formats, music began to be featured more with some gospel artists appearing on the shows. However, the urge for each preacher to dominate and control his own show prevailed and the preachers all began to develop talent within their organization to appear on their programs. They could control these singers, dictate what songs they sang, what music they played, and not have to pay them much. Thus the medium with potentially the greatest influence has had little, if any, influence on gospel music.

With the exception of Jimmy Swaggart, none of the televangelists have been particularly musical, most barely able to carry a tune. Instead they have seen themselves as preachers and the thrust of their operation was themselves and their messages. Swaggart had a strong musical background and he initially built his following on his ability to play and sing, becoming well known through his records as well as through radio and television. Along the way, he became the most successful artist in the southern gospel, or country gospel vein, dominating the airwaves and selling large numbers of albums outside his own shows.

Swaggart's background is interesting because he came from the Pentecostal tradition. This tradition also provided many of the major performers in the early days of rock 'n' roll. Artists like Elvis Presley, Little Richard, Swaggart's cousin Jerry Lee Lewis, and numerous others came from Pentecostal backgrounds and the fervid emotionalism of that heritage gave early rock 'n' roll some of its most dramatic qualities. Additionally, Pentecostalism also provided a number of preachers who became successful as TV evangelists.

Pentecostalism began at the beginning of the twentieth century and it spread like wildfire across the country. It found its most receptive adherents in the south, which has a long history of revivalism and a strong streak of emotionalism in religion. Fundamentalist in nature, Pentecostalism is set apart by its emphasis on speaking in tongues or glossolalia, a prayer language that sounds like gibberish

to the non-initiated with Hebraic sounding phrases coming forth from the speaker
For the Pentecostal believer, it is proof of the Holy Spirit, the evidence tha
the speaker is one of the chosen.

A number of Pentecostal churches soon sprang up in the early twentietl
century, including the Four Square Church headed by evangelist Aimee Sempk
McPhearson, and the Assembly of God churches. It was this latter branch o
Pentecostalism which came to Ferriday, Louisiana, hometown of Jimm
Swaggart, during the Depression.

Mother Sumrall and her daughter, Leona, came from Mississippi to Ferriday
in the spring of 1936. On a vacant lot on Texas Avenue they pulled weeds anc
cleared the lot for some chairs and benches. Lee Calhoun, local big wheel
bootlegger and relative of the Swaggarts, happened to drive by in his truck on
afternoon when the Sumralls were busy fixing up the lot. He asked Mothe
Sumrall who she was and what she was doing; the evangelist replied that sh
was making a church. Calhoun replied that the town already had four churches
she countered that there would soon be five. Calhoun, always interested ir
finances, asked who would be supplying the money for this project. "God" wa:
the answer Mother Sumrall gave. After a few more pleasantries, Mother Sumral
made it plain that she was doing the will of God. Calhoun drove on.

When summer came there was a tent for the services. Mother Sumrall hac
begun preaching with just her daughter in the audience, but soon people begar
stopping by, curious about what was going on. In a short while there was a
small rag-tag congregation from Ferriday and the neighboring area. To them
Mother Sumrall preached the Pentecostal doctrine and through prayer, song
exhortation, and altar calls encouraged them to repent of their sins and giv
their life to Jesus.

The Swaggarts were not church folk, but Jimmy's father, Willie Leon wa:
always attracted to music. Pulled like a magnet to the singing in the tent, Willi
Leon was soon standing at the front playing his fiddle. His wife, Minnie Bel
played rhythm guitar and Jimmy Lee hung around, close by. It was the firs
time the family had attended church and they soon became regulars.

The tent became the Assembly of God church, built in Ferriday in 1941
financed by Lee Calhoun. It was a small wooden church, painted white witl
a cross formed from seven panes of glass in each of the two front doors. Th
Sumrall women left after the church was constructed to begin evangelistic effort:
all over again elsewhere. Tom Holcome, a young minister, came to lead th
congregation but it was soon obvious the small congregation was too poor tc
afford to pay their minister full-time. Holcome commuted to Ferriday every weel
from his day-job in Texas. This was not unusual—many ministers in the poo:
rural south had to have regular jobs in addition to their preaching duties
Preaching was a calling, but it didn't always pay well, or sometimes at all fo
that matter. Those who went into it did so for God, not for money. It wa
a test of faith.

Brother Holcome's young son died of pneumonia after he had ministerec
a short while so he gave up the Ferriday ministry after the boy's death. Holcom
was replaced by Henry Culbreth, described as a "quiet, brooding" man (Tosche
43). It was under his tutelage that the Holy Ghost arrived in full force in Ferriday
Louisiana. The Swaggarts were not there when the first fires occurred, howeve

because they had moved to Temple, Texas in December, 1941, where Willie Leon began working in a defense plant after the outbreak of World War II. Temple had grown rapidly because of the high wages paid to defense workers in the plants there. The Swaggarts who had an addition to the family (Jeanette) was soon desperately homesick for Ferriday. Jimmy Lee was seven when his family packed all their belongings once again and headed back to Louisiana.

The first Swaggart to be baptized was Jimmy Lee's grandmother, Ada. She had returned from a revival in Snake Ridge speaking in tongues and telling others about her experience. Jimmy Lee was enthralled by the stories of her experience and he spent a lot of time at her house on Mississippi Avenue.

Nannie, as young Jimmy Lee called her, had been nearly as wild as the rest of the Calhoun-Lewis-Swaggart-Gilley clan, enjoying booze, cigarettes and even some gambling. But when she came back from that Church of God camp meeting all those vices were gone. She was forty-five years old and on fire for the Lord.

Nannie's revelations shocked the family, especially Willie Leon and Minnie Bell, who had never heard tell of such goings on. And the twenty-five member congregation of the Assembly of God church where they attended branded her a fanatic and openly rejected her. Her family was openly antagonistic and skeptical; all except young Jimmy Lee who admitted, "I was thrilled about it." He kept asking her to tell him over and over again the story about "the experience."

Swaggart recounts this story in his autobiography, *To Cross a River*. She would say:

Jimmy, you know when I went to that camp meeting I was so hungry for the Lord. Those services lasted almost twenty-four hours a day. When one preacher finished, we'd sing and then another would start. The services never seemed to end. But one day I was standing outside the little tabernacle near a grove of trees praying with my brother John and his wife. The presence of God became so real. Suddenly it seemed as if I had been struck by a bolt of lightning. Lying flat on my back, I raised my hands to praise the Lord. No English came out. Only unknown tongues (27-28).

Willie Leon, concerned about the influence of his mother-in-law on the young boy and dubious about her newfound faith—would shake his head openly and say "Nannie's gone crazy over religion" and tell Jimmy Lee "She's filling your head full of junk." He finally forbade Jimmy to go over to Ada's house.

Itinerant evangelist J.M. Cason came to the little Assembly of God church to hold a revival later in that 1943 summer. At the revival was Willie Leon and Minnie Bell, Elmo and Mamie Lewis, and the Gilleys. Jimmy Lee and Jerry Lee were a few blocks away playing with their friends, Mack and Huey P. Stone when suddenly they heard a piercing scream coming from the church. Jimmy Lee instantly knew it was his mother.

At the church the young boys witnessed a powerful scene—the Holy Spirit had broken loose and was pouring itself out upon the congregation. Brother Cason was standing at the front, leading the congregation in singing after having given the altar call when Minnie Bell Swaggart let loose her howl and bolted from her seat. Mamie Lewis, who was coming back to her seat from the altar where she had answered the call, suddenly leaped in the air and turned back towards the altar. Irene Gilley (Mickey's mother) was kneeling at the altar in front of brother Cason speaking in tongues. The rest of the congregation had begun to dance, yell, sing, and howl in spiritual jubilation. Minnie Bell danced past Mamie, who had fallen to the floor, and both were speaking in tongues. Willie Leon was standing still, a huge smile on his face while he shouted at the top of his lungs. The whole church kept getting louder and louder and all the activity kept gathering speed, like a huge ball rolling down a steep hill. Everyone was in his or her own private world, moving, talking in tongues, dancing, running, shouting, waving arms, heads back shaking their hair, their bodies beyond their control. Never had that little church seen such frenzied activity and never would it be the same.

Thelma Wiggins, a woman preacher from Houston, came to Ferriday for another revival and again the Swaggarts went. Jimmy Lee made trip after trip to the altar, all to no avail. Then, on the final night of the services, something happened. It was like he was being released, like chains were coming off him and he was slipping out of a straitjacket. He began to feel light and free—all the pressure that had built up inside him began leaking out, like a steam kettle whose vapor was shooting into the air. He was kneeling down at the altar and praying, just like he had done time and time before, but things were different this time. He became aware of what seemed like a bright shaft of light coming out of heaven. It was like a spotlight and it was focused right on him.

Jimmy Lee opened his mouth and a torrent of sounds came out. The language was not the words he spoke everyday but a rushing stream of sound that felt like it was coming right from heaven straight through him. His heart was beating fast and his body was twitching and he was no longer Jimmy Lee Swaggart of Ferriday, Louisiana but an instrument of God which the Lord Almighty was playing fast and furious. His mouth stayed open and the sounds kept coming and Jimmy Lee knew that God had given him His greatest gift, the baptism of the Holy Spirit.

Jimmy married Frances Anderson of Wisner, Alabama when he was seventeen years old. By this time, Willie Leon was a Pentecostal preacher but Jimmy Lee was a wild teenager. He had quit school because he didn't like it; he had quit church because he didn't like that either. Something about other people telling him what to do just didn't sit well with the hotheaded young man. He had been doing odd jobs to pick up a dollar here and there but didn't have a steady job. He was cocky and full of fight and figured he'd make a way someway, though he didn't know how.

Jimmy's parents did not want him to get married. They knew their rebellious son would have a hard time making a living, let alone getting along with another human being in an institution like marriage. The Andersons weren't too keen either; they wanted Frances to finish high school and go to college. Those plans ended when Jimmy and Frances found a Baptist minister to marry them on a Friday night. The ring he slipped on her finger was his mother's, which he had borrowed for the occasion. Willie Leon, who could have married them, refused because he felt they were too young and knew his son to be wild, reckless, and irresponsible. It was all wrong but Jimmy was as hardheaded as they come and when he made up his mind to do something he was going to do it even if everybody else was against it.

Jimmy Swaggart began his public ministry standing outside a grocery store in a little town on a Saturday and preaching to those who had come into town to do their weekly shopping. The place was Mangham, Louisiana, where his father had been born. It was a small town, only about 500 inhabitants. Then, as always, his wife stood behind him, her strong will a support for him.

Before he stood in front of the grocery store and began preaching, Swaggart had asked the town's only policeman for permission. The man just looked at him and shrugged. Whatever you want to do, just go ahead and do it was the message he gave.

Jimmy had his accordion and he began playing. Several of the young members of the church had guitars and the rag-tag band began singing "There Is Power In The Blood." After a few more songs, as fifteen or twenty people gathered around, Jimmy began to preach. He told them about Hitler invading Poland. He told them about World War II and how America was dragged into the picture. He covered the years up to 1953. Then he told them that America was deep in sin and was coming under God's judgment. As he preached he began to sweat. His nerves showed and if you looked close you could see his hands trembling. But they were not just trembling because he was nervous—he was talking about the wrath and judgment of God and such things make a body tremble and shake. His knees felt wobbly, his collar was wet with sweat but he preached on. Louder, faster, the words came out. He knew he had said some of those things before just a few minutes earlier, but he said them again. He drove home his point with his hands chopping the air, his fingers pointing. When he finished, the policeman, who had been watching from the edge of the crowd, came up, shook his hand and said, "Son, you've got the fire." A friendly pat on the back and then a smile. "No question about that," he said. Jimmy Swaggart just stood there, drained (Swaggart 75).

Jimmy Swaggart had long dreamed of being a travelling evangelist, having been influenced by people such as Jack Coe, William Branham and Gordon Lindsay (publisher of *Voice of Healing* magazine) who were prominent in the early 1950s. Since 1954 he had been working as a "swamper" in the Franklin Parish ("oiling and greasing the dragline" Swaggart 84) and preaching on the weekends. Finally, on January 1, 1958 he quit his job and began evangelistic work full-time.

Swaggart had been approached by several gospel quartets to play piano for them but turned them down. He wanted to preach and be more than just a piano player. By 1960 he had been ordained by the Assembly of God as a preacher. He moved to Baton Rouge to be near his father after his mother's death. Because he was advertising himself as Jerry Lee Lewis' cousin, he was getting a lot of attention and offers to preach revivals. He drew crowds with his honky-tonk style of gospel playing and singing but that style also had its drawbacks and he notes that some in the church "didn't like my piano playing and singing. They thought it wasn't churchy sounding enough. There seemed to be more rhythm in it than they thought the four walls of the church could stand" (Swaggart 124).

Jerry Lee was a major star in rock 'n' roll by this time, recording on Sun Records in Memphis, the label that had also been home for Elvis Presley, Johnny Cash, Roy Orbison, Carl Perkins, Charlie Rich and others. Sun had offered

Swaggart a chance to record, too, but he turned them down, uncomfortable with the rock'n roll atmosphere. Swaggart's other cousin, Mickey Gilley, had been on Dot Records but had not been a hit like Jerry Lee so had moved to Houston to begin a club.

It was Gilley's connections in Houston that led to Swaggart's first album being recorded there. He had previously recorded one song, "At the End of the Trail," in the radio station studio in Ferriday, accompanied by his piano, a washtub bass and three girl singers. In Houston he recorded his first album, *Some Golden Daybreak*, which included songs like the title cut, "What a Day That Will Be," "He Bought My Soul" and "Stranger" (Swaggart 138).

The album did well at Swaggart's revivals and he recorded a second album the next year in Memphis at the Sun studios. The engineer for this session was Scotty Moore, who had been Elvis' lead guitar player.

This album also sold well on the sawdust trail and received an added boost from Floyd Miles and Chuck Cossin on WMUZ in Detroit when they began playing "God Took Away My Yesterdays." Orders began coming in for the album and Jimmy and his wife Frances were labeling and shipping the orders out from motel rooms and wherever else they would stop during Swaggart's preaching schedule. Several labels offered him recording deals but Swaggart turned them all down, preferring to keep creative control. Soon stores and distributors began calling him for the album on his custom label and as a result of this exposure, more people began coming to his revivals. This meant that he was now preaching revivals four to six weeks long instead of the previous one or two week long revivals.

"God Took Away My Yesterdays" was the record that opened doors for Swaggart. Soon he was preaching at Assembly of God Camp Meetings and recording more albums, which sold well at his revivals.

At the beginning of 1969, Swaggart began his radio program, "The Camp Meeting Hour" on stations in Atlanta, Houston and Minneapolis-St. Paul. Swaggart had purchased some equipment from Houston and set up a small, make-shift studio in his home to record the radio programs. He used the song "Someone To Care," which he had just recorded, as his theme song. The initial response was zero—no cards or letters—but later, after an appeal from one of the stations, Swaggart received nine hundred letters and $3000 for the program to continue (Swaggart 189).

The radio program grew rapidly and soon Swaggart moved the operations out of his home and into a building he had constructed in Baton Rouge. The radio program featured a good dose of Swaggart's music and album sales mushroomed. In 1971 "This Is Just What Heaven Means To Me" topped the charts and in 1972 Swaggart had a hit with "There Is A River," receiving exposure on radio outside of his program.

Soon "The Camp Meeting Hour" was in most major markets in the United States and Swaggart moved out of churches and into Civic auditoriums with his revivals. He added a band and bought a tractor trailer to carry equipment, also expanding his offices in Baton Rouge. In 1973 he began production of his television program.

Swaggart tried to tape the program originally in Baton Rouge and then New Orleans but the facilities did not offer him the quality he wanted. Finally, he settled on Nashville, taping the program in the same studios where "Hee Haw" was taped. The thirty-minute format featured about twenty minutes of music, ten minutes of preaching, and the rest of the time devoted to pitches for albums and announcements about his revival meetings.

By 1976, Swaggart's radio program was on 550 stations, he was selling over a million albums a year, and his operating budget was $35,000 a day.

By 1988 Swaggart was on television all over the world, broadcasting from the elaborate studios he had built in Baton Rouge. He was the founder of the Jimmy Swaggart Bible College, planning a Seminary, boss to 1200 employees, and head of an empire that was bringing in over $150 million annually. He was also the major spokesperson against contemporary Christian music.

Early in 1988, Swaggart stated in his magazine, *The Evangelist*, "I definitely feel all contemporary gospel music is inappropriate for the worship of the Lord" adding that "contemporary music" has "a meandering, dislocated melody which means, in everyday terminology, there is no harmony" ("Brother Swaggart..." 9) To those who insist that contemporary music attracts an audience to hear the gospel message—an argument Swaggart used for his own music in the 1960s— he answered in 1988 that "sacred music was never meant by God to draw the unsaved or to address itself to the unsaved...The *primary purpose* of music is to *worship God* (italics are his) (10). He concluded that contemporary music will lead to "spiritual death" because "the melody is...discordant; consequently it affects the harmony and it would be totally impossible for people to worship God with it" (10).

In early 1988, Jimmy Swaggart achieved national notoriety for "moral failure" and was suspended for three months from preaching. Eventually, he resigned from the Assemblies of God Church to continue his TV shows, crusades, and worldwide evangelism.

More than any other musician and singer in the 1970s and 1980s, Jimmy Swaggart used the media—especially television—to take his music and his message all over the world. He is an important figure in gospel music because he is a musician and a preacher, unlike the "teams" of Moody-Sankey, Sunday-Rodeheaver, or Graham-Shea, Swaggart has been able to be a musician and a preacher. He is a man who has combined the elements of early rock 'n' roll, southern gospel, country music, and Pentecostalism to present a music that has appealed to a number of people. And, through his outspoken views against contemporary Christian music, Swaggart became a controversial figure, opinionated, but influential among those who share a distaste for contemporary music but do not have the platform or are unable to articulate their views.

To a large degree, the music of Jimmy Swaggart has played a major role in him becoming the most widely known, seen and heard evangelist in the twentieth century, opening doors for him in this country as well as other countries around the world.

Chapter 28
Country and Gospel:
Johnny Cash and Barbara Mandrell

Gospel has often been cited as the long tap root amongst the roots of country music. As twentieth century country music began to evolve from the British ballads and folk music transplanted in the south to the commercially recorded music of the middle of the century, gospel songs were an integral part of the music. The mostly rural people who gave birth to early country music considered religion an important part of their life, thus gospel songs were as much a part of their heritage as the secular songs. Early field recordings reflect this as many groups and individuals often recorded gospel and country songs from the same repertoire. However, as early "hillbilly" music, as it was called, began to become more commercially successful, some differences emerged. First, there was the problem among some members of the audience from mixing the sacred with the secular; second, as country music emerged as a music for honky tonks and beer joints, there was a reluctance by these patrons to hear a gospel song on the jukebox because of the conviction or guilt it would bring. But more importantly, there emerged two different markets for gospel and country which drew influences from each and occasionally intertwined but were, by and large, separate.

Still, a number of country music performers acknowledge their gospel roots by recording some gospel songs, or even gospel albums, and including gospel songs in their stage shows. In the early 1970s, one of the most successful acts in southern gospel music, the Oak Ridge Boys, signed with the Nashville division of CBS and attempted to record gospel music for the country market. They reasoned that a music this popular—they were selling over 100,000 copies of each album—would find a home on country music radio and with the country consumers. After several years of near starvation, they were proven to be resoundingly wrong and had to choose between returning to the gospel market via a gospel label or recording country songs for a country label. They chose the latter.

Reflecting on that decision, ex-Oaks member Bill Golden stated, "Rather than sit around and fuss and fight and argue with certain people in those situations, we decided to expand our music and deal with the other six days of the week...Some people didn't want to be reminded of a Sunday message on Wednesday" (See "Notes" re: quotes from Oaks). Duane Allen continued: "Just as you move from one house to another and just as you occasionally change from one job to another, we made a step to country." Both men admit that, financially, there was much more money in country music for them as well

177

as less conflict in their stage show. Golden states, "The gospel business got to a point that they started demanding that they want to know all these things on all the people in the group, like testimonies and all those things, and I just can't pretend to be any better than anyone else. I just loved the music and what the music does." Golden further admitted that he had never been "born again" or felt particularly religious and as southern gospel began to demand more ministry and not just entertainment, he felt uncomfortable. However, Allen stated that religion is still a major part of his life, though not in the same public way, and that he felt comfortable with it this way.

One country artist who has made a strong public stand for his Christianity is Johnny Cash, although he has never left the country music field to devote himself totally to gospel music. For Cash, gospel music is important because of his boyhood roots as well as his current life.

Johnny Cash grew up in a strong, Christian home and was a dedicated, conscientious and practicing Christian during his childhood and early adult life. He grew up in Dyess, Arkansas, during the Great Depression; his father was a sharecropper on a 40-acre government project. There were seven children in the family, and young J.R. (he became John when he joined the Air Force and needed a first name, then became Johnny when he released his first record and the label thought it sounded more appealing) was especially close to his older brother Jack, a very devout youth who died at the age of 14 in a sawmill accident.

Cash graduated from high school and went to Detroit where he worked briefly in an auto assembly plant. Then he joined the Air Force spending most of his tour in Germany. Here, Cash bought his first guitar and learned to play, singing old country songs he heard on the radio and old gospel songs he remembered from his youth in the church.

In 1955, Johnny Cash and the Tennessee Two—bass player Marshall Grant and lead guitarist Luther Perkins—formed a gospel group. Living in Memphis and working as an appliance salesman and at other odd jobs to support his wife and daughters, Cash sought an audition with Sam Phillips at Sun Records. Phillips and Sun were already a minor legend with their early rockabilly recordings and the growing popularity of Elvis Presley, Carl Perkins, Jerry Lee Lewis and Charlie Rich. Cash camped in Phillip's office until he was given an audition.

Phillips had already tried to sell gospel and had been unsuccessful so he was reluctant to repeat that effort. After being turned down, Cash went home and began writing and practicing some country songs. He returned to Phillips for another audition with his country material and was signed to Sun Records, where his first record—"Hey Porter" backed by "Cry, Cry, Cry"—was released on June 21, 1955.

Other hit records followed and then he hit the road. Cash was still a strong Christian and determined to stay that way. His first big hit, "I Walk The Line," was about marital fidelity. But during the ten years that followed his initial recordings, traveling took its toll, and Cash backslid into drugs (primarily uppers and downers) and into a very unchristian life.

My policy of aloneness and severed fellowship from other committed Christians weakened me spiritually. Not that missing church necessarily meant missing God. It was just that Jesus never meant for us to try and make it on our own. There is something important in worshipping together with other believers. And missing it left me vulnerable and easy prey for all the temptations and destructive vices that the backstage of the entertainment world has to offer. (Cash stated in *Man in Black*, 87)

By 1967 Johnny Cash had destroyed so many hotel rooms that some hotel and motel owners refused to rent rooms to country acts. His body was emaciated—all skin and bones—and he looked like walking death. He was downing an incredible number of pills and staying up for days at a stretch. He was sometimes incoherent on stage. Home was a Nashville apartment he shared with Waylon Jennings. When one or the other forgot the apartment key he broke the door down.

June Carter was the girl singer on Cash's road show at the time and she had been fighting the pills. Said Cash:

The one person who could get to me and talk to me when no one else could was June Carter, and everybody knew it. And when the pill habit got really bad, she started fighting it because she could see what it was doing to me...In the name of God, she claimed my recovery which she began fighting to bring about...June was never afraid of me, and she was serious about the battle she was waging against the pills. 'I'm just trying to help,' she'd say. 'God has His hand on you, and I'm going to try to help you become what you are whether you want me to or not.' (Cash 118)

Finally, Cash gave up. He was found hugging a tree, nearly frozen, beside the tractor he had been driving near an icy lake below. After that, June Carter and her parents—E.J. Carter and Mother Maybelle—moved in with Cash and gave him emotional support. June chased the pushers away and a friend, Dr. Nat Winston provided professional counseling. Day after day and night after night, Johnny Cash fought the demons of drug addiction. Many times he wanted to give in but he was buffered by the support he was receiving from the Carters. Finally, in November 1967, Cash emerged and gave his first concert without the support of pills, an important victory.

The next year, 1968, Johnny Cash married June Carter in March. He kicked the pill habit and vowed to again live a Christian life. In 1969 he recorded "A Boy Named Sue" and began working on a weekly show on ABC-TV that made him a household name. At the year's end, he swept the Country Music Association Awards Show, winning five of those awards (the only artist to do so) and two Grammy's. In 1971 his son, John Carter Cash, was born and Cash formally committed his life to Christ at the Evangel Temple. He quit his TV show (which prominently featured young singer-songwriters such as Kris Kristofferson, as well as gospel music) because of network interference with the content.

In the years since 1971 Cash has continued to tour, record and be a Christian witness. He wrote and produced the movie, *Gospel Road*, now distributed by Worldwide Films. In his autobiography, *Man In Black*, and in 1980 he was elected to the Country Music Hall of Fame. He also wrote a novel about the apostle Paul titled *Man in White*.

Cash said:

I just hope I sow the proper seed wherever I go. I'm not a gleaner. I'm not so much of a gleaner because if you really want to get into religion, I believe people who have a need, if we touch them and show them how that need can be fulfilled, then the Holy Spirit will do his work. It's up to Him to do the gleaning anyway, not me. I don't think that a human being should take the credit for the Holy Spirit's work. I can't see where a preacher should boast saying, 'I've had 71 converted in my church last week.' He is giving himself and the church credit. I think the credit should go to the Holy Spirit. Because there is no conversion without the Holy Spirit's work. (See "Notes" re: Cash quotes not documented)

Cash admits that fame carries burdens and obligations he must face. He said:

I do have an obligation with that fame. That fame has its price. It has a lot of pride and a lot of fees that have to be paid. Fame has its price for sure. You have a lot of obligations. I wrote a song called 'Sit On The Porch and Pick On My Old Guitar.' One day I was up at my farm in Bon Aqua (Tennessee) and I was so tired from touring and everything, I just couldn't see where I'd ever want to do anything the rest of my life but sit on my porch and pick my guitar. It doesn't take but a few hours of that for me to get bored, and then I want to get back where the action is.
I enjoy the obligation and the responsibility. He said, 'To whom much is given, much will be required.' I'm all set to try to fulfill those requirements. I got my head on straight and I still have a lot of strength left in this body. I don't feel any ebbing of energy or strength, so far as it is required to do my job. Of course, I'm not saying I feel 25. I don't. My daddy is 83 years old and probably has more energy than I do. I think I inherited it a lot from him. I feel like I have a little staying power. I've been told that I do. I never lose interest in my work, never. I think about it all the time, about my work and what I'm going to do here and there, this and that move. I do pray for guidance and I get it.

Johnny Cash tasted the sweet glory of success as well as the bitter defeat of drugs in his life. During those dark days, however, Cash never really turned his back on the truth and never totally left his Christian beliefs. He stated:

I never really turned my back on it, inside personally. So far as the world was concerned it looked like I had. But, I never turned my back on it, and I was always susceptible to communication with God. I was in Nickajack Cave in Chattanooga once, and I was in there alone, and I just laid down and said, 'Go ahead and take me. I'd just as soon die than be like this.' I felt a warm, sweet presence and that silent inner voice said, 'You're not going yet Cash. I got work for you to do. You can't die yet.' I then felt a complete peace because I knew I was not abandoned by Him. It was just I was struggling with human temptations and problems. I felt Him waiting. If it was going to be three months or three years, I felt His patience waiting for me, and smiling at me and my human weaknesses and waiting 'til a time of strength and renewal came from Him.

Nearly every country artist has done a gospel album, or at least expressed an interest in doing one. There are several reasons—spiritual as well as materialistic—for this. But the major reason is probably the deep-seated faith that rests in the hearts of many country music artists.

Ironically, it is a faith at odds with that of most contemporary country music. Country artists do songs about cheating, drinking, hurting, and loving because they are a reflection of life. Many do gospel music for the same reason. For them, the Gospel is part of life too—an important one to be sure—but one often relegated to once a week or in times of need.

Gospel is the conscience of country music, and woven into the hell-raisin' shenanigans many country artists sing about is the thread of belief in God and the forgiveness of sins. They seem to admit their sins and hope for a righteous life while at the same time confessing they can't obtain it. So the vicious cycle of sin and salvation spins round and round.

Country music star Barbara Mandrell is obviously aware of the dilemma of having Christian faith in a secular world. She has been untouched by scandal, married to the same man for over twenty years, and she is known throughout the industry for being hard-working, "straight," and a Christian. She featured gospel songs on her network television show, in her concerts, and she has recorded an all-gospel album. And she always professes to live her faith even while she is singing about some unchristian ways of life.

The question obviously arises about whether performing country music conflicts with her Christian beliefs. "No, not at all," she replies. "The guys that were out here to my house a few months ago fixing my swimming pool or the guys here painting the house don't just work on Christian homes. Where you witness is not really in church" (See "Notes" about quotes from Mandrell).

The biggest thing I have learned in the last few years is not to judge others and I don't, so I can't say it for anybody else but I really feel like if He meant for me to be totally in gospel music, that is where I would be. Because He doesn't pull any punches with me. Besides, I reach so many, many people, and I don't say this in any ugly way—I am just stating fact—that I would never reach if I were not a secular singer.
In concert, I average about 10,000 people a night and I always do at least one gospel song during those performances. In a television show I reach 3 to 4 million people. My mind is just not capable of comprehending those numbers—even if I took off my shoes I couldn't count that many. But the mail I get, especially from teenagers and young people who turn to me—and I don't know why—but I have thought about it and maybe it's because they see me as 'not a square.' I'm fun, I'm silly and I allow people to see me get a pie in the face or be bald on TV or do all these things so they know I am fun and that I enjoy life. And then, when I sing the gospel songs, they see something in my eyes that lets them know I mean what I am singing about. I think that is why they turn to me. I've had kids who have gone back to church, that have gotten over family problems. Do you think they would have tuned into me had I been on a 'gospel' music show?

Through the years Barbara has done a number of "bedroom" songs such as "Woman to Woman," "If Loving You Is Wrong (I Don't Want To Be Right)," "Midnight Oil" and others. Isn't there a conflict with her faith in doing these songs?

"I don't condone it, but I agree with the lyrics. They're about things that go on in this world." She paused, then explained further.

What I do is sit back and listen as a fan, and it's how the song, the lyrics, melody, the whole thing hits me. I am real big on first impressions. Then I use my judgment as to whether I think it's got a viewpoint. Is it in good taste? There have been songs I have turned down because they were not...perhaps they said the same thing but they were not in good taste. It is whether or not I think it will be a hit.

You see, I don't record for me. I am a public servant and I record—we are talking about my music and not my gospel music. The gospel album is where I put my foot down and said, 'This is an exception. I am making this album for me.' But with my other music I am simply trying to be a commercial success, and by being a commercial success I know that I am doing my job.

I am not some brilliant, philosophical person. I am not trying to get great teachings through my music. I am just trying to do one thing and that is to entertain.

Indeed, Mandrell works hard as an entertainer, perfecting her show and performing extensively. She said:

I am very ambitious. Some people think it is very good. All the upbringing I ever had, even in terms of spiritual life, is that hard work never hurt anybody. This is respected. You can want, but He gives you the talent and ability to go for it.

I know when I saw my son for the first time work out in his karate class, I saw how difficult what he was doing was, and I saw how well he was doing at it. I smiled and was réally proud of him. And I think that my Heavenly Father is proud of me like that when I do something.

Barbara's born-again experience occurred when she was a child. "I believe I was ten," she said.

I can't place the time exactly but I remember the experience vividly. I was raised basically what people call Pentecostal, but I was saved in a Lutheran church. It was in Lancaster, California, and we had gone because we liked the minister there. I guess I had reached that age in my life as a child when I realized what it was all about. There was a visiting missionary in the church talking to all of us about the crucifixion and why Jesus died for us. Then he said, 'What are you going to do for Him?' And it just really hit me for the first time what it was all about. I wasn't sitting with my parents at the time, I was with some girlfriends and a boy at that point. But in your life at the moment you don't care who is looking, you just get up and do it.

Talking about her music and her faith she said:

Different music gives me different feelings as vividly as if you were to say something to me to spark an emotion. But with gospel music, the music itself sometimes can touch me more deeply than even a really good sermon with a really good message. And I am hungry for that message, and I find a growing need everyday. I don't know if it is because of my age, my maturity, or what. I don't know what it is.

Maybe it is because the more you learn, the more you want to know, and the more you want to grow as a Christian. We have cable TV in our house and I often find the Christian channel is such good food for thought. I have heard some good music, too. We socialize with my minister and his wife and very often the topic of conversation has nothing to do with music or Christianity. See, you are not just a Christian when you are talking about it. I don't respond to what other people tell me I need to be. I only respond to however He leads me.

But the point is, the Lord didn't tell me...and I don't care about anyone else, that isn't my concern...The biggest thing I have learned in the last few years is not to judge others. I have trouble enough just taking care of me and keeping myself straight and doing what I'm supposed to do. I just thank goodness that He loves me enough to forgive the things I do that aren't right.

Barbara admits a general disdain for denominations. "I have been to Methodist, Episcopal, Catholic, Baptist and Presbyterian churches," she said. "I was raised Pentecostal, but I was married in a Presbyterian. I am not big on denominations, period. I am just hungry to be around any church where it is for real—where they put Him first instead of doctrine or buildings and offerings."

Barbara doesn't often speak out publicly on abortion, gun control, nuclear war, foreign affairs, the interest rates or any other political issue.

She said:

First of all, I think it is very bad business. And also I feel quite honestly, who am I? Where do I get off telling somebody else who they should vote for or what we should do about ...Now, I feel that I have every right to vote, and I exercise that right. I have a right to my opinion and I am very opinionated, but I would never begin to impose those ideas on other people. I don't think it is right for me, and I am to speak out, that is fine. I can only answer for me in what I do, and I don't feel like that is anybody's business.

Barbara dislikes controversy intensely, and the thing that probably upsets her most is being in the midst of unrest and controversy. Yet, at the same time, she has taken a stand for her faith that sets her apart from many of her cohorts in country music, while maybe not endearing her to those who have given their talents totally to Christian music. It could easily turn out that Barbara finds dreaded controversy both from Christians and the secular world from the very thing that brings her strength and comfort—her faith.

Some in Christian music would argue with her about the choices she's made— some of her decisions and opinions and, perhaps, some of her beliefs. However, she doesn't ponder those things about the people in Christian music. She has learned "never to judge others" and she is content to let the Lord work as He will in other lives, even if it is a completely different way from her own life.

The question finally came about what she would like to be remembered for. She thought a few moments, then replied,

Making people smile and tap their toes. Making them forget anything that may be bothering them for the length of time that I have gotten their attention. I want to be remembered as an entertainer.

Chapter 29
Amy Grant

Amy Grant's concert crowd and record buyers are composed primarily of churchgoers, but they are not from Puritan stock; the closest they come to Calvin is having designer jeans with that name on the hip. She does not water down her Christianity but has made it more palatable by being straightforward and unembarrassed by it, as a matter-of-fact aspect of her everyday life. Furthermore, she doesn't just talk about it, she honestly believes and lives it.

Amy's Christian faith is at the center of her life and spills out in her private conversations, her public performances, on her records and oozes through her whole career. She does not feel that she compromises her faith as an entertainer; still, she has not let the traditional church put a barrier around her career like it has done to so many others.

Amy had sung in front of a crowd only once in her life before she was signed to Word Records—the CBS of gospel music. That appearance was at a school chapel service when she was 15. She had begun writing songs to share her faith with friends and schoolmates, openly admitting "the Lord was the author." She did not dream of bright lights, a record deal, touring to packed concert houses, or hearing her tunes blaring from the radio or stereo speakers. She really did not know enough about the record business to even be aware of these fine points.

Growing up in Nashville, Amy was part of a high school Christian fellowship headed by Brown Bannister. Brown worked with Chris Christian at Home Sweet Home Productions and they had just begun their association with Word Records producing acts, the first being B.J. Thomas. A family friend of Amy's wanted a tape copy of her songs so she asked Brown—and Brown agreed—to let her put them down in the studio as a favor. He had heard her sing some songs once and was impressed by her sincerity and ability to communicate through music.

Once the songs were on tape, Brown became excited at the result and played them for Chris Christian, who also became excited and called the head of A & R at Word. Word Records had just signed an agreement with Christian where he would bring several new acts to the label, so Amy became the first act in that deal. Myrrh Records, a division of Word, signed her to a recording contract when she was 15 years old after hearing a tape played over the phone.

Amy was not a performing artist, an accomplished songwriter, or a known personality; she was a schoolgirl. She did not have to audition, play songs for producers, call label executives, send press kits or any of the number of activities would-be artists engage in attempting to land a recording contract. Amy Grant was simply a high school student trying hard to be a good Christian and to communicate what she believed to be His message and His love through some songs to her high school friends. With the release of her first album, the songs immediately became hits on radio—"Old Man's Rubble," "What a Difference You've Made in My Life" and "Beautiful Music." Meanwhile, the record label were caught by surprise that this high school kid might have a hit on her hands. At this point, Amy's father hired an independent promoter to call radio stations and help the album along.

Gospel radio has always been a rather strange animal when compared to secular radio. Although there are a few nonprofit stations, most gospel stations are commercially licensed by the FCC, just like all others. However, because the audience is so small (gospel radio accounts for about 2 percent of total radio in America) they cannot attract big advertisers. They depend upon selling broadcast time to "preaching and teaching" programs—blocks of time (usually 15 to 30 minutes) to local or national preachers and figures in the Christian world who have their own shows. These people often ask for donations, which in turn serves to pay for the time. It has been an economic necessity for gospel radio to do this to stay on the air. Gospel radio views itself as a ministry and a certain part of their audience tunes in regularly to these programs.

Gospel radio is also stubbornly independent. Until the 1980s, they had refused to acknowledge national trade charts and instead programmed what they felt to be effective for their audience. This is in marked contrast to secular radio, which keeps a close eye on the charts and whose local playlists often reflect the national trade charts from *Billboard* and other magazines. Gospel radio has traditionally demanded albums instead of singles and the prerogative to choose which cuts to play. There is little regulation about rotation, so the disc jockeys are often free to choose what cuts to play and when. This has meant a listener could hear a song on the radio once and not hear it again for several weeks. Or a song could be doing very well at some radio stations, but not heard on others. It was quite likely that three different radio stations would be playing three different songs from an album. Because airplay was so scattered, it was very difficult for an artist to become well known through gospel radio. Before Amy Grant came along, few if any, gospel artists had achieved popularity primarily due to radio airplay. The others usually did it by extensive touring over a long period of time. For Amy Grant to have three hit songs on gospel radio was a remarkable achievement and one that propelled her from oblivion to an almost overnight success. The gospel industry sat up and took notice.

With a surprisingly successful first album under Amy's belt, there was a demand for a follow-up. By this time, Word Records had gotten the hint and was figuring out ways for the album to get maximum support. They made it a priority release and it was named "Album of the Month"—an almost unheard of event for an artist who had only one release.

The second album had attractive pictures of Amy on the front and back covers and was filled with excellent songs. Titled *My Father's Eyes*, a song that has since become a trademark, the album also had great production, thanks to the expertise of Brown Bannister. At this time, Brown and Amy had a unique relationship—they were young producer and young artist as well as young man and young lady who had eyes for each other. These albums were a labor of love in more ways than one. Later, the eyes didn't have it and Brown's and

Amy's relationship developed into a strong friendship and solid professional relationship as each married someone else. Still, those first albums reflect an artist/producer relationship that was deeper than just a working studio relationship.

On the second album, Amy emerged as a songwriter, writing four of the songs herself and co-writing another four with Brown. She also included the song, "O Sacred Head," an old hymn she recorded with her three sisters. In the background of this track you can hear rain and thunder. The way and manner the storm got on this cut constitutes a minor miracle in itself.

It was four in the morning at the studio and everyone was bone-weary tired, exhausted and calling it quits when someone remarked it was raining outside. Brown immediately decided that a touch of the natural element was what the song needed. He took a studio microphone and placed it outside the door. Turning on the recording machine, the thunder rolled just as the song began, rumbled a bit during some key phrases in the middle and, as the song ended, rumbled once again to provide a perfect ending to the recording.

When *My Father's Eyes* was released, Amy was a college student at Furman University in South Carolina. Later, she transferred to Vanderbilt University in Nashville for her last two years, but stopped just short of graduating with a degree in English. While in college she made occasional appearances on weekends, touring full-time only during her summer vacations.

The daughter of a physician, Amy Grant grew up in Belle Meade, a wealthy suburb of Nashville. She attended private schools and, growing up in a strongly religious family, accepted Christianity at an early age. It was in the seventh grade, at a Wednesday night church service, that Amy "just felt that I needed to make a commitment to the Lord and be baptized so I did, but I really didn't know or understand all that it meant at the time" (See "Notes" re: quotes). About two years later, in high school, there were "some feelings of rebellion" within her personal life and she felt a little mixed up—she had committed herself to the Lord yet really didn't want to live with that commitment. This was when she became involved in the high school fellowship with some others from her church headed by Brown Bannister. "It was here I started hearing about 'quiet time' and 'worship' and 'prayer time' and it really turned me around because I realized I should be spending quality time with the Lord drawing closer to Him—and I hadn't been doing it," she said. It was right after this she began writing songs, and, then, a year later, recording them.

Amy has been privileged in many respects. When her first album began to receive attention her father paid an independent promotion person to help— an advantage many beginning Christian artists can not afford. Later, when she began to tour with a full band, her father again provided financial support— a necessity since her first two major tours lost money. However, they generated a lot of excitement and a gospel artist touring with a full band putting on a first-class show won her a huge following. Still, most gospel artists could not afford the initial investment required for this groundbreaking move.

As her second album was released, Amy's brother-in-law, Dan Harrell, was joined by Mike Blanton, who was the head of Word's Nashville office and instrumental in orchestrating the marketing of the second album, to form a management firm with Amy as the first artist. It is rare for a gospel artist to have management. Both Blanton and Harrell are extremely qualified and dedicated and have made a mark on Christian music with their management organization. However, they also had the advantage of being underwritten by Dr. Grant, allowing them the money and time to develop as managers—an advantage many such firms don't have.

With strong management and crucial financial backing, Amy has been allowed to concentrate on her songwriting, recording, and performing while the details of her business affairs are in trusted hands. The management company has pursued additional opportunities for her—such as major TV appearances. Amy is surrounded by what few gospel artists—but most major superstars themselves have—a complete career development team. Yet is is talent that counts and she has an abundance. The direction planned by her management company was for exposure in the secular field and they viewed her as a Christian entertainer, rather than a minister. Still, she remains with a gospel record label and, until 1986, about 90 percent of her records were purchased in Christian bookstores. A large degree of her initial success came from making a concentrated and successful effort to reach the youth involved in churches—not by tapping the traditional youth market or rebellious teenagers. And while she seems to have a broad appeal, her primary market still seems to be the Christian yuppie.

Growing up in the public eye took its toll on Amy, but she weathered the storms and learned to handle herself well. She said:

When I started seeing articles written about me, I read every one. But I don't read them anymore. From the time I was seventeen and a half until my nineteenth birthday, I went through an identity crisis because I was claiming something I hadn't laid hold of yet. I was splashing around in a big ocean. I didn't accept myself and something as nebulous and insignificant as a young girl coming up to me at a concert and saying, 'You're not half as pretty as your album covers' or 'Why can't you be more like Evie' or arriving at a concert and performing hideously on just a piano and guitar and not sounding like my records—it all seeped into my personal life and suddenly I was a basket case. I'd go to a party or social group and I wouldn't quite feel comfortable until someone acknowledged I'm a singer because it gave me worth in this life. I would feel a burden to make everyone feel comfortable because if anybody went away uncomfortable and I was there, I felt responsible because I was the public figure. I felt a burden to have everyone like me. And what made me so insecure was reading magazine articles and seeing the image of Amy Grant and then I would look inside and think, 'I'll never measure up to that.'

Self-confidence and self-acceptance was a big change in Amy's life. "It's hard growing up when you have an audience," she reflected. "I'm so glad I was encouraged to just be myself. That's what my parents told me the first time I got on stage—just be myself." Being a Christian celebrity had had its drawbacks as well as rewards. "I get tired of Christians trying to tell me what being a Christian is," she stated. "I get tired of that kind of Christianity. I don't mean that in a disrespectful way, but it's especially true in the college-age group. We have such a regimented idea of what Christianity is. Sometimes I feel like Christians are boxing themselves in. The way we talk about Christianity is so much less than what Christ is."

Amy has also learned to accept other drawbacks in public life. She said:

There are people who are not going to like me. So many times from stage I've said 'God is my audience.' But just recognizing the fact that I'm going to walk into a crowd and some people are going to say, 'The big haughty jerk. Got a record contract when she was 15 and she's conceited, selfish, and self-centered.' I don't need to worry about that. I've been scrutinized and picked apart so much that I hope I don't do that to other people. I remember the story in Matthew when Jesus asked a man something and the gospel states 'seeking to justify himself he said.' Reading that made me realize that all my life I had been seeking to justify myself. I think of all the times Jesus was accused of things and He didn't make a move to say 'you're wrong.' I think there's a fine line between still being sensitive and loving and not seeking to justify yourself and turning your back on people and saying 'I'm just going to live my own life.' That's not what Jesus meant for us to do.

We give our hearts to Jesus and He makes our life a thoroughfare. He says, 'I'm going to walk everybody and their dog through your life and the only way I can do that is because I'm doing miracles in you. I want them to see Me in you.' As we let ourselves be led by the Lord, He'll rip us open for everyone to see.

Somehow, being a singer whose name has become one of the hottest items in popular music seems rather far removed from the young lady who expressed those thoughts, but Amy is aware of her calling and aware of the power of mixing the music and the gospel. She said:

Through music, God is making strides in the Christian world. It's teaching people to worship. Singers walk into battle with their armor on. They can get into a concert hall with people who have had hideous days and sing a worship song and the Lord is there and Satan is chased away. Suddenly, all those people are freed up to be ministered to by the Lord.

Possibly the biggest change in Amy's life occurred when she married Gary Chapman. Musically, as well as spiritually, he has been a great influence on her and some of her more recent music adventurism can be attributed to him.

"Father's Eyes" was the first hit Gary Chapman wrote. It was, coincidentally, the first major hit for Amy Grant as an artist, the song that established her as a major gospel recording act. The two met at a listening party where the album was previewed.

Chapman hails from DeLeon, Texas, where his father was a minister. He attended Southwestern Assemblies of God College in Waxahachie, Texas, before joining The Downings, a southern gospel group, as a guitar player. That was his first move to Nashville but four months later moved back to Texas. He had met some members of Buck and Dottie Rambo's band so when an opening occurred in that group, they called Gary. At the time, it was August and Gary was planning on going back to school. But, he said, he figured the Bible college would be there longer than the job so he took the job.

It was while playing guitar for the Rambos that Gary came under the influence of Dottie Rambo. "I was really captured by the way Dottie constructed her songs," he said. "I never knew there was that much to it. It's like the words are all there and you just have to get them in the right order" (See "Notes" re: quotes from Chapman). Chapman calls Dottie "a genius" as a songwriter and she inspired him to try his hand at writing songs.

Chapman went on tour with Amy Grant, serving as an opening act in 1980. Soon romance developed and he was pushed off her concert package because of a rule imposed by Dan Harrell, Grant's brother-in-law and manager, about mixing business with pleasure. Amy and Gary had an on-again off-again romance until one night she ran into him at a movie. She wanted to talk and the two decided their friendship was more important than the romance. Ironically, the romance bloomed again as Gary became part of the Grant entourage and in June, 1982, the two were married.

The two did not click immediately in marriage—Amy had never left the privileged home where she grew up while Gary had been on his own a number of years before they married—but, as they now admit, they "learned how to fight."

Within Christian music there is an endless debate on entertainment vs. ministry. Should the role of a gospel artist be to entertain an audience or should it be to minister the gospel? Is a gospel artist really a "Minister" or an "Entertainer" who is a Christian? This debate has caused problems within the gospel community since artists—who must be entertaining before a crowd and use the tools of show biz like promotion and publicity—try to be a little of both and all of neither. Amy Grant is the first gospel artist to be comfortable as a Christian entertainer, openly admitting the entertainment aspect of her career and throwing off claims to be first and foremost a minister to a record-buying congregation.

Other artists have felt uncomfortable as entertainers, thereby limiting themselves to the Christian sub-culture, unable to break out of a market that often has an underlying philosophy that anything fun or enjoyable must be sinful or at least avoided. Amy is far less inhibited in her career, less narrow in her vision of Christianity, and more at home in the youth culture that has made entertainment a need rather than an extravagant want in contemporary America. Because she has been willing to place herself at the forefront of the Christian entertainment industry, she has met the need for good, clean Christian entertainment within a secular context.

Amy Grant and Gary Chapman were major forces in gospel music before they married; together they have become a team and, although Amy is the one primarily in the spotlight, much of her success is helped by him. These two have made Christian entertainment acceptable to the gospel mainstream while showing the secular industry there is a greater demand for gospel music than was once thought possible. They have attracted a young crowd to their music—an audience once considered impossible to reach with gospel music. They have given these church youth positive images to relate to. They are comfortable in their roles, clearly ambitious and anxious to reach out further. Unlike many other gospel artists, they are not afraid of success, especially in the public sector. They have the ability to live their beliefs and still appeal to a large cross-section of people. Their fans are the silent majority youth and they have been inspired to buy their recordings in record numbers. Although both have remained essentially gospel artists, they have also gained acceptance in the pop market, a market which has not openly embraced Christianity. It is as a bridge between these two markets that Amy Grant has made a major impact in gospel music and her major mark as an artist.

Chapter 30
The Rock That Doesn't Roll:
Imperials, Petra and Michael W. Smith

Tracing the history of contemporary Christian music, many see it as an offshoot of the late 60s peace movement, coming out of secular rock 'n' roll and using popular culture to proclaim the Christian message. The gospel world embraced popular culture in an effort to catch up with the times and reflect the '60s revolution in thought, music, and fashion. The southern gospel world had been caught in a time warp, left behind by the flower children who could not believe in such an outdated, outmoded and outlandish form of rural religion. Even the Jesus music revolution could not relate to those in the southern gospel world—this was a music and culture of the past and the Jesus people wanted a current, hip Jesus, not an old-fashioned historic icon. The Imperials were leaders in bridging this gap and ultimately this movement within the gospel world would begin to join the elements from the rock music culture to fuse contemporary Christian music in the Christian culture.

But all that lay ahead. In the mid-'60s there was no contemporary Christian music as it became known and so, in essence, the Imperials and the Oak Ridge Boys were contemporary Christian music. These moves to contemporize were more than just changes in the music—they were changes in attitudes and appearances. The Imperials were able to make some major moves because of the popularity and acceptance of Jake Hess.

The Imperials were formed in 1964, begun by the hottest gospel singer of the day. Jake Hess wanted a super group and had his own theory of how a gospel group should look and perform. He handpicked what he felt were the best talents from other groups for the Imperials—Armand Morales (from the Weatherford Quartet), Shirl Neilson, Gary McSpadden, and pianist Henry Slaughter.

The southern gospel world at that time was riddled with hypocrisy so Hess required all group members to sign moral contracts, stating that they would not dally with members of the opposite sex they were not married to or otherwise conduct themselves in a manner fast, loose, libertine, or unbecoming to a personal representative of God. Since the other groups all dressed alike in shiny matching suits, the Imperials dressed more casual, wearing sports coats of different colors while their vocal harmonies were smooth and tight instead of the more ragged sound prevalent at the time. Because of the tremendous popularity of Hess, the group immediately had a full schedule of bookings and because of the new look and sound, they soon took the southern gospel world by storm, ushering in a new era in this music.

191

After the Imperials had been formed for about a year, Shirl Neilson left the group and was replaced by Jim Murray. A short while later Henry Slaughter resigned and Joe Moscheo was hired to play piano. At this time, the format for gospel quartets still consisted of four singers and a piano and, at this point, the Imperials were pioneers in a social and cultural revolution more than a musical one.

The next step for the Imperials was to sign a recording contract with a major label—in this case, The Benson Company. The Benson Company helped the group buy a bus for touring and released a record as the Imperials became one of the first professional groups on what had previously been basically a custom record company. (A custom record is one where the artist or group pays for the recording out of his own pocket instead of the label paying the initial costs. Then, the artist is responsible for selling the albums himself. This is usually done by selling the records at live appearances and wherever the artist can find willing buyers. The custom record is widely accepted in gospel music and often serves as a sort of audition. The custom record business serves like a farm club system for gospel acts and labels keep their eyes on these performers—when they can sell a large number on their own, the company is then willing to sign them.)

To give an idea of the relative wealth of gospel performers during this time, pianist Joe Moscheo was hired for $150 a week while each of the singers was making $200-250 per week. This was c. 1966-1976. Then, as now, with a number of southern gospel groups, someone owned the group and was responsible for management, maintaining an office, buying the clothes, paying the hotel bills and generally running the group like a small private business. That someone was Jake Hess. At this time the Imperials were doing well in the southern gospel world, making anywhere from $600-1000 a night performing.

Hess had health problems—a bad heart—and in 1965 decided to quit the road so Moscheo, Jim Murray, and Armand Morales purchased the group from him. When Hess left the group there was an immediate reaction in the gospel world and 93 scheduled dates were cancelled by gospel promoters who had booked the Imperials because Hess was the lead singer. This left the group in dire financial straits, broke with hardly any dates for the coming year. They played some churches for love offerings (collections where the audience can put in what they wish at the end of a performance), getting $50-100 a night sometimes, trying to keep the group together and themselves alive.

During this time, the Imperials' office was in the RCA building on Music Row in Nashville. Through their friendship with Mary Lynch, Chet Atkins' secretary, they were booked on an Elvis Presley session—the one that yielded the gospel album *How Great Thou Art*. For these sessions, RCA wanted a choir sound so the Jordanaires—Elvis' long time back-up group—were hired as well as the Imperials and some female background singers. This was the Imperials' first contact with Elvis and it allowed them to make some money singing background on studio sessions.

Mary Lynch also connected the Imperials with Jimmy Dean, hot off his ABC-TV show, who had a recording date scheduled but did not know any of the songs. The Imperials worked with him, teaching him the songs, and for this were given the job of singing back-up for Dean. Dean and the Imperials got along so well that he invited the group to travel with him to California where he was performing. There, they were to sing in his show as part of The Cimaron Singers, a group of background singers from New York dressed in cowboy garb. For the Dean trip, the Imperials were given $1000 for a week's work. Since they were making much less than that in Nashville, they gladly took it. Dean quickly dropped the rest of the Cimaron Singers (there were about 12) and hired the Imperials alone to sing behind him as well as perform some opening numbers in his show. At this time, Jimmy Dean was a very hot country act, having had "Big Bad John" and a number of other hits, and soon the Imperials found themselves playing Las Vegas, Lake Tahoe, Reno, state fairs, rodeos, and the top theaters in the country.

In 1969, Elvis called the Imperials to perform in his show and soon the group was performing with Elvis as well as Dean—which meant even more Vegas appearances. Working with Elvis was very prestigious, but the Imperials made a lot of sacrifices too. Colonel Tom Parker, Presley's manager, would call two weeks before a tour and tell the group where they would play. The problem was that the group often had other bookings in the gospel world. They would scramble to cancel these bookings, making a lot of people in the gospel industry angry.

After several years of doing this, the conflict of performing with Dean and Elvis became so great that the Imperials had to reevaluate their position. Elvis offered only a background slot and lots of glamour while Jimmy Dean offered the same amount of money, a back-up slot and a solo part in his show as well as participation in his new syndicated TV show. The Imperials decided it was a better move for their career to stick with Jimmy Dean.

Their resignation from Elvis raised more than a few eyebrows because of the glamour and prestige involved, but the group felt strongly they should do it. After they left, Elvis hired J.D. Sumner and the Stamps Quartet to be part of his show, another gospel group from the southern gospel world, who remained with him until his death.

In 1975, the Imperials reached a crossroads. There were two groups in gospel music who were at the top of the field—the Imperials and the Oak Ridge Boys. The talk was strong that gospel music could hit the secular world in a big way with one of these groups. Because of the exposure each group had received, both within and outside the gospel community, it was thought secular success was just around the corner.

The Oaks decided to make that move. They took their music to the secular marketplace and after starving for a couple years hit it big in country music. But they had to abandon gospel music to achieve success thus proving that the secular industry would not buy a gospel artist as they had originally thought. Meanwhile, the Christian audience who have been known to bury their wounded, abandoned the Oaks and cut them off from that world.

It was at this time that the Imperials decided they did not want to go after the secular world but would continue to immerse themselves more deeply in the gospel industry, continuing to record for gospel labels. Imperials' member Jim Murray admits the group had an identity crisis during this time. "Sometimes we didn't know who we were or who we wanted to be," he said (See "Notes" re: quotes from the Imperials). The Vegas circuit was very lucrative financially and some of the lounges where they had performed wanted them to return. TV shows such as Merv Griffin, Mike Douglas, and Dinah had them on and welcomed them back. But the Imperials decided not to go that route.

It has been said that when people say they want to serve God, they often mean in an advisory capacity. Gospel audiences frowned heavily on Christian groups performing in Las Vegas and with secular artists. It's all or nothing, they say, and the Imperials decided to stake their all in the Christian world—a move they have not regretted. They believed God was calling them to sing about Him and not perform the Vegas circuit. Too, they desired to be more heavily involved in the ministry, less in show biz entertainment, so they stayed with gospel music.

The group proved their progressive thinking by hiring Sherman Andrus, a black, to sing with the group in 1972. Andrus was the first black to enter the southern gospel world and, like Jackie Robinson and James Meredith, he paid a price. The Imperials were rewarded for this move by having a number of dates cancelled and being forbidden to play in a number of places where they had once performed. But that was part of the Christian way of life in the south during the early 1970s.

But the Imperials became accepted not only in the southern gospel world, but also the contemporary Christian world—two worlds which were not always compatible in the past. For a long time the southern gospel world looked on the Jesus Movement of the late '60s and early '70s as a bunch of hippies polluting gospel music. The Jesus People responded by accusing the southern gospel world of carrying on a religion riddled with hypocrisy and following a conservative redneck Jesus who, they felt, did not capture the true spirit of the original.

The bridge the Imperials built between the contemporary and southern gospel worlds and even the secular world seems to be their greatest contribution. They showed there are no boundary lines—that these worlds which were once so far apart had far more in common than either one had originally thought possible. They proved their talent as well as their faith and priorities, arriving at a point where they were possibly the group who reached more people with more diverse tastes with the Christian message than any other musical ministry in Christian music.

This desire to promote the ministry is shared by a number of the groups and individuals who see contemporary Christian music as a way of reaching kids with a gospel message. Many of these groups come from strong Christian backgrounds, growing up with the radio on a rock'n roll station. For them, playing gospel rock'n roll is somewhat like missionary work, but instead of going to a foreign country, they go to the church world. Unfortunately, they often find some ugly Americans in the Christian world.

Bruce Springsteen told a story during some of his concerts about growing up with a guitar, wanting to play rock 'n' roll. He was told he shouldn't do it but he continues his search, finding God in a house way out in the darkened countryside with loud music coming from within. God tells Bruce that actually there were eleven commandments Moses was supposed to bring down from the mountain but that Moses, in his haste, only brought down ten. The eleventh commandment, according to God via Bruce Springsteen, is "Let it rock!" (Marsh 230).

The powerhouse Christian band Petra has adhered to all eleven of these Great Commandments. Still, they did not become a rock band who happened to play Christian music; they became dedicated, evangelistic Christians who happened to play in a rock band. That's the way they started and that's the direction they're still heading.

Petra began in Fort Wayne, Indiana, in 1972, at the Christian Training Academy. Bob Hartman, a young Christian who played the guitar, formed a group there consisting of himself, John DeGroff, Bill Glover, and Greg Hough—all students at the Academy—and the four went out to spread the gospel through rock songs to those around Ft. Wayne.

It wasn't easy—what with the church's belief that rock music was from the devil—but the group did play some places and received the backing of school officials who knew the young men were dedicated more to the gospel than they were to the music.

After playing around Ft. Wayne for several years, Petra gradually became more aware of the music business. In late 1973, they drove to Nashville to audition for a major gospel label at a small church. They were being managed by Paul Paino, Honeytree's manager, who had just gotten Honeytree signed to Word through Billy Ray Hearn. Hearn was a leader in signing contemporary Christian acts to Word's newly formed Myrrh label. Later, Hearn began Sparrow Records, which would become one of the dominant labels in contemporary Christian music.

Hearn signed Petra and produced their debut album. It was recorded in South Pekin, Illinois, and marked the first time the band had ever been in a recording studio. Hearn was a novice rock producer and the Jesus rock band's first LP suffered some birth pains. It was released in early 1974 and the result was less than overwhelming.

Christian bookstores were reluctant to stock an album which was so overtly rock; their basically conservative clientele just didn't trust rock music. That was the music of the world, of the devil, and represented sin. How could sanctified folk play—or even listen—to such stuff? Since most considered it an elaborate hoax on true Christianity, getting the album stocked, advertised and promoted was extremely difficult. Suffice it to say it wasn't done very well.

Myrrh was reluctant to do another Petra album considering the initial problems and the reactions to the first release. They finally recorded and released *Come and Join Us*. It was on this album that vocalist Greg. X. Volz made his Petra debut and this former member of the group "e" would continue to handle the lead vocal chores for the next ten years.

Feeling they should aim for the unchristian, unchurched, diehard rock fan, the group recorded loud and powerful. Feeling their competition was the reigning royalty of rock—REO Speedwagon, Rush, Styx—Petra went after a comparable sound. The result was one small step towards rock, one giant leap off the label. As they say in record company offices, "If you don't sell, you smell," and Petra was raising a stink Myrrh couldn't cope with. Those Christian bookstore managers who didn't particularly care for the first Petra album liked the second one even less, and since the distribution system for gospel rock hadn't yet been developed, there was nowhere for Petra to go but home. It wasn't all Myrrh's fault—they too were suffering growing pains in trying to find this market.

Two executives from Word, Darrell Harris and Wayne Donowho, left to form another label, Star Song. These men had a vision of what Petra could do, signed them to Star Song, teamed them with their third producer, George Atwell, and sent them to Bee Jay Studios in Florida for their third album, *Washes Whiter Than*, distributed by a Kansas City based company. It was not serviced properly so disappointing sales again resulted. But it did have one thing going for it—a hit single, "Why Should The Father Bother"—which gave them much needed airplay and let people hear them who had never heard them before.

Petra's fourth album teamed them with producer Jonathan David Brown, a producer they finally felt comfortable with and who allowed them to be themselves and inspired their best work. *Never Say Die* yielded a number one song on Christian radio, "The Coloring Song," a rather mellow song by rock standards, which won them a whole new audience.

The best way for a rock band to achieve popularity is through extensive touring. Rock fans don't want just a concert, they want an event that is social, musical and, above all, memorable. Successful rock acts get on the road and stay there, playing night after night across the country until they have built a large following who demand encore performances. Audiences spread the word about the group and buy their albums. Since radio in general—and Christian radio in particular—has generally been adverse to playing hard rock on the airwaves, touring has often been the only way a rock act can break. Since Petra hardly toured during the years when they recorded their first four albums, they were not using the primary means available to break as an act. It wasn't all their fault, of course. They wanted to be on the road playing, but nobody was calling them to come. During this time (1983) Petra moved to Nashville and broke up. When they did perform, it was Hartman, Volz and whoever they could find at the time for bass and drums. Petra's members were in school, so playing gigs had to be limited to an occasional weekend, and Hartman had a regular job as well, one which he was reluctant to lose considering the vagaries of the music industry.

Hartman met Mark Kelly and John Slick through a Bible study and found they all had the same outlook—they were Christians first, earnestly desiring to communicate the gospel any way possible, and musicians after that. Hartman jammed with the two—Slick on keyboard and Kelly on bass—and discovered they were quite good. After rehearsals, and the addition of drummer Louis Weaver, the new Petra was off and running.

A break came for Petra in the form of another gospel rock band, Servant. Servant was on a national tour and invited Petra to join them. The group blossomed on stage and was finally able to realize their full potential as a gospel rock band.

Surrounding themselves with capable people, Petra launched a series of national tours, promoting their own concerts. In 1982 they spent 300 days on the road and in 1983, 240 days. Their sixth album, *More Power To Ya* was released with the support of a full tour that saw the group become an "overnight success" after ten hard years of struggle.

The Christian world still doesn't completely trust rock music. Gospel artists playing loud rock 'n' roll must also proclaim the gospel loud and clear, with a heavy emphasis on converting the young. It must be ministry over entertainment using the music as a tool to reach the young with the gospel message and not just as an end itself. This has suited Petra fine because they are content—honored, really—to be ministers. As Hartman has said, "What we're doing now is what we've always felt called to do...I think our message is pretty much straight ahead: knowing Christ and living for Christ" (See "Notes" re: Petra quotes). Hartman adds that "We definitely acknowledge and seek to improve the entertainment aspects of what we do; we are no less entertaining though we are primarily ministry motivated," although he admits that "this thrust toward ministry probably hurts us as far as secular success."

A major change in Petra occurred in 1986 when lead vocalist Greg Voltz left and was replaced by John Schlitt, formerly of Head East. This gave the band a fresh start, so to speak, and once in the studio, the band quickly went back to it's rock roots, moving away from the synthesized sound of their *Beat the System* album. They released the two-album live set, *Captured in Time and Space* that put on tape the energy of their live show before beginning on their next studio album, *Back to the Street*.

Along the way Petra has logged a lot of miles and made thousands of fans. They also saw a lot of changes in the Christian music business as Christians began to accept rock as a viable medium for the gospel. The change came through a grassroots movement among the kids. Said Hartman "Kids were really responding to rock spiritually. There was really fruit coming from it—the kids were really receiving something beneficial from the music—and because church members saw that as well, they would get behind it." The industry also opened its arms to Christian rock and Hartman notes that "different types of ministry are accepted more now than they used to be. The industry accepts a lot more kinds of music than it used to."

Petra blazed the trail for gospel rock for a number of other acts. Although the group was not the first Christian rockers, they were the first truly successful act to sell large numbers of records and have large, successful tours which attracted thousands of kids to gospel concerts. It is often an uneasy alliance between rock and gospel, ministry and entertainment, but the 1980s saw an increasing number of acts who provided entertainment in a Christian concert setting. And the acts who rocked the best were often the most successful with the kids whose souls were saved but whose bodies were still restless.

Christianity has been known for infusing its members with guilt, especially in terms of physical expression, but in the 1980s, a new liberation theology broke loose that set the feet of a lot of the kids free. One of the leaders in this trend in Christian entertainment is Michael W. Smith, who became a teen idol for many young Christians through his recordings and concerts. On stage he ran, danced, jumped, paced, and led the band and audience in concert aerobics, pouring his all into a concert until the audience was at a fever pitch. There were a few older people in the audience—probably because some of the kids were too young to drive and because the older generation wanted to check out all the hullabaloo their siblings were raving about. But, for the most part, the concert halls were filled with 13-20 year-olds, some of whom remained standing in front of the stage the entire concert, offering up shrieks and screams throughout the whole performance.

It wasn't always this way for Smith, a handsome young man who grew up in West Virginia and who came to Nashville after being encouraged by studio keyboard whiz Shane Keister. Earlier he had been discouraged because things were not happening fast enough.

Michael grew up in his grandmother's house, where his parents lived from the time they were married. His grandmother was a piano teacher so it was natural he would be attracted to that instrument and at the age of four he began to pick out tunes. He began learning how to sight read when he was eight but even at that age had an aversion to practice, something which continues to be part of his make-up. Indeed, playing by ear, by feel, and by spontaneous combustion is the essence of Michael W. Smith.

Michael became a Christian at the age of ten and committed himself to full time service. But after high school graduation, he suffered a wild streak and ran loose for awhile. He moved to Nashville in 1978 to be part of the music scene and joined the gospel group, Higher Ground, where he wrote "I Am," his first major song. He was soon signed to a publishing company by Randy Cox and when Cox started his own publishing firm, Michael came along, Before long, the duo decided to do a pop album with Cox producing. Some tapes were made, they went to Los Angeles, and there was some interest shown. But Michael began to realize he wasn't cut out to be a pop star, he had to be a Christian artist.

A connection with Mike Blanton and Dan Harrell, managers of Amy Grant, proved crucial and soon they had signed Michael to management and a recording contract with their fledgling Reunion label. Michael's musical prowess had already established him and his writing ability was becoming apparent on albums by a number of Christian artists, including Amy Grant and Gary Chapman. Michael would spend two years working as Amy's keyboard player as well as being a major musical influence on her.

His first album, titled simply *Michael W. Smith*, was geared to young people—high energy techno-pop rock 'n' roll. It was a natural extension of Michael—he enjoys communicating with high school students and had been part of church groups working with them. Now his music would be another part of his appeal to Christian youth. And they bought it like they'd never bought any other new artist—the first two albums combined to sell almost half a million units. Then there was the tour.

Rock is more than a music; it is an attitude. So is gospel. Rock is high energy, a touch of the rebel, living fast and on the outside. Smith's audience is mostly churchgoing, clean-cut, well-scrubbed kids who keep the energy but discard the rebellion. The result is wholesome rock 'n' roll, which is not a contradiction in terms as some insist. The attitude of gospel is that it is all being done as a ministry—for God—and not just entertainment. The attitude of gospel is that there's a message and it needs to be heard, the performers know the Truth and must proclaim it. Smith does a particularly good job of conveying his faith and his message without being overbearing. He lets the audience know where he stands and he gently prods and encourages them to keep the faith. They yell approvingly.

Michael W. Smith, Amy Grant and others on the cutting edge of contemporary gospel music acknowledge and embrace what many other "ministry" oriented acts could never admit—that there is a need and demand for Christian entertainment, a demand for good, clean fun. Christian youth are similar to their secular counterparts with an important philosophical difference—they're rebels with a cause. This new music does not make demands on philosophy or faith, it accepts the audience and merely chides them to live what they believe.

The result is the secularization of gospel music—a music in which many of the artists have stated their purpose is to Christianize secular music. Christian rock, formerly a contradiction in terms, is now providing music the youth demand with lyrics the parents are comfortable with. It still copies secular music, but it is no longer five years behind—the gap has now closed to a year or two.

Within the gospel industry, the performers and executives came to realize that what they thought was a conspiracy against them and their music was actually paranoia. Nobody was holding gospel music back except the performers themselves, who continued to have identity crises about whether they're supposed to be entertainers or ministers.

In the end, it is Gospop—high energy music with a moral message—played by musicians with a mission. It reflected the musical preferences of the kids of the '80s who wanted to hear the timeless message dressed up in the fashion of "now." It was the *Old Testament* in *Gentleman's Quarterly*, new wine in new wineskins, played fast but not loose. And it had a whole lot more in common with Bruce Springsteen than it did with George Beverly Shea as the new breed cut loose and the walls reverberated with the message, "Let it rock!"

Chapter 31
The Music Missionaries

There have been missionaries as long as there has been Christianity: the original Apostles were the first and the Apostle Paul the best known. Great Britain's domination of the world was helped along by their missionaries, who, while they did not necessarily see themselves in this light, helped the colonization process. Many of the first settlers in America viewed the new land as a missionary field.

Great Britain has played an integral part in rock 'n' roll becoming a global music. The popularity of the Beatles heralded the British invasion of the 1960s. The Jesus Revolution of the latter part of the '60s and early '70s saw many Christian musicians view the mission field in terms of global music. They combined a social awareness and missionary zeal with a desire to write and play music and they created a new creature: the musical missionary. This missionary is a musician who travels around the world spreading the gospel through music via concerts and performances. It is a new twist to the old concept of missions and one whose birth in the late 1970s was especially apropos to the Christian tradition of missions and the 1980s concept of global interdependence. It is a belief rooted in the idea that the power of the gospel combined with the power of music can transcend culture, language, politics, economics and numerous other barriers and obstacles to deliver the Christian message to the rest of the world.

Two contemporary Christian musicians who have made a commitment to missions are Karen Lafferty and Scott Wesley Brown. They approach it from two perspectives: Lafferty moved to Europe to actually live outside the United States on the mission field while Brown lived in the United States and made yearly trips overseas.

"I think being a missionary is just being a Christian in another place," said Karen Lafferty. "If there's not much light somewhere, you should go and add a little light to that place and just learn from there" (See "Notes" re: Lafferty quotes).

Karen Lafferty has been a missionary for several years, although she does not fit the traditional role of a missionary who goes into the wilds of Africa, builds a church and converts the natives. Karen Lafferty is a musician living in Amsterdam and she travels doing concerts. She is also the founder of Musicians for Missions, an organization dedicated to bringing musicians to the mission field.

Lafferty grew up loving music and performing in folk groups. The southern New Mexico native took music lessons when she was young and majored in music education at East New Mexico State. Her first experience on the road came as a member of her college choir when the group toured Greenland, Iceland, and the Arctic Circle. "That was a real good experience seeing what it is to be on the road, performing every night in a new place," she said. "I think travelling really got in my blood then."

After college, she began entertaining in bars with her guitar. It was while she was doing this in New Orleans that a life-changing visit occurred. Karen said:

Even though I was raised in a Christian home and made a commitment to the Lord pretty young, I was like a lot of kids sowing my oats and stuff. I was entertaining down in New Orleans and some friends out in Campus Crusade came and visited me. They were talking to me about a spirit-filled life, walking in the spirit—a daily thing with the Lord—and I saw I'd really gotten into a game-playing thing of putting on a different hat to fit into who I was with. I was a barroom entertainer one night, then I would go to church the next day. And I really desired to see how they could incorporate the Lord into life, but I don't know if I didn't have examples or wasn't looking at them. These friends were really used to help me make a firm commitment to follow the ways of the Lord. That was in 1971 and I went to a Campus Crusade Music Conference and wanted to join immediately. I saw a music ministry and knew that's where I belonged— but I wasn't accepted and that was very good for me because I wouldn't have had the understanding I needed from my spiritual growth.

So Karen decided to be a secular entertainer with a witness "like Johnny Cash and Pat Boone." She moved to California to pursue her musical dreams and landed in Costa Mesa, living with some cousins. "On the second day I was there they took me over to Calvary Chapel, which was five minutes from where I lived and I've been there ever since," she said.

Still, she continued to pursue a career in the music industry and made appointments with managers and booking agencies, finally landing a job as an entertainer in a restaurant chain. She said:

I only worked there about two months and pursued these things just a little while longer and just felt very strongly the Lord was calling me out of the entertainment thing to go more directly into ministry. I really believe that Christians can be in the entertainment world although I think it's difficult at times because there's pressure to compromise your life, and yet I know that the first people I led to the Lord were in bars I was working in.

She begun to attend Calvary Chapel and was there during the early stages of Maranatha Music.

I just started writing some Christian songs and one day I just talked to the pastors and asked if it would be alright to share a couple of songs. Then I just started meeting some people and since I play oboe and they were starting their second album and needed some of that kind of accompaniment, I played on that and started going to their Bible studies. Finally, I talked to the leadership again and said 'I believe the Lord is giving me this kind of ministry' and they encouraged me.

Lafferty's first album came as a result of her growth and involvement in Maranatha Music and Calvary Chapel.

I had been on one Maranatha album so I just went and submitted it to Chuck Smith. I said 'I feel like it would be time for me to do an album. Do you think I'm being crazy or off the wall or do you think it's time?' I think a lot of musicians go through that, wondering if they're exalting themselves. Especially when you've had a desire in your past to give in to the recording thing. But when you're wanting to serve the Lord, you're thinking, 'I don't want those worldly motives. I really do want the Lord in there and glorified.' Anyway, Chuck said he felt good about it so we did it. I got Peter Jacobs to produce it and it was a real learning experience because it was fairly low budget. Peter and I did over half the stuff—background vocals and I played saxophone and oboe and all kinds of stuff.

Prior to that first album, Karen had made her first trip as a musical minister to Europe, performing in Holland with Children of the Day. She said:

Actually, one of the reasons I had been invited was because they had two children travelling with them and they needed help with them. I was a friend of theirs so we just thought the combination of me taking care of the kids when they were on stage and opening up their shows was a good idea. I was free but I didn't feel any great calling overseas. But I had always felt a calling to go places that didn't get very much ministry, kinda like a pioneering spirit.

That was in 1973 and she returned to Europe in 1978. In the meantime, she had gone to Australia with another group, Phoenix Sunshine. On her second trip to Europe, she came over alone for a three-month tour. "I had some problems because I was travelling by myself," she said. "My concert sponsors could always speak English but I stayed in German and French speaking homes and they couldn't speak English and you can only smile at each other across the table for so long. It was a very lonely time for me."

It was at this time Karen began to seriously consider working as a music missionary. She also began working with Youth With a Mission. Said Karen:

I met some Youth With a Mission people at my concerts and knew about them beforehand. I met Floyd McClung and he had invited me to come to the farm for a rest. I called a YWAM base and asked if they could provide a French/English speaking girl to travel with me to interpret in homes and help me minister to people after a concert. That worked very well and I've been doing it ever since.

Lafferty's tour was organized by the record distributors of her Maranatha albums. The album had received some attention and they had encouraged her to come. It was at this time that the concept of Musicians for Missions came into being. Karen said:

I'd go places and ask 'Do you have concerts like this regularly?' and they'd say 'Oh yeah. We had one last year.' That was a lot to them. And I saw how effective it is because we're a novelty as Americans. A lot of times non-Christians will come because of that—they've grown up on that style of music. You know, young people are growing up on the same styles of music and a lot of it is in English. Every time I talk to a missionary from some far off island or a Christian from some exotic place, I ask what do young people listen to and they'll listen to the same pop and rock groups. And that's when I felt like a light turned on in my head. I said, 'Lord, here's this thing called contemporary Christian music that has been birthed the past few years and there is a wide open door to the whole world.'

Karen returned to Europe again in 1979 with a friend.

I felt like this time the Lord said, 'Don't travel alone.' I began asking missionaries, 'What if a music group would come and just offer their services to you, work under you, would that be helpful to your ministry?' So often people had not thought of it because they always thought it was so costly they could never afford to do that. So that's when I saw it had to be approached as mission work.

Karen approached several other missionary organizations as well as individuals about Musicians for Missions before talking with Floyd McClung, head of YWAM's Amsterdam office. She said:

I met Floyd and shared with him this vision of Musicians for Missions. I felt YWAM's vision of reaching the world was very much like how I felt. We needed to get out to the people with music and go right to where the people are, to the streets. I knew it wasn't enough to just provide a booking agency to musicians because I had been involved in Christian music long enough and I had discovered in my own life and seen in other people's lives that it's very dangerous for us personally to get out there on the road all the time and not have a home base and a spiritual covering.

Floyd caught Karen's vision immediately. She said:

I had all kinds of reasons why I was uncomfortable with that. Because I was a woman, and a musician, but he said, 'I believe this vision is of the Lord and we'll do all we can to see it come about.' So Floyd and I came to an agreement that I would start this ministry through Youth With a Mission. It's been quite a change for me, coming from such an independent type ministry where I called all the shots to now being part of a world-wide mission group and needing to be supportive of different projects, not just musical projects, and really be family—and then not to be so project-oriented but relationship-oriented.

Karen has learned a lot about music missions in the years since. She said:

Dave Garrett gave a seminar once and he said, 'When musicians start being serious about their ministries to the point of really seeing it as a ministry, not just a musical opportunity, and really see that as a ministry we are a type of leader and we have to be in contact with other spiritual leaders, when we start approaching it like that, then the music ministry will be recognized with the leadership in the church.' I've seen that to be true. So I believe the ideal way is for musicians to be a regular Christian in a fellowship and be in touch spiritually with their leadership there, because we're called first to do that and be part of the body of Christ and know how to worship the Lord ourself. Then the Lord uses particular ministries as musicians and writers or whatever we're going to do.

Musicians for Missions is open to working with other musicians who come over for a Summer of Service as well as those who serve full-time on staff. But while she is open to American musicians wanting to come over to Europe to play, she feels a need to be careful about choosing musicians to be part of MFM. She said:

I want to know through some kind of communication just why somebody wants to come over. It's a tender time for music here because even though it's been developing pretty good, there's certain aspects that have been developed in America that I hope don't come over here, like the stardom type aspect. I don't think there's anything wrong with being known—Paul the Apostle was well known and we are to honor one another—and yet when you can sense that Christians are getting more into the area of idolizing or worshipping than just honoring, I think we've got to realize our responsibility not to promote that.

Karen also feels a desire to work with established ministries on a limited basis. She said:

This really is mission type work. And people will have to raise their own support and not expect to come over and play for a thousand dollars a night because they just can't afford that over here. We don't want to become a booking agency but we do want to work with musicians in the states who want Europe to be part of their ministry.

In her own concert ministry, Karen had adapted her performances to the European audiences.

I always try to do some songs in the language of the country where I am performing, no matter how bad I do them. You know, we expect everybody to speak English even when we're in their country. That's some of the things that have turned Europeans off to Americans.

She also states that "I like doing concerts where I'm pretty direct about the gospel," preferring that her concerts not be publicized as just musical events. "I want to let them know I'm not going to just give them music. I want to give the gospel."

Karen Lafferty has blazed a unique trail in music missions with Musicians for Missions and feels that music can play an important role in future mission efforts. "I think it's a very important time in world history for us in contemporary Christian music for us to be involved." she said. "We can go so many places, but we have to have the willingness to go and finance our own ways, be patient with places that aren't as developed. I hear a world vision coming out in people's songs." For Karen, that world vision means taking the gospel in music all over the world, something she is doing through her own concerts and through working with other musicians in Musicians for Missions.

Scott Wesley Brown has also been moved by his experiences outside the United States, although he continues to live in the States. "I think I'm more Christian and less American now." said Scott Wesley Brown (See "Notes" re: quotes from Brown). He was discussing his trips to the eastern European communist countries, especially the Soviet Union, where he has gone to help other Christian musicians and encourage their efforts to spread the gospel.

Brown says that it is two different kinds of Christianity that he has faced: a Soviet Christianity and an American Christianity. The differences are startling. He said:

I find the Christians in the Soviet Union like little sheep. I think the verse, 'Like sheep we are being led to the slaughter all day long,' describes them. They are very innocent, naive—yet very gentle, loving, caring. A lot of them are frightened and it hurts me to see that fear in their eyes. It's hard to sit there and say to them, 'Jesus takes our fears away.' As an American, I think we have a different perception of the scriptures because we don't have to deal with real hard, tough situations everyday like they do over there.

Brown described the Russian Christian further stating:

I think it's just a firm grip on the fact of what Jesus said, 'If any man wants to follow me he must deny all rights to himself, pick up his cross and follow me.' You see that kind of Christianity—a suffering kind where people see that following Jesus is not getting into a social club and putting on your leisure suit, or joining the choir and playing on the church softball team. It is not a Republican Jesus at all. It is almost a mournful kind of life, very sacrificial and selfless and, in many cases, tortured and persecuted and oppressed by the government. It is serious. In church services, particularly in Moscow, when people prayed they wept. And when people praise, they fall to their knees before the altar crying. It's not the joyful, free praise we often see here. I never saw that before and at first it really frightened me. I thought 'what is going on?' But there is such tension between the church and the state and these people are living in friction, with society. But to me, that's where the church needs to be. The church is friction to society. We end up letting society squeeze us into their own mold and we end up going along with it, or much of it. We think the abortion issue is friction, but every single thing in life is friction in the Soviet Union. So when you become a Christian, it is for keeps. There's no playing the fence.

That is in marked contrast to American Christianity and Scott notes that the freedom for the church in the West has taken its toll.

I think oppression has made the church a stronger church. It's not a compromised church like the Americans. We're a social club church. I mean, we're into choir robes and softball teams and bowling alleys, having movie theaters in our churches. We've got everything at the touch of a button, but their churches have nothing. They've just got each other, so you see the living stones coming to life. You see fellowship and koinonia in a whole different sense than you see it here in America. I don't know that a little persecution wouldn't be a healthy thing for the American church. There's a saying that the Christians in Russia are being persecuted but the Christians in America are being seduced. I think that's a real applicable analogy to illustrate what the situation is. Because we're seduced into prosperity and God only travels first class and Jesus drives a Mercedes Benz kind of philosophy. Even Christians in the Soviet Union have a tendency to want material things—I think man is just greedy by nature and you can't take away basic human nature— and Satan works in their lives just like he does in our lives. But at the same time, over there I think there's a more realistic view of life and there's a little bit more of a compassion towards other people. And they'll die for one another. I mean, rather than turn a congregation in, one pastor we know of was nailed to the floor and urinated on by the KGB, but he would not give the names.

This message is tough to give to American Christians in churches. Said Brown:

I see people wanting to be more international. But it's amazing how American we really are. I'm almost afraid sometimes to say something negative about America for fear people will come up and accuse me of not even loving God. It's almost like God and America are synonymous. People don't understand the world, they don't understand Beirut, Central America, Iran and Iraq, the Soviet Union, Africa and the drought, Calcutta and Mother Teresa. The world is so far removed and all it is is a 12-inch square in our living room. It's amazing how many misconceptions there are about the Soviet Union. People here ask me such ridiculous questions about the Soviet Union; it's amazing. 'Do guys really walk around in trench coats and machine guns?' 'Is everything black and white over there?' They picture the Soviet Union as a black and white country where the grass isn't green. Sure it's definitely an oppressed nation, but it's a beautiful nation. It's gorgeous.

One of the moments of true beauty for Scott and his wife came when they were walking around Moscow. Brown described it,

We went to the back side of the Kremlin and we saw at least two or three thousand girls dressed in white. They were all brides and all the guys were dressed up in their Sunday suits. All the little kids were dressed up and there were flowers everywhere. It's a real honorable thing to be married at the Kremlin; it's a state wedding and that's the ceremony. There's a big row of flowers and the bride and groom jump over the flowers and they're married. All the guys were laughing and punching each other and all the girls were giggling and the mothers and fathers were crying and I thought to myself, 'This is life and these people are human beings and no different than we are here in America. They get excited when their hockey team scores a goal like we do when our football team scores a touchdown. They have the same needs and desires we have. They want to put food on the table for their family. They want to have a good education and grow up and have a happy life.' I think most Americans have a hard time picturing the Russians like that. They picture him as a real devout Communist with a gun who wants to kill everybody. The Communist party is such a minute part of the population. There are 70 million Christians in the Soviet Union and, according to polls in America— which I don't believe—there are 50 million Christians here.

Scott only stays a few days in the communist countries where he visits. He stated:

You need visas and it's not safe to stay in an area for too long. Get in, do your business, then get out. It's hard on them. Everywhere we went, they'd just go out of their way. They'd save sugar and meat, salt, flour. They'd ration their food a long time before you came so that when you came they'd have enough food to feed you. It's a real hardship for them—a lot of them take off work. And it's hard because they don't make a lot of money.

It is amazing that Christianity has survived the purge it has undergone; it is also amazing that there are spiritual movements in those countries. Said Brown:

I think there's a quiet revival amongst the youth particularly in Czechoslovakia. They told me the churches were getting packed out on Sunday mornings with kids. In the Soviet Union we talked with several churches which are now getting into having a Sunday afternoon youth service. They can't say it's a youth service, but the kids know it's youth oriented because they have guitars in the service. Kinda like the folk mass that was here in the '60s. I think there's a real curiosity towards western thought and western things and naturally western religion. People are wanting to know about this Christian faith. It's been hidden from them for many generations. A lot of families pass down the faith, but that's more in the Pentecostal movement. A lot of kids told me if their parents found out they were going to church they'd get into a lot of trouble. The parents would whip them or punish them in some way. A lot are afraid of those things because their parents could lose their jobs or their kids could be kicked out of school and that would humiliate the parents, so a lot of them become Christians through their friends and they have to secretly be Christian. And they sneak out and get around like the kids do in America.

Although Bibles are not in great numbers, there is evidence that a number of people do have access to Bibles, according to Brown. Scott said:

Statistics say one out of eight people have access to a Bible. When we were at the Moscow Baptist Church we were asked a few times by people if we had Bibles to give them. In Estonia, there were more Bibles because in Moscow the revolution took place in 1917 and there was a great purge of religion by Stalin and lots of church burnings. So they've had to go through it for a lot longer. In some of the western countries like Czechoslovakia or Poland or Yugoslavia or Lithuania, it's only been in the last 30 to 40 years they've had to undergo this real rigid communist structure. Therefore, they've got more Bibles. I found that Bibles were more common the further west you got. Also, Christianity was stronger the further west you got with more churches operating.

Yet, even though Soviet Christians are bound by the common thread of their outlawed faith, there is still strife and discord. Said Brown:

There's division. I wish I could say there wasn't. I think there's mistrust. Even in fellowships there can be a lot of mistrust because I think fear is just ingrained in their lifestyle and they just operate out of fear, intimidation, and suspicion. There's not the doctrinal divisions like here, although it's hard for new churches to get founded. New things threaten them.

Scott began life in Washington D.C. and was active in the peace marches in the '60s. It was hard to reconcile the contradictions of some in the movement though—wanting peace and throwing a Molotov cocktail at the same time. As a high school student, he accepted Jesus in 1970. He soon became involved with Young Life and began singing and playing, expressing his faith.

But Scott was not content to be a local hero. He made a record when he was still in high school and dreamed of a record deal. Yet, he continued to see himself as a missionary and travelled to Appalachia and Puerto Rico, helping people build porches and trying to reach people with his music.

Scott Wesley Brown made his first trip to the Soviet Union in 1983 and since then has continued to keep in contact with musicians in the eastern bloc countries and help them. He stated:

You can mail some religious material in. One or two Christian cassettes aren't going to really hassle them. They can't monitor all that mail, especially small packages. Getting through borders with battery operated things isn't too hard and we've dropped off lots of stuff like that. There has been a problem with guitars—my guitar was taken by the KGB in Moscow and returned to me four months after I returned to the U.S. That was when the KAL flight was shot down. One year we went in with a small Yamaha synthesizer and they took that right away from me at the border. I said 'I need to practice.' They said 'You don't need to practice. That's too small a time. You'll get it back when you leave the country.' So I said 'How about if I just wanted to take it in and give it away?' They did some figuring and said '600 Rubles.' which at their exchange rate is about $1.35 per ruble and I only paid about $300 for it, so it would have cost me $7-800. They inflate everything. The way I got my guitar in, I met an East German in Holland at the Christian Artists convention in DeBron and just gave him my guitar...he told me his personal need was a guitar. It was the most incredible experience to see his eyes—they just teared up. An ovation electric with all these guitar cords and about ten packs of strings. Since then, he's written and given a list of needs of all the Christian musicians he knows of in East Germany and right now we're working on getting a Fender Rhodes, 12 mics, 12 mic stands, a DX7 and some other stuff.

Although Scott goes into the Soviet Union and performs, that is not his major goal. He said:

I don't necessarily want to go to the Soviet Union and perform for all these people. I think it's like the old adage, 'If you give a man a fish, he'll eat for a day; if you teach him how to fish, he'll eat for a lifetime.' We're trying to give them the tools necessary so they can begin their own Christian music scene over there and use it for evangelism and body ministry.

But even when Scott does perform in Russia, it is not like an American concert. Scott said:

Concerts are outlawed there. The way kids have a concert over there is they'll take a Christian music album and invite friends over to their house and play cut for cut and in between cuts they'll discuss it and have Bible study. I perform mostly in churches and homes. In churches, I was a guest from America and the way they would do it— it was really against the law for me to preach without permission from the government— was that I would stand up and bring greetings. It is legal for a foreigner to bring greetings and I would stand up and share maybe a minute of greetings. Then I would sit down and the pastor would get up, smile and say, 'Some more greetings.' So I would stand up and greet them for another couple of minutes, maybe sing a song and sit back down. Then the pastor would say 'Maybe some more greetings after we pray' so they'd pray and then I'd greet them again for about ten minutes. So I'd end up spending about an hour greeting people, standing up and sitting down.

He stated the largest concert crowd was "about 60 people crammed into somebody's living room."

In America it is a different story and Scott likes to use his platform to somehow unite both worlds.

I have a platform here in America to get up in front of several thousand kids every week and tell them, 'Hey, look what's going on here. Can you help me? Can you help me get instruments in? Can you help me pray for these kids? Write letters?' The reaction has been overwhelming.

The commitment of Scott Wesley Brown has also been overwhelming and through his organization, "I Care," he intends to continue making an annual trip to the European communist countries as well as to a third world country. "These people have become special friends," said Scott. "I mean they are really precious friends. I don't think in my life I'd be willing to say I'd lay my life down for somebody, but I would for these people."

Part 4

Chapter 32
The Christian Culture

In a 1976 survey, the Gallup Poll found that one out of every three Americans considered themselves "born again" Christians. In 1976, for the first time since World War II, church attendance increased rather than decreased. Topping off all this, in 1976, a "born again" Christian was elected to the White House.

These revelations caught the mainstream press off guard. Scrambling quickly to recover, they discovered a huge Christian culture that included books, records, television, radio, bookstores and churches all doing a booming business. They discovered a culture in America that had size as well as strength—led by no less than the President of the United States and accounting for hundreds of millions of dollars in revenue.

In the mid-1960s the church had been on the decline with attendance decreasing and interest from youth waning. The Jesus Revolution of the late '60s and early '70s took the gospel back to the street, largely via music. At this time, Christian musicians had a hard time making ends meet—their commitment to spreading the message of the gospel kept them going in spite of a rejection from both the church and society towards their gospel music in the pop/rock format. The church, accustomed to 200-year-old hymns, generally considered the music to be from the Devil and those involved with street level Christianity to be cultish and suspect while the secular culture simply did not want to hear about Jesus through their loudspeakers. Because the gospel record companies and Christian radio stations generally sided with the conservative churches, the result was a stifling of Christian music by the Christian culture itself.

By the mid-1970s that had changed dramatically, with the churches realizing that contemporary music was a way to reach the youth while the record companies and radio realized there was a demand for this kind of music. Too, many of the musicians and others involved in the Jesus Movement proved themselves to be sincere, dedicated Christians who became involved in local churches, so the fears of conservative church members were generally quieted as they realized this movement was not composed of wild hippies on the loose.

America underwent a spiritual awakening during this time and a more radical Christianity became acceptable—a Christianity that was fundamental in its beliefs, active in its faith, and more in touch with the contemporary culture than the Sunday morning services of churches whose traditions from the past dictated their services at the expense of contemporary societal questions and needs. The term "born again" became known, accepted, and practiced, with many Americans going through a rebirth in their spiritual lives. This was highlighted by publication of the book *Born Again* by Nixon's former hatchet man, Chuck Colson, and the election of Jimmy Carter as president. Carter's campaign and presidency made the born-again movement known and accepted to a wide cross-section of Americans who had looked with disfavor at the contemporary Christian culture. It also forced the press to seriously examine the Christian culture. Unfortunately, the secular press—trained to be skeptical—could not really comprehend this movement and initially refused to acknowledge it as an ongoing news story. Instead, they attacked and looked for skeletons in the closet, ignoring a social change that was as radical as the changes of the '60s which altered the social fabric in American lives.

Still, Carter's presidency and open admission of being born again highlighted the born-again movement and made it socially desirable in middle America. This manifested itself in the growing number of Christian bookstores—which moved into malls—the proliferation of Christian books, and the widespread acceptance of Christian music. This music industry reaped the rewards of this boom through a large number of acts selling vast numbers of Christian records. In short, the Christian culture became big business as it moved from retail outlets into homes via recordings, books, assorted trinkets and artifacts to be worn or hung on walls. Television evangelists became leading populist figures and magazines by, about, and for Christians delivered their messages straight to the living room.

The Christian culture initially expanded as many converts joined the faith. But during the early 1980s, the Christian culture began to turn inward and view Christianity as a target audience, intent on reaching believers and convincing them to buy Christian products. With television this meant the development of cable channels devoted exclusively to Christian programming. For Christian bookstores, it meant an expansion into shopping malls. In radio it meant more music and less talk.

At one time it was felt the key to growth for gospel music was in reaching secular consumers who had not yet heard gospel. There were some attempts to enter the secular marketplace and reach the consumer who was buying non-gospel albums, but as the '70s ended and the '80s began, the industry realized that growth actually depended upon reaching the Christian consumer more effectively. It became obvious there was a large Christian market, but the question remained how to reach them. The answer lay in the church and the Christian bookstore.

The Christian Bookseller's Association had begun in 1950 with about 25 stores. By 1985 they had 3400 member stores out of a total 5200-5500 bookstores that sold Christian products. Criteria for membership in the CBA is that a store must be open at least 40 hours a week, have a sign out front, and 75 percent of the products offered must be Christian-related. The CBA stores generated $1.269 billion in sales in 1985, which means the average store generated $235,000 in business, higher than their secular counterpart in the American Bookseller's Association.

The biggest spurt of growth for Christian bookstores came in the mid-seventies. In 1976, the CBA represented 2800 members, which generated $500 million in sales, up from $100 million in 1971. During this period, average annual revenue jumped 17.4 percent per year, almost twice the secular bookstore's growth, which was listed at nine percent per year.

In 1985 Christian bookstores were mostly family-owned with about 56 percent in shopping or strip malls and about five percent in regional malls. The average owner was 37 years old, compared to the 59-year old average owner in 1965. The new breed often came armed with degrees in business and saw themselves as retailers and businessmen, although they still saw the 'ministry' aspect of their business. This contrasted sharply with the Christian bookstores of the late-60s which saw themselves as primarily a ministry which offered some religious books for sale to support that ministry.

When the Christian Bookseller's Association began it represented stores which sold books. In 1985 book sales accounted for 29 percent of sales with music accounting for 23 percent. Other items include Bibles, which account for 16 percent of sales; Sunday School curriculums, which account for six percent; greeting cards, four percent; jewelry, two percent; and gifts, ten percent.

While the Christian bookstore is the backbone for the Christian culture, it is not the most visible part. That honor belongs to Gospel TV, especially the well-known television evangelists who have brought Christianity into America's living rooms and created, in essence, a fourth network that generates billions of dollars. This network is comprised of about 200 local TV stations, 1,134 radio stations, and numerous production companies that purchase time on secular stations. In 1977, estimates were that $500 million was spent by gospel evangelists to purchase time on TV stations; by 1985 that figure had grown to about two billion. The major programs depend upon viewers to send in contributions in order to stay on the air and the viewers do so in astounding numbers and amounts. The Christian Broadcasting Network, headed by Pat Robertson and his "700 Club," had an annual income of $223 million; Jimmy Swaggert took in $140 million a year; Robert Schuller and his "Hour of Power" had a television budget of $37 million annually; Jim Bakker and his "PTL Club" took in over $100 million each year; Jerry Falwell counted receipts that exceeded $100 million a year; and Oral Roberts oversaw a budget of $120 million a year (1986 figures).

Gospel television, also called "Pray TV," reached an estimated 13.3 million people, or 6.2 percent of the national TV audience, regularly. Additionally, 21 percent of American households "tune(ed) in...for at least six minutes a week" and 40 percent "for at least six minutes a month," adding up to 61 million Americans "with at least minimal exposure," according to *Time* magazine ("Gospel TV" Feb. 17, 1986).

The growth of the Christian bookstore can be attributed to the grassroots strength of the Christian movement. They provide Christian products basically unavailable in other outlets. The growth of Gospel TV also reflects this grassroots movement of American Christianity as well as the fact that the personalities are dynamic and appealing. Too, the Federal Communication Commission now gives public service credit to stations for paid religious shows. Cable and VHS outlets have grown dramatically in the 1980s, the technology of videotaping has lowered productions costs significantly, and the computer has made massive fund raising relatively easy with its bank of names, addresses and phone numbers— all contributing to growth.

It has been said that in times of great technological growth, people yearn for a "return to the basics," a desire to simplify their life with basic values. The growth of American Christianity in the latter half of the twentieth century may be explained by the fact that America remains a Christian nation with Christian ethics and morals still dominant, despite protestations to the contrary by many in the Christian culture who appeal for donations as a way to set the nation back on its Christian course. Another factor is the spiritual revival that occurred in the United States beginning in the late '60s—like the spiritual revivals of George Whitefield, Charles Finney, Dwight Moody, and Billy Sunday in times past.

Ironically, the Christian Culture has used this technological revolution to turn this spiritual revival into a major industry generating billions of dollars in revenue and carrying Christianity from the church or revival tent right into the living room of the electronic cottage.

In addition to books and television, the Christian culture also includes a number of periodicals, many connected to denominations, but others offering a Christian version of periodicals found on the newsstands. These magazines are generally slanted to the right politically. They are an important line of communication to Christian consumers because that is the way Christian celebrities, authors, and speakers maintain their bases of support.

In education, there are a large number of Christian colleges, most affiliated with a denomination, which offer students courses in Bible and ministry-related studies as well as degrees in business, the liberal arts, and sciences. This network provides an outlet for speakers, musicians, and authors who wish to penetrate the Christian market. It is not unusual for a youth to be educated in Christian schools from kindergarten through post-graduate studies, receive Christian periodicals in the home, buy Christian books at a Christian bookstore, gospel albums to be played on the stereo, and tune into Gospel TV regularly. For a job, he may work in a Christian organization that markets Christian products or at least be involved in a number of organizations that center their activities and purposes around Christian ideals. Indeed, the Christian culture is a large network of like-minded people connected to each other by the church, the Christian bookstores and the Christian media. It is a culture that is insular and self-perpetuating and has made its influence felt in the political, social, and cultural arena.

While there are some black Christian speakers, authors and TV personalities, the Christian culture remains predominantly white. The common bond between black and white Christianity—if there is a common bond—is music, with musicians from both fields influencing each other. Still, there is a radical difference between black gospel for the black audience and white gospel for the white audiences. The end result is that black gospel artists do not really benefit from the Christian bookstore network to any degree.

Black gospel in the latter part of the twentieth century seems to have split into two different camps called "traditional" and "contemporary." The traditional artists have their roots in the church choir and, musically, in blues and the older R&B sound while the contemporary artists have been influenced more directly by the modern R&B sound, the Motown influences, jazz and disco—or dance—music heard on the radio. The contemporary sound generally appeals to the younger audiences whose ties to the church are not as strong, while the traditional sounds appeal to the older audiences and those who grew up with strong ties to the church, although no hard fast lines can be drawn defining who listens to what.

Although these two paths exist in black gospel, they are not two totally separate roads but rather intertwining paths that lie close together. The music is often played on the same gospel radio programs, often back to back, and sold together in record bins at retail outlets. The difference is mostly a matter of attitude, from the artists as well as the audiences, manifesting itself in music that either scorns pop (traditional) or embraces it (contemporary).

There is also within black gospel, as well as black music in general, a move towards a smoother sound that appeals to white audiences as opposed to the harsher, more primitive rhythmic sound that appeals strictly to black audiences. It is this smoother sound that has permeated the white gospel market and provided the initial impetus for traditionally white gospel labels to embrace this music and sell it through the mainstream white Christian outlets of the Christian bookstores. Many music marketing executives have picked up the clue from Sam Phillips and his Sun Records of the '50s and sought to market black music to white audiences. It has enabled several black gospel acts to enjoy followings of white audiences.

The term "crossover" generally means a music that can appeal to several different audiences and can appeal on several different charts—country and pop, R&B and pop, jazz and R&B, rock and easy listening—and therefore can sell in much greater numbers. Within black gospel, the term "crossover" has a twofold meaning. First, there is the crossover into the white gospel market. The crossover into the pop market has generally come from artists who have gone from being black gospel artists to pop artists. These artists have had to abandon gospel to cross over; however, the gospel market looks at such activity with a jaundiced eye and once these artists switch they're not considered "gospel" anymore. The key factor in the success of a gospel artist is commitment to the Christian way of life—which shuns the trappings of the world—and to the fans and audiences who want to hear gospel, not pop music. This means that when an artist forsakes gospel music the audience generally forsakes that artist.

The crossover into the white gospel market has become a much more lucrative and viable alternative for black gospel artists because it allows them to expand their market while staying true to their Christian commitment. The white audience has been reasonably receptive to the black artist whose music is smoother and influenced by popular music.

Black gospel is generally sold in independently owned retail record stores (called "Mom and Pop" stores) or in chain stores located in the black sections of a city. The albums are located in the same bins as R&B, soul, dance, and secular music. Black gospel doesn't sell in huge numbers but with production costs kept down, and tour support and other record company financial amenities virtually non-existent, a label can produce a profit. Artists who consistently sell 40-50,000 albums are considered major stars. These units reflect album sales and not singles (or 45's). The single, which has always had large sales in black pop music, is almost non-existent in gospel, with hits generally emerging from an album through live appearances and radio airplay.

Most black gospel is heard on black radio stations that will play an hour or two of gospel each day. These programs are generally funded by brokers who pay for the time and then either sell ads or gain revenue from promoting concerts or other related activities. There are only a handful (12-15) of radio stations that program black gospel full-time. The remainder of radio airplay for this music comes from Sunday programs provided by black radio stations and a few white contemporary stations who will program a black contemporary artist.

There is a limited consistency of radio programming within the ranks of gospel programming and a general feeling that the black gospel market isn't large enough to support very much radio time. The diversity of artists and records makes it impossible—according to critics—to program a commercial sounding station and represent all the artists or to appeal to all segments of the black gospel audience without offending and turning off others.

The church is still the center of black gospel music, although artists performing in concerts and making studio records have become the center pieces. The black market has created a steady demand for the choirs that record for black gospel labels, although most of these albums sell better regionally than nationally.

For their part, black gospel artists are faithful to gospel music, to the church and to their audiences. For this, they are rewarded by having audiences who are faithful to them for a number of years. The audience and performer are, in a certain sense, married and the only grounds for divorce are a desertion into secular music. This is the only unforgivable sin. However, if performers leave pop or soul music for gospel—visibly demonstrating their new commitment—then they are generally welcomed with open arms by the gospel community.

This commitment to gospel music is the key to success for an artist in black gospel. The commitment should manifest itself through touring, which continues to provide the bulk of exposure (and therefore record sales) in black gospel. This makes black gospel an integral part of the world of black music—providing deep roots and a strong heritage for performers. But it also sets black gospel apart from black music, letting it keep its own identity, integrity and values. And that's what keeps black gospel a breed apart from the pop spectrum of black music. Black gospel is separate from white gospel because it appeals to different audiences. Also, white gospel has created its own indigenous world while black gospel has remained part of the black culture.

In a world dominated by celebrities and celebrity-consciousness, the Christian culture has generated its own coterie of celebrities who remain basically unknown outside Christian circles. Indeed, there are Christian superstars who remain virtually anonymous in the secular culture. There are even circles within circles and the gospel music industry is similar to the secular music industry in that it produces recordings and gets them sold and played on the radio. However, it is vastly different in numerous other ways, including where the records are sold, how the artists reach their public, and even why the records are made.

Gospel music has influenced the pop music world—and is influenced by the pop music world—yet the two remain strangely separate, keeping their distance. There are a few instances of musicians functioning in both worlds but, for the most part, it is an either/or situation and an artist must choose one side or the other. Gospel is a very jealous music, wanting a total commitment from its artists. You can't be part-time gospel, part-time pop; it's either all of one or the other.

For Christian musicians, the musical world is divided into two segments—gospel and secular. Gospel music is the music that deals lyrically with Jesus Christ and the Christian life. Secular music is everything else.

In a certain sense, there is really no such thing as gospel music because gospel embraces all musical forms. From heavy metal to light rock, from country to jazz, from dance music to church choirs, gospel encompasses all forms of music. The only really definable gospel music forms are the old hymns, the worship or praise songs, and black gospel. The rest changes with the tastes of the times.

White gospel is divided into several camps. First, there is the inspirational market where choirs and soloists perform primarily for churches. Then there's southern gospel, which is akin to country music in its sound, and finally there is contemporary Christian music, which is pop music—everything from heavy metal and hard rock to soft rock—with Christian lyrics.

The differences in musical tastes are often differences in the self-image of the consumer. The classical enthusiast generally sees himself as more sophisticated, more educated, more appreciative of the finer things of life; the jazz aficionado sees himself as having superior musical taste, being able to appreciate and distinguish great music over merely commercial; the bluegrass fan sees himself as down-to-earth, without pretenses, able to simplify the complexities of life; the gospel fan views himself as a member of the family of God, a person whose religion is the most important part of his life. Gospel music views itself as a ministry rather than entertainment, having a message the world needs to hear, serving God instead of man, representing God's point of view.

This leads to a certain schizophrenia within the gospel world—trying to live in the world but not be of the world—and a certain distrust from those outside this world—how can anyone know what God is thinking or be sure there is only one absolute truth that fits everybody and everything? Contradictions and conflicts abound within the Christian culture but at the core is an absolute certainty that Jesus is the Son of God, the Bible is the Word of God, and that God communicates to man through the Holy Spirit—a silent voice that whispers only to believers.

This mysticism is difficult to accept by the rationalist mind or a scientific society that demands empirical proof for solutions. Still, part of man is a spiritual being and this Christian culture has provided spiritual answers and direction for some. Most of those involved in gospel music are not wealthy and certainly do not do it for money. They do it because they feel called and compelled to do so, for a love that transcends earthly explanations and a commitment to spread the gospel message that defies earthly barriers. It is a mission for those armed with the "Answer" who seek to convince a questioning world. However, in the midst of this spiritual quest, it is also the music biz.

Overall, gospel radio accounts for about two percent of the total radio audience in America and sales of gospel recordings (black and white) accounts for about five to seven percent of the total sales of prerecorded product in this country. For contemporary Christian music, which is predominantly white with some black artists, it must depend upon the Christian bookstore for eighty percent of its sales. Overall, music accounts for 23 percent of Christian bookstore sales with 19 percent in prerecorded products and the remaining four percent from print music sold to churches and their choirs (1985 figures).

Just as the secular music industry produces stars, so does the gospel music industry. The essential difference is that the secular star views himself as an entertainer with music the most important thing in his life while the gospel music star generally views himself as a minister with music secondary to his own relationship with God. It is his role to convey the gospel to those who don't believe or to encourage those who do believe to keep the faith.

The gospel artist must be sincere and must truly believe what he is singing about. He may acknowledge the troubles of life, but never doubt the great truth; he may sometimes question aspects of his faith but never abandon the faith. The gospel artist is more gospel than artist, a conduit for God speaking to the world, a spiritual salesman and a shining example that God is alive and working within an individual's life. The performance is not just a show, it is a service too and the recordings are not just to listen to—they are to be accepted and agreed with. In short, the career must emphasize ministry and the records are just part of the service to God.

There are, of course, a wide range of possibilities and diversions within gospel music. There are those who prefer to be Christian entertainers, or entertainers with a Christian message, or entertainers who serve the saints—providing the church with entertainment. There are also those who preach as much as they sing and who witness to the unbeliever, intent on correcting the error of his ways. It would be foolish to state that all the motives are totally pure, but at least it must be acknowledged that at the root of most gospel artists there is a firm commitment to live a Godly life and have a close relationship with God.

Those outside the gospel industry often don't see this and cast a jaundiced eye at the gospel world, viewing gospel artists as hypocrites or frauds. But that hypocrisy usually comes from trying to serve both man and God and the fraud comes when a gospel artist deceives himself. It is more than a music, it is a way of life and the gospel artist must live it as well as believe it. It is not an easy life.

The Christian culture cannot be underestimated in America. Its marketing network is responsible for billions of dollars in business each year while the development of its own media (and media stars) allows it to communicate to fellow believers and affect issues in the world at large. It provides a base of support for those involved in entertainment and has given gospel music in the latter part of the twentieth century the ways and means to reach a like-minded audience, providing entertainment with a message compatible to the audience's beliefs. Although it may be argued that the role of Christian music is to evangelize and attract new believers—and some musicians claim that as their purpose—in reality, the thrust of the gospel industry is "music for the saints" and they provide this service through the church, the Christian bookstore, and the Christian media.

Chapter 33
Rewards and Awards:
Marketing the Movement

As gospel music embraced the technology of the twentieth century—radio, television, records—it became a major music form of its own, isolated from the secular world, but Big Business for the Christian consumer. The number of Christian bookstores grew phenomenally in the mid-1970s and by the 1980s the stores were into malls. Gospel music became an accepted part of the American music scene. But the acceptance did not come easy and the growth came after fighting barriers erected between the secular and gospel worlds. The gospel world was responsible for erecting some of those barriers but the secular world put up a wall too: the fact is, neither world is quite comfortable with the other.

The Gospel Music Association has been the major driving force in bringing gospel music to the masses, making it acceptable to the American music culture. It has done this primarily through the Dove Awards, given annually to the top performers in the gospel music field. Ironically it is these awards—given in a field which supposedly disdains earthly "awards" and whose recipients have often felt uncomfortable about competing for and acquiring awards and accolades for "God's work"—and not the numerous efforts by the organization to unite the gospel industry into one cohesive force that has given the gospel industry its major recognition.

In the early 1960s, there were several groups of people aware of the need for an association of gospel music performers and business people. The success of the Country Music Association in Nashville served as an excellent role model. In Memphis, the Blackwood Brothers' organization was trying to pull an organization together while in Nashville, a group headed by Don Light was also moving in that direction. The Blackwoods and the Statesmen, two southern gospel groups, had the decided advantage of owning the National Quartet Convention, which had first been held in 1956 in Memphis. This convention brought together all those involved in southern gospel music for a weekend of fellowship, fun, showcasing, and business. Later, the event grew to cover four days, then a week, and then a ten-day event in Nashville.

The first Quartet Convention was held in October, 1956 in Memphis and was a joint venture of the Blackwoods and Statesmen quartets, who owned it and viewed it as a business venture. This same group sowed the seeds for the Gospel Music Association and obtained a charter from the state of Tennessee in 1964, joining forces with the group in Nashville to elect the first board of directors. Among the founding fathers were James Blackwood, J.D. Sumner,

Cecil Blackwood, and Don Butler; Tennessee Ernie Ford was elected the first president.

The idea of an awards ceremony honoring those in gospel music was first presented by Bill Gaither at a GMA quarterly board meeting in 1968 at the Third National Bank Building offices in Nashville. J.D. Sumner, Bob MacKenzie, and Les Beasley were all enthusiastic and the first ceremony was set for October 10, 1969. The event was held in the penthouse of the Peabody Hotel in Memphis and approximately 665 guests attended. That first Dove Awards was not a lavish affair: the afternoon of the show, members of the Dove Committee had to put on work clothes and mop floors, wash windows, scrub, sweep, and decorate because the penthouse was in disastrous shape. The crew finished in time to shower and dress for the awards show.

The name "Dove" came from Bill Gaither while the design came from Les Beasley, who worked with an artist on the concept. That first year reflected the fact that this was basically a southern gospel organization as the winners came from that field of gospel music.

The next year, the Doves were held at the Rivermont Hotel in Memphis and again the winners came from the southern gospel world. In the third year, 1971 disaster struck when it was discovered that the Blackwood Brothers had caused some discrepancies in voting. The result was that the awards were all deemed invalid and that year was wiped off the slate. As a result, the GMA does not count 1971 as a Dove year and the winners from that year do not appear on any of the GMA's official releases of past Dove winners.

The Dove Awards continued to grow and moved to Nashville, where the gospel music business was increasingly centered. In the following years, there were awards shows held in a giant tent over the plaza between the Capital Park Inn and Municipal Auditorium, at the War Memorial Auditorium, Ryman, Hyatt Regency, Opry House, Opryland complex, and Tennessee Performing Arts Center. In 1984, the show was first televised. A contract had first been signed with a production company in 1980 but no TV network was interested. After several years of being turned down by networks, the Gospel Music Association signed with the Christian Broadcasting Network to broadcast over cable.

1979 was also a key year in the development of the Doves because there were no Dove Awards that year because of a shift in time for the event from the fall to the spring of the year. Since the first shift would have meant awards only a few months apart, it was decided to skip 1979 and begin anew in the spring of 1980. Major changes were afoot as the Gospel Music Association was going through severe growing pains, wrenching itself away from the domain of the southern gospel people, to a more contemporary direction. It was beginning to reflect the growth in contemporary Christian music and the movement of the industry towards a more pop/rock attitude and sound. The southern gospel people, who began the organization, were reluctant to bend and grow and most were eventually eased out—to their chagrin—until by 1986 there was only one award aimed directly at southern gospel music. Changes had begun in 1978 when several contemporary artists won awards.

Gospel was beginning to flex its muscles and exert its influence on the overall music industry. In October, 1977, *Record World*, a music industry trade magazine, devoted a special issue to gospel music. This was the first real acknowledgment on a major scale of gospel music by the secular industry; the result was that suddenly the secular people were much more aware of what was happening in gospel music, retailers began ordering gospel music for record stores, and the gospel industry itself received a major boost in self-image as it began to consider itself a major part of the whole music industry and not just a second class cousin, isolated in its own world. The idea of tapping the pop market was in the minds of a number of those in gospel music and, spurred by the success of Debbie Boone's "You Light Up My Life" and the inauguration of Jimmy Carter, the first "born-again" president, Christianity became a hot topic and gospel music was "in."

In 1978, *Contemporary Christian Music*, a magazine aimed directly at that field of gospel music, was begun by Jim Willems, owner of Maranatha Bookstore in Orange County California. This magazine, edited by John Styll, (who would eventually take over ownership) became a major vehicle for the promotion and exposure of contemporary Christian acts. It also played a leading role in the shift in the gospel audience from an older age group to young people—12-25—who had never been attracted to gospel in any great numbers before. Another publication, *The Singing News*, based in Pensacola, Florida, had long been the major publication in gospel music, but they were a southern gospel publication and though they attempted to expand their coverage and include all facets of gospel, their support and audience was too firmly rooted in the southern gospel world to change. As a result, they have remained the major publication for southern gospel music but have not made a major impact on the contemporary Christian world.

Billboard, the major music industry trade, published a special edition on gospel music about two years after *Record World* and *Cashbox*, another trade, followed the others in 1980. Since so many retailers buy from these charts (particularly *Billboard*'s) this meant an increased presence of gospel music in normal retail record outlets, although the Christian bookstores would still account for about 80 percent of gospel sales overall. With the advent of airplay charts for singles in *Contemporary Christian Music*, gospel radio began to shift towards the pop-type format of "hit" radio and away from album play.

Traditionally, the gospel market has been an album market with hit singles virtually unheard of. Retailers and consumers insisted on buying the artist and not just the song, so the emphasis was naturally on the album. But radio required an independence to play whatever cut the disk jockey chose from an album, guided only by what they felt their audience needed and the "spirit." As a result, it was possible to hear ten different songs from an album on ten different radio stations, and if you did hear a song you liked it might be two weeks before you heard it again. This contrasts sharply with pop radio which insists on high rotation—the same small select collection of songs (all "hits") over and over again. While this tends to annoy a long-term listener, it has a strong appeal for the person who will only listen to the radio for 10-15 minutes at a time; for instance, driving in the car across town. Too, the high rotation assured that a lot of people would hear the song and, through the repetition, be persuaded to buy the record. The sales of gospel albums had suffered from this lack of focus on a single song from an album.

Since gospel radio viewed itself primarily as a ministry, stations were often reluctant to program with an emphasis on music. The economics of a gospel radio station also discouraged this: most of the income came from preachers and others who purchased time on the station to present their programs. These shows, termed "preaching and teaching" programs, usually make a plea for money on the show and receive enough donations to buy more time, thus staying on the air. If their pleas are not successful, they must go off the air.

This began to change when the younger audience started tuning into gospel radio in larger numbers: this age group did not want to hear the "preaching and teaching" programs (which are generally geared to an older audience), they wanted music. The stations, realizing this, began to program for this audience.

Since *Contemporary Christian Music* and, later, *MusicLine*, an off-shoot aimed at the trade audience, began compiling radio airplay charts, the radio industry gradually shifted towards the "hit" format, using the charts to determine what to program (like pop stations). This, in turn, created a greater demand for the "hit" acts at the Christian bookstores with the result that several artists achieved gold and platinum status in the 1980s. This whole movement, in turn, manifested itself at the Gospel Music Association's Dove Awards beginning in 1978 but taking firm hold in 1980 as the young audience and pop-type music grew to dominate the industry.

The Grammy Awards, presented by the National Association of Recording Arts and Sciences (NARAS) also reflected this surge in contemporary Christian music as their categories for gospel grew from one to eight and gospel performers were increasingly asked to perform on the nationally telecast show. The Grammys, more than any other award, gave gospel music the greatest exposure to a national music audience and caused the secular media to pay closer attention, thus creating even more awareness through national media coverage.

The Dove Awards benefited from all this because more people became aware of the awards. And when the Doves began receiving television exposure in 1984, it was the icing on the cake for gospel music. Unfortunately, because gospel is such a diverse music (embracing the sounds of country, rock, black, jazz and other forms of music) several areas got left behind—notably black gospel (which has never really broken into the Gospel Music Association crowd) and the founding fathers from southern gospel, who were, understandably disgruntled and attempted to form their own separate organization and present their own awards.

Awards are perhaps the best way to bring attention to music and the Dove Awards have served this function well, bringing recognition to those within gospel music and publicizing the music and artists to those outside the field. The Doves have allowed the media to focus their attention on this event and thus created national coverage for gospel music. The gospel industry, by following the trends of the pop music world (videos, compact discs, big production road shows, etc.) have managed to continue to appeal to a young audience and take advantage of this national media exposure.

Conclusion

American Christianity has long been inundated with the "bigger is better" syndrome and the assumption that success is an affirmation of the blessing of God. This is reflected in the huge television ministries and the number of churches who will witness to 20,000 (or more) worshipers on a Sunday morning. For those in gospel music, this has meant seeking larger audiences for their music. It is not acceptable to have a small, local ministry—a ministry must be national in scope and reach the far corners of the USA to be considered truly effective. Musicians put pressure on themselves and their record companies to provide an outlet for this kind of visibility; conversely, record companies demand that artists be national (at least potentially) before they will sign them.

The emergence of the record company as the all-powerful arbiter of commercial taste and acceptance follows the rise in power of the secular record company in America. If an artist is worth his salt, then he will have a record contract with a major label. This leads to booking agents being interested in booking them, concert promoters willing to risk finances for a concert, and radio and TV making the air waves available to them. In contemporary Christian music, the competition is fierce to be signed with a major record label.

While Christian artists are noted for proclaiming themselves different from their secular counterparts, the fact remains that they are amazingly similar. There is competitive pressure to get the attention of the record company and be signed, then pressure to get the product shipped to radio and TV stations for exposure and to retail outlets to be sold. The difference is that the Christian record company only signs gospel acts, the radio and TV stations only program gospel music or Christian personalities, and the retail outlets are Christian book and record stores, which only sell Christian "products." The bookers only book Christian concerts and the audiences—though many listen to and buy secular acts—demand that artists and all those around them be untainted by the secular world. In order for the artist to be successful and make a living, he must consent to this marketing structure and strategy.

The Christian artist trying to reach the secular world is forced to appeal to secular companies and outlets—who are generally not interested in promoting the Christian message. The Christian culture often casts a jaundiced eye at those who would become immersed in the world of unbelievers. It is generally an either/or situation and the Christian culture is very possessive of its own. It fears that the sheep will stray. They will go to great lengths to discipline and bring back to the fold those they believe have erred in their ways with musical adventurism. Therefore, in order to survive artists must either subjugate their Christianity and become a secular act or direct their energies and efforts to the Christian culture. Even those exceptions who find acceptance in both worlds

226

must have a firm commitment to one world while they make forays into the other.

Although contemporary Christian musicians have attempted to be non-denominational, the boundary lines are often drawn quite clearly in the churches. As George Bernard Shaw once observed, "There is one Truth, but a hundred different versions." This makes the Christian culture and audience difficult to deal with—no matter what is said or done, someone takes offense. This has forced artists to take safe topics for their songs—the conversion experience, a personal walk with Jesus, how and why others should be Christians or re-telling the ageless gospel story—for commercial acceptance. Musically, the contemporary Christian artists must conform to whatever is popular in the secular world—so there is really no difference musically except in lyric content. And, with Christian artist limited in these topics, there has developed a sameness that causes them to break no new ground artistically.

The church has always stifled artistic growth, basically because its leaders have felt it hinders a person's personal spiritual growth. Music in the form we know it today developed in the Age of Faith around 1000. This is when the concept of the musical staff and the multiple tones in songs developed, realizing all music did not have to be Gregorian chants, which were monotonic. Most of these breakthroughs came through in the church at a time when the church dominated society, serving as the educational, cultural and political center. However, although monks birthed many musical breakthroughs, these were kept from the common people. Thus, it was left to secular society to appeal to the masses in song. In order to reach the masses with a Christian message, the church later copied the secular society.

The arts blossomed in the Renaissance, but at the expense of spirituality in the church. The Popes during that time used wars and art to further themselves at the expense of providing spiritual leadership. Although the church was a leader in art (particularly painting and architecture), the result was the Protestant Reformation led by Luther, who capitalized on the disenchantment within a church which had promoted individual greed and political gain. The Puritans of early America relegated music to a position that was secondary to preaching. They stifled musical creativity by insisting that only Psalms be sung to a handful of tunes. When the revivals brought forth hymns, making religion more personal and music the product of individual composers, the following generations took hold of these hymns and stopped musical development—hanging onto those as the only music fit and proper for the church. The church has traditionally been conservative and resistant to change—in music as well as in a myriad of other matters—until a new generation comes along who bring a spiritual revival, often led by music. But as soon as this new wave becomes accepted—after the initial rejection—Christians adopt this as part of their religion and resist further change, stifling musical growth.

The result is that although music often leads spiritual revivals, the role remains secondary and functional—the real thrust of spiritual revivals is people accepting the gospel, not accepting, developing and pursuing art and music. The manifestation is music first reaching outward to the non-believers (or marginal believers) then turning inward to the believers, until a complacency sets in, bound in tradition and acceptance, until another spiritual revival shakes the foundations and breathes new life into Christianity. Music of the Christian culture will always play a major role in spiritual revivals but almost never play a major role in artistic development. This is because the Christian world must use secular forms in order to make the gospel message contemporary, then throw away the contemporary culture to separate itself from secular, Godless pursuits. The role, therefore, of Christian musicians is not artistic, but rather spiritual and the role of music is secondary to that of the gospel message. While music can and does draw attention to the gospel, it can never overshadow it, in spite of the desires of artists who continue to expand artistic visions.

Because music strikes an emotional chord in listeners, it has always been a leader in spiritual revivals, but as churches are established and the second and third generations take over the reins, it is generally relegated and its influence downplayed as established congregations tend to discard emotionalism for rationalism. In revivals, music precedes the message, although it must remain secondary to the message. In established churches it is often a notch further down the line as the service itself—with an orderliness and tradition—carries the main thrust of the religion.

Most established congregations are conservative and against emotional outbursts—hence they are against new music being introduced. They dislike secular music for the same reasons—its appeal to the heart and emotions—and concentrate instead on an appeal to the soul through the mind. For that reason, music will continue to play a major role in religious revivals while new music will be frowned upon by established churches because it disrupts their order and takes the control of the service out of the hands of the preacher. However, revivals spring from the people, and the people will continue to demand music as part of their religion and whenever and wherever there is a spiritual revival, music will play a major part.

In the past, gospel songs were geared to the gathering of believers—committed, marginal, or hopeful. However, in the contemporary Christian music culture, many songs are developed for records and radio and may never be sung by a church congregation. The emphasis on individuals and groups singing from a stage to a passive audience is the norm, not the exception, but the inturning of gospel music towards the church changes that as new music written and developed for the church becomes more accepted. If the future is like the past, the songs that will survive and make a long-range impact will be the ones which will be sung by church congregations and choirs, not the ones where they must sit and listen to a recording, because gospel music needs to be an active part of religious faith.

Notes

Since 1974, I have done countless interviews and written articles on gospel music or gospel performers for *Billboard, Record World, Contemporary Christian Music, Music City News, Cashbox, Christian Life, Christian Review, Christian Retailer,* and a number of other publications as well as presented papers on gospel music for the Popular Culture Association and Popular Culture of the South Association meetings. This book is a culmination of all those interviews, articles, conferences, readings and research. This makes it difficult to document many parts of this book, particularly the chapters on contemporary Christian music, because the information has been assimilated, digested and in many cases recycled until original sources have been lost. Also, my ideas have developed over a long period of time and often I am not sure exactly when or where I came to a particular idea or conclusion except to say that it has been a long, growing process that has come from ideas presented to others, tossed around in conversations, and modified through numerous discussions and articles.

In these "Notes" I have given sources I have quoted from directly as well as "Major sources," which means those works which have had a particularly significant influence on me. In no case have I included all of the sources I have used in any chapter simply because that would be impossible. Too, many of these sources have influenced not just one chapter but many, although I usually only mention them once. Finally, the greatest source has been a regular exposure to the gospel music industry through conversations with artists, executives, and writers, listening to albums, and reading periodicals, especially *Billboard* and *Contemporary Christian Music.* This, of course, cannot be adequately documented.

Chapter 1

The passages from the Bible in this chapter are taken from the New International Version (Grand Rapids, Michigan: The Zondervan Corp., 1978) with the help of *Cruden's Complete Concordance,* also published by Zondervan (1977, nineteenth printing).

Chapter 2

Sources quoted in this chapter are *Music in the History of the Western Church* by Edward Dickinson (New York: Charles Scribner's Sons, 1902).

Chapter 3

Sources quoted directly here are *The Reign of Elizabeth* by J.R. Black (Oxford: Clarendon, 1959); *Henry VIII and Luther* by Erwin Doernberg (Stanford: Stanford University, 1961); and *The Reformation* by Will Durant (Volume 6 of *The Story of Civilization*) (New York: Simon and Schuster, 1957). Other major sources for this chapter are *The Elizabethan Renaissance* by A.L. Rowse; "The Enduring Relevance of Martin Luther 500 Years After His Birth" by Jaroslav Pelikan *(New York Times Magazine,* Sept. 18, 1983) and discussions with Professor William Holland of Middle Tennessee State University.

Chapter 4

Sources quoted directly for this chapter are "When You Sing Next Sunday, Thank Luther" by Richard D. Dinwiddie *(Christianity Today*, 21 October. 1983: 18-21); *Luther and Music* by Paul Nettl (New York: Russell and Russell, 1948), *The Handbook to the Lutheran Hymnal* by W.G. Pollack (St. Louis: Concordia, 1975) and *Christian Singers of Germany* by Catherine Winkworth (Freeport, N.Y.: Books for Libraries, 1977). The songs came from *A Treasury of Hymns* edited by Marie Leiper and Henry W. Simon (New York: Simon and Schuster, 1953). Other sources include *Readings in Luther for Laymen* by Charles S. Anderson; *Music in the History of the Western Church* by Edward Dickinson, *Luther: An Experiment in Biography* by H.G. Haile, and "How One Man's Pen Changed the World" by Henry Zecher.

Chapter 5

Sources quoted directly are the two volume work, *American Hymns Old and New* by Albert Christ-Janer, Charles W. Hughes, and Carlton Sprague (New York: Columbia U P, 1980); *Early New England Psalmody* by Hamilton C. Macdougal (New York: De Capo, 1969); "Mainstreams and Backwaters in American Psalmody" and "Music of the American Revolution" by Richard Crawford; "White Spirituals from the Sacred Harp" by Allen Lomax; *Americans and Their Songs* by Frank Luther (New York: Harper Brothers, 1942). Other major sources consulted include *The Gospel in Hymns* by Albert Bailey, *The Oxford History of the American People* by Samuel Eliot Morison and conversations with Professor William Beasley (now deceased) at Middle Tennessee State University.

Chapter 6

The only source quoted directly in this chapter is *The Gospel in Hymns* by Albert Bailey (New York: Charles Scribner's Sons, 1950). Other sources include *Make a Joyful Noise Unto the Lord* by Susan S. Tamke; and *A Treasury of Hymns*, edited by Leiper and Simon.

Chapter 7

Sources quoted directly here are *The Gospel in Hymns* by Bailey; "Two Brothers..." by Richard Dinwiddie, and *A Treasury of Hymns* edited by Marie Leiper and Henry W. Simon.

Chapter 8

Sources quoted here are *Yesterdays* by Charles Hamm (New York: W.W. Norton, 1979); *Francis Hopkinson and James Lyon* by Oscar G.T. Sonneck (New York: De Capo, 1967); *American Hymns Old and New* by Christ-Janer, Hughes and Sprague; "Mainstreams and Backwaters in American Psalmody" (Jacket notes to *Make a Joyful Noise*, New World Records, NW 255) and "Music of the American Revolution" (Jacket notes for *The Birth of Liberty*, New World Records, NW 276) by Richard Crawford; *Early New England Psalmody* by Hamilton C. Macdougal (New York: De Capo, 1969); *Americans and Their Songs* by Frank Luther (New York: Harper Brothers, 1942); and "White Spirituals from the Sacred Harp" (Jacket notes for *White Spirituals from the Sacred Harp*, New World, NW 205) by Alan Lomax.

Chapter 9

Sources quoted directly are *White and Negro Spirituals* by George Pullen Jackson (Locust Valley, N.Y.: J.J. Augustin, 1943) and *American Hymns Old and New* by Christ-Janer et. al.

Chapter 10

Sources quoted directly are *Pilgrims in Our Own Land* by Martin Marty (Boston: Little, Brown, 1985); *The General Next to God* by Richard Collins (Glasgow: Fantana/Collins, 1965); and *My Life and the Story of the Hymns* by Ira Sankey (Philadelphia: The Sunday School Times, 1907).

Chapter 11

The source quoted directly here is *Billy Sunday Was His Real Name* by William G. McLoughlin (Chicago: U of Chicago P, 1955). Other major sources include *Vision of the Disinherited: The Making of American Pentecostalism* by Robert Anderson, *Bright Wind of the Spirit: Pentecostalisms Today* by Steve Durasoff, "White Urban Hymnody" by Harry Eskew, and *The Holiness Pentecostal Movement* by Vinson Synan.

Chapter 12

The source quoted directly in this chapter is *The Electric Church* by Ben Armstrong (Nashville: Thomas Nelson, 1979); other major sources are *American Popular Song* by Alec Wilder and *From Tin Foil to Stereo* by Oliver Read and Walter L. Welch.

Chapter 13

Sources quoted directly in this chapter are *Pilgrims in Their Own Land* by Martin Marty (Boston: Little, Brown, 1985); *The Gospel Sound* by Tony Heilbut (New York: Simon and Schuster, 1971); *Sing Your Heart Out Country Boy* by Dorothy Horstman (New York: E.P. Dutton, 1975); and *Some Aspects of the Religious Music of the United States Negro* by George R. Ricks (New York: Arno Press, 1977). Other major sources include the books by George Pullen Jackson, especially *Spiritual Folk Songs of Early America* and *White and Negro Spirituals*; and "Black Urban Hymnody" by Anthony Heilbut.

Chapter 14

Sources quoted directly here are "Gospel Boogie: White Southern Gospel Music in Transition" and "Columbia Records and Old-Time Music," both by Charles Wolfe. Other major sources include *Wings of a Dove* by Lois Blackwell and conversations with Charles Wolfe.

Chapter 15

The source directly here is *Above All* by Kree Jack Racine. Other major sources include *The James Blackwood Story* by James Blackwood, *Let The Song Go On* by Paula Becker, and conversations with Brock Speer, James Blackwood, and Charles Wolfe.

Chapter 16

Major sources for this chapter are *Why Should The Devil Have All the Good Music* by Paul Baker, the books by Joel Whitburn on the *Billboard* charts, and "Gold and Platinum Awards" from the RIAA.

Chapter 17

The sources quoted directly in this chapter are *Elvis: The Final Years* by Jerry Hopkins; "Three chords and a cloud of dust" by Bob Terrell in *The Singing News* and an interview with J.D. Sumner in January, 1988 and not published previously. Other major sources include an interview with Joe Moscheo done for the article "The Imperials: Building a Musical Bridge."

Chapter 18

The source quoted directly in this chapter is *The Gospel Sound* by Tony Heilbut (New York: Simon and Schuster, 1971). Other major sources are *Just Mahalia, Baby* by Laurraine Goreau, and *Sweet Soul Music* by Peter Guralnick.

Chapter 19

Major sources for this chapter are *Why Should The Devil Have All the Good Music*, "The New Rebel Cry: Jesus is Coming!" in *Time*, an interview with Larry Norman conducted in 1978 which has never been published, and conversations with Paul Baker.

Chapter 20

Major sources include *Pilgrims in Their Own Land* by Martin Marty, and a personal interview with Ray Bruno of the North American Liturgy Resources published as "The New Movement in Catholic Music" and "St. Louis Jesuits: Music with Mass Appeal" both in *Contemporary Christian Music*.

Chapter 21

Quotes from Jarrell McCracken in this chapter came from an interview published in *Record World*, "Jarrell McCracken on Spreading the Word." Quotes from Marvin Norcross came from an interview in March, 1982, shortly before he died and not published previously. Major sources for the Benson Company section came from interviews with John T. Benson III and Bob Benson, both published in *Record World's* Oct. 1, 1977 issue. Another major source was "The Benson Company: 75 Years of Growth," written by the company and published in *Record World* in the Oct. 1, 1977 issue.

Chapter 22

Quotes from this chapter came from an interview with Bill Gaither in June, 1986 and not published previously.

Chapter 23

Sources quoted in this chapter are "Stepping Out Into Freedom: The Life of Fanny Lou Hamer" and "Prophet of Hope for the Sick and Tired," both by Danny Collum and "Voice of Calm" by Charles McLaurin *(Sojourners* December, 1982), and excerpts from a personal interview conducted with James Cleveland and published as "James Cleveland on Expanding Gospel's Audience" in *Record World*, November 11, 1978. Other major sources include *The Gospel Sound* by Tony Heilbut, the article "GMWA: Where 'Everybody is Somebody' " published in *Record World* Oct. 1, 1977 and conversations with Fred Mendelsohn, president of Savoy Records.

Chapter 24

The quotes from the Cathedrals in this chapter came from personal interviews with Glen Payne and George Younce in 1982 and published in a record company biography for them as well as "The Cathedrals: At the Top of Today's Southern Gospel" in *Rejoice*; I have also used quotes on the Florida Boys from a personal interview with Les Beasley, October, 1987, and an interview with Jim Hamill, September, 1987. Other sources quoted are "The Kingsmen...A Spiritual Explosion" by Jeanne Coffman *(Singing News* November, 1986) and "Three Chords and a cloud of dust: The Jim Hamill Story" by Bob Terrell *(Singing News* February, 1988). Other major sources include "Eldridge Fox

Receives Norcross Award" by Bob Terrell *(Singing News* September 1986) and conversations with Marvin Norcross (now deceased).

Chapter 25

Quotes from Billy Ray Hearn in this chapter come from an interview published in *Record World*, "Billy Ray Hearn on Sparrow's Takeoff" on November 11, 1978. I have also had a number of conversations and interviews with Mr. Hearn in the ensuing years which have been invaluable. The information on Keith Green came from a number of articles published in *Contemporary Christian Music.* Particularly helpful was the special issue devoted to Green in September, 1982.

Chapter 26

The source quoted in this book is *Then Sings My Soul* by George Beverly Shea and Fred Bauer. I also did an interview with Mr. Shea published in *Music City News* in May, 1985. The major sources for the section on Sandi Patti came from research for the book I did on her, *Sandi Patti: The Voice of Gospel*, published by Doubleday/Dolphin. An interview with Elwyn Ramer with Lorenz Music was the major source for the section on church music publishing.

Chapter 27

Sources quoted directly in this chapter are *To Cross a River* by Jimmy Swaggart with Robert Paul Lamb (Baton Rouge: Jimmy Swaggart Ministries, 1984); *Hellfire* by Nick Tosches; and "Brother Swaggart, Here's My Question" from *The Evangelist* (Feb. 1988 Vol. 20 No. 3: 9-10).

Chapter 28

The quotes from Johnny Cash in this chapter came from a series of interviews I did with him in Spring, 1980 and published in *Cashbox* ("Johnny Cash: The First 25 Years") on June 14, 1980; in *Contemporary Christian Music* ("Johnny Cash") in April, 1981; and in *Music City News* ("Johnny Cash Carries a Message in Song") in September, 1980. The quotes from Barbara Mandrell came from an interview with her previously published in *Contemporary Christian Music,* "Barbara Mandrell: Making People Smile and Tap Their Toes" in November, 1982.

Chapter 29

Quotes in this chapter came from several interviews done with Amy Grant and published in "Amy Grant" in *Contemporary Christian Music* in June, 1979 and "Amy Grant—Reaching Out" published in *Christian Life* in June, 1981. The quotes from Gary Chapman came from an interview previously published as "Gary Chapman" in *CCM* in June, 1981.

Chapter 30

The section on the Imperials came from an article I wrote for *Contemporary Christian Music* in February, 1980, "The Imperials: Building a Musical Bridge." The information on Petra came from a number of articles written about them in *CCM* and from a personal interview I did in 1987. The information on Michael W. Smith came from interviews done with him, never published previously, and an article by Bill Littleton in *CCM*, "Michael W. Smith."

Chapter 31

Quotes from this chapter were taken from a personal interview with Karen Lafferty, in Amsterdam in June, 1983 as well as conversations with her that summer and published in *CCM* as "Karen Lafferty: Musician with a Mission" in September, 1984; the quotes from Scott Wesley Brown came from a personal interview previously published in *CCM*, "Scott Wesley Brown: Back From the U.S.S.R." in January, 1986.

Chapter 32

This chapter was originally done for a class taught by Charles Wolfe. The source quoted directly here is an article from *Time*, "Gospel TV." Other major sources include the Gallup Report and *The Search for America's Faith* by George Gallup, Jr. and David Poling and interviews with Shannon Williams and executives with the Christian Bookseller's Association.

Chapter 33

Most of the information on the Gospel Music Association in this chapter came from an interview with Don Butler, published in *Record World*, "Don Butler: Spreading the Word Through GMA," on Nov. 11, 1978.

Bibliography

Anderson, Charles S. *Reading in Luther for Laymen*. Minneapolis: Augsburg, 1967.

Anderson, Robert Mapes. *Vision of the Disinherited: The Making of American Pentecostalism*. New York: Oxford, 1979.

Anderson, Robert and Gail North. *Gospel Music Encyclopedia*. New York: Sterling, 1979.

Andrews, Edward D. *The Gift To Be Simple*. New York: Dover Pub. 1940.

Appell, Richard G. *The Music of the Bay Psalm Book*. New York: Institute to Studies in American Music, 1975.

"Are Hits Holy? Radio Stations, Record Labels Feud Over Use of Singles." *CCM* Aug/ Sept. 1981 Vol. 4 Nos. 2 & 3: 31.

Armstrong, Ben. *The Electric Church*. Nashville: Thomas Nelson, 1979.

——— "How Big is the Religious Radio-TV Audience?" *Religious Broadcasting*. May, 1981.

"Back to That Old Time Religion." *Time*. December 26, 1977: 52-58.

Baer, Hans A. *The Black Spiritual Movement: A Religious Response to Racism*. Knoxville: U. of Tennessee P, 1974.

Bailey, Albert Edward. *The Gospel in Hymns*. New York: Charles Scribner's Sons, 1950.

Baker, Paul. "Bass Sees Bright Future for Gospel in Christian Market." *CB* March 29, 1980: G-6, G-16.

——— "Can Gospel Increase Airplay and Climb the Secular Pop Charts?" *CCM* Aug. 1980 Vol. 3 No. 2: 16-17.

——— "Can Preaching Programs Be Hip?" (Radio) *CCM* Feb. 1981 Vol. 3 No. 8: 16, 36.

——— "Can Preaching Programs Help?" (Radio) *CCM* July 1981 Vol. 4 No. 1: 15.

——— "Contemporary Christian Field Faces Big Challenges in 80s." *CB* March 29, 1980: G-6, 17.

——— *Contemporary Christian Music*. Westchester, Ill.: Crossways, 1985.

——— Gospel Music Today: Going in Many Directions At Once." *BB* Oct. 11, 1986.

——— *I've Got a New Song*. San Diego: Scandinavia, 1983.

——— "Jesus Music: A New Dimension in Pop and Gospel." *RW* Oct. 1, 1977: 12, 88, 98.

——— "The National Gospel Radio Seminar: Growing Together in St. Louis." *CCM* Aug. 1979 Vol. 2 No. 3: 30, 32.

——— "Religious Radio: Ain't What It Used to Be." *BB* July 28, 1979: R-28, R-43, R-45.

——— "Setting the Good Word to Modern Music." *BB* July 28, 1979: R-4, R-12.

——— "Sparrow Records: 10th Anniversary Brings New Luster to Roster of Largest Gospel Independent." *BB* Oct. 11, 1986: G-6.

——— *Topical Index of Contemporary Christian Music*. Pinson, Alabama: Music Helps, 1987.

——— *Why Should The Devil Have All The Good Music*. Waco: Word, 1979.

Barbour, James. *The Music of William Billings*. New York: De Capo, 1972.

Barton, William E. *Old Plantation Hymns*. New York: AMS Press, 1972.

Becker, Paula. *Let The Song Go On.* (Biography of the Speer Family). Nashville: Impact, 1971.

Belknap, Alan. "Catholic Communications: Linking Tradition with Relevancy." *CCM* Oct. 1979 Vol. 2 No. 4: 19, 25.

"The Benson Company: 75 Years of Growth: *RW.* Oct. 1, 1977: 3, 30.

Benware, David. "Christian Radio in Focus: Part 1." *CCM.* Dec. 1978 Vol. 1 No. 2: 18, 22.

———— "Christian Radio: Part 2." *CCM* Jan. 1979 Vol. 1 No. 7: 16, 28.

———— "Christian Radio: Part 3." *CCM* Feb. 1979 Vol. 1 No. 8: 18, 25.

———— "Christian Radio: Part 4." *CCM* March 1979 Vol. 1 No. 9: 16-21.

———— "Christian Radio: Part 5." *CCM* April 1979 Vol. 1 No. 10: 13, 31.

———— "Christian Radio: Part 6." *CCM* May 1979 Vol. 1 No. 11: 17, 23.

Berkman, Dave. "Long Before Falwell: Early Radio and Religion—As reported by the Nation's Periodical Press." *Journal of Popular Culture.* Vol. 21 No. 4 Spring 1988: 1-11.

"The Bill Gaither Trio: At The Forefront of the Gospel Field." *RW* Oct. 1, 1977: 8.

"Bill Gaither's Pinebrook Studio." *CCM* May 1981 Vol. 3 No. 11: 31.

Billings, William. *The Psalm-Singers Amusement.* New York: De Capo, 1975.

"Billy Ray Hearn." *CCM* May 1980 Vol. 2 No. 11: 11, 32.

Bisher, Furman. "They Put Rhythm in Religion." *Saturday Evening Post,* c. 1953.

Blanchard, John. *Pop Goes the Gospel.*

Bock, Al. *I Saw The Light: The Gospel Life of Hank Williams.* Nashville: Green Valley Record Store, 1977.

Blackwell, Lois S. *The Wings of the Dove.* Norfolk, Va.: The Donning Co., 1978.

Blackwood, James, with Dan Martin. *The James Blackwood Story.* Monroeville, Penn.: Whitaker House, 1975.

"Bob Dylan," *CCM* Aug. 1980 Vol. 3 No. 2: 11.

Broughton, Viv. *Black Gospel.* Pool, England: Blandford, 1985.

Brown, Theron and Hezekiah Butterworth. *The Story of the Hymns and Tunes.* New York: American Tract Society, 1906.

Bruce, Dickson D. Jr. *And They All Sang Hallelujah.* Knoxville: U. of Tennessee P, 1974.

Burt, Jesse and Duane Allen. *The History of Gospel Music.* Nashville: K & S Press, 1971.

Carr, Patrick. *The Illustrated History of Country Music.* Garden City, New York: Dolphin and Doubleday, 1980.

Cash, Johnny. *Man in Black.* Grand Rapids, Mich.: Zondervan, 1975.

Cash, June Carter. *Among My Klediments.* Grand Rapids, Mich.: Zondervan, 1979.

Cash, Rita. "Reverend James Cleveland". *Soul.* August 15, 1977.

"CBA Slights Music Sales." *CCM* May 1980 Vol. 2, No. 12: 31.

Chandler, Russell. "The Good News in Gospel Music." *Saturday Evening Post.* April 1982: 18-19, 22, 115.

Chase, Gilbert. *America's Music.* New York: McGraw-Hill, 1955.

Christ-Janer, Albert, Charles W. Hughes, and Carleton Sprague Smith. *American Hymns Old and New.* New York: Columbia University P, 1980.

Claghorn, Gene. *Women Composers and Hymnists: A Concise Bibliographical Dictionary.* Metuchen, J.J.: The Scarecrow Press, 1984.

Clower, Jerry with Gerry Wood. *Ain't God Good.* Waco: Word, 1975.

Cobb, Buell E. Jr. *The Sacred Harp: A Tradition and It's Music.* Athens, Ga.: University of Georgia P, 1981.

Coffman, Jeanne. "The Kingsmen...A Spiritual Explosion." (*Singing News,* November, 1986).

Collins, Richard. *The General Next To God.* Glasgow: Fantana/Collins, 1965.

Collum, Danny. "Prophet of Hope for the Sick and Tired." (Fanny Lou Hamer) *(Sojourners,* Vol. 11 No. 11 December, 1982: 3-4).

———— "Stepping Out Into Freedom: The life of Fanny Lou Hamer". *Sojourners.* Vol. 11 No. 11 December, 1982: 11-16.

Cone, James H. *The Spirituals and the Blues.* Westport, Ct.: Greenwood P, 1972.

Conn, Charles Paul. *The New Johnny Cash.* Old Tappan, N.J.: Spire, 1976.

"Convention Report: National Religious Broadcasters." *CCM* March 1979 Vol. 1 No. 9: 16.

Crawford, Richard A. *Andrew Law, American Psalmist.* New York: De Capo, 1981.

———— *The Core Repertory of Early American Psalmody.* Madison, Wi.: A.R. Editions, 1984.

———— "Mainstreams and Backwaters in American Psalmody." Jacket notes to *Make a Joyful Noise.* New World Records, NW 255.

———— "Music of the American Revolution." Jacket notes for *The Birth of Liberty.* New World Records, NW 276.

"Creative Merchandising in the Christian Store." *CCM* July 1980 Vol. 3 No. 1: 11, 15.

Crews, Harry. *The Gospel Singer.* (fiction) New York: William Morrow & Co., 1968.

Crosby, Fanny. *Memories of Eighty Hymns.* Boston: James H. Earle & Co., 1906.

Crouch, Andrae with Nina Ball. *Through It All.* Waco: Word, 1974.

Curtis, J. Scott. "NRB: Can Music Be Plugged Into the Electric Church?" *CCM* April 1979 Vol. 1, No. 10: 18.

Cusic, Don. "Amy Grant—Reaching Out." *Christian Life* June 1981 Vol. 43, No. 2: 18-20.

———— "Barbara Mandrell: Making People Smile and Tap Their Toes." *CCM* Nov. 1982 Vol. 5 No. 5: 10-13.

———— "Billy Ray Hearn on Sparrow's Takeoff." *RW* Nov. 11, 1978: 24, 48, 51, 60.

———— "Bob Benson on Building the Gospel Market." *RW* Oct. 1, 1977: 6, 22, 28.

———— "Brown Bannister." *CCM* June 1982 Vol. 5, No. 12.

———— "Cash Discusses Christianity and the Gospel Message." *CB.* June 14, 1980: C-10, 28.

———— "Cash On Stage: Combination of Styles, Moods, and Subjects." *CB.* June 14, 1980: C-10, 30.

———— "The Cathedrals: At the Top of Today's Southern Gospel." *Rejoice.* Winter 1987 Vol. 1, No. 1: 31-32.

———— "Don Butler: Spreading the Word Through GMA." *RW* Nov. 11, 1978: 22, 52, 60.

———— "Gary Chapman." *CCM* June 1981 Vol. 3 No. 12: 10, 12.

———— "Gospel Music Goes Back to Church with a Return to Tradition." *Rejoice* Winter 1987 Vol. 1, No. 1: 42-43.

———— "Gospel Faces Important Issues Following Growth of 70s." *CB* March 29, 1980: G-3, G-12.

———— "Gospel Music Seeks Ways to Unite and Publicize Its Various Styles." *RW* Nov. 11, 1978: 16, 64.

———— "Gospel: Music With a Timeless Message." *RW* Oct. 1, 1977: 4, 99.

———— "Gospel Radio at Crossroads Between Music and Message." *CB* March 29, 1980: G-9.

———— "Greg Nelson: A Vital Relationship With The Lord." *BMI: The Many Worlds of Music.* Fall 1987: 28-30.

———— "The Imperials: Building a Musical Bridge." *CCM* Feb. 1980 Vol. 2 No. 8: 6-7.

_____ "James Cleveland on Expanding Gospel's Audience." *RW* Nov. 11, 1978: 32, 48.

_____ "Jarrell McCracken on Spreading the Word." *RW* Oct. 1, 1977: 14, 78, 92, 101.

_____ "John T. Benson III on the Future of the Benson Co." *RW* Oct. 1, 1977: 4, 31.

_____ "Johnny Cash." *CCM* April 1981 Vol. 3 No. 10: 8-9.

_____"Johnny Cash: The First 25 Years." *CB*. June 14, 1980: C-5, 22.

_____ "Johnny Cash Carries A Message In Song." *Music City News*. Vol. XVII No. 3 September, 1980: 16-17.

_____ "June Carter Cash: The Lady Behind the Man in Black." *CB*. June 14, 1980: C-14, 30.

_____ "Karen Lafferty: Musician With a Mission." *CCM* Sept. 1984 Vol. 7 No. 3.

_____ "A Market Divided" (Black gospel) *CB* Aug. 7, 1982: G-14.

_____ "Music That Fulfills a Need." *CB* Aug. 7, 1982: G-4, 5.

_____ "The New Movement in Catholic Music." *CCM* July 1979 Vol. 2 No. 1: 27-28.

_____ "Ralph Carmichael Examines the Evolution of Gospel." *CB* March 29, 1980: G-3, 17.

_____ "Sandi Patti." *Rejoice*. Spring 1988 Vol. 1, No. 2: 4-7.

_____ *Sandi Patti: The Voice of Gospel*. New York: Dolphin/Doubleday, 1988.

_____ "Scott Wesley Brown: Back from the U.S.S.R." *CCM* Jan. 1986 Vol. 8, No. 7.

_____ "Shannon Williams Traces the History of Nashboro Records." *CB* March 29, 1980: G-3, 14.

_____ "Southern Gospel: An Historical Review." *Rejoice* Winter 1987 Vol. 1 No. 1: 29-30.

_____ "Southern Gospel Grows From Rural Roots." *BB* July 28, 1979: R-16, R-45.

_____ "Stan Moser on the Changing Face of Gospel." *RW* Oct. 1, 1977: 34, 94, 100.

_____ "St. Louis Jesuits: Music With Mass Appeal." *CCM* Oct. 1979 Vol. 2 No. 4: 32.

_____ "White Christian Market Continues to Grow." *RW* Oct. 1, 1977: 83.

_____ "Zondervan Corp. Announces Major Record Expansion." *CB* March 29, 1980: G-19.

Dabney, Dick. "God's Own Network." *Harper's*. August, 1980: 33-52.

Daniel, Ralph T. *The Anthem in New England Before 1800*. New York: De Capo, 1979.

Darden, Bob. "Word Records: A 30-Year Success Story." *CCM* Jan. 1981 Vol. 3 No. 7: W-4, 5.

_____ "Word Records: Breaking Down Barriers Still Top Priority in Campaign to Capture New Musical Trends." *BB* Oct. 11, 1986: G-4.

_____ "Word's 30 Years Net 70% of Christian Records Sold." *CCM* Jan. 1981 Vol. 3 No. 7: W-17, 18.

"David Serey—NALR." *CCM* Oct. 1979 Vol. 2 No. 4: 10, 17.

Deller, Fred, Roy Thompson and Doug Green. *The Illustrated Encyclopedia of Country Music*. New York: Harmony, 1977.

Dickinson, Edward, *Music in the History of the Western Church*. New York: Charles Scribner's Sons, 1902 and 1927.

Dinwiddie, Richard D. "Two Brothers...Who Changed the Course of Church Singing." *Christianity Today*, 21 Sept. 1984: 30-34.

_____ "When You Sing Next Sunday, Thank Luther." *Christianity Today*, 21 Oct. 1983: 18-21.

"Does Rock 'n' Roll Lead to Rack 'n' Ruin?" *CCM* Aug./Sept. 1981 Vol. 4 Nos. 2 & 3: 15.

Donaldson, Devlin. "Petra." *CCM* Nov. 1983 Vol. 6 No. 5.

Dorsey, L.C. "A Prophet Who Believed." (Fanny Lou Hamer) *Sojourners* Vol. 11 No. 11 December 1982: 21.

Dowley, Tim, ed. *Eerdman's Handbook to the History of Christianity.* Grand Rapids, Mich.: Wm. B. Eerdman's, 1977.

Durasoff, Steve. *Bright Wind of the Spirit: Pentecostalism Today.* Englewood Cliffs: Prentice-Hall, 1972.

"Dylan Retrospective Unfulfilled...Almost." (Bob Dylan concert review). *CCM* Dec. 1980 Vol. 3 No. 6: 32-33.

"Dylan Tells Story of Conversion." *CCM* Feb. 1981 Vol. 3 No. 8: 11, 22.

Edwards, Jim. "Amy Grant Concert Review." *CCM* April 1981 Vol. 3 No. 10: 41.

——— "Dylan Injects a Shot of Love Into His Music." *CCM* Aug./Sept. 1981 Vol. 4 Nos. 2 & 3: 19, 24.

——— "Keith Green Concert Review." *CCM* May 1979 Vol. 1 No. 11: 25, 27.

Elson, Louis C. *The History of American Music.* New York: MacMillan, 1925.

Eskew, Harry. "White Urban Hymnody." Jacket notes on *Brighten the Corner Where You Are.* New World, NW 224.

"Facing the Challenges of a Burgeoning Industry." *CCM* Aug. 1978 Vol. 1, No. 2: 10, 15.

Findlay, James F. Jr. *Dwight Moody: American Evangelist, 1837-1899.* Chicago: U of Chicago P, 1969.

Fischer, John. "Biblical Foundations for a Music Ministry (I Corin.)" *CCM* Dec. 1979 Vol. 2, No. 6: 25-26.

——— *Dark Horse: The Story of a Winner.*

Flake, Carol. *Redemptorama: Culture, Politics and the New Evangelism.* Garden City, N.Y.: Anchor and Doubleday, 1984.

Foote, Henry Wilder. *Three Centuries of American Hymnody.* Cambridge: Harvard U P, 1940.

Ford, Tennessee Ernie. *This is My Story, This is My Song.* Englewood Cliffs: Prentice-Hall, 1963.

Gaillard, Frye. *Race, Rock & Religion.* Charlotte, N.C.: East Woods Press, 1977.

Gaither, Gloria. *Because He Lives.* Fleming H. Revell, 1977.

Gallup, George Jr. and David Poling. *The Search for America's Faith.* (Nashville: Abingdon, 1980).

"Gallup Poll Profiles Christian Market." *CCM* May 1980 Vol. 2, No. 12: 31.

Gallup Report. "Religion in America." No. 236: May, 1985.

Geer, E. Harold. *Hymnal for Colleges and Schools.* New Haven: Yale, 1956.

Gentry, Linnell. *A History and Encyclopedia of Country, Western, and Gospel Music.* Nashville: Clairmont Corp., 1969.

Gillespie, Paul E., ed. *Foxfire 7.* Garden City: Anchor/Doubleday, 1982.

"GMWA: Where 'Everybody is Somebody.' " *RW* Oct. 1, 1977: 103.

Goldberg, Michael. "Amy Grant Wants to Put God on the Charts." *Rolling Stone.* June 6, 1985.

Goreau, Laurraine. *Just Mahalia, Baby.* Waco, Word, 1975.

"The Gospel Boom." *Saturday Evening Post.* April, 1979: 34-36, 40, 136.

"Gospel Music: A Potential Retail Giant." *RW* Oct. 1, 1977: 82.

"Gospel TV: Religion, Politics and Money." *Time.* February 17, 1986: 62-69.

Gould, Nathaniel D. *Church Music in America.* New York: A.N. Johnson, 1853.

Great Songs of the Church (Number Two). Chicago: Great Songs Press, 1965.

"The Greatest Story Ever told...and Retold, and Retold..." *New Times.* September 16, 1977: 14-15.

Green, Douglas. *Country Roots.* New York: Hawthorn, 1976.

Green, Keith. "Music or Mission." *CCM* Oct. 1978 Vol. 1, No. 4: 32.

Green, Melody. "A letter from. . . ." *CCM* Sept. 1982 Vol. 5 No. 3: 36-37.

Gulliksen, Kenn. "A Perplexing Dilemma: Can This Tragedy Be God's Will?" (Keith Green). *CCM* Sept. 1982 Vol. 5, No. 3: 30, 37.

Guralnick, Peter. *Sweet Soul Music.* New York: Harper & Row, 1986.

Hafer, Jack. "A Christian Look at the Arts." *CCM* July 1980 Vol 3, No. 1: 45, 49.

———— "The Importance of Entertainment." *CCM* Sept. 1980 Vol. 3, No. 3: 22, 29.

———— "Lyrics: Honest, Deep and Christian Too?" *CCM* Nov. 1980 Vol, 3, No. 4: 10, 25.

———— "The Purpose of Music." *CCM.* Aug. 1980 Vol. 3, No. 2: 28, 33.

———— "The Spiritual Power of Rock'n Roll." *CCM* Oct. 1980 Vol. 3, No. 4: 37.

Haile, H.G. *Luther: An Experiment in Biography.* Garden City, N.J.: Doubleday, 1980.

Hamm, Charles. *Yesterdays: Popular Song in America.* New York: W.W. Norton, 1979.

Hamm, Charles, Bruno Nettl and Ronald Byrnside. *Contemporary Music and Music Cultures.* Englewood Cliffs: Prentice-Hall, 1975.

"HeartWarming: First Label." *RW* Oct. 1, 1977: 3, 18, 30.

Heilbut, Anthony. "Black Urban Hymnody." Jacket notes on *Brighten the Corner Where You Are.* New World, NW 224.

———— *The Gospel Sound.* New York: Simon and Schuster, 1971.

Hinkle, Sally. "Musical Conversion: From Pop to Praising the Lord." *BB* July 28, 1979: R-18, 41.

Hopkins, Jerry. *Elvis: A Biography.* New York: Warner, 1971.

———— *Elvis: The Final Years.* New York: Playboy, 1981.

Horn, Dorothy D. *Sing To Me of Heaven.* Gainesville: U of Florida P, 1970.

Horsfield, Peter G. *Religious Television: An American Experience.* New York: Longman, 1984.

Horstman, Dorothy. *Sing Your Heart Out Country Boy.* New York: E.P. Dutton, 1975.

Ingalls, Jeremiah. *The Christian Harmony.* New York: De Capo, 1981.

Inserra, Lorraine and Hitchcock, H. Wiley. *The Music of Ainsworth Psalter.* New York: Institute for Studies in American Music, 1981.

Jackson, Clyde Owen. *The Songs of Our Years: A Study of Negro Folk Music.* New York: Exposition, 1968.

Jackson, George Pullen. *Another Sheaf of White Spirituals.* Gainesville: University of Florida P, 1952.

———— *Down-East Spirituals and Others.* New York: J.J. Augustin, 1939.

———— *Spiritual Folk Songs of Early America.* New York: J.J. Augustin, 1937.

———— *White and Negro Spirituals.* Locust Valley, N.Y.: J.J. Augustin, 1943.

———— *White Spirituals in the Southern Uplands.* New York: Dover, 1965.

Jackson, Irene. *Afro-American Religious Music.* Westport, Ct.: Greenwood P, 1979.

Jantz, Stan. "CBA Report: A Merchandiser's Dream." *CCM* Sept. 1978 Vol. 1, No. 3: 11.

Johnson, Guye. *Treasury of Great Hymns and Their Stories.* Greenville, S.C.: Bob Jones U P, 1986.

Johnson, James Weldon and J. Rosamond Johnson. *American Negro Spirituals.* New York: Viking, 1925.

Johnson, June. "Broken Barriers and Billy Sticks." (Fanny Lou Hamer) *Sojourners* Vol. 11, No. 11 December 1982: 16-17.

Julian, John. *Dictionary of Hymnology Volume I: A-O.* Grand Rapids, Mich.: Kregel, 1985.

———— *Dictionary of Hymnology Volume II: P-Z.* Grand Rapids, Mich.: Kregal, 1985.

Hall, Sammy with Charles Paul Conn. *Hooked on a Good Thing.* Old Tappan, N.J.: Fleming H. Revell, 1972.

Hicks, Hillary. "Black Gospel: Meeting the Challenges of Change." *BB*. Oct. 11, 1986: G-8.

Holm, Dallas. *This is My Story*. Nashville: Benson.

Howard, John Tasker. *Our American Music: Three Hundred Years of It*. New York: Thomas Y. Crowell, 1930.

Knaack, Twila. *I Touched a Sparrow: Ethel Waters*. Waco, Tx.,: Word, 1978.

"Karen Lafferty Has a Mission for Musicians in Europe." *CCM* May 1981 Vol. 3, No. 11: 17.

"Keith Green's Next Album Not to Be Available in Stores." *CCM* Dec. 1979 Vol. 2, No. 6: 31.

"Keith Green." *CCM* Sept. 1982 Vol. 5, No. 3: 32-33.

"Keith Green's Musical Journey." *RW* Oct. 1, 1977: 69.

"Keith Green: A Tribute." *CCM* Sept. 1982 Vol. 5, No. 3: 36-37.

King, Edwin. "Go Tell It On The Mountain: A Prophet from the Delta." (Fanny Lou Hamer) *Sojourners* Vol. 11, No. 11 December 1982: 18-20.

"Larry Norman: The Original Christian Street Rocker." *CCM* March 1981 Vol. 3, No. 9: 8-11, 25.

Larson, Bob. *Rock*. Wheaton, Ill.: Tyndale House, 1980.

Lawhead, Steve. "Beyond the Statistics." *CCM* Nov. 1979 Vol. 2, No. 5: 30, 32.

_____. "The Consumer: Christian Music's Most Wanted Person." *CCM* Sept. 1979 Vol. 2, No. 3: 30, 32.

_____. "Selling the Message in the Marketplace." *CCM* May 1980 Vol. 2, No. 12: 21.

_____. "Who is the Consumer?" *CCM* Aug. 1979 Vol. 2, No. 2: 22.

Leach, MacEdward, ed. *The Ballad Book*. New York: A.S. Barnes, 1955.

Lee, Pam. "The Imperials at Home and On the Road." *CCM*. Aug. 1982 Vol. 5, No. 2: 8-12.

Leiper, Maria and Henry W. Simon, eds. *A Treasury of Hymns*. New York: Simon and Schuster, 1953.

Littleton, Bill. "Michael W. Smith." *CCM* April 1985 Vol. 7, No. 10.

Livgren, Kerry and Kenneth Boa. *Seeds of Change*.

Lomax, Alan. "Baptist Hymns and White Spirituals from the Southern Mountains." Jacket notes for *The Gospel Ship*. New World, NW 294.

_____. "White Spirituals From the Sacred Harp," Jacket notes for *White Spirituals from the Sacred Harp*. New World, NW 205.

Lorenz, Ellen Jane. *Glory, Hallelujah*. Nashville: Abingdon, 1978.

Luther, Frank. *Americans and Their Songs*. New York: Harper Brothers, 1942.

McLaurin, Charles. "Voice of Calm." (Fanny Lou Hamer) *Sojourners* Vol. 11, No. 11 December 1982: 12-13.

MacDonald, John D. *One More Sunday*. (fiction) New York: Knopf, 1984.

MacDougal, Hamilton C. *Early New England Psalmody*. New York: De Capo, 1969.

Malone, Bill. *Country Music U.S.A.* Austin: University of Texas Press, 1968.

_____. *Southern Music, American Music*. Lexington: University Press of Kentucky, 1979.

Marsh, Dave. *Born to Run: The Bruce Springsteen Story*. New York: Dell, 1981.

Marsh, J.B.T. *The Story of the Jubilee Singers With Their Songs*. New York: AMS P, 1971.

Marshall, Madeleine Forell and Janet Todd. *Hymns in the Eighteenth Century*. Lexington: University of Kentucky P, 1982.

Martin, Rob. "Keith Green: Sold Out to Jesus." *CCM* Oct. 1978 Vol. 1, No. 4: 1, 6.

Marty, Martin. *Pilgrims in Their Own Land*. Boston: Little, Brown, 1985.

McCall, Michael. "Smitty Gets Gritty." (Michael W. Smith) *CCM.* June 1986 Vol. 8, No. 12.

McKay, David P. and Richard Crawford. *William Billings of Boston.* Princeton: Princeton U P, 1975.

McLoughlin, William G., Jr. *Billy Sunday Was His Real Name.* Chicago: The University of Chicago Press, 1955.

Medema, Ken with Joyce Norman. *Come and See.* Waco: Word, 1976.

Metcalf, Frank. *American Psalmody.* New York: De Capo, 1968.

Millard, Bob. *Amy Grant.* New York: Dolphin/Doubleday, 1986.

Morris, Edward. "Oaks Translate Gospel to Secular Success." *BB* July 28, 1979: R-34, 50.

Morison, Samuel Eliot. *The Oxford History of the American People.* New York: Oxford, 1965.

Murphy, Cullen. "Who Do Men Say That I Am?" *The Atlantic.* December, 1986: 37-58.

Murrells, Joseph. *Million Selling Records.* New York: Arco, 1984.

"Music Companies Actively Pursue Catholic Market." *CCM* May 1980 Vol. 2, No. 12: 9, 11, 14.

Naisbitt, John. *Megatrends.* New York: Warner, 1982.

"NALR Institute Revitalizes Worship Music." *CCM* Dec. 1980 Vol. 3, No. 6: 31.

"NALR President Ray Bruno." *CCM* Oct. 1980 Vol. 3, No. 4: 12-14.

Nathan, Hans. *William Billings: Data and Documents.* Detroit: The College Music Society, 1976.

Nettl, Paul. *Luther and Music.* New York: Russell and Russell, 1948.

"New Gaither Vocal Band." *CCM* May 1981 Vol. 3, No. 11: 50.

"The New Rebel Cry: Jesus is Coming!" *Time.* June 21, 1971: 56-63.

Newcomb, Brian Quincy. "Petra: Back to the Rock." *CCM* Oct. 1986 Vol. 9, No. 4.

——— "Petra Wages a New War." *CCM* Oct. 1987 Vol. 10, No. 4.

Nichol, John Thomas. *Pentecostalism.* Plainfield, N.J.: Logos, 1966.

Nobel, E. Maron. *The Gospel of Music.* Washington, D.C.: MARP, 1971.

"NRB Members Restless, Dissatisfied with Gospel Music Industry." *CCM* Aug. 1980 Vol. 3, No. 2: 35.

Nutt, Grady. *So Good, So Far. . .* Nashville: Impact, 1979.

Nye, Russel Blaine. *The Cultural Life of the New Nation.* New York: Harper & Brothers, 1960.

——— *The Unembarrassed Muse: The Popular Arts in America.* (New York: The Dial Press, 1970).

Oldham, Doug with Fred Bauer. *I Don't Live There Anymore.* Nashville: Impact, 1973.

Oliver, Paul, Max Harrison, William Bolcom. *The New Grove Gospel, Blues and Jazz.* New York: W.W. Norton, 1986.

O'Neill, Dan. *Troubadour for the Lord: The Story of John Michael Talbot.*

Orgill, Michael. *Anchored in Love: The Carter Family.* Old Tappan: Fleming H. Revell, 1975.

Owens, J. Garfield. *All God's Chillun.* New York: Abington, 1971.

Palaosaari, Jim. "The Christian Radio-Record Connection." *CCM* May 1981 Vol. 3, No. 11: 42, 46.

Patterson, Daniel W. *The Shaker Spiritual.* Princeton: Princeton U P, 1979.

Patti, Sandi. *The Book of Words.* Milwaukee, Wisc.: Hal Leonard, 1986.

Pelikan, Jaroslav. "The Enduring Relevance of Martin Luther 500 Years After His Birth." *New York Times Magazine* 18 Sept. 1983: 43-45, 99-104.

Pemberton, Carol Ann. *Lowell Mason: His Life and Work.* Ann Arbor, Michigan: UMI Research P, 1985.

Peters, Dan, Steve Peters, Cher Merrill. *What About Christian Rock?* Minneapolis: Bethany House, 1986.

Pike, G.D. *The Jubilee Singers.* New York: AMS P, 1974.

Platt, Karen Marie. "Bob Dylan: Saved: A Sovereign Act of God." *CCM* Aug. 1980 Vol. 3, No. 2: 6-7, 12.

———— "Catholic Music: Going Into the World." *CCM* Oct. 1979 Vol. 2, No. 4: 32.

———— "Catholic Records Since Vatican II." *CCM* Oct. 1980 Vol. 3, No. 4: 16, 21, 42.

———— "Church Musicals: A Case of Dramatic Anemia." *CCM* Dec. 1980 Vol. 3, No. 6: 10, 28.

"The Doves: What Kind of Strange Birds Are They?" *CCM* April 1981 Vol. 3, No. 10: 29.

Pollack, W.G. *The Handbook to the Lutheran Hymnal.* St. Louis: Concordia, 1975.

"Power, Glory—And Politics." *Time.* February 17, 1986: 62-69.

Pugh, John. "Gospel Now." *Country Music.* January, 1975: 25-31.

Racine, Kree Jack. *Above All.* Memphis: Jarodoce, 1967.

"Ralph Carmichael Looks at the Future of the Musical." *CCM* Dec. 1980 Vol. 3, No. 6: 10, 28.

Rabey, Steve. *The Heart of Rock 'n' Roll.* Old Tappan, J.J.: Fleming H. Revell, 1986.

———— "Keith Green," *CCM* Dec. 1987 Vol. 10, No. 6.

———— "Rock 'n' Roll Bar-B-Que." *CCM* Aug./Sept. 1981 Vol. 4, Nos. 2 & 3: 15.

———— "Test Driving the 1987 Imperials." *CCM* Feb. 1987 Vol. 9, No. 8: PPSIII

———— "An Update with John Michael Talbot." *CCM* Oct. 1980 Vol. 3, No. 4: 14.

Read, Oliver and Walter L. Welch. *From Tin Foil to Stereo.* Indianapolis: Howard W. Sams, 1959 and 1976.

Reagon, Bernice Johnson and Linn Shapiro, eds. *Robert Martin and the Roberta Martin Singers: The Legacy and The Music.* Washington D.C.: Smithsonian, 1982.

"Recording Positive Pop in the Secular Market." *CCM.* Aug. 1980 Vol. 3, No. 2: 9.

Reeves, Jeremiah Bascom. *The Hymn as Literature.* New York: The Century Co., 1924.

Reich, Charles A. *The Greening of America.* New York: Bantam, 1970.

"Rev. James Cleveland." *CCM* June 1981 Vol. 3, No. 12: 11, 16.

"Rev. James Cleveland: Gospel Artist Extraordinaire." *RW* Oct. 1, 1977: 103.

Revitt, Paul *The George Pullen Jackson Collection of Southern Hymnody.* Los Angeles: U of California Library, 1964.

RIAA. *Gold and Platinum Awards.* New York: Recording Industry Association of America, Inc., 1988.

Ricks, George Robinson. *Some Aspects of the Religious Music of the United States Negro.* New York: Arno Press, 1977.

Roach, Hildred. *Black American Music.* Boston: Crescendo, 1973.

Robberson, Jan. "Larry Norman/Randy Stonehill Concert Review." *CCM* Dec. 1980 Vol. 3, No. 6: 34.

Roberts, Patti. *Ashes to Gold.*

Rogal, Samuel J. *Sisters of Sacred Song.* New York: Garland, 1981.

Rookmakker, Hans. *Art Needs No Justification.* Intervarsity: 1978.

———— *The Creative Gift.* Cornerstone, 1981.

Routley, Erik. *An English Speaking Hymnal Guide.* Collegeville, Minn.: The Liturgical P, 1979.

———— *The Music of Christian Hymns.* Chicago: G.I.A. Publications, 1981.

Sankey, Ira D. *My Life and The Story of the Gospel Hymns.* Philadelphia: The Sunday School Times, 1907.

Sankey, Ira, James McGranahan, George C. Stebbins and Phillip Bibbs. *Gospel Hymns Nos. 1 to 6 Complete.* New York: De Capo, 1972.

Sasson, Diane. *The Shaker Spiritual Narrative.* Knoxville: U of Tennessee P, 1983.

Schaeffer, Franky. *Addicted to Mediocrity: Twentieth Century Christians and the Arts.* Cornerstone.

Schaeffer, Franky and Harold Fickett. *A Modest Proposal.*

Schalk, Carl. "The Seduction of Church Music: Perspective on the American Scene." *Church Music* 79: 2-10.

Seay, Davin. "Amy Grant: Where's She Headed?" *CCM.* March 1984 Vol. 6, No. 9: 22-26.

_____ "One Year Later" (Melody Green on Keith). *CCM* July 1983 Vol. 6, No. 1: 12-19.

_____ "Sandi Patti: Songs for the Family." *CCM* Dec. 1984 Vol. 7, No. 6.

Seay, Davin and Mary Neely. *Stairway to Heaven.* New York: Ballantine, 1986.

Shaw, Arnold. *The World of Soul.* New York: Paperback Library, 1971.

Shea, George Beverly with Fred Bauer. *Songs That Lift The Heart.* Old Tappan, J.J.: Fleming H. Revell, 1972.

Shea, George Beverly with Fred Bauer. *Then Sings My Soul.* Old Tappan, N.J.: Fleming H. Revell, 1968.

Shelton, Robert. *No Direction Home: The Life and Music of Bob Dylan.* New York: Beech Tree/William Morrow, 1986.

Sizer, Sandra S. *Gospel Hymns and Social Religion.* Philadelphia: Temple University Press, 1978.

Southern, Eileen, ed. *Readings in Black American Music.* No publisher or date listed.

Smith, Huston. *The Religion of Man.* New York: Harper & Row, 1958.

Smith, Jane Stuard and Betty Carlson. *A Gift of Music.* Cornerstone Books, 1981.

Smith, Michael S. "Apocalypse Now." *New West.* March 12, 1979: SC-1-3.

Smith, Michael W. *Old Enough to Know.* Sweet, 1987.

Sonneck, Oscar G.T. *Francis Hopkinson and James Lyon.* New York: De Capo, 1967.

Sonneck, Oscar George Theodore and William Treat Upton. *A Bibliography of Early Secular American Music.* Washington D.C.: Library of Congress, 1945.

"Sparrow to Release New Keith Green Album." *CCM* June 1981 Vol. 3, No. 12: 30.

"Stan Moser." *CCM.* Nov. 1978 Vol. 1, No. 5: 14.

"Stan Moser: Direction for the 80s." *CCM* Jan. 1981 Vol. 3, No. 4.

Stevenson, Arthur L. *The Story of Southern Hymnology.* Roanoke: A.L. Stevenson (self-published), 1931.

Styll, John W. "Amy Grant: The *CCM* Interview." *CCM* July/Aug. 1986. Vol. 9, Nos. 1 & 2: 30-39.

_____ "The Bill Gaither Trio: Making Concerts in the Round." *CCM* Jan. 1980 Vol. 2, No. 7: 29, 34.

_____ "The Bill Gaither Trio: Making It Work at Home." *CCM* May 1979 Vol. 1, No. 11: 6-7.

_____ "B.J. Thomas' Road Home." *CCM* Dec. 1978 Vol. 1, No. 6: 1, 24, 28.

_____ "Bob Dylan's Controversial Concerts." *CCM* Dec. 1979 Vol. 2, No. 6: 27.

_____ "CBA Convention: A Sense of Purpose." *CCM* Aug. 1979 Vol. 2, No. 2: 8, 25.

_____ "CBA Fever: Close Encounters of a Profitable Kind." *CCM* July 1979 Vol. 2, No. 2: 12.

———— "Christian Music: Who Sets the Standards?" *CCM* Aug. 1978 Vol. 1, No. 2: 10, 15.

———— "Christian Rock Wars: Evangelist Jimmy Swaggart tells why he hates today's Christian rock." *CCM* June 1985 Vol. 7, No. 12: 14-17.

———— "Frustrations and Boredom at NRB." *CCM* March 1981 Vol. 3, No. 9: 26.

———— "Good News About Catholic Music." *CCM* Oct. 1980 Vol. 3, No. 4: 5.

———— "Jesus Christ's 'Superstars." ' *CCM* Aug. 1980 Vol. 3, No. 2: 5, 8.

———— "Keith Green: An Exclusive Interview." *CCM* March 1980 Vol. 2, No. 9: 6-7.

———— "Many Important Lessons to Learn." (Keith Green). *CCM* Sept. 1982 Vol. 5, No. 3: 6.

———— "Pop and Rock: The Language of the Young." *CCM* Nov. 1980 Vol. 3, No. 4: 5.

———— "Swaggart: One Man's Opinion." *CCM* Sept. 1980 Vol. 3, No. 3: 5.

———— "Trials, Tribulations, and Happy Endings" (Larry Norman). *CCM* March 1981 Vol. 3, No. 9: 5.

———— "What Makes Music Christian?" *CCM* April 1987 Vol. 9, No. 10: 35-36.

Swaggart, Jimmy. "Brother Swaggart, Here is My Question." *The Evangelist.* Feb. 1988, Vol. 20, No. 2: 9-10.

Swaggart, Jimmy with Robert Paul Lamb. *To Cross a River.* Plainfield, N.J.: Logos International, 1977.

———— *To Cross a River.* Baton Rouge: Jimmy Swaggart Ministries, 1984.

———— *Religious Rock 'n' Roll: A Wolf in Sheep's Clothing.* Baton Rouge: Jimmy Swaggart Ministries, 1987.

Synan, Vinson, *The Holiness Pentecostal Movement.* Grand Rapids, Michigan: William B. Eerdmans, 1971.

Tamke, Susan S. *Make a Joyful Noise Unto The Lord.* No Publisher Listed, 1978.

Tepper, Ron, "Retail Witnesses Financial and Distribution Challenges." *BB* July 28, 1979: R-20, 46.

Terrell, Bob. "Eldridge Fox Receives Norcross Award." *Singing News,* September, 1986.

———— "Three chords and a cloud of dust: The Jim Hamill Story." *Singing News,* February, 1988.

Thomas, B.J. *Home Where I Belong.* Waco: Word.

———— "The Power of Positive Pop," *CCM* Aug. 1980 Vol. 3, No. 2: 28, 30.

Toffler, Alvin. *The Third Wave.* New York: Bantam, 1980.

Topp, Dale. *Music in the Christian Community.*

Tosches, Nick. *Hellfire: The Jerry Lee Lewis Story.* New York: Delacorte, 1982.

Velten, Ron. "The Confessions of John Michael Talbot." *CCM.* Oct. 1979 Vol. 2, No. 4: 6-7, 39.

Walton, Samuel B. "People Like Honest Sounds" (The Bill Gaither Trio). *Saturday Evening Post.* April, 1977: 46-47, 99, 102.

Walsh, Sheila. *Never Give It Up.* Old Tappan, N.J.: Fleming H. Revell, 1986.

Ward, Ed, Geoffrey Stokes, and Ken Tucker. *Rock of Ages: The Rolling Stone History of Rock & Roll.* New York: Rolling Stone P/Summit, 1986.

Warner, Brian. "Why Audiences Aren't Ready For Contemporary Christian Music." *CCM* Jan. 1980 Vol. 2, No. 7: 18, 24.

Warnke, Mike. *Hitchhiking on Hope Street.* Garden City, New York: Doubleday & Co., 1979.

Warnke, Mike. *The Satan Seller.*

Weill, Gus. *You Are My Sunshine: The Jimmie Davis Story.* Waco: Word, 1977.

Whitburn, Joel. *Pop Memories 1890-1954*. Menomonee Falls, Wisc.: Record Research, Inc.: 1986.

———— *Top 40 Hits*. New York: Billboard Publications, 1987.

———— *Top Pop 1955-1982*. Menomonee Falls, Wisc.: Record Research, 1982.

———— *Top Pop Albums 1955-1985*. Menomonee Falls, Wisc.: Record Research, 1985.

———— *Top Pop Singles 1955-1986*. Menomonee Falls, Wisc.: Record Research, 1987.

Widner, Ellis and Walter Carter. *The Oak Ridge Boys: Our Story*. Chicago: Contemporary Books, 1987.

Wilder, Alec. *American Popular Song*. New York: Oxford, 1972.

Willems, Betty. "Pat Robertson on Christian Music." *CCM* Nov. 1978 Vol. 1, No. 5: 20, 24, 30.

Willems, Jim. "Christian Retailing: Book Store or Record Store?" *CCM* April 1979 Vol. 1, No. 10: 8.

———— "1980 NARM Convention Faces the Issues." *CCM* May 1980 Vol. 2, No. 11: 18-19.

Willems, Jim and Betty. "Convention Report: National Association of Recording Merchandisers." *CCM* May 1979 Vol. 1, No. 11: 12.

Williams-Jones, Pearl. "Black Gospel Blends Social Change and Ethnic Roots." *BB* July 28, 1979: R-12, 16.

Winkworth, Catherine. *Christian Singers of Germany*. Freeport, N.Y.: Books for Libraries, 1977.

Witter, Evelyn. *Mahalia Jackson*. Milford, Mich.: Mott Media, 1985.

Wolfe, Charles K. "Columbia Records and Old-Time Music." *JEMF Quarterly*. 118-125, 144.

———— "Early Gospel Quartets: The Case of the McDonald Brothers." *Rejoice*. Spring 1988, Vol. 1, No. 2: 14-17.

———— "Gospel Boogie: White Southern Gospel Music in Transition." *Popular Music*. Cambridge, 1981.

———— *Kentucky Country*. Lexington: University of Kentucky P, 1982.

———— *Tennessee Strings*. Knoxville: University of Tennessee P.

Wood, Gerry. "A Joyful Noise Rises to New Heights." *BB*. July 28, 1979: R-4, 12.

"Word Nudges World Awake to Rise of Contemporary Gospel." *CCM* Jan. 1981 Vol. 3, No. 7: W-7, 12.

Work, John W. ed. *American Negro Songs and Spirituals*. New York: Bonanza, 1940.

Zecher, Henry. "How One Many's Pen Changed the World." *Christianity Today* 21 Oct. 1983: 10-13.

Index

Index-A

ABC Records, 137, 138, 159
ABC-TV, 137, 165, 179, 192
Aberdeen (Scotland), 27
Africa, 9, 84, 86, 200
Age of Faith, 227
Ainsworth Psalter, 20
Akron, Ohio, 149
Alabama, 100
Aldergate (London), 33
Alexandria, 7
all day singing, 50, 100, 104
All Day Singing Conventions, 103
all night sings, 98, 143
American Bible Society, 167
American Christianity, i, ii,
    iii, 10, 205, 215, 216, 226
American Colonization Society, 86
American Culture, 136, 160
American Society of Composers,
    Authors and Publishers (ASCAP),
    78
American-European Culture, 84
Ames, Iowa, 69
Amsterdam, 200, 203
Anderson College (Indiana), 139, 168
Anderson, Indiana, 126, 139, 140,
    142
Angel Records, 136
Anglican church, 11, 32
Anglicans, 24, 130
anthems, 42
Apollo Records, 94
Apostolic Faith Gospel Mission,
    The, 76
Apostolic Age, 7
Arkansas, 105
Ashville (N.C.), 156
Assembly of God, 171, 172, 174, 176
Assertion of Seven Sacraments, 13
Association of Christian
    Brothers, 13
Athens, Alabama, 100
Atkerman, Mississippi, 104

Atlanta (Ga.), 89, 96, 97, 98,
    102, 143, 156, 166, 175
Australia, 202
Azusa Street (L.A.), 76

Back to God Hour (radio show), 80
Back to the Bible (radio show), 80
ballad opera, 43
Baltimore (Md.), 85
Baptist Seminary in Fort Worth,
    158, 175
Baptists, 23, 48, 50, 56, 89,
    92, 93, 103, 121, 131
Baton Rouge (La.), 174, 175, 176
Bay Psalm Book, The, 20, 23
Baylor Univ. (Tx.), 134, 135, 158
Beaumont, Texas, 158
Beckley, West Va., 151
Benson Co., The, 102, 129, 136,
    139, 140, 141, 192
Berkeley (Calif.), 126, 132
Bethel Bible School, 75
Bible, 3, 13, 18, 27, 34, 62, 73,
    75, 76, 126, 127, 161, 207,
    216, 219
Bible, Authorized Version
    (King James), 13
Bible, Latin Vulgate, 13, 16
Big Stone Gap, Va., 156
Billboard, 98, 112, 113, 185,
    224
Billy Graham Crusades, 164,
    166, 167
Birdwing (Records), 159
Birmingham (Ala.), 101, 104
black gospel (music), i, 84, 86,
    88, 89, 91, 92, 121, 123,
    134, 138, 143, 146, 147,
    148, 216, 217, 218, 219, 225
black music, 81, 82, 92, 124,
    147, 148, 217, 218, 225
bluegrass, 219
blues, 55, 78, 81, 82, 89, 91,
    121, 146, 216
Boaz, Alabama, 105

247

Book of Common Prayer, 34
Born Again, 213
Boston (Mass.), 22, 23, 40, 42,
  43, 58
British Isles, 84, 165
Broadcast Music, Inc. (BMI), 78
broadside ballads, i, 42, 43, 50
Brooklyn (N.Y.), 60
Brunswick (Records), 97
Brussels (Belgium), 13
Bullett Records, 102

California, 105, 132, 151, 193, 201
call-and-response, 49
Calvary Chapel (Calif.), 128,
  129, 201, 202
Calvinism, 11, 26, 28, 30, 64
Camp Meeting Hour, The (radio
  show), 175
camp meeting songs, 86
camp meeting(s), 47, 50, 56,
  86, 93, 192
Campus Crusade, 128, 201
Canaan Records, 136, 137, 145
Canada, 105
Capitol (Records), 127, 129
Cashbox, 224
Cathedral of Tomorrow (Ohio), 149
Catholic church, 8, 9, 10, 11,
  12, 17, 130, 131
Catholic folk mass, 131
Catholic music, 132, 133
Catholics, 50, 56, 130
CBS (TV & radio), 107
CBS, 162, 184
Center Point, Tennessee, 100
Certayne Psalms, 20
Charleston (S.C.), 19, 23, 40,
  85, 144
Charlotte (N.C.), 166
Chattanooga (Tn.), 106, 180
Chattanooga Medicine Company, 154
Chicago (Ill.), 58, 59, 60, 62,
  69, 79, 80, 88, 89, 90, 93,
  122, 123, 145, 146, 165
Chicagoland Youth For Christ, 165
children's albums, 141, 159
children's choirs, 71
children's music, 168
children's records, 136
Choice Hymns and Spiritual
  Songs, 23
choir(s), 74, 118, 145, 164,
  167, 168, 228
Christ Church, Oxford (Eng.), 33

Christian Artists Convention, 208
Christian Bookseller's Assoc., 215
Christian Bookseller's
  Convention, 159
Christian bookstore(s), i, 99,
  134, 137, 138, 140, 148, 158,
  159, 162, 187, 195, 214, 215,
  216, 217, 220, 221, 222, 224,
  225, 226
Christian Broadcasting Network,
  215, 223
Christian Culture, i, iii, 75,
  87, 144, 160, 169, 213, 214,
  215, 216, 218, 219, 220, 226,
  227, 228
Christian music, iv, 9, 134,
  136, 137, 183, 189, 194, 195,
  197, 203, 208, 213, 214, 220
Christian musicians, i, 129,
  200, 213, 219
Christian revival(s), i, iii, 3,
  6, 56, 75, 112, 126, 130
Christian rock, 197
Christian Science, 161
Christian sub-culture, 189
Christian Training Academy
  (Indiana), 195
Christian World Liberation Front, 126
Christian-Minstrel, 94
Christianity, i, ii, 56, 57, 58,
  60, 62, 63, 112, 120, 126,
  130, 160, 163, 164, 169, 184,
  186, 189, 213, 214, 228
Christy Minstrels, 81
Cincinnati (Oh.), 81, 91, 154
Cinco Hollow, Ohio, 70
circuit riders, 85
Civil Rights Movement, 123, 125,
  143, 144, 145
Civil War, ii, 50, 52, 56, 81,
  82, 85, 86, 88
Clanton, Alabama, 107
classical music, i, 135, 219
Cleveland (Oh.), 131
Club Time (radio show), 165, 166
coin-slot phonograph, 77, 78
Collection of Hymns for the Use
  of the People Called
  Methodists, A, 34
Collection of Psalms and Hymns, 33
Columbia (Records), 74, 77, 97, 122
Compilation of the Litanies,
  Vesper Hymns, and Anthems, as
  sung in the Catholic Church, A, 23
Connecticut, 165

contemporary Christian music, i,
99, 113, 128, 133, 134, 136,
137, 138, 139, 148, 158, 160,
176, 191, 194, 203, 204, 220,
223, 225, 228
Contemporary Christian Music
Magazine, 224, 225
Continental Congress, 44
Copyright Act of 1909, 78
Costa Mesa, Calif., 128, 201
Cotillion Records, 128, 129
Council of Laodicea, 8
country (music), i, 55, 78, 79,
95, 98, 99, 107, 149, 176,
177, 178, 181, 217, 219, 225
Country Music Association Awards
Show, 179
cowboy music, 82
Crickett Records, 135
Cullman County, Alabama, 100
cylinders, 77

Dallas (Tx.), 97, 101, 135, 145
Dalton, Georgia, 95
dance (music), 216, 217, 219
Darwin's theory of evolution,
56, 79
Davenport, Iowa, 69
Day of Doom, 20
Dayspring (Records), 137
Dayton, Tennessee, 79
DeBron, Holland, 208
Decca (Records), 161, 165
Declaration of Independence, 41
DeLeon, Texas, 188
Denver (Co.), 132
Depression (Great), 78, 89, 101,
164, 171, 178
Detroit (Mich.), 131, 132, 145,
175, 178
Devil, 17, 18, 28, 32, 71, 87,
92, 96, 116, 129, 145, 179,
195, 213
disco, 146, 216
Dissenters, 29
Divine and Moral Songs, 26
Dot Records, 175
Dothan, Alabama, 155
Dove award(s), 139, 154, 168,
169, 222, 223, 225
Dyess, Arkansas, 179

Easter, 168
Edinburg, Pennsylvania, 59
Edinburgh (Scotland), 27

Edison Phonograph Company, The, 77
Eisenach (Germany), 15, 18
EMI (Records), 136
England, 10, 12, 13, 20, 22, 32,
42, 45, 48, 49, 55, 58, 62, 130
English garden music, 44, 45
English musical theatre, 43
English Reformation, 14
Episcopal(s), 23, 183
Erfurt, University of (Germany),
12, 15
Europe, 12, 18, 30, 40, 43, 44,
50, 131, 158, 200, 202, 203, 204
Evenings with Dorsey, 91

Faith Music Co., 156
Faith-At-Word, 137
Family Bookstores, 138
Family Record Club, 135
Fayette County, Georgia, 100
Federal Communication Commission
(FCC), 185, 215
Federal Radio Commission (FRC),
79, 80
Fentress, Mississippi, 102
Ferriday (La.), 171, 172, 173, 175
field recordings, 82, 97, 177
First Baptist Church in Hearn,
Tx., 134
First Baptist Church of
Thomasville, Ga., 158
First Wesleyan Methodist Church
in Jersey City, 164
Florida, 196
Florissent, Missouri, 132
folk (music), i, 45, 78, 82, 84, 110
folk mass, 130, 131, 207
folk movement, 112, 127
folk song tradition, 49, 84
folk songs, 45, 48, 50, 115, 140
foot washing, 93
Fort Wayne, Indiana, 195
Fort Worth, (Tx.), 104, 107, 135,
158
Four Square Church, 171
France, 10, 100
Free Africa Society, 85
Freedom Farm Cooperative, 145
French Academy, 122
French Revolution, 47
fuguing tunes, 42, 45
Fundamentalism, 75, 93, 170
Fundamentalists, 26, 93

Gaels, 48

Gainesville, N. C., 150

Gallup Poll, 213

Garner, Iowa, 70

Geneva (Switzerland), 20

Gennett (Music Co.), 97

Georgia, 94, 97, 100

German folk songs, 16

Germany, 12, 130, 178

God, 6, 28, 32, 57, 58, 63, 84,
86, 93, 95, 97, 140, 142, 144,
145, 152, 153, 161, 162, 171,
174, 176, 179, 181, 188, 191,
194, 195, 206, 220, 226

Godfrey, Arthur Talent Show, 107

Godspell, 114

Gold record (album), 111, 112,
115, 139, 167, 225

Good New (Records), 128, 129, 137

Good News (mag.), 154

Good News (musical), 127, 158

Gospel Broadcasting Association, 80

Gospel Caravan (TV show), 102

Gospel Music Association (GMA),
154, 222, 223, 225

gospel music, i, iii, 26, 73,
74, 75, 80, 88, 89, 92, 95,
96, 97, 98, 100, 101, 102,
106, 107, 110, 111, 119,
120, 123, 124, 125, 134,
138, 139, 140, 142, 146,
147, 148, 150, 151, 154,
155, 158, 160, 163, 167,
168, 169, 170, 176, 178,
179, 181, 182, 184, 189,
190, 213, 214, 217, 218,
219, 220, 222, 223, 224,
225, 226, 228

gospel music industry, 160, 162,
169, 193, 195, 218, 220, 222,
224, 225

Gospel Music Workshop of America,
145

Gospel of Wealth, The, 56

gospel radio, 80, 148, 185, 217,
220, 224, 225

Gospel Road, 179

gospel rock, 195, 196, 197

Gospel Singer's Convention
(Dorsey), 90

gospel song(s), i, 50, 53, 71,
72, 73, 74, 89, 97, 98, 112,
116, 119, 123, 128, 177, 181, 228

Grammy Awards, 139, 167, 179, 225

Grand Ole Opry, 116

Great Awakening, ii, 21, 32, 40,
49, 75

Great Britain, ii, 23, 30, 43,
48, 49, 130, 165, 200

Great Revival, 25, 45, 58, 59

Greek and Roman song tradition, 8

Greentree (Records), 138

Greenville, S.C. 119, 154

Gregorian chant, 19, 227

Haight-Ashbury (San Francisco), 126

Hair, 113

hard rock (music), 129, 196, 219

Harmonia American, 23

Harmonia-Sacra, 94

Haven of Rest (radio show), 80

Hearn, Tx., 134

HeartWarming (Records), 102, 138

Heaven and Home Hour (radio show),
80

heavy metal (music), 219

Hebrew melodies, 7

Hee Haw, 176

Henson (Music Co.), 96, 156

hillbilly music, 78, 82, 172

holiness church(es), ii, 84, 87,
92

Holland, 20, 202, 208

Hollywood (Calif.), 118

Holy Ghost, 94, 171

holy rollers, 87, 93

Holy Spirit, 75, 76, 87, 170,
172, 180, 219

hootenannies, 127

Houlka, Mississippi, 104

Hour of Decision (radio show), 166

Houston (Tx.), 75, 173, 175

Huguenots, 19

hymn(s), 26, 29, 37, 40, 42, 66,
71, 72, 74, 78, 80, 88, 121,
127, 144, 164, 165, 167, 168,
213, 219, 227

Hymnal 1940, The, 55

Hymns and Sacred Poems, 35, 36

Hymns and Spiritual Songs, 23, 27

Hymns for Our Lord's Resurrection,
37

Hymns for Those That Seek and
Those That Have Redemption in
the Blood of Christ, 38

Hymns From the Chapel (radio show),
165

Imitations of the Psalms, 27

Impact (Records), 138

Indiana, 91

Indianapolis (Ind.), 59, 60
Indianola, Miss., 143
Industrial Revolution, 50, 56, 58, 79
Institutes of Christianity, ii, 10
Introduction to the Singing of Psalm-Tunes, An, 23
Iowa, 70, 105, 107
Ireland, 42,48
Irish, 45, 48
Israel, 3, 4, 27, 30, 161
Israelites, 3, 55

Jackson, Miss., 104
Jacksonville, (Tx.), 95
Jamestown, (Va.), 19, 20
jazz, i, 81, 82, 89, 91, 121, 135, 146, 216, 217, 219, 225
Jellico, Tennessee, 70
Jersey City, (N.J.), 164
Jesus Christ, 5, 6, 28, 29, 86, 87, 94, 113, 120, 127, 152, 160, 162, 171, 188, 205, 207, 219, 227
Jesus Christ Superstar, 113
Jesus Movement, i, ii, 16, 99, 110, 115, 127, 128, 129, 131, 194, 213
Jesus Revolution, 115, 126, 127, 130, 131, 133, 136, 191, 200, 213
Jesus rock, 127, 129, 131, 134, 137
jig and cakewalk music, 81
Jim (Records), 137
Johnson City, Tennessee, 97
Joseph and the Amazing Technicolor Dreamcoat, 113
Jubilee Singers and Their Songs, 53
jubilee songs, 123
Jubilee Songs, 52
jubilee singers, 88
jukebox, 77, 78, 172

Kansas, 105
Kansas City (Ks.), 75, 145
KDKA (Pittsburgh, Pa.), 79
Keen Records, 97
Kentucky, 48
Kentucky Revival, ii, 48, 49
KFGQ (Boone, Iowa), 79
KFUO (St. Louis), 79
King Records, 154
KMA (Shenandoah, Iowa), 157
Knowledge of the heavens and Earth Made Easy, The, 26

Kosciusko, Mississippi, 104
KPOF (Denver), 79
KPPC (Pasadena, Ca.), 79
KRM, 106
KWKH (Shreveport, La.), 105

Lake Tahoe, 193
Lamb and Lion (Records), 137
Lancaster, California, 182
Las Vegas (Nv.), 119, 193, 194
Last Days Ministries, 162, 163
Last Days Newsletter, 162
Latter Rain Movement, 87
Lawrence County, Tennessee, 100
Lawrenceburg, Tn., 73, 95, 101
Lawrenceville, Penn., 81
Lenoir, North Carolina, 150
Leoma, Tennessee, 100
Let's Go Back To the Bible (radio show), 165
Lexicon Music, 136
Lexington, (Ky.), 48
Liberty Records, 128
Life, 166
Light Records, 137
Lindale, Texas, 162
lined out, 27
Living Water Songs, 138
Logic, 26
London, (Eng.), 13, 26, 33, 43, 45, 57, 62, 113, 166
Los Angeles, (Calif.), 75, 125, 128, 135, 137, 141, 147, 158, 159, 162, 198
Louisiana, 105, 155, 172, 173
Love Me Tender, 155
Lutheran Hour, The (radio show), 80
Lutheran(s), 19, 24, 64, 131, 182

Madgeburg, (Germany), 15
Mangham, Louisiana, 174
Manhattan, (N.Y.), 174
Mansfield, (Germany), 15
Maranatha Music, 128, 129, 137, 201, 202, 224
Marshalltown, (Iowa), 69
Maryland, 130
Mass for Young Americans, 131
Mass(es), 8, 131, 133
Massachusetts, 20, 21
MCA Records, 113, 138
Meditations, 20
Meditations in the Psalms (radio show), 164
Memphis, (Tn.), 97, 107, 108, 116,

117, 118, 119, 120, 124, 156,
174, 175, 178, 222, 223
Methodist Church, 76
Methodist Episcopal Church, 59, 85
Methodist General Conference
(for free blacks), 85
Methodist TV, Radio and Film
Commission, 141
Methodists, 21, 50, 56, 85, 92,
93, 131, 183
Millenial Excitement, 49, 50
Miller Madness, 50
Milwaukee (Wisc.), 108
Minneapolis-St. Paul (Minn.), 175
Minnesota, 105, 132
minstrel shows, 81
Mississippi, 100, 104, 106, 123,
143, 171
Missouri, 105, 132
Monterey, Tenn., 155
Montogmery, Alabama, 101, 143
Moody Bible Institute (Chicago),
80, 165
Moravians, 19, 33
Mormons, 50
Moscow (Soviet Union), 205, 206,
208
Moses, 3, 4, 6, 55, 85, 194
Motown, 216
Muncie, Ind., 139
Music in Miniature, 41
Musicians for Missions, 200, 202,
204
MusicLine, 225
Mutual Broadcasting Network, 80
Myrrh Records, 136, 137, 158, 159,
195, 196

Nashville, (Tn.), 101, 102, 117,
119, 135, 137, 138, 142, 144,
176, 177, 179, 184, 186, 188, 192,
193, 195, 196, 198, 222, 223
National Association of Recording
Arts and Sciences (NARAS), 225
National Baptist Convention
(Negro), 88, 89
National Phonograph Company, 77
National Quartet Convention, 222
NBC-TV, 78
Nebraska, 105
Nevada, Iowa, 69
New England, 19, 21, 22, 24, 25,
40, 84
New England Psalm Singer, 41
New Jersey, 21, 45, 165

New Mexico, 200
New Orleans, (La.), 97, 121, 122,
155, 176, 201
New Pax (Records), 137
New York, 23, 35, 40, 43, 87, 81,
122, 164, 165, 193
Newcastle, (Pa.), 59
Newport Jazz Festival, 123
North American Liturgy Resources, 132
North Dakota, 105
Northfield, Massachusetts, 58
Norway, 122
Noxapater, Mississippi, 104
Nutley, New Jersey, 146

Oakland, (Calif.), 113
Ohio, 150
Okeh (Records), 97
Oklahoma City, (Ok.), 168
old time religion, 50, 56, 59
Omaha, Nebraska, 79, 132
oral tradition, 45, 49, 55, 62,
77, 75, 92
Orange County, California, 224
Ottawa, Canada, 164
Ozark Jubilee TV show, 157

Pacific Garden Mission (Chicago), 69
Paragon (Records), 137
Parliament, 13, 14
Paul (Apostle), 5, 7, 8, 11, 160,
179, 200, 204
Pensacola, Fla., 153, 154, 158, 224
Pentecostal, 93, 118, 170, 182
Pentecostalism, 75, 76, 170, 171,
176
Philadelphia, (Pa.), 23, 40, 41,
42, 45, 69, 85, 111, 145
phonograph, ii, 77, 82
phonograph records, 73, 134
Pickwick Records, 136
Pickering and Inglis, Ltd., 166
Pilgrim Baptist Church (Chicago),
88, 89, 90
Pilgrims, ii
Pittsburgh, (Pa.), 69, 81
Plantinum records, 111, 167, 225
player pianos, 78
Plymouth, (Mass.), 19
Plymouth Church in Brooklyn, 38, 57
Plymouth Colony, 20
Poland, 174, 207
pop charts, 112, 125, 127
pop market, 168, 189, 217, 224
pop music, 121, 125, 139, 141,

142, 217, 218
Pope, The, 12, 13, 14, 130,
    131, 227
popular culture, i, 117, 191
popular music, 44, 45, 59, 78,
    81, 110, 120, 131, 188
Port Royal, South Carolina, 19
praise music, 128, 219
Presbyterian, 93, 183
Presbyterians, Scottish, 20
Prohibition, 73, 82
Protestant Reformation, ii, iii,
    10, 12, 15, 17, 18, 19, 127,
    130
Protestant(s), 56, 57, 85, 130
Protestantism, 18, 50, 93, 130
Psalm(s), 4, 5, 7, 16, 27, 29, 30,
    86
Psalms of David Imitated in the
    Language of the New Testament,
    and Apply'd to the Christian
    State and Worship, The, 29
Psalms, Hymns and Spiritual Songs,
    23
Puerto Rico, 207
Puritans, 19, 25, 40, 48, 49, 55,
    130, 227

R&B (music), i, 146, 216, 217
R&B charts, 125
race records, 78
Radio Bible Class (radio show), 80
Radio Chapel Service (radio show), 79
radio, ii, 75, 78, 79, 80, 97,
    101, 110, 111, 112, 113, 145,
    147, 164, 167, 170, 176, 177,
    178, 184, 196, 213, 214, 218,
    222, 226, 228
Radio Revival (radio show), 80
ragtime, 81, 82
Rainbow Records, 73
RCA (Records), 74, 77, 78, 107,
    116, 117, 120, 125, 166, 167, 192
record stores, 99, 148, 217
Record World, 224
Recording Industry Association of
    America (RIAA), 111
Reformed Church (Calvin), 11
religious music, 40, 45, 49, 75, 136
Renaissance, 227
Reno, (Nv.), 193
Restless Ones, The, 127
Reunion (Records), 198
revivalist tunes, 45
revival(s), 47, 49, 50, 59, 63, 70,

74, 93, 161, 173, 174, 175, 176,
    226, 228
Revolutionary War, 41, 43, 44, 45,
    47, 48
rock music, i, 107, 113, 127, 129,
    196, 197, 217, 225
rock 'n' roll, 55, 76, 78, 110,
    116, 117, 120, 124, 125, 128,
    137, 170, 174, 175, 176, 191,
    194, 197, 198, 200
rockabilly, 178
Rodeheaver Company, 137
Roman Catholic Church, 9, 19, 24,
    130
Rome, (Italy), 7, 12, 13, 131
Ruebush-Kieffer School, 94, 95
Ruleville, (Miss.), 143, 144, 145

Sacred Harp, 25, 50, 94, 94
sacred music, 24, 40, 45, 136,
    137, 176
Sacred Records, 136
Sacred Singing School, 41
Salem, (Mass.), 22, 49
Salisbury, England, 57
Salvation Army, 57
San Antonio, (Tx.), 158
San Diego, California, 106
San Francisco, (Calif.), 20, 126
Satan, 188
Savannah, Georgia, 33
Savoy Records, 146
scientific revolution, 79
Scopes Monkey Trial, 79
Scotland, 20, 42, 48
Scottish balladry, 42
Scottish Psalter, 20
secular, 9, 123, 135, 139, 142,
    181, 183, 169, 193, 194, 214,
    219, 222, 227
secular culture, i, 9, 110, 126,
    218
secular music, 43, 45, 88, 96,
    199, 217, 219, 228
Selection of Psalms with
    Occasional Hymns, A, 23
SESAC, 78
Seventh-Day Adventists, 50
sex symbol, 71, 123, 125
Shady Grove Hill, Alabama, 100
shaped note, 95, 150
shaped-note songbooks, 94, 95
sheet music, 73, 92, 168, 169
Shenandoah Valley, (Va.), 94
Shenandoah, Iowa, 105, 106, 107,

156

Showalter, A.J. Music Company, 95

Shreveport, (La.), 105

sight singing, 22, 101

singing convention(s), 95, 96,
  100, 101, 150

singing master, 22

Singing Master's Assistant, The, 41

Singing News, The, 153, 224

singing school(s), 21, 22, 40,
  94, 95, 100, 101, 150

Singing Time in Dixie (TV show), 102

Skylite Company, 102

Slave songs of the United States,
  52, 86

slavery, ii, 54, 55, 84, 85

snake handling, 93

Snake Ridge, (La.), 172

Soldier's Orphan Home (Iowa), 69

Solid Rock (Records), 137

Song of Deliverance, 20

songbooks, 49, 62, 72, 73, 75,
  101, 102, 105, 131, 150, 168

Song for the Nursery or Mother
  Goose Melodies for Children, 42

Songs in the Night (radio show),
  165, 166

soul music, 92, 125, 217, 218

South Carolina, 94, 186

South Dakota, 105

South Pekin, Illinois, 195

southern gospel, i, 25, 95, 96,
  98, 99, 100, 106, 107, 117,
  118, 119, 120, 128, 134, 136,
  137, 138, 149, 153, 155, 156,
  157, 170, 176, 177, 178, 191,
  192, 193, 194, 219, 222, 223,
  224, 225

Southern Harmony, 50, 96

southern religion, 93, 94, 120

Soviet Union, 204, 206, 207, 208

Spanish-American War, 70

Sparrow Records, 158, 159, 160, 162

speaking in tongues, 87, 93, 94,
  170, 173

Specialty Records, 125

spiritual-jubilee tradition, 88

spirituals, 50, 52, 53, 75, 81, 84,
  86, 116, 123, 144

St. Bonifacius, Minnesota, 133

St. Louis, (Me.), 90, 132, 145

Stamps Music School, 95

Stamps organization, 101, 105

Stamps Quartet Music Company, 95

Stamps, V.O. Music Company, 95

Stamps-Baxter, 90, 95, 101, 155

Star Song Records, 196

Sternhold and Hopkins Psalter
  (The Old Version), 20, 30

Stoughton, Massachusetts, 41

Stow, Ohio, 108

Student Non-Violent Coordinating
  Committee (SNCC), 99, 143

Suffolk Harmony, The, 41

Sumar Talent, 119

Sun Records, 116, 117, 118, 124,
  174, 175, 178, 217

Sunday School, 58, 59, 81, 215

Sweden, 166

Taste of New Wine, The, 136

Tate and Brady (New Version), 30

Tate and Brady Psalter (The New
  Version Psalter), 23

televangelists, 170, 214, 215

television (TV), ii, iii, 76, 78,
  80, 102, 120, 122, 143, 148,
  154, 155, 164, 170, 175, 176,
  179, 181, 182, 187, 193, 194,
  213, 222, 223, 225, 226

Tell It Like It Is, 127, 137, 158

Temple, (Tx.), 172

Tennessee, 100, 222

Testament, New, 5, 6, 94

Testament, Old, 6, 142, 161, 199

Texas, 95, 105, 150, 155

The Beggar's Opera, 43

The Book of Common Prayer, 14

The Divine Hymns or Spiritual
  Songs, 23

The Evangelist, 176

The Graduate, 113

Time, 215

Tonight Show, The, 128

Topeka, Kansas, 75

Toronto (Canada), 132

Tri-State Singing Convention, 156

Trinity, Texas, 123

tune books, 23

Tupelo, Mississippi, 107

Ukraine, 167

Union army, 59, 69

Unitarian, 58

United Kingdom, 33

United States, ii, 48, 58, 78, 79,
  81, 94, 131, 154, 200, 204, 215

Universalists, 23

Up With People, 127

Urania, 42

WSIX (Nashville), 102
WWBL (Richmond), 79

York, (Eng.), 62
Young Men's Christian Association
 (YMCA), 58, 59, 60, 69
Youth for Christ, 127, 155, 165
Youth With a Mission (YWAM), 202,
 203

Zondervan Corporation, 138

Index-N

Proper Names
Abee, Charles, 156
Abernathy, Lee Roy, 96
Abney, Sir Thomas, 26
Ackley, B.D., 71
Adams, J.T., 135
Adams, John, 46
Agape, 128
Aiken, Jesse, 105
Ainsworth, Henry, 20
Aitkin, John, 23
Alaimo, Steve, 112
Albertina Walker's Caravans,
 146
Alexander, Charles, 70, 71
Alexander, J.W., 125
Allen, Duane, 177, 178
Allen, Jimmy, 134
Allen, Richard (Bishop), 85
Allen, Steve, 117
Alline, Henry, 23
Allred, Glen, 153, 155
Alpert, Herb and the Tijuana
 Brass, 112
Ambassadors, The, 156
Anderson, Robert, 146
Andrews, Inez, 146
Andrus, Sherman, 194
Angelic Choir of Nutley, New
 Jersey, 146
Anka, Paul, 114
Anthony, Dick, 135
Apollo 100, 114
Arminius, 34
Armstrong, Louis, 146
Arne, Thomas, 44
Arnold, Samuel, 45
Asberry, Richard and Ruth, 76
Asbury, Francis, 85
Atkins, Chet, 116, 118, 192
Atwell, George, 196

Vatican II, 131
Vaughan, James D. Music Company,
 95, 96, 101, 155
Vep Ellis Music Co., 156
Victor Records, 77, 97
Victrola, 103
Vietnam, 136
Villa Rica, Georgia, 89
Village Hymns, 23
Virginia, 84, 94
Virginia Normal School, 94
Vocalion Records, 97
Voice of Healing, 274

Waco, (Tx.), 135, 137, 155, 158
Wales, 21, 48
WAPO, (Chattanooga), 106
Washington D.C., 145, 207
Waxahachie, Texas, 188
WCAL (Northfield, Minn.), 80
WCFL (Chicago), 165, 166
West Virginia, 151, 198
Western Springs, Ill., 165
Westminster Records, 135
Wheaton College, (Illinois), 165
WHEF (Kosciusko, Mississippi), 104
white gospel, i, 148, 216, 217,
 218, 219
WHK (Cleveland), 80
WHN (New York), 165
Whole Booke of Psalmes Faithfully
 translated into English Metre,
 The (Bay Psalm Book), 20
Williamsburg, (Va.), 42
Winona Lake, Indiana, 137
Winsett Music Co., 96
Wisner, Alabama, 173
Wittenberg, (Germany), 10, 12, 13,
 16, 18
WJDX (Jackson, Ms.), 104
WKBO (Jersey City), 164
WLAC (TV Nashville), 102
WMBI (Chicago), 80, 165, 166
WMCA (New York), 164
WMPS (Memphis), 107
WMUZ (Detroit), 175
Word Records, 129, 134, 135, 136,
 137, 138, 155, 158, 159, 184,
 185, 195, 196
World War I, 73, 100
World War II, 78, 79, 97, 102,
 105, 106, 153, 165, 172, 174, 213
worship music, 128, 219
WSFA (Montgomery), 101

Bach, 15, 44, 45
Bachelors, The, 112
Bagwell, Wendy, 137
Bailey, Albert, 27, 32, 34
Baize, Bill, 119
Baker, Paul, 126
Baker, Richard, 135
Baker, Seth, 159
Bakker, Jim, 76, 215
Ballouw, Silas, 23
Bannister, Brown, 184, 185, 186
Barkmeyer, Paul, 166
Barlow, Joel, 23
Barnard, John, 23
Barnhouse, Donald Grey, 80
Barrows, Cliff, 166
Baxter, J.R., 95
Baxter, Les, 112
Beasley, Bill, 154
Beasley, Les, 153, 154, 155, 223
Beatles, 112, 200
Beecher, Henry Ward, 38, 57, 58
Beiderwolf, William E., 70
Benson, Bob, 138, 139, 140
Benson, Eva, 138
Benson, John T., 136, 138
Benson, John T. III, 138
Benson, John T. Jr., 138
Berle, Milton, 117
Berlin, Irving, 82, 89
Berliner, Emile, 77
Berman, Bess, 122
Berry, Chuck, 124
Biles Brothers, 98
Bilhorn, P.P., 70
Billings, William, 41, 43
Black, Bill, 116
Blackwell, Bumps, 125
Blackwood Brothers, 100, 102,
    103, 104, 105, 106, 107, 114,
    119, 155, 156, 222, 223
Blackwood Brothers Stamps Quartet,
    105
Blackwood, Cecil, 107, 118, 156,
    223
Blackwood, Doyle, 102, 103, 104,
    106, 107
Blackwood, James, 102, 103, 104,
    106, 107, 120, 222
Blackwood, Lena, 102
Blackwood, R.W., 103, 104, 106,
    107, 156
Blackwood, Roy, 102, 103, 104,
    105, 106, 107

Blackwood, Susan, 104
Blackwood, William Emmett and
    Carrie, 102
Blake, Eubie, 82
Bland, James A., 82
Blanton, Mike, 186, 187, 198
Blessed Hope, 128
Bliss, P.P., 64
Blue Ridge Quartet, 149, 151, 157
Boggs, Frank, 135
Boone, Debbie, 115, 224
Boone, Pat, 112, 115, 201
Booth, William, 57
Bradstreet, Anne, 20
Brady, Nicholas, 23
Branham, William, 174
Brock, Dwight, 101
Brock, Lena, 100, 101
Brooklyn Bridge, 113
Brown, Aaron, 137
Brown, Johnathan David, 196
Brown, R.R., 79
Brown, Scott Wesley, 200, 204,
    205, 206, 207, 208, 209
Butler, Don, 223
Butler, Jerry, 96
Byrds, 112

Calhoun, Lee, 171
Calvert, Cecil, 130
Calvert, George, 130
Calverts, The, 130
Calvin, John, ii, 10, 26, 28, 184
Campbell, Glen, 114, 115
Campbell, Lucie, 89
Candle, 159
Canton, Eddie, 161
Carmichael, Ralph, 127, 136, 137,
    158
Carson, Johnny, 128
Carter, E.J., 179
Carter, Jimmy, 115, 213, 214, 224
Carter, June, 179
Carter, Mother Maybelle, 179
Cartwright, Peter, 51, 52
Caruso, Enrico, 78
Carwall, John, 37
Cash, Jack, 178
Cash, John Carter, 179
Cash, Johnny, 163, 174, 178, 179,
    201
Cason, J.M., 172
Cathedrals, 149, 151, 160,
Catherine of Aragon, 13
Catledge, Gene, 103

Chapman, Gary, 188, 189, 198
Chapman, J. Wilbur, 69, 70
Charles, Emperor of Italy, 13, 14
Charles, Ray, 124
Children of the Day, 128, 202
Christian, Chris, 184
Christy, E.P., 81
Cimaron Singers, The, 193
Clapton, Eric, 114
Clark, Alan, 122
Clark, Bobby, 149, 151
Clark, Paul, 128
Clark, Petula, 114
Cleveland All-Stars, 146
Cleveland, James, 145, 146, 147, 148
Coasters, 124
Cobb, Ty, 69
Coe, Jack, 174
Cole, Nat King, 112
Collier, Charles, 156
Collier, Richard, 57
Collins, Judy, 113, 114
Colson, Chuck, 213
Como, Perry, 111
Conniff, Ray, 111
Cook, Dale, 125
Cook, Martin, 156
Cooke, Sam, 122, 123, 124, 125, 151
Cooley, Haskell, 151
Coombs, Tom, 128
Cornell, Don, 112
Cossin, Chuck, 175
Cotton, Joseph, 20
Cotton, Seaborn, 40
Coughlin, Father Charles E., 80
Country Faith, 128
Cox, Randy, 198
Cravens, Rupert, 96
Crawford, Mrs. Percy (Ruth), 165
Crawford, Richard, 20, 24, 25, 40,
    41, 42, 43
Crew Cuts, 112
Crosby, Bing, 112
Crosby, Fanny J., 64
Crouch, Andrae, 148
Crouch, Andrae and the Disciples, 128
Culbreth, Henry, 171
Cutshall, Charles, 156
Cutshall, Frank, 156

Darin, Bobby, 112
Darwin, 79
Davanaugh, John, 132
Davies, Mary Johnson, 122
De Forest, Lee, 78

Dean, Jimmy, 192, 193
DeGroff, John, 195
Delmore Brothers, 102
Dick & Deedee, 112
Dickinson, Edward, 8
DiMucci, Dion, 113
Dino (Kartsonakis), 168
Dinwiddie, Richard, 34
Dixie Drifters, 155
Dixie Rhythm Quartet, 155
Dixon, Jessy, 146
Dixon, Johnny, 106
Dodd, Guy, 153
Domino, Fats, 112, 124
Donowho, Wayne, 196
Doobie Brothers, 113, 115
Dorsey bands, 161
Dorsey, Reverend T.M., 89
Dorsey, Etta, 89
Dorsey, Thomas Andrew, 88, 89, 90,
    91, 93, 94, 145, 146
Doughten, Jane, 154
Douglas, Mike, 194
Drake, Sir Francis, 20
Dufford, Bob, 132
Duke, William, 23
Dykes, Bill, 151
Dylan, Bob, 114, 115

Eades, Elmer, 166
Edison, Thomas, 77
Edwards, Fanny, 59
Edwards, Jonathan, ii, 20, 21, 39,
    40
Elliman, Yvonne, 113
Elliot, Lena, 156
Enoch, Ed, 119
Erasmus, 13
Evie (Tornquist), 187

Faith, Percy, 123
Falls, Mildred, 123
Falwell, Jerry, 215
Farley, Jesse, 123
Field, Fred, 128
Finney, Charles, 216
Fischer, Fred, 70
Fisk Jubilee Singers, 52, 82, 86
Fleet, Thomas, 42
Fletcher, Francis, 20
Florida Boys, 120, 136, 153, 154,
    155
Foggy River Boys, 157
Foley, John, 132
Foley, Red, 90, 98, 157

Fontana, D.J., 116
Ford, Tennessee Ernie, 98, 111, 116, 223
Foster, Stephen, 46, 81
Fowler, Andrew, 23
Fowler, Wally, 98, 153, 156
Fox, Eldridge, 156, 157
Franklin, Aretha, 114
Franklin, Benjamin, 41, 47
Frederick the Wise, 16
Freedom Singers, 144
Freeman, "Cat", 106
Frisbee, Lonnie, 128
Fry, Charles William, 57
Fry, Fred, Ernest, Bertram, 57
Frye, Theodore, 91
Fuller, Charles, 80
Funk, Joseph, 94, 95

Gabriel, Charles, 71
Gaither Trio, Bill, 138, 139, 140, 168
Gaither, Bill, 126, 139, 140, 141, 142, 223
Gaither, Danny, 126, 140
Gaither, Gloria (Sickle), 126, 139, 142
Gaither, Mary Ann, 140
Gaithers, The, 140
Galloway, Sigmund, 123
Garrett, Dave, 203
Garstain, Jim, 151
Gay, John, 43
Gentle Faith, 128
Georgia Tom, 89
Gerhardt, Paul, 33
Gilley, Irene, 173
Gilley, Mickey, 173, 175
Gilleys, The, 172
Girard, Chuck, 128
Gleason, Jackie, 117
Glehn, Manfred von, 167
Glover, Bill, 195
Golden, Bill, 177, 178
Goldsboro, Bobby, 114
Good News, 128
Goose, Elizabeth, 42
Gospel Chimes, 146
Gospel Melody Boys, 155
Gospel Melody Quartet, 153
Graham, Bill, 154
Graham, Billy, 127, 142, 161, 165, 166, 176, 196
Grant, Amy, 169, 184, 185, 186, 187, 188, 189, 190, 198, 199

Grant, Dr. Burton, 187
Grant, Marshall, 178
Gray, George, 166, 167
Greaves, R.B., 114
Green, Imogene, 146
Green, Keith, 160, 161, 162
Gregory the Great, 8
Grein, Janny, 159
Grewin, Billy, 106
Griffin, Merv, 194
Griswold, Hilton, 105, 106, 107
Gulliksen, Kenn, 128
Guralnick, Peter, 125

Hackenhull, Isaac, 121
Haley, Bill and the Comets, 110, 124
Hall, Connor, 96
Hall, Tom T., 114
Hamblen, Stuart, 166
Hamer, Fanny Lou, 143, 144, 145
Hamer, Pap, 144
Hamill, Jim, 118, 149, 155, 156, 157
Hamilton, Roy, 124
Hamm, Charles, 44
Hampton, Lionel, 89
Handel, 44
Handy, W.C., 82, 99
Happy Hitters, 153
Harmoneers, 150
Harrell, Dan, 186, 187, 189, 198
Harris, Darrell, 196
Harris, Howell, 21
Harris, Larnelle, 168
Harris, R.H., 123, 124
Harrison, George, 114
Hartman, Bob, 195, 196, 197
Hawkins, Edwin Singers, 113
Hawkins, Hoyt, 116
Head East, 197
Hearn, Billy Ray, 127, 136, 158, 159, 160, 195
Heilbut, Tony, 89, 121, 122
Helvering, John, 167
Henry VIII, ii, 10, 11, 12, 13, 14
Herbert, George, 37
Herring, Annie, 159
Hess, Jake, 118, 120, 191, 192
Hibbler, Al, 112
Higher Ground, 198
Highway QC's, 123
Highwaymen, The, 112
Hildebrand, Ray, 136
Hine, Mr. & Mrs. Stuart K., 167
Hite, Les, 89
Hitler, 91, 175

Hockensmith, Hadley, 128
Hodge, Charlie, 119
Holcome, Tom, 171
Holmes, Warren, 106
Holyoke, Samuel, 23
Homeland Harmony Quartet, 96, 104
Honeytree, 195
Hopkins, Jerry, 117
Hopkins, John, 20
Hopkinson, Francis, 41, 42, 43,
    44, 45
Hopkinson, Judge Joseph, 45
Horne, Roger, 151
Hough, Greg, 195
Houghton, Dr. Will, 165
Howard, Roy, 153
Humbard, Rex, 149, 150, 151
Humphries, A.T., 106
Humphries, LaVera, 107
Hurst, Madame Lula Mae, 122
Huskey, Ferlin, 112

Ihrig, Faye, 102
Imperials, 118, 119, 140, 190,
    191, 192, 193, 194
Impressions, 112
Ingalls, Jeremiah, 23
Ink Spots, 124
Inspirations, 156
Isaac, E.W., 89

Jackson, George Pullen, 48, 49, 86
Jackson, Mahalia, 88, 89, 91,
    111, 121, 122, 123
Jacobs, Peter, 202
James, Joni, 112
James, Tommy and the Shondells
    113, 114
Jarette, Hugh, 114
Jefferson, Thomas, 41, 46, 47
Jennings, Waylon, 179
Johnny and Jack, 98
Johnson Gospel Singers, 121
Johnson, James P., 82
Johnson, Prince, 121
Johnson, Robert, 121
Johnson, Torrey, 165
Johnson, Wilbur, 121
Jordan, Glen, 166
Jordanaires, 116, 117, 118, 119,
    192

Kaiser, Kurt, 127, 136, 137, 158
Kapp, Jack, 165
Keister, Shane, 198

Kelly, Mark, 196
Kelly, Paul, 114
Kennedy, John, 123, 130
Kerner, Debby, 128
Key, Francis Scott, 45
Kieffer, Aldine, 94, 95
Kilby, Diane, 114
Kimble, Edward, 58
King Charles I, 130
King James I, 130
King, Martin Luther, Jr., 123, 143
Kingsmen, The, 149, 155, 156, 157
Kingston Trio, 110
Kirby, Jim, 156
Koker, Danny, 149, 151
Kristofferson, Kris, 115, 179

LaBelle, Patti and the Blue Belles
    112
Lafferty, Karen, 128, 200, 201,
    202, 203, 204
Lane, Frankie, 113
Lee, James, 122
LeFevre, Mylon, 128, 129
LeFevres, The, 102, 128, 154, 155
Lemon, Louise Barry, 121, 122
Leonetti, Tommy, 113
Lewis, Elmo, 172
Lewis, Jerry Lee, 76, 170, 174,
    175, 178
Lewis, Mamie, 172, 173
Light, Don, 222
Lindsay, Gordon, 174
Lindsey, Holy Hubert, 126
Lister, Hovie, 96, 156
Little Richard, 76, 124, 170
Little, William, 94
Lomax, Alan, 25, 43, 45
Lombardo, Guy, 91
London, Laurie, 111
Lopez, Trini, 112
Lord Baltimore, 130
Lorimer, Miss Mamie, 70
Love Song, 128, 129
Loveless, Wendall, 80
Luce, Henry, 183
Luther, Frank, 21
Luther, Hans and Grethe, 12
Luther, Martin, i, ii, 10, 11, 12,
    13, 14, 15, 16, 18, 26, 130, 227
Lyles, Bill, 106, 107, 156
Lynch, Mary, 118, 192
Lyon, James, 42, 44

MacDougal, Hamilton C., 21

MacKenzie, Bob, 223
Maier, Walter A., 80
Mandrell, Barbara, 181, 182, 183
Manion, Tim, 132
Mantovani, 111
Marconi, Guglielmo, 78
Marsh, Simeon B., 35
Marshall, Jack, 107
Martin, Dean, 111
Martin, Roberta, 91, 122, 146
Martin, Sallie, 90, 91, 122, 146
Martin, Tallmadge, 149
Martindale, Wink, 112
Mather, Cotton, 20, 23, 24, 40, 84
Mather, Richard, 20
Mathews, Charles, 156
Mathis, Johnny, 111
Matthews, Lorne, 151
Matthews, Neal, 116
Matthews, Randy, 129, 137
Maxwell, Bill, 128
McClung, Floyd, 202, 203
McClurkan, Rev. J.O. 138
McCoy, James, 96
McCoy, Otis, 96
McCracken, Jarrell, 134, 135, 136,
    137, 138, 155, 158
McCuen, Brad, 166
McGee, Cecil, 127
McGuire, Barry, 112, 158, 159
McGuire Sisters, 112
McKinney, Louis, 156
McKinney, Raymond, 156
McKinney, Reese, 156
McKissick, Norsalus, 146
McLauring, Charles, 143
McManus Trio, 155
McPhearson, Aimee Semple, 171
McSpadden, Gary, 140, 191
Meade, Sister Janet, 115
Mears, Buddy, 153
Melody Four Quartet, 135
Melodymen, 157
Mendelsohn, Fred, 146
Mendelsohn-Bartholdy, Felix, 38
Meredith, James, 194
Merrell, Tiny, 153
Miles, Floyd, 175
Miller, Keith, 136
Miller, Mrs. Rhea, 164
Miller, William, 50
Milligan, Wallace, 105
Mills Brothers, 124
Monterey Quartet, 155
Moody, Dwight, ii, 57, 58, 59,

60, 61, 62, 63, 64, 66, 70,
    71, 88, 161, 176, 216
Moore, Scotty, 116, 175
Morales, Armand, 191, 192
More, Sir Thomas, 12
Mormon Tabernacle Choir, 112
Morrison, Dorothy, 114
Moscheo, Joe, 192
Moss, Terry, 106
Mother Goose, 42
Mother Teresa, 206
Murray, Jim, 192, 193
Murray, John, 23
Mustard Seed Faith, 128
Mycall, John, 23

Nabors, Jim, 112, 115
Neal, Bob, 116
Neilson, Shirl, 191, 192
Nettl, Paul, 16
Nettleton, Asahel, 23
Nichols, Ted, 134
Nixon, Richard, 213
Norcross, Marvin, 135, 136, 137,
    155
Norman, Larry, 127, 129
Norwood, Dorothy, 146
Nowlin, W.B., 154

O'Connor, Roc, 132
O'Day, Molly, 98
Oak Ridge Boys, 119, 155, 157,
    177, 191, 193
Ocean, 114
Oglethorpe, Governor, 33
Oldenburg, Bob, 127
Oldham, Doug, 140, 168
Olsen, Erling C., 164
Orbison, Roy, 174
Orell, Lloyd, 154
Orioles, 124
Ormandy, Eugene and the
    Philadelphia Orchestra, 111
Ozman, Miss Agnes, 75

Pacific Gas & Electric, 114
Page, Patti, 112
Paino, Paul, 195
Parker, Colonel Tom, 116, 117, 193
Parker, Emory, 153
Parnham, Charles Fox, 75, 76
Patti, Sandi, 167, 169
Patty Family, The Ron, 168
Patty, Ron, 198
Paul and Paula, 136

Payne, Glen, 149, 150, 152
Pearce, Billy, 135
Penn, Gov. John, 42
People, 127
Perkins, Carl, 174, 178
Perkins, Luther, 178
Peter, Paul and Mary, 112
Petra, 195, 196, 197
Phillips, Sam, 116, 118, 124, 178, 217
Phoenix Sunshine, 202
Pilgrim Travelers, 125
Platters, 124
Pope Clement VIII, 13
Pope John XXIII, 131
Pope Paul VI, 131
Pratney, Winkie, 161
Presley, Elvis, 76, 90, 98, 112, 114, 116, 117, 118, 119, 120, 124, 128, 140, 156, 170, 174, 175, 178, 192, 193,
Preston, Billy, 113, 114, 145, 146
Pride, Charley, 115
Prince, Thomas, 23
Prokhanoff, Reverend Ivan S., 167

Racine, Kree Jack, 102
Radar, Paul, 79
Rainey, Ma, 89
Rambo, Buck, 188
Rambo, Dottie, 168, 188, 189
Rambos, The, 138, 188
Rawls, Lou, 124
Ray, Mr., 103
Rebels, The, 157
Redd, Jerry, 156
Reddy, Helen, 113, 115
Reese, Ray Dean, 156
Reich, Charles, 111
REO Speedwagon, 195
Repp, Ray, 131
Rettino, Ernie, 128
Rex Nelon Singers, 155
Reynolds, Lawrence, 113
Rice, Darol, 166
Rice, Tim, 113
Rich, Charlie, 174, 178
Richards, George, 23
Richards, Turley, 114
Ricks, George Robinson, 88
Rivers, Johnny, 114, 118
Robert, Reverend Carl, 166
Roberts, Oral, 215
Robertson, Pat, 215
Robinson, B.C., 96

Robinson, Jackie, 194
Robinson, R.B., 123
Rodeheaver, Homer Alvin, 70, 71, 72, 73, 74, 75, 164, 176
Rodgers, Jimmie, 103
Rodgers, Kenny and the First Edition, 114
Rodgers, Harlan, 128
Roosevelt, Franklin D., 78
Roper, Joe, 105
Routley, Erik, 34
Royal Scots Dragoon Guards, 114
Ruebush, Ephraim, 94
Ruffin, David, 124
Rupe, Art, 125
Rupf, Conrad, 16
Rush, 195

Salerno, Tony, 159
Sankey, Ira, ii, 58, 59, 60, 61, 63, 64, 65, 66, 70, 71, 75, 88, 161, 164, 176
Schlitt, John, 193
Schuler, Robert "Fighting Bob", 80
Schuller, Robert, 215
Schutte, Dan, 132
Scott, Colonel John, 69
Scott, Myrtle, 146
Second Chapter of Acts, 158, 159
Selah, 128
Servant, 196
Sewall, Samuel, 43
Seymour, Mary Estes, 100
Seymour, William J., 75, 76
Sha Na Na, 114
Shaw, George Bernard, 227
Shaw, Robert, 111
Shea, George Beverly, 135, 140, 161, 164, 165, 166, 167, 169, 176, 199
Shoals, Stephen H. (Steve), 107, 116, 166
Shore, Dinah, 194
Showalter, A.J., 95
Silvertones, The, 156
Simeone, Harry, 112
Simon and Garfunkle, 112
Singing Children, The, 123
Singing Nun, The, 112
Singletary, Edward, 153
Slaughter, Henry, 191, 192
Slick, John, 196
Smith, Bessie, 121, 122
Smith, Chuck, 128, 202

Smith, Don, 106
Smith, Eugene, 146
Smith, Joshua, 23
Smith, Kate, 105
Smith, Michael W., 197, 198, 199
Smith, Mrs. Albert, 60
Smith, William, 94
Smith, William Mae Ford, 122
Snider, Ted, 135
Songfellows, The, 156, 157, 158
Sonlight, 128
Sonneck, Oscar G.T., 40, 44
Soul Stirrers, 123, 124, 125
Speer Family, The, 100, 101,
    102, 136, 138, 155
Speer, Ben, 100
Speer, Brock, 100, 102
Speer, Emma, 100
Speer, J.J., 100
Speer, Mary Tom, 100
Speer, Mom and Dad, 100
Speer, Rosa Nell, 100
Speer, Tom "Dad", 100, 111, 155
Spiritualaires, 150
Springfield, Rick, 114
Springsteen, Bruce, 194, 195, 199
St. Augustine, 28
St. Louis Jesuits, 132
Stafford, John, 45
Stamps Quartet, 100, 117, 119,
    120, 150, 193
Stamps Quartet, Lester, 150
Stamps, Frank, 95, 105, 150
Stamps, V.O., 105
Stamps-Baxter, 90, 101, 105, 155
Stamps-Ozark Quartet, 150
Staple Singers, 114
Starr, Kay, 112
Statesmen, 102, 118, 120, 156, 222
Stebbins, George C., 64
Steiner, Melody, 162
Sterban, Richard, 119
Sternhold, Thomas, 20
Stevens, Cat, 114
Stevens, Ray, 114
Stewart, Derrell, 153, 155
Stoker, Gordon, 116, 117
Stoll, Charles, 156
Stone, Huey P., 172
Stone, Mack, 172
Stonehill, Randy, 128
Stookey, Noel Paul, 114
Styll, John, 224
Styx, 195
Sullivan, Ed, 117

Sumner, Donnie, 119
Sumner, J.D., 102, 117, 119, 120,
    154, 193, 222, 223
Sumrall, Leona, 171
Sumrall, Mother, 171
Sunday, William Ashley "Billy",
    69, 70, 71, 72, 73, 74,
    166, 176, 216
Sunshine Boys Quartet, 107
Sunshine Quartet, 119
Supremes, 114
Swaggart, Ada, 172
Swaggart, Frances (Anderson),
    173, 175
Swaggart, Jeanette, 172
Swaggart, Jimmy Lee, 76, 170, 171,
    172, 173, 174, 175, 176, 215
Swaggart, Minnie Bell, 171, 172
Swaggart, Willie Leon, 171, 172,
    173
Sweet Inspirations, 119

Talbot, John Michael, 133, 159
Talbot, Terry, 159
Talley, Kirk, 151
Tampa Red, 89
Tate, Nahum, 23
Taunton, Mack, 151
Taylor, Edward, 20
Taylor, James, 114
Taylor, Johnny, 124
Tennessee Two, 178
Terkel, Studs, 122
Terry, Neeley, 75, 76
Tersteegen, 33
Thomas, B.J., 114, 184
Tindley, C. Albert, 88
Toney, Aldon, 107
Torrey, Reuben A., 70
Tremble, Roy, 151
Truax, Jay, 128
Truman, Harry, 166
Tudor, Mary, 20
Tufts, John, 21
Turner, Nat, 85
Tyndale, 13

Vail, S.J., 60
Van Winkle, Joseph E., 70
Vaughan, James D., 73, 95, 96,
    100, 101
Vaus, Jim, 166
Vesey, Denmark, 85
Volz, Greg X., 195, 196, 197

Walbert, James D., 155
Walker, William, 94
Wallace, Sam, 166
Waller, Fats, 82
Walter, Thomas, 21
Walther, Johann, 16
Washington, Dinah, 124, 146
Washington, George, 41, 42, 47
Watchmen quartet, 149, 151
Watts, Isaac, ii, 21, 23, 26, 27,
    28, 29, 31, 32, 34, 38, 45, 89
Way, The, 128
Weatherford Quartet, 149, 150, 157,
    191
Weaver, Louis, 196
Webber, Andrew Lloyd, 113
Webster, George Amon, 151
Wesley, Charles, 32, 33, 34, 37
Wesley, John, 32, 33, 34, 35, 85
Welsey, Samuel (brother), 33
Wesley, Samuel (father), 32
Wesleys, The, ii, 21, 28, 30, 32,
    37, 39, 40, 43, 45
Westmoreland, Kathy, 120
White Sisters, The, 135
White, Benjamin Franklin, 94
Whitefield, George, ii, 21, 32,
    37, 39, 216
Whitfield, J. G., 153
Whittemore, Rev. Lewis B., 79
Wiggins, Thelma, 173
Wigglesworth, Michael, 20
Wilder, Alex, 81
Wiley, Fletch, 128
Willems, Jim, 224
Williams, Andy, 111
Williams, Hank, 98, 101
Wilson, John, 20
Winkworth, Catherine, 16
Winsett, R.E., 90, 96
Winston, Dr. Nat, 179
Winterhalter, Hugo Orchestra, 166
Withers, Bill, 114
Wolfe, Charles, 95, 96, 97
Wolsey, Cardinal, 13, 14
Wonder, Stevie, 112
Wycliff, 13
Wyrtzen, Jack, 164, 165

Younce, George, 149, 150, 151, 152
Youngbloods, 114

Zamperini, Louis, 116
Zinzendorf, 33
Zundel, John, 38

Index-S

Songs
"Abraham, Martin and John", 113
"Ah Lovely Appearance of Death",
    43
"Ain't Gonna Let Nobody Turn Me
    Around", 144
"Alexander's Ragtime Band", 82
"All My Trials", 112, 114
"All You Need is Love", 112
"Amazing Grace", 114, 142
"Amen", 112, 127
"America", 73
"Angels in the Sky", 112
"Are You Ready", 114
"At the End of the Trail", 175

"Baa Baa Black Sheep", 42
"Battle Hymn of the Republic",
    71, 112
"Beautiful Dreamer", 81
"Beautiful Music", 185
"Because He Lives", 139
"Before Jehovah's Awful Throne",
    30, text: 30-31
"Begin, My Tongue, Some Heavenly
    Theme", 31
"Bible Tells Me So, The", 112
"Big Bad John", 193
"Blessed Assurance", 62
"Blowin' in the Wind", 112, 115,
    125, 143
"Boy Named Sue, A", 179
"Brighten the Corner", 71,
    text: 72
"Bringing in the Sheaves", 71
"Bye Baby Bunting", 42

"Carry Me Back to Old Virginny", 82
"Chain Gang", 125
"Change is Gonna Come, A", 125
"Chester", 41
"Child of God", 112
"Christ is My Redeemer", 71
"Christ the Lord is Risen Today",
    35, text: 34-35
"Christian People", 128
"Church Street Soul Revival", 114
"Clock O' the North", 42
"Coloring Song, The", 196
"Columbia", 41
"Come Back Home", 114
"Cry, Cry, Cry", 178

"Crying in the Chapel", 112, 124
"Crystal Blue Persuasion", 113

"Dammit Isn't God's Last Name",
113
"Day by Day", 114
"De Brewer's Big Horses", text:
73-74
"De Camptown Races", 81
"Dear Christians, One and All,
Rejoice", 18
"Deck of Cards", 112
"Deep Enough For Me", 114
"Did You See My Savior", 88
"Didn't My Lord Deliver Daniel",
(text), 53-54
"Do Lord", 127
"Dominque", 112

"Eve of Destruction", 112, 158
"Every Time (I Feel His Spirit)",
112
"Everybody Love to Cha Cha Cha",
125

"Family of God, The", 140
"Fight is On, The", 71
"Fire and Rain", 114
"From Depths of Woe I Cry to
Thee", 18

"Game of Life, The", 134, 135
"Get Together", 114
"Give Me Oil in My Lamp", 127
"Give Us This Day", 112
"God Took Away My Yesterdays",
175
"God Understands", 165
"God's Gonna Separate the Wheat
from the Tares", 122
"Good Book, The", 112
"Gospel Boogie", 96
"Grandma's Hands", 114
"Greensleeves", 42

"Hail, Columbia", 45
"Hark! The Herald Angels Sing",
text: 37
"Have You Talked To The Man
Upstairs", 107
"He Bought My Soul", 175
"He Touched Me", 139
"He", 112
"He's Everything to Me", 127
"He's Got the Whole World in His

Hands", 111, 112
"Heartbreak Hotel", 117
"Help Me Make It Through the
Night", 139
"Here's To Good Old Whiskey", 57
"Hey Porter", 178
"Hey, Hey Paula", 136
"Hickory Dickory Dock", 42
"Holy Man", 114
"How About You", 88
"How Could They Live Without
Jesus", 161
"How Great Thou Art", 120,
166, 167
"How Many Times", 91
"Hurry on, My Weary Soul", text:
52-53

"I Am", 198
"I Am A Promise", 139
"I Am Loved", 139
"I Believe", 112
"I Can Put My Trust in Jesus", 122
"I Do, Don't You", 89
"I Don't Know How to Love Him",
113, 115
"I Got A Woman, 124
"I Heard the Voice of Jesus", 114
"I Knew Jesus Before He Was a
Superstar", 115
"I Love You (but the Words Won't
Come)", 127
"I Surely Know There's Been a
Change in Me", 91
"I Walk the Line", 178
"I Walk with the King,
Hallelujah!", 71
"I Want You, I Need You, I Love
You", 117
"I Was the One", 117
"I Wish We'd All Been Ready",
127
"I'd Like to Teach the World to
Sing", 114, 164, 165
"I'll Overcome", 88
"I'll Take You There", 114
"I'm a Believer", 112
"I'm Gonna Live the Life I Sing
About in My Song", 91
"I've Got the Joy, Joy, Joy",
127
"If I Had a Hammer", 112
"If Loving You Is Wrong (I Don't
Want To Be Right)", 181
"If You Know the Lord", 166

"If You See My Savior, Tell Him
  That You Saw Me", 89, 122
"If Your Heart Keeps Right",
  text: 72-73
"In The Evening By The Moonlight",
  82
"In the Sweet By and By", 70
"Is There No Balm in Christian
  Lands, 43
"It Is No Secret", 166
"It is Well With My Soul", 62
"It's My Desire", 91
"Ivory Palaces", 166

"Jack Spratt", 42
"Jeannie With The Light Brown
  Hair", 81
"Jesus Gave Me Water", 124
"Jesus is a Soul Man", 113
"Jesus Is Just Alright", 114,
  115
"Jesus Lover of My Soul",
  (text), 35
"Jesus Loves Me", 62, 168
"Jesus Whispers Peace", 165
"Joy to the World", 29
"Joy", 114
"Joy, Freedom, Peace and
  Ceaseless Blessing", 57
"Jubilation", 114

"Keep Me Every Day", 122
"King is Coming, The", 126,
  139, 140
"Known Only to Him", 120, 166
"Kum Ba Ya" ("Kumbaya"), 113,
  127

"Last Lamentation of the
  Languishing Squire, The", 40
"Lead Me Gently Home, Father",
  165
"Lemon Tree", 112
"Life Can Be Beautiful", 91
"Life", 114
"Little Boy Blue", 42
"Little Robin Redbreast", 42
"Lord Will Make Way, The", 91
"Love Divine, All Loves
  Excelling", (text 38)
"Love-Sick Maid, The" (song), 40
"Loveable", 125

"Me and Jesus", 114
"Michael", 112

"Midnight Oil", 181
"Mighty Clouds of Joy", 113
"Mighty Fortress is Our God, A",
  16, text: 17
"Morning Has Broken", 114
"Move On Up a Little Higher",
  122
"Mrs. Robinson", 113
"My Days Have Been So Wondrous
  Free", 41, 42
"My Father's Eyes", 188
"My Heavenly Father Watches Over
  Me", 120
"My Shepherd Will Supply My
  Need", 30
"My Sweet Lord", 114

"Ninety and Nine, The", text:
  62-63, 71

"O For a Thousand Tongues to
  Sing", 38, text: 38-39
"O Sacred Head", 186
"O Store Gud", (O Heart God)",
  166
"O, Dem Golden Slippers",
  82
"Oh Happy Day", 113, 114
"Oh Rock My Soul", 112
"Oh! Susanna", 81
"Oh, To Be Nothing", 71
"Old Black Joe", 81
"Old Man's Rubble", 185
"Old Rugged Cross, The", 74
"Once More Our God Vouchsafe to
  Shine", 43
"One, Two, Buckle My Shoe", 42
"Only Sixteen", 125
"Onward Christian Soldiers",
  62, 71
"Out of the Depths I Cry to
  Thee", 16
"Out of the Shadow Land", text:
  65-66

"Peace in the Valley", 90,
  text: 91, 98, 112
"People Get Ready", 112
"Peter, Peter, Pumpkin Eater", 42
"Picture of Life's Other Side,
  A", 97
"Precious Lord, Take My Hand",
  text: 90, 122, 123
"Pull From the Shore", 71
"Put Your Hand in the Hand", 114

"Rattlesnake Remedy, The", 137

"Rejoice, The Lord is King",
36, text: 36-37

"Remember Sinful Youth", text:
50-51

"Ring the Bells of Heaven", 71

"Rock Around the Clock", 110, 124

"Rock of Ages", 62

"Safe From the Law", 71

"Saved By Grace", 64, text:
64-65

"Scatter Seeds of Kindness",
text: 60-61

"Sellingers' Round", 42

"Silent Night", 122

"Sing a Song of Six Pence", 42

"Singing in My Soul", 91

"Sinner Man", 112

"Sit on the Porch and Pick On
My Old Guitar", 180

"Sixteen Tons", 111

"Snail, Snail", 42

"Someone To Care", 175

"Song to the Flag", 73

"Speak to the Sky", 114

"Spirit in the Sky", 114

"Stand By Me", 88

"Star Spangled Banner, The",
45, 46

"Stealing in the Name of the
Lord", 114

"Stoned Love", 114

"Storm the Forts of Darkness", 57

"Stormy Sea Blues, The", 89

"Stranger", 175

"Strathspey's Reel", 42

"Superstar", 113

"Surely I Will", 155

"Sweet Cherry Wine", 113

"Sweet Sweet Spirit", 120

"Take My Hand", 114

"Tell It On The Mountain", 112

"Tenderly He Watches", 166

"That's The Way God Planned It",
114

"The Old Folks at Home", 57

"The Prodigal Child", text: 64

"There Are No Flies on Jesus",
57

"There is a Fountain Filled With
Blood", 60, 71

"There is a Redeemer", 161

"There Is a River", 175

"There Is Power in the Blood",
174

"There's a Leak in This Old
Building", 155

"There's Just Something About That
Name", 139, 140, 141

"Think His Name", 114

"This Is Just What Heaven Means
To Me", 175

"This Little Light of Mine", 144

"Tight Like That", 89

"To Anacreon in Heaven", 45

"To Market, To Market", 42

"Tom Dooley", 110, 111

"Top 40 of the Lordy", 114

"Turn Your Radio On", 114

"Turn, Turn, Turn", 112, 113

"Two Faithful Lovers", 40

"Way-Worn Traveller, The", 42

"We Shall Behold Him", 168

"We Shall Overcome", 88, 143

"We'll Gather By the River", 70

"Wedding Song (There is Love)",
114

"Were You There", text: 55

"What a Day That Will Be", 175

"What a Difference You've Made in
My Life", 185

"What a Friend We Have in Jesus",
92

"When I Survey That Wondrous
Cross", 28, text: 28-29

"When I've Done the Best I Can",
91

"When Israel Was in Egypt's Land
(Go Down, Moses)", 53, text:
54-55

"When the Roll is Called Up
Yonder, 70

"When the Saints Go Marching In",
112, 127

"Where Are the Hebrew Children",
text: 51-52

"Where Shall My Wandering Soul
Begin", 34

"Whiter Than Snow", 62

"Wholly Holy", 114

"Why Me, Lord", 115

"Why Should the Devil Have All
the Good Music", 127

"Wings of a Dove", 112

"Without Him", 128

"Woman to Woman", 181

"Wonderful Time Up There, A", 112
"Wonderful World", 125

"Yankee Doodle", 41
"You Light Up My Life", 115, 224
"You Send Me", 125
"You'll Never Walk Alone", 112, 114, 124

Albums
Agape (Agape), 128
Alleluia—Praise Gathering for Believers (Bill Gaither Trio), 115, 139
Armageddon Experience, The (Armageddon Experience), 128

Back to the Street (Petra), 197
Beat the System (Petra), 197
Born Twice (Randy Stonehill), 128

Captured in Time and Space (Petra), 197
Chief Musician (Candle), 159
Christmas (Tennessee Ernie Ford), 111
Come and Join Us (Petra), 195
Concert for Bangla Desh (George Harrison and Friends), 114

Did You Think to Pray (Charley Pride), 115

Earthen Vessels (St. Louis Jesuits), 132
Eleventh Anniversary, The (Florida Boys), 155
Everlastin' Living Jesus Concert, The (Maranatha), 128

For My Friends (Sandi Patti), 167
For Those Who Have Ears (Keith Green), 160, 162

His Hand in Mine (Elvis Presley), 117
How Great Thou Art (Elvis Presley), 112, 118, 192
Hymns (Tennessee Ernie Ford), 111

Jesus Christ Superstar (Cast) album, 115
Jesus Was a Capricorn (Kris Kristofferson), 115
John Wesley Harding (Bob Dylan), 115

Lord's Prayer, The (Jim Nabors), 115
Lord's Prayer, The (Mormon Tabernacle Choir), 112

Michael W. Smith (Michael W. Smith), 198
More Power To Ya (Petra), 196
Music Machine, The (Candle), 159
My Father's Eyes (Amy Grant), 185, 186

Nearer the Cross (Tennessee Ernie Ford), 111
Neither Silver Nor Gold (St. Louis Jesuits), 132
Never Say Die (Petra), 196

Sandi's Songs (Sandi Patti), 167
Some Golden Daybreak (Jimmy Swaggart), 175
Songs From the Savior (Paul Clark), 128
Spirituals (Tennessee Ernie Ford), 111
Star Carol (Tennessee Ernie Ford), 111

Truth of Truths (cast), 128

Upon This Rock (Larry Norman), 127

Washes Whiter Than (Petra), 196
Why Should The Father Bother (Petra), 196
Wish We'd All Been Ready (Randy Stonehill), 137

You Light Up My Life (Debbie Boone), 115

CPSIA information can be obtained
at www.ICGtesting.com
Printed in the USA
FSOW02n1330081016
25764FS